There was a time w
The earth and every

       To me did
Apparel'd in celestial light
The glory and the freshness of a dream
It is not now as it has been of yore
Turn wheresoe'er I may
       By night or day
The things which I have seen I see them no

      The Rainbow comes and goes
And lovely is the rose
The moon doth with delight
Look round her when the heavens are ba
      Waters on a starry night
Are beautiful and fair
      The sunshine is a glorious birth
But yet I know where'er I go
That there hath pass'd away a glory from

Now while the Birds thus sing a joyous
    And while the young lambs bound
    As to the tabor's sound
To me alone there came a thought of grief
A timely utterance gave that thought rel
    And I again am strong
The cataracts blow their trumpets from th
No more shall grief of mine the season wron
I hear the echoes through the mountains thr
The winds come to me from the fields of sle
    And all the earth is gay

THE FRIENDSHIP

BY THE SAME AUTHOR

A.J.P. Taylor: A Biography

Boswell's Presumptuous Task

The two poems illustrated on the endpapers exhibit the kind of intimate poetic dialogue that took place between Coleridge (left) and Wordsworth (right) on several occasions. Coleridge's 'A Letter to —' (addressed to his beloved Sara Hutchinson, and later reworked into the poem published six months later as 'Dejection: An Ode') was written in response to hearing the first few stanzas of a then untitled poem of Wordsworth's, which had been written only days before (see pages 344–7). Wordsworth did not complete the poem until some years later, and it was published in his 1807 collection under the title 'Ode: Intimations of Immortality from Recollections of Early Childhood'. The two poems explore the same theme of lost creativity and the search for inspiration, but reach very different conclusions. This is the first page of one of two surviving manuscripts of 'A Letter to —', and is written in Coleridge's hand; the 'Immortality' ode is taken from a book of Wordsworth's manuscript poems thought to be the one copied out for Coleridge and taken by him to Malta in 1804. It is almost certainly in Sara Hutchinson's hand; Wordsworth very much disliked the act of writing, and usually asked his wife Mary, her sister Sara or his sister Dorothy to write down his poems from his dictation. *(Both poems reproduced courtesy of Dove Cottage, The Wordsworth Trust)*

THE FRIENDSHIP

Wordsworth and Coleridge

ADAM SISMAN

VIKING

VIKING
Published by the Penguin Group
Penguin Group (USA) Inc., 375 Hudson Street,
New York, New York 10014, U.S.A.
Penguin Group (Canada), 90 Eglinton Avenue East, Suite 700,
Toronto, Ontario, Canada M4P 2Y3 (a division of Pearson
Penguin Canada Inc.)
Penguin Books Ltd, 80 Strand, London WC2R 0RL, England
Penguin Ireland, 25 St. Stephen's Green, Dublin 2, Ireland
(a division of Penguin Books Ltd)
Penguin Books Australia Ltd, 250 Camberwell Road, Camberwell,
Victoria 3124, Australia
(a division of Pearson Australia Group Pty Ltd)
Penguin Books India Pvt Ltd, 11 Community Centre, Panchsheel Park,
New Delhi – 110 017, India
Penguin Group (NZ), 67 Apollo Drive, Mairangi Bay,
Auckland 1311, New Zealand
(a division of Pearson New Zealand Ltd)
Penguin Books (South Africa) (Pty) Ltd, 24 Sturdee Avenue,
Rosebank, Johannesburg 2196, South Africa

Penguin Books Ltd, Registered Offices:
80 Strand, London WC2R 0RL, England

First American edition
Published in 2007 by Viking Penguin,
a member of Penguin Group (USA) Inc.

10   9   8   7   6   5   4   3   2   1

Copyright © Adam Sisman, 2006
All rights reserved

Map illustrations by John Gilkes

ISBN 978-0-670-03822-0

Printed in the United States of America

To George Misiewicz

CONTENTS

ILLUSTRATIONS

The Bristol lodgings shared by the Pantisocrats for most of 1795. Line
drawing by Edmund New.

Racedown Lodge in Dorset, occupied by Wordsworth and his sister
Dorothy from 1795 to 1797. Line drawing by Edmund New.

The Nether Stowey cottage, home of the Coleridge family from the end
of 1796 until the middle of 1799. Line drawing by Edmund New, 1914.

Alfoxden Park, rented by William and Dorothy Wordsworth in 1797–98.
Line drawing by Edmund New, 1914.

Wordsworth at the age of twenty-eight, by William Shuter. *(Courtesy of
the Division of Rare and Manuscript Collections, Cornell University
Library)*

Wordsworth aged thirty-six. Drawing by Henry Edridge. *(Dove Cottage,
The Wordsworth Trust)*

Coleridge in 1798, by an unknown German artist. *(Mrs Gardner)*

Coleridge early in 1804, by James Northcote. *(Dove Cottage, The
Wordsworth Trust)*

Silhouettes of Dorothy Wordsworth in 1806, and of Sara Hutchinson
and Mary Wordsworth in 1827. *(Dove Cottage, The Wordsworth
Trust)*

Miniatures of Sara Coleridge in 1809 *(Getty Images)* and of Annette
Vallon, date unknown. *(Dove Cottage, The Wordsworth Trust)*

Hartley Coleridge, aged ten. *(Frontispiece to Vol. 1 of Hartley Coleridge's
Poems, 1851)*

The Great Track over the top of the Quantocks, photographed in the
1930s. *(Kit Houghton)*

'Alfoxton Park' by Miss Sweeting, from a book of views published in
the 1830s.

Greta Hall, illustrated in 1887. Postcard from *Souvenir of the English Lakes*. *(Jeronime Palmer and Scott Ligertwood of Greta Hall, Keswick)*
Landscape surrounding Greta Hall. Engraving from W. Westall's original drawing. *(Dove Cottage, The Wordsworth Trust)*

Portrait of Robert Southey by James Sharples, probably painted in 1795. *(Bristol Museums, Galleries & Archives)*
Self-portrait by William Hazlitt, painted *c*.1802. *(Maidstone Museum and Art Gallery, Kent/The Bridgeman Art Library)*

Thomas Poole. *(Frontispiece to* Thomas Poole and his Friends *by Mrs Henry Sandford, 1888)*
Charles Lamb, after an original drawing by Robert Hancock, 1798. *(From* Reminiscences of Samuel Taylor Coleridge and Robert Southey *by Joseph Cottle, 1847)*
Joseph Cottle. *(Dove Cottage, The Wordsworth Trust)*

Leathes Water (Thirlmere), a mezzotint based on a pencil and wash drawing by John Constable made in 1806. *(Dove Cottage, The Wordsworth Trust)*
Grasmere in the early nineteenth century, by George Fennel Robson. *(Dove Cottage, The Wordsworth Trust)*
Ullswater. Engraving by Miller after Allom, *c*.1830. *(Getty Images)*

Three contemporary drawings by John Harden of Brathay Hall, not far from Grasmere. *(Abbot Hall Art Gallery, Kendal/The Bridgeman Art Library)*

Dove Cottage, photographed early in the twentieth century. *(Getty Images)*

Part-title portraits: Southey (page 1) and Wordsworth (page 121) after original drawings by Robert Hancock, 1796 and 1798 respectively; Coleridge (page 327) after an original painting by Peter Vandyke, 1795. From *Reminiscences of Samuel Taylor Coleridge and Robert Southey* by Joseph Cottle (1847).

MAPS

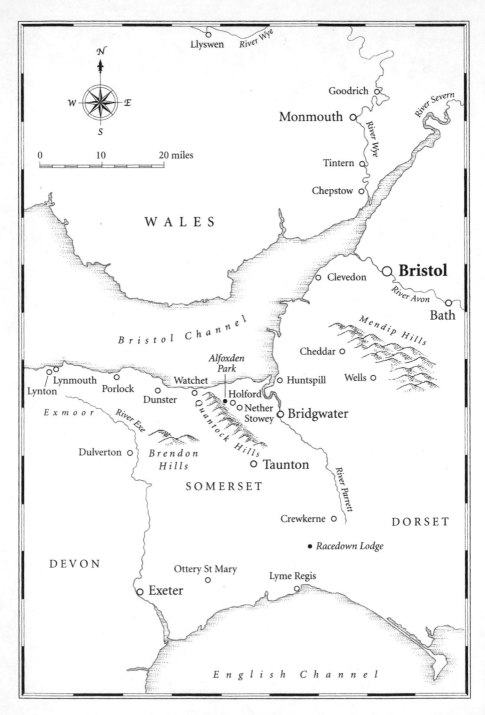

The West Country

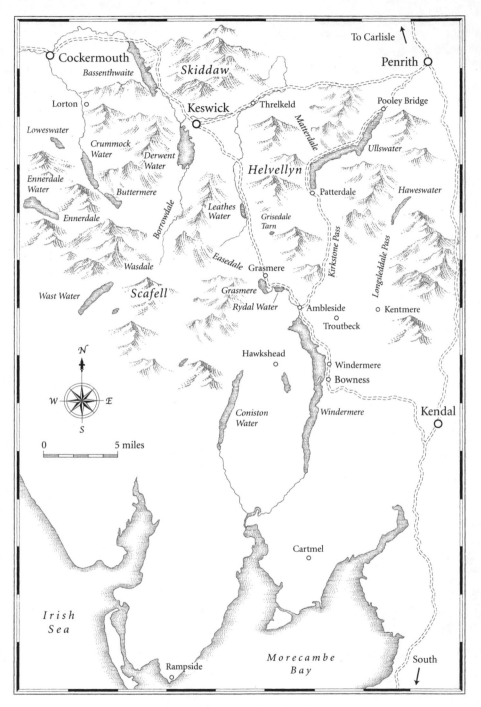

Wordsworth and Coleridge's Lakes

INTRODUCTION

One June afternoon, more than two hundred years ago, a young man halted by a field-gate overlooking an isolated Dorset valley. His name was Samuel Taylor Coleridge, and he was twenty-four years old. He had walked forty miles since leaving his cottage in the Quantock Hills early the previous morning.

Beyond the gate, a cornfield stretched downhill towards the side of a substantial house, built in brick and partly covered by grey stucco render. In the kitchen garden two figures, a man and a woman, both about his own age, could be seen working; first one, then the other, paused and looked up towards where he stood.

The lane continued in a wide arc to the front of the house. Too impatient to take this long way round, Coleridge vaulted over the gate and bounded across the field towards the waiting figures, leaping through the corn. The two watchers, William Wordsworth and his sister Dorothy, retained a distinct memory of this sight almost half a century afterwards.[1]

Until this moment, Wordsworth and Coleridge had met only a handful of times. Now Coleridge planned to stay several days with his new friend – but they soon found that this was not enough, and he repeatedly postponed his departure. The two had much to say to each other, and after more than three weeks neither wanted to part; so it was rapidly arranged that the Wordsworths would move to the Quantocks. There the poets lived in close proximity, meeting almost daily, composing and developing their work together. This was an intensely creative time for them both. Under the constant stimulus of the other, each man would write some of his finest poetry. Ideas, themes and images would pass back and forth between them, one poem prompting a response from the other in exhilarating succession. And though this miraculously fertile period lasted only sixteen months, it was the seed-time of fruit that would ripen through the subsequent decade. Two years later their association would be renewed in the Lakes, where there would be a brief reprise of their poetic duet.

If Coleridge's arrival on that June afternoon in 1797 was not the beginning of their acquaintance, it was the beginning of their intimacy. Previously they had exchanged ideas, expressed mutual regard, and offered friendly criticism. Now the relationship became much closer, one of dialogue and collaboration, of sharing plans and dreams.

The names of Wordsworth and Coleridge have been linked ever since. They have passed into legend as a pair, like Boswell and Johnson, or Lennon and McCartney. The myth-making began while they were still living, and has continued uninterrupted. The image of these two young geniuses, the progenitors of English Romanticism, roaming the Quantock Hills in an ecstasy of shared understanding and creative fulfilment, is irresistibly romantic. Their subsequent estrangement, quarrel, and superficial reconciliation complete a story as poignant as any love affair.

A shared ambition dominated the friendship between the two men. Both believed ardently that poetry could occupy a central place in the culture of the age. The visionary Coleridge dreamed of a great poem – perhaps greater than any yet written. It would encompass all human knowledge, and take twenty years to write. It would ensure the poet a place among the immortals; more important, it would hasten in the 'blessed day' of Mankind's redemption, 'the day fairer than this': beginning where Milton left off.

Coleridge had scarcely sketched his utopian scheme before deciding that his friend was better suited to realise it. Wordsworth accepted the commission. For many years he struggled heroically to write this impossible poem, until at last he abandoned it, bitterly disappointed. The friendship that had been so productive at the beginning would end in failure.

'Why do people have to like Wordsworth and hate Coleridge and *vice versa*?' asked Edmund Blunden.[2] The residual bitterness after their falling out has tended to distort subsequent interpretation of the relations between the poets. As a stimulating scholar who has written recently on relations between the two men has pointed out, understanding of them has been bedevilled by partisanship: 'The practice of elevating one figure over the other has dominated Coleridge and Wordsworth biography for decades; to some extent because the very closeness of the two writers was later wrecked by savage disagreement. Interpreting one of them sympathetically almost inevitably means showing the other in a bad light.'[3]

My book is an attempt to escape from this biographical impasse, by concentrating on the friendship itself, at its most intense when both men were young and full of hope. Its core is the period of six and a half years between Coleridge's exuberant arrival at Racedown Lodge and his sad departure for Malta. This is the story of two marvellously gifted young men, for whom anything seemed possible. At the outset, their friendship was beneficial to both, pushing each to higher aspirations. Overhanging all was their joint mission, to fulfil the hopes of a generation disappointed at the failure of the French Revolution: nothing less than a poem that would change the world.

THE FRIENDSHIP

PROLOGUE

'How much the greatest event it is that ever happened in the world!' exclaimed Charles James Fox on hearing of the fall of the Bastille, 'and how much the best!' The long struggle between Britain and France that began in 1793 has obscured the fact that most Britons (many of whom subsequently modified or concealed their enthusiasm) welcomed the outbreak of the French Revolution in 1789. Few then predicted how it would end. Some saw the changes transforming France as overdue, introducing the French to the liberties long enjoyed by Englishmen; others rather more excitedly as a precursor of the millennium, when the brotherhood of man would be established on earth. Half a lifetime afterwards, Robert Southey, though by then a staunch Tory, could still vividly recall the excitement of that time: 'Few persons but those who lived in it can conceive or comprehend what the memory of the French Revolution was, nor what a visionary world seemed to open upon those who were just entering it. Old things seemed passing away, and nothing was dreamt of but the regeneration of the human race.'[1]

Even the Prime Minister William Pitt, later the most determined enemy of the French Republic, then looked forward to a reconstructed and free France as 'one of the most brilliant powers of Europe'. France was arguably the most powerful nation in the world, certainly the centre of European culture and thought. Indeed, the events in France seemed likely to spread a beneficial influence everywhere. 'The French, Sir, are not only asserting their own rights, but they are advancing the general liberties of mankind,' declared John Cartwright, the Lincolnshire reformer. Like Cartwright, the nonconformist minister Richard Price was a veteran in the cause of liberty; according to him, the success of the American colonies in winning their independence was 'one step ordained by providence' towards the millennium. In a sermon preached to the London Revolution Society on 4 November 1789, Price gave thanks that he had lived to see this 'eventful period'.* He predicted 'a general amendment beginning in human affairs; the dominion of kings changed for the dominion of laws, and the dominion of priests giving way to the dominion of reason and conscience'.[2]

In almost every country of pre-Revolutionary Europe, princes ruled without check; their subjects suffered, unprotected by laws; perhaps worst of all, taxes were raised without consulting those who would have to pay them. France had been one of the most lamentable examples. In England, by contrast, the 'Glorious Revolution' of 1688 had limited the power of the monarchy, and established the rights of its subjects: liberty of conscience, the right to be governed by elected representatives, the freedom to make money and to hold property. Now, at last (a century after the British), the French were catching up. The rest of Europe would surely follow.

Such was the British view. There was a widespread complacency about the British way of doing things. How could the *status quo* be at fault when the nation was so rich? The struggles of the seventeenth century had been absorbed into the political culture, and were no longer threatening; on the contrary, they were a source of pride, evidence of superiority. However absurd this might seem to Americans, and indeed to peoples still subject to British rule, Britons were generally united in seeing their country as a lighthouse of liberty and prosperity on the edge of a benighted continent.

Even so, the unreformed House of Commons was hard to defend. Many MPs held sinecures granted by the Crown, which ensured that they would support the King's government, right or wrong. Men went into Parliament expressly to obtain such posts. Elections were flagrantly corrupt; with only a small number of electors, who were easily bought, often by the simple expedient of providing free drink. Some seats had a mere handful of voters, and in one notorious example, none at all. In rural constituencies, a large proportion

---

* He was sixty-six, and died two years later.

of the electorate owed their livelihoods to powerful landowners, who as a result virtually controlled elections. Such abuses, distressing in themselves, were (in the view of many) symptomatic of a deeper problem: as constituted, the House of Commons failed to represent the nation as a whole. Parliament was controlled by a self-perpetuating oligarchy, one that left significant sections of society without a voice. Pitt introduced a Bill to reform some of the more obvious abuses, only to have it thrown out by a suspicious House of Commons. Radicals called for bolder constitutional reforms, including secret ballots, regular elections, extension of the franchise, and restrictions on the power of the Crown to make appointments. Yet there was little popular pressure for change. A great many Britons agreed with Dr Johnson when he remarked that most schemes of political improvement were very laughable things.

The apparent success of the French Revolution encouraged British radicals. The dormant Society for Constitutional Information revived; a group of well-meaning young aristocrats designated themselves the Society of Friends of the People; and at the other end of the social scale a London shoemaker founded a Corresponding Society for the encouragement of constitutional discussion, which in time gave birth to similar societies around the country. Messages of solidarity were sent to France at each revolutionary development. The presses ran hot with political pamphlets. In dissenting circles, where many of the radicals were to be found, there was a strong hope that the laws barring from public office those who refused to conform to the Thirty-Nine Articles of the Church of England might be abolished, or at least relaxed. Dissenters in England were traditionally progressive; and increasingly discontented with an established order from which they were to a large extent excluded. Toleration was not enough; participation was what they wanted. Unitarians, who formed the intellectual elite of the dissenting movement, were rational Christians, preaching science, enlightenment and tolerance, and rejecting the mysticism of the Trinity. Not content with eventual salvation, they hoped for a better life on earth. For a Unitarian like the philosopher-chemist Joseph Priestley, the need for reform was self-evident; the system was clearly rotten.

Of course there were differences between these radicals: while some harked back to 1688, to the establishment of a constitutional monarchy, others looked back further, to 1649, and the foundation of a republic. Another strand of radical opinion daringly discarded historical precedent, and asserted instead the natural and inalienable rights of man. Such differences, not always obvious at first, would become more distinct as the Revolution developed.

Even those John Bulls (and there were plenty of them) who believed that the British constitution could not be bettered had cause to welcome the news from France. For the century that preceded the Revolution, France had been Britain's principal enemy in wartime and chief rival for empire. With a population almost three times that of Britain and a comparable overseas trade, plus revenues twenty-five times those of the new United States, France possessed resources unmatched by any country in the world. She had been contained only by heroic effort; she remained a dangerous Catholic power, a permanent menace to British security and Protestant freedoms. Now, perhaps, the long struggle was over. Until 1789, French strength had been concentrated in the hands of the French king. Within a matter of months, the French monarchy had been weakened; French despotism overthrown; the French threat seemingly diminished.

To the young, the tumultuous events in Paris – the gathering of the Estates-General, the tennis court oath, the formation of the National Assembly, the jostling crowds in the streets, the passionate rhetoric, the Declaration of the Rights of Man and of the Citizen, the sweeping reforms, the sudden collapse of the *ancien régime* – seemed irresistibly dramatic. The solemn ceremonies that took place throughout France promised an end to the abuses of the past. Above all, the storming of the Bastille, and the release of prisoners arbitrarily detained there, symbolised the liberation of the people as a whole. This inspiring moment was commemorated by the teenage Samuel Taylor Coleridge in one his earliest poems, 'The Destruction of the Bastille':

> I see, I see! glad Liberty succeed
> With every patriot* Virtue in her train!

For him, as for so many Britons, the French were simply following where Englishmen had gone before:

> And still, as erst, let favour'd Britain be
> First ever of the first and freest of the free!

---

* In the eighteenth century, a 'patriot' was one prepared to put duty to one's country above personal or sectional interest. During the Revolution, the term came to have a more specific meaning: one willing to defend the Republic against foreign invasion.

PART I

Strangers

Bliss was it in that dawn to be alive,
But to be young was very heaven![1]

1

REVOLUTION

In the summer of 1790, William Wordsworth, then twenty years old and a commoner at St John's College, Cambridge, together with Robert Jones, another Cambridge undergraduate, made a vacation walking tour across Europe. They set out from Calais on 14 July, the first anniversary of the fall of the Bastille. This was the climax of the week-long *Fête de la Fédération*, culminating in a tremendous spectacle in the capital, attended by 400,000 delegates from all over the country, and celebrated throughout France. The two undergraduates walked through towns and villages decorated with triumphal arcs and window-garlands; the whole nation seemed 'mad with joy'.[1] Wordsworth was a self-confessedly stiff young man, proud and prickly, but even he found it hard to resist the intoxicating mood:

> ... 'twas a time when Europe was rejoiced,
> France standing on the top of golden hours,
> And human nature seeming born again.[2]

The thoroughfares of France were crowded with *fédérés* returning home from the festivities in Paris. Wordsworth and his companion fell in with a 'merry crowd' of these; after supper on a riverbank they danced around the table, hand in hand with the celebrants:

> All hearts were open, every tongue was loud
> With amity and glee. We bore a name
> Honoured in France, the name of Englishmen,

3

And hospitably did they give us hail
As their forerunners in a glorious course;
And round and round the Board they danced again.[3]

At such a moment it was easy to assume that the Revolution had run its course, that a healthy France had purged itself, that monarch and people were united in a delightful new equilibrium. Had not the King sworn to uphold the decrees of the Assembly in front of a vast crowd at the Champ de Mars? Had he and his family not decamped from the magnificent Palace of Versailles to the Tuileries, in the very heart of Paris (albeit under duress)? Had he not appeared in public to greet the Mayor at the Hôtel de Ville, his hat adorned with the Revolutionary red-and-blue cockade?

'It was a most interesting period to be in France,' Wordsworth wrote to his sister from the shores of Lake Constance.[4] But not *that* interesting: he and his friend Jones bypassed Paris, even though their route took them close to the capital, where all the most interesting events were happening. The Revolution was not their affair; they were headed for the Alps, then a sacred destination in the cult of the sublime. The young Englishmen joined in the Revolutionary festivities as guests, rather than participants. In his great autobiographical poem *The Prelude*, most of which was written a decade or more after the events described, Wordsworth admitted that

> . . . I looked upon these things
> As from a distance – heard, and saw, and felt,
> Was touched, but with no intimate concern –[5]

(At this point a cautionary note is appropriate. On the one hand, *The Prelude* dramatises what Wordsworth called 'spots in time' – moments of special significance from his inner life. It is the principal source for the biography of his youth, particularly some obscure years of his young manhood for which the poem provides almost the only illumination. On the other hand, it cannot be wholly relied upon, and in at least some aspects is misleading. The emotional and psychological aspects of the poem may be more trustworthy than the merely factual and chronological – though perhaps not entirely so. In *The*

Prelude, Wordsworth plots the 'growth of a poet's mind', from his infancy until he came into contact with Coleridge in his late twenties. But Wordsworth was writing in retrospect, trying to make sense of his past from the perspective of his mid-thirties. He had become a different man from the youth he was writing about. Not only was his memory fallible; there was a tendency in him, as in all of us, to manipulate the past in order to explain the present. Wordsworth's biographers cannot avoid using *The Prelude*, but they need to do so cautiously, and to seek for confirmatory evidence elsewhere.)

The two undergraduates returned home in October for their final term at Cambridge, after trudging more than a thousand miles* through France, Switzerland, Italy, Germany and Belgium in just under three months (Wordsworth's admiring sister Dorothy traced his path on the map). This was a poor man's Grand Tour, directed towards natural rather than cultural wonders, and undertaken on foot rather than by coach. Walking holidays were then coming into vogue, particularly for undergraduates and young clergymen – though few undertook a journey as ambitious as this one. Many of Wordsworth's Cambridge friends had thought the scheme mad and impractical, with so many difficulties as to render it impossible. Nevertheless, such tours were not completely unknown: two years before, William Frend and his old schoolmate Richard Tylden had trodden a similar route. Frend was a Cambridge Fellow, and it is possible that his example inspired Wordsworth. The poet William Lisle Bowles was another who had made a recent walking tour of the Continent. Wordsworth's school friend Joshua Wilkinson would undertake two walking tours in Europe in the following three years, and in 1798 would publish *The Wanderer*, a book based on his experiences. But walking tours were still something new; indeed the *Oxford English Dictionary* credits Wordsworth, in speaking of this tour, as the first to use the word 'pedestrian' in its literal rather than its metaphorical sense. A few years later an anonymous reviewer in the *Monthly Magazine* noted approvingly the 'increasing frequency of

---

* This is a low estimate. They travelled about two thousand miles in all, but some of the journey was by boat.

these pedestrian tours'. By 1815 the editor of the *Bristol Journal* could refer to 'this age of Pedestrianism'.[6]

Most of these new walkers did not venture abroad. Boswell's *Journal of a Tour to the Hebrides*, published in 1785, had helped to popularise the notion of internal tourism, exploring the wild and remote corners of the British Isles, until then generally assumed to be not worth going to see. Even before this, back in 1769, Thomas Gray had made a tour of the Lake District, and by the end of the century the Lakes had begun to attract tourists.* A succession of guidebooks to the regions of Britain appeared. Young men clad in sturdy boots and heavy coats strode up hills and along valleys, admiring landscapes previously unconsidered. Walking provided access to picturesque vistas otherwise inaccessible. Moreover, it was a form of escapism, disapproved of by the respectable. There was something intrinsically egalitarian – almost democratic – about this new habit. While the Grand Tour was available only to the very wealthy, walking tours, especially tours in Britain, could be made by anyone with the necessary leisure and modest funds to cover essential expenses. Such tours brought the middle-class walker into contact with the common people who shared the roads, while the rich rattled past in their coaches.† Dressed like tramps, the new walkers endured the same hardships and privations.

There was camaraderie on the road, as Wordsworth and Jones had discovered. Towards the end of their journey they passed through another country in revolt; the Belgians, inspired by their French neighbours, had risen against their ruler, the Austrian Emperor.

> . . . a glorious time,
> A happy time that was. Triumphant looks
> Were then the common language of all eyes:
> As if awaked from sleep, the nations hailed
> Their great expectancy; the fife of war
> Was then a spirit-stirring sound indeed,
> A blackbird's whistle in a vernal grove.[7]

---

* The term came into usage around 1800.
† Coach travel cost 2d or 3d per mile, a prohibitive expense for all but the wealthy.

Edmund Burke's *Reflections on the Revolution in France* appeared in print within weeks of Wordsworth's return to England. (This was a response to Richard Price's address to the London Revolution Society, now published as a pamphlet.) Burke was then in his sixtieth year; his *Reflections* were delivered with the authority of an elder statesman, the most intellectual of the Whigs, an exponent of principle in politics, a champion of liberty, and a philosopher of the sublime. Assessing what had happened in France, he argued that nothing good could come from a complete break with the past: on the contrary, such an upheaval must inevitably lead to bloodshed, war and tyranny. He did not oppose change of any kind; but he believed it must be gradual rather than sudden, and rooted in the traditions of the people. His book became a bestseller, and his ideas were much discussed, but by no means generally accepted; the Prince of Wales, for example, then a young radical, scorned it as a jeremiad, 'a farrago of nonsense'. In the House of Commons, the Prince's mentor Fox could not resist describing the new government of France as 'the most stupendous and glorious edifice of liberty which had been erected on the found- ation of human integrity in any time or country'. Fox and Burke had long been political allies, and when an indignant Burke voiced his opposition to 'all systems built on abstract rights' in the debate, Fox whispered his hope that though they disagreed, they might still remain friends. Burke spurned his appeal, declaring aloud that their friendship was at an end. Fox rose to reply, but was so hurt that he could not speak for some minutes, while tears trickled down his cheeks.

Burke's *Reflections* infuriated radicals, all the more so because Burke had been such an eloquent critic of the British government at the time of the American Revolution, fifteen years earlier. It provoked any number of hostile responses – including an essay written by Robert Southey, then a Westminster schoolboy – the most famous being Tom Paine's colossally successful *Rights of Man*. These in turn inspired further ripostes, one delivered by Richard Watson, Bishop of Llandaff, who had initially lauded the French attempts to free them- selves from arbitrary rule, but who had come, like Burke, to deplore the results when the passions of human nature were 'not regulated by religion, or controlled by law'.

Meanwhile Wordsworth had left Cambridge with a mere pass degree, a disappointment to his relatives who had hoped that he might have done well enough to be elected to the Fellowship reserved for men from Cumberland, succeeding his uncle William Cookson. They castigated him for having undertaken such an arduous walking tour in his final long vacation, when he should have been studying. Wordsworth's future was not a matter for him alone; a successful career would bring influence that could be used for the benefit of the whole family. But he was stubborn. The more his seniors tried to guide him, the more he resisted. An orphan from the age of thirteen, he had since been dependent on his grandfather and two uncles who acted as guardians; with no home of their own, he and his siblings had suffered slights from tactless relatives and insolent servants. Pride and restraint were at war within him. Open rebellion was not an option for Wordsworth; he could not afford to defy his uncles while he remained reliant on them. The most that he could do was to thwart their plans for him.

After quitting Cambridge, Wordsworth spent some months in London, where 'Free as a colt at pasture on the hills/I ranged at large'.[8] He feasted greedily on the spectacle offered by what was then the greatest city in the world: the bustle, the theatres, the shops, the pleasure gardens of Vauxhall and Ranelagh, the prostitutes and the fashionable ladies, the destitute and the wealthy, the extraordinary variety of sights and sounds and smells, all the more extraordinary to one who had grown up in the remote Lakes. As a spectator he attended the law courts, and watched the debates in Parliament, where he marvelled at Pitt's sustained oratory and was inspired by Burke's evergreen eloquence.[9] His reactions suggest that on the great issues of the moment he was not yet *parti pris*, even though he was mixing with radicals sympathetic to the French revolutionaries. On Sundays he would often dine with Samuel Nicholson, a Unitarian and a member of the Society for Constitutional Information, afterwards going on with him to hear the popular sermons preached by the minister Joseph Fawcett at the dissenters' meeting house in Old Jewry. It was probably at this time too that he met another radical dissenter, the bookseller-publisher Joseph Johnson, who lived above his shop in St Paul's Churchyard.[10] Johnson, who would be Wordsworth's first publisher, combined business acumen with good taste; among the eminent writers he published were Richard Price, Joseph Priestley, William Cowper, Erasmus Darwin, Thomas Malthus, William Godwin, Mary Wollstonecraft and Maria Edgeworth. He was also publisher of the liberal monthly the *Analytical Review*, and was then in the process of publishing the first part of Paine's *Rights of Man*.

In the late spring of 1791 Wordsworth left London for Wales, to stay with his walking companion Robert Jones and his sisters. 'He seems so happy that it is probable he will remain there all the summer,' observed his sister Dorothy. 'Who would not be happy enjoying the company of three young ladies in the Vale of Clewyd [*sic*] and without a rival?'[11] Despite these attractions, Wordsworth was able to tear himself away; he and Jones went on a walking tour of north Wales, and made a memorable night ascent of Snowdon to see the sunrise from the summit.*

To his friends at this time, Wordsworth affected a devil-may-care nonchalance. 'I am doomed to be an idler throughout my whole life,' he boasted to another Cambridge friend, William Mathews, after a year in which he cheerfully admitted to doing very little. His family was now trying to steer him towards the Church, but Wordsworth did not relish the prospect of 'vegetating on a paltry curacy'. Fortunately he was still, at the age of twenty-one, too young to take holy orders; he could afford to look about him a while yet. He appeared to be thinking as much of his own prospects when he urged Mathews to find 'some method of obtaining an Independence', which would 'enable you to get your bread unshackled by the necessity of professing a particular system of opinions...The field of Letters is very extensive, and it is astonishing if we cannot find some little corner, which with

---

* It seems likely to have been on this trip that Wordsworth visited the celebrated travel writer Thomas Pennant, whose *Tour in Scotland* had stimulated Johnson and Boswell to make their journey to the Western Isles.

a little tillage will produce us enough for the necessities, nay even the comforts, of life.'[12]

Wordsworth counted himself a 'philosopher', in the original sense of a lover of wisdom, one devoted to the search for fundamental truth. In the parlance of the time, the term might equally be applied to a scientist or a naturalist as to a student of political or moral philosophy, or metaphysics. At this stage Wordsworth was far from certain what kind of life lay ahead of him. While at Cambridge he had become increasingly aware of his poetic gifts. The 'instinctive humbleness' he felt at the very thought of publication began to 'melt away'; his 'dread awe of mighty names' softened; increasingly he felt a 'fellowship' with the authors he revered, and he was filled with 'a thousand hopes', 'a thousand tender dreams', as 'a morning gladness' settled on his mind. He had already completed one long poem, 'An Evening Walk'; this achievement encouraged the 'daring thought' that he

> . . . might leave
> Some monument behind me which pure hearts
> Should reverence . . .'[13]

Yet his feeling of fellowship with the great poets of the past was accompanied by a sense of alienation in the present. At Cambridge he had often been melancholy, conscious that he did not belong. There was 'a strangeness in my mind', a solitariness, an impression that he was different. Sometimes he would leave his university friends and walk out into the surrounding country, 'turning the mind in upon itself'. Then again he would feel

> The strength and consolation which were mine.

The swelling appreciation of the powers latent within him strengthened his conviction that he was 'a chosen son' of Nature.[14]

Towards the end of the year Wordsworth returned to France, to pass the year in Orléans, which until the Revolution had been a fashionable destination for young Englishmen, but where now (as he would discover) only a handful remained. It seems that he had no particular plan beyond that of improving his French, in the vague hope that this would qualify him for the post of travelling companion to some young gentleman. His uncles would have preferred him to return to Cambridge, to study oriental literature. 'William has a great attachment to poetry,' remarked his sister Dorothy to her friend Jane Pollard, 'which is not the most likely thing to produce his advancement in the world.'[15]

The country to which he returned in November 1791 was very different from the one he had left the year before. France was in a state of turbulence; the apparent equilibrium had proved illusory. The National Assembly was supplanted by a Legislative Assembly, which would be replaced while Wordsworth was still in France by a National Convention. Each new body proved more susceptible than its predecessor to Revolutionary rhetoric, and each member tried to outdo his peers in crowd-pleasing Revolutionary zeal. The debate was increasingly histrionic. Publications such as Jean-Paul Marat's *L'Ami du peuple* set a tone of vituperative abuse. Factions began to form: the most radical grouping found a permanent place on the left side – the 'left wing' – of the *Manège* (the converted riding school where the Assembly met), the most conservative on the right. The King had displayed his commitment to constitutional monarchy by attempting to flee the country, only to be escorted back from Varennes (not far from the border) under restraint; National Guardsmen had opened fire on their fellow citizens in suppressing a demonstration at the Champ de Mars. Frenchman had fired on Frenchman; brother had killed brother. It became clear that the Revolution was not yet complete.

This time Wordsworth travelled through France by coach rather than on foot. His route to Orléans took him through Paris, where he spent a few days exploring, hastening to the Champ de Mars to sniff the grapeshot, listening to the debates in the Jacobin Club* and the Assembly, pocketing a stone as a relic from the ruins of the Bastille. There he sat in the sunshine, 'affecting more emotion than I felt'. He

---

* Generally known as such after the place where members of the club met in the rue St Jacques. Their official name was the Society of the Friends of the Revolution.

admitted to being more moved by a painting, the baroque Magdalene de Le Brun, displayed in a Carmelite convent while religious music played in the background for the benefit of visitors – now almost forgotten, but then one of the must-see sights of Paris.[16]

At this moment the young Wordsworth appears to have had no more than a vague sympathy for the Revolution. By the time he left France a year later he was ready to take up service for the cause, however dangerous – even, if necessary, to sacrifice his life.[17] Such a change could not have occurred overnight; it seems more plausible that Wordsworth's loyalties were won gradually during his stay in France. As he became more familiar with the language, so he was better able to comprehend what was being said and written all around him. And as a result he was better able to form his own judgements about the behaviour and character of those he encountered. It was natural that the longer he stayed in France, the more he should identify with French concerns. At first he felt as if he had arrived at a theatre when the play was already far advanced. By the end of his stay he felt ready to act a part himself.

The Revolution reached its crisis while Wordsworth was in France. Since his flight to Varennes the King was no longer trusted; there were persistent rumours that he was conspiring with *émigrés* and foreign powers to usurp the new constitution. In April the nation declared war on 'the King of Bohemia and Hungary' (the Austrian Emperor Leopold, brother of the hated Marie Antoinette); by the summer the French were at war with the Emperor's allies, the Prussians, as well. Shouting demonstrators burst into the Tuileries, forcing Louis to don a red bonnet and drink a glass of wine with them, which he did with courage and good humour. The Prussians issued a manifesto calling on the French to rise up against their Revolutionary 'oppressors', and threatening an 'exemplary and unforgettable act of vengeance' against the capital in the event of further outrages against the royal family. Morale in the old royal army was as low as could be; two-thirds of the officer corps had abandoned their commands, many to avoid a compulsory oath of allegiance to the new constitution, others in despair of disciplining the new 'patriot' recruits.* Generals and their staffs defected *en masse* to the enemy. The Prussian army marched towards the border, crossing into France in mid-July. The Assembly formally decreed a state of emergency, '*La Patrie en Danger*', and appealed for volunteers. These flocked to Paris from the provinces, aflame with Revolutionary ardour. A further decree allowed all citizens to enrol in the National Guard, creating 'a nation in arms'. Excitement crackled in the streets, and on the morning of 10 August an angry crowd gathered in front of the Tuileries. The King's Swiss Guards retreated inside the palace. The royal family fled to the Assembly, where the King appealed for shelter. After a flurry of shots, Louis sent an order to his Guards to stand down. The crowd stormed the palace, pursuing the Guards and courtiers out into the streets, where they were hunted down and slaughtered.

Now that his authority had collapsed, Louis XVI was no longer relevant; the monarchy was suspended, and soon abolished. The royal family was imprisoned in the Temple, the gloomy medieval home of the Knights Templar. The Assembly accepted Robespierre's proposal to summon a National Convention, elected by universal (male) suffrage, for the purpose of framing a new constitution. Meanwhile the Prussians advanced steadily. First one fortress, then another fell to them. The mood in Paris became jittery. More than a thousand suspected 'counter-revolutionaries' were taken into custody. A guillotine was erected outside the Tuileries.

It was difficult for Wordsworth to follow the changing situation in Paris and the fighting on the borders. In a letter home he confessed that, 'in London you have perhaps a better opportunity of being informed of the general concerns of France, than in a petty provincial town in the heart of the kingdom itself'.[18] Nevertheless, it was impossible for any resident of France not to be aware of the upsurge in patriotic feeling at this time. Every town saw parades and ceremonies, introduced by speeches of lofty rhetoric; Revolutionary clubs like the ubiquitous Jacobins began to usurp the powers of local government:

---

* Until the Revolution, commissions in the army had been reserved for scions of families whose aristocratic lineage went back at least four generations.

> . . . 'Twas in truth an hour
> Of universal ferment; mildest men
> Were agitated; and commotions, strife
> Of passion and opinion, filled the walls
> Of peaceful houses with unquiet sounds.[19]

This was a cultural revolution. The young men in its vanguard aimed to introduce a sterner moral code into public life, in place of the lax cynicism of the *ancien régime*. These zealots were steeped in the classics, whose authors presented an ideal of civic virtue, of loyalty to the Republic triumphing over selfish attachments. Their values were those of self-sacrifice, purity, duty, integrity, patriotism, stoicism and austerity; their model the Roman Republic; their heroes unimpeachable citizens like Cato or Cicero, whose oratory echoed down the centuries. Indeed, the revolutionaries identified themselves with the Roman Republic to what now seems a ludicrous extent. Had they not cast off a line of tyrannical kings, as the Romans had done? Had they not established a Senate? Had they not sworn solemn oaths, like the Horatii? Had they not defeated conspiracy after conspiracy to undermine the Republic?

The changes taking place extended into every area of life. A severe neoclassicism became the predominant style in painting, in sculpture, in architecture, in fashion. The artificiality of the eighteenth century was replaced by an emphasis on naturalness. Wigs began to disappear. Men wore their own hair, often short and straight, perhaps brushed forward in the Roman style, without powder or curls. (While at Cambridge Wordsworth had powdered his hair, but now he too cut it short.) Women wore loose, flowing, high-waisted dresses, in contrast to the ornate and cumbersome constructions favoured by fashionable ladies in pre-Revolutionary France. It became *de rigueur* to address everyone as '*tu*', no matter how distant the relationship; while the titles '*monsieur*' and '*madame*' made way for the more democratic '*citoyen*' and '*citoyenne*'.[20] These usages, though offensive or embarrassing to many, were enforced by the new authorities. Even the calendar would be replaced while Wordsworth was in France: Sunday was abolished and a ten-day week introduced. Year 1 began with the founding of the Republic, on 22 September 1792.

In Orléans Wordsworth lodged above a shop in the rue Royale owned by M. Gellet-Duvivier, a vociferous opponent of the Revolution. The other lodgers, three Cavalry officers and 'a gentleman from Paris', were of like mind. After a fortnight in Orléans, an apparently surprised Wordsworth reported that he had not met a single person 'of wealth and circumstance' favourable to the Revolution. 'All the people of any opulence are aristocrates* [sic] and all the others democrats,' he informed his brother Richard.[21] His fellow lodgers introduced Wordsworth to the society of other officers stationed in the city. All were well-born, all 'were bent upon undoing what was done', and some spoke openly to this young foreigner of leaving to join the émigrés mustering with the enemy armies on the borders.

If the officers assumed that the Englishman (being an Englishman) would share their contempt for the lower orders, they were mistaken. Wordsworth was not one for whom rank and wealth commanded automatic respect, having grown up in the Lake District,

> . . . which yet
> Retaineth more of ancient homeliness,
> Manners erect, and frank simplicity,
> Than any other nook of English land.[22]

Moreover, he and his siblings had a long-standing grievance against one of the 'great': the notoriously mean Earl of Lonsdale, the most powerful landowner in the north-west of England, who used his enormous wealth to exert absolute control over nine seats in Parliament,† enough in the chaotic politics of the eighteenth century to give him considerable political leverage. As an attorney, Wordsworth's father

* Confusion is caused by the term 'aristocrat'. The French noblesse was not the same as the English aristocracy: even allowing for the difference in population size, they were far more numerous – perhaps a quarter of a million people, compared to the 10,000 or so in Britain. By no means all 'aristocrats' were wealthy, despite occupying a privileged position under the ancien régime. It was not unknown for a French 'aristocrat' to push his own plough. In Britain, the term 'aristocrat' had a political as well as a social meaning; it was used as shorthand to denote anyone opposed to reform; while a 'democrat' was defined as one who demanded radical changes to the constitution, together with an immediate peace with France and recognition of the French Republic.
† His MPs were known as 'Lonsdale's ninepins'.

John, a widower, had been Lonsdale's* man of business, and in this capacity he had freely disbursed his own money on his employer's behalf. After John Wordsworth's sudden death in 1783 Lonsdale had refused to honour the outstanding sum, amounting to several thousand pounds. The Wordsworth orphans were left impoverished, dependent on relatives. Having been raised with certain expectations, they had been disappointed; a sense of injustice coloured their lives. Wordsworth had therefore the strongest personal reasons for resenting the power and the privileges of the wealthy, and his formative experience of the ruling class was of an especially odious specimen. This was an upbringing that might have been devised for the raising of a revolutionary. Many of the leading deputies in the Assembly were young men like Wordsworth: from the middle ranks of society, alienated from their families, well educated but carrying some form of grievance.

Cambridge had encouraged Wordsworth's democratic inclinations, being 'something . . .

> Of a Republic, where all stood thus far
> Upon equal ground, that they were brothers all
> In honour, as in one community –
> Scholars and Gentlemen – where, furthermore,
> Distinction lay open to all that came,
> And wealth and titles were in less esteem
> Than talents and successful industry.[23]

Nothing in Wordsworth's background led him to share the officers' assumptions about the innate superiority of the landowning classes. On the contrary, their disdain for the uncouth masses rankled with him.[24]

But anyway, Wordsworth felt that it would be impossible to 'undo what was done', whatever the outcome of the war. The Revolutionary reforms were belated and inevitable. As he wrote to Mathews:

> . . . suppose that the German army is at the gates of Paris, what will be the consequence? It will be impossible to make

* Lonsdale was Sir James Lowther until ennobled in 1784.

16

any material alteration in the constitution, impossible to reinstate the clergy in its ancient guilty splendor, impossible to give an existence to the *noblesse* similar to that it before enjoyed, impossible to add much to the authority of the King: Yet there are in France some [?millions – this word is indecipherable] – I speak without exaggeration – who expect that this will take place.[25]

It seems likely that he was thinking of the officers when he wrote these words.

Wordsworth could not refrain from contrasting such disillusioned and resentful reactionaries with the gallant volunteers for the citizen army. Once again, as in 1790, he saw the roads of France crowded, this time not with *fédérés* returning from Paris, but with 'the bravest Youth of France' flocking to the frontier, in response to urgent appeals to defend the motherland from invasion. He witnessed many poignant scenes of farewell, the memory of which would move him to tears more than a decade afterwards. News from the front that summer was of disaster after disaster: the patriot army seemed unable to match the superior discipline of their opponents, all professional soldiers. To Wordsworth, the volunteers appeared as martyrs, going willingly to their certain doom.

> . . . they seem'd
> Like arguments from Heaven that 'twas a cause
> Good, and which no one could stand up against
> Who was not lost, abandoned, selfish, proud,
> Mean, miserable, wilfully depraved,
> Hater perverse of equity and truth.[26]

Such idealism could scarcely fail to move an open-hearted young man. The fine principles for which the volunteers fought, dressed in heady rhetoric, were universal. The French were fighting to defend their country, but they were fighting in the name of all Mankind. The fire had been kindled in France, but it seemed possible, indeed likely, that the blaze would spread across Europe, perhaps even to England. In such circumstances, it is scarcely surprising that Wordsworth should have come to see himself as 'a Patriot':

> . . . my heart was all
> Given to the People, and my love was theirs.[27]

Wordsworth was then a child of Rousseau; he was inclined to believe that men are naturally good, that the existing institutions of society are artificial, tending to perpetuate idleness, luxury and flattery: a rotten carapace that could be peeled back to reveal the healthy flesh underneath. The violence that accompanied the Revolution was not characteristic; it was simply necessary to correct the unnatural abuses of the past. A new social contract would be founded on Justice, Equality and Reason. Government would be by the 'general will', for the common good, and by consent of the citizenry. In making a new constitution, free from any encumbrances of the past, the Convention would be making a new kind of Man. For the young Wordsworth, the Revolution promised heaven on earth:

> O pleasant exercise of hope and joy!
> For great were the auxiliars which then stood
> Upon our side, we who were strong in love.
> Bliss was it in that dawn to be alive,
> But to be young was very heaven! O times,
> In which the meagre, stale, forbidding ways
> Of custom, law, and statute took at once
> The attraction of a country in romance –
> When Reason seemed the most to assert her rights
> When most intent of making of herself
> A prime enchanter to assist the work
> Which then was going forwards in her name.
> Not favoured spots alone, but the whole earth,
> The beauty wore of promise . . .[28]

In Orléans Wordsworth became involved with a woman at least four years his senior, Annette Vallon, and it was probably on her account that he moved early in 1792 to her home town of Blois, some thirty miles down the Loire. It seems likely that he was one of the two Englishmen admitted on 3 February to the Revolutionary club in Blois, Les Amis de la Constitution.[29] Its President was Henri Grégoire, a radical cleric closely identified with the iconography of the Revolution: his image appears at the centre of Jacques-Louis David's famous composition *The Tennis-Court Oath*.* As 'Constitutional Bishop' of Blois he had served as a member of the Constituent Assembly until its dissolution in September 1791. Former members of the Constituent Assembly were debarred from sitting in the new Legislative Assembly, so after its dissolution Grégoire had returned to Blois. On 14 July 1792, Federation Day, he delivered a fiery speech to Les Amis de la Constitution in which he prophesied that the Revolution would spread across the world. He hailed the patriot armies fighting for '*la liberté de l'univers*':

> The present augurs well for the future. Soon we shall witness the liberation of all humankind. Everything confirms that the coming revolution will set all of Europe free, and prove a consolation for the whole human race. Liberty has been fettered to thrones for far too long! She will burst those irons and chains and as she extends her influence beyond our horizons, will inaugurate the federation of all mankind![30]

Whether Wordsworth was present while this speech was being delivered is unknown. If not, he may well have read the transcript when it was published soon afterwards. In any case, Grégoire's rhetoric gives a sense of the millenarian atmosphere in Revolutionary Blois at the time. Wordsworth was certainly aware of Grégoire; he later referred to him admiringly and quoted his words with approval.

In Blois, Wordsworth again lodged in a house with army officers, but here he met one different from the rest (and ostracised as a result): Michel Beaupuy, a captain who, though an aristocrat by birth, embraced the changes brought by the Revolution wholeheartedly. Beaupuy was thirty-seven, fifteen years older than Wordsworth, and he became a mentor to the younger man. Together they walked many a mile along the banks of the Loire, or in the forests

---

* Commissioned by the Jacobin Club but never completed (in part because of the need for constant changes; some of those who had been present became *personae non gratae*, and thus had to be excluded, while others, who had not, now wished to be included): existing only in the form of David's preliminary (but detailed) sketches, some of which portray the assembled oath-swearers as classically severe nudes.

that grew along the valley, engaged in 'earnest dialogues', putting the world to rights:

> Why should I not confess that earth was then
> To me what an inheritance new-fallen
> Seems, when the first time visited, to one
> Who thither comes to find in it his home?
> He walks about and looks upon the place
> With cordial transport – moulds it and remoulds –
> And is half pleased with things that are amiss,
> T'will be such joy to see them disappear.[31]

In this spirit of comradely idealism, Wordsworth may even have fantasised about joining Beaupuy in an armed crusade to liberate Britain from monarchy and aristocracy. There is a passage in *The Prelude* that seems to hint at such a possibility, when he writes of a 'philosophic war/Led by philosophers'.[32] And why not? However unrealistic, Wordsworth's dream of revolution in Britain was consistent with the rhetoric used by men like Grégoire.

Among Beaupuy's qualities that impressed Wordsworth was his compassion for the poor, 'a courtesy which had no air/Of condescension'. On one of their walks they chanced on a 'hunger-bitten girl', leading a heifer by a cord.

> . . . at the sight my friend
> In agitation said, ' 'Tis against *that*
> Which we are fighting,' I with him believed
> Devoutly that a spirit was abroad
> Which could not be withstood, that poverty,
> At least like this, would in a little time
> Be found no more . . .'[33]

Such sympathies would linger in Wordsworth's heart long after he had abandoned hope of revolutionary change.

On 2 September 1792, the fortress of Verdun fell to the Prussians. The French army prepared to make a last stand; if this failed, the road to Paris lay open before the invaders. Panic seized the capital; rumour spread that as the enemy arrived at the gates a 'fifth column' of aristocrats and priests would emerge from prison to murder the defenceless families of citizens away fighting. Marat fed the paranoia, urging the people to eliminate this threat from within. Mobs stormed prisons across the city, dragging out the inmates and slaughtering them in the street: old and young, men and women alike. The often mutilated corpses were stripped of their clothing, then loaded onto wagons and carted away for disposal. The newly severed head of one of Marie Antoinette's closest friends, her former lady-in-waiting the Princesse de Lamballe, was impaled on a pike and waved jeeringly outside the Queen's window. About half of all those imprisoned in Paris were massacred, among them more than two hundred priests. Three years before,the Revolution had begun with the joyous release of prisoners from their dark cells; now prisoners were hauled out into the light to be butchered.

The September Massacres, as they became known, shocked even the by-now hardened French public. More than a thousand people were murdered before the frenzy faded. Among the dead were fifty or so prisoners being transferred from Orléans, ambushed by a band of armed Parisians at Versailles. Blood was shed in Orléans itself in early September: a mob protesting against the high price of bread went on the rampage, burning and looting houses. The city authorities imposed a curfew and declared martial law, but by the time the National Guard had restored order, thirteen people had been killed in the riots. Wordsworth returned to Orléans from Blois some time in September; it is not known whether he was in time to witness the violence. He was then putting the finishing touches to his poem 'Descriptive Sketches'; its conclusion welcomed the proclamation of the Republic by the Convention on 21 September:

Lo! From th'innocuous flames, a lovely birth!

It seems probable that these lines were written even as bloodstains were being scrubbed from the pavements of Paris.

Wordsworth was preparing to return to England. By this time it must have been obvious that Annette Vallon was pregnant; she would give birth to a daughter on 15 December. So why did Wordsworth leave France, just as he was about to become a father? He was certainly short of money. He may have believed that the time was ripe to publish his poems. Maybe he felt that he must return home to secure his future, to establish himself in the Church or some other profession, so that he would be able to provide for Annette and his child. Possibly he intended to marry her once he was established; Annette's subsequent letters suggest that she expected him to do so. But she may have been deluding herself. It would have been difficult for him to make a career in the Church, with a foreign, Catholic wife and a child born out of wedlock. Perhaps he made promises to Annette that he did not mean to keep. The frustrating truth is that there is not enough evidence on which to base anything more than guesses at Wordsworth's intentions.

The very day before the proclamation of the Republic, the French repelled the Prussians at Valmy, about a hundred miles east of Paris. This was the turn of the tide; the crisis had passed. Goethe, who was accompanying his patron, a general in the defeated army, immediately recognised the significance of the Revolutionary victory. That same evening, sitting in a circle of demoralised Prussian soldiers around a damp campfire, he attempted to lift the prevalent gloom by telling them: 'From this place and this time forth commences a new era in world history and you can all say that you were present at its birth.'[34]

In the House of Commons, Fox did not hide his delight at the French victory. For him, the 'conspiracy' of the reactionary powers (Prussia and Austria) threatened 'not merely the ruin of liberty in France, but the ruin of liberty in England; the ruin of the liberty of man'. Like Fox, Wordsworth had come to see the fate of mankind as being bound up with that of the Revolution; he 'laid this faith to heart',

> That if France prospered good men would not long
> Pay fruitless worship to humanity.[35]

In late October Wordsworth, 'enflam'd with hope', arrived in Paris on his way back to England. It was a moment of high political tension. The majority in the new Convention was attempting to assert its authority over those extra-parliamentary forces that had so recently wrought havoc in the capital. One of the most prominent of those trying to re-establish the rule of law was the leader of the loosely organised 'Girondin' group of deputies, Jacques Pierre Brissot. In this he was resisted by Maximilien Robespierre, who by a process of manipulation and intimidation dominated the Jacobin clubs and the Commune. Robespierre's supporters were known as 'the Mountain', after the position they took in the new chamber in the Tuileries, on the benches high up against the wall. The majority of uncommitted deputies sat lower down, close to the debating floor, and thus became known as 'the Plain'. Brissot and his allies had already made one attempt to rein in Robespierre, which failed when Marat brandished a pistol in the Convention chamber and melodramatically threatened to blow out his own brains.

On his first morning in the capital, after a disturbed night dreaming of the massacres, Wordsworth emerged onto the street to find hawkers selling copies of a speech denouncing Robespierre. In the Convention, Robespierre dared his opponents to identify themselves – and, after a silence, the Girondin journalist Louvet stepped forward to the tribune to accuse him, amongst other crimes, of encouraging the creation of a personality cult, and aspiring to a dictatorship.

In *The Prelude*, Wordsworth chose to dramatise this as a decisive scene in the Revolution, the moment when its future would be decided, for good or ill. He may have overestimated its significance – historians disagree on the subject – but there seems little reason to doubt his sincerity. It was clearly an important moment for *him*.* He bemoaned the fact that 'Louvet was left alone without support/Of his irresolute friends'. Though 'an insignificant stranger', Wordsworth contemplated taking sides in this struggle:

* It may be significant that Louvet had been elected to the Convention to represent the Loiret, the *département* in which Wordsworth had been living; perhaps this fact contributed to Wordsworth's interest in him.

Mean as I was, and little graced with powers
Of eloquence even in my native speech,
And all unfit for tumult and intrigue,
Yet would I willingly have taken up
A service at this time for cause so great,
However dangerous.[36]

It was not unprecedented for an Englishman to engage in French politics. Tom Paine, for example, had been elected to the Convention after receiving a letter from the President of the Assembly announcing that 'France calls you to its bosom,' as well as invitations from no fewer than three different *départements* to stand as one of their deputies. In August the Assembly had conferred on Paine the title of 'French citizen'.* It is possible that Wordsworth had already met Paine in 1791 through his publisher Joseph Johnson, the original publisher of *Rights of Man*; possible too that Wordsworth attended the dinner of expatriate Englishmen at White's Hotel in Paris on 18 November, at which Paine was toasted and diners offered their 'fraternal homage' to the new Republic. Ten days later, a delegation from the Society for Constitutional Information in London presented a congratulatory address to the Convention. In response, Grégoire evoked the memory of the English revolutionaries of the 1640s. 'The moment is at hand,' he declared, 'when the French Nation will send its own congratulations to the National Convention of Great Britain.'[37]

Nearly fifty years afterwards, an elderly Wordsworth chucklingly confessed that he had been *'pretty hot in it'* while in Paris, but what he meant by this is unclear. In a letter to his brother Richard written soon after his first visit to the French capital, he had referred to an unnamed member who had introduced him to the Assembly, 'of whose acquaintance I shall profit on my return to Paris'.[38] This was probably Brissot. Thomas De Quincey, who first met Wordsworth in 1807 and whose source was likely to have been Wordsworth himself, recorded that Wordsworth 'had been sufficiently connected with public men to have drawn upon himself some notice from those who

---

* Joseph Priestley was made a citizen of France in September. He too was elected to the Convention, but declined the election.

afterwards composed the Committee of Public Safety', i.e. Robespierre and his associates. He implied that Wordsworth had been prominent enough to be in danger had he remained longer in France.[39] In *The Prelude* Wordsworth would later suggest that had he stayed in Paris he 'doubtless should have made a common cause/with some who perished' – and maybe would have perished himself.[40]

As well as Brissot, Wordsworth knew at least one other prominent Girondin deputy, the journalist Jean-Antoine Gorsas. Moreover, he was familiar with and may have known Grégoire, who in September had returned to Paris from Blois to sit in the Convention as deputy for Loir-et-Cher. It was Grégoire who had proposed the motion to abolish the monarchy, initiating the Republic. On 16 November he would be elected President of the Convention.

Robespierre replied to the charges against him in a speech to the Convention a week later. It was delivered in his usual style: self-dramatising, paranoid, brimming with righteous indignation. Far from seeking power for himself, he claimed to be no more than a repository of Historical Truth. He defended the recent violence, and dismissed the charges of illegality, pointing out that the Revolution was from its outset 'illegal'. To judge the Revolution by standards of conventional morality was to rob the people's uprising of its *natural* legitimacy. He concluded with a rhetorical flourish: 'Do you want a Revolution without a revolution?'[41]

The speech carried the Convention; his accusers melted under the heat of Robespierre's high-minded rhetoric. He now turned his attention to the fate of the King, demanding that he should face trial. Robespierre's protégé, the young fanatic Louis-Antoine Saint-Just, went further: he asserted that a trial was unnecessary, because Louis was by definition guilty: 'one cannot reign innocently'. There was only one possible solution: the surgical removal of this excrescence from the body of the nation.

Another prominent deputy, the Minister of the Interior Jean Marie Roland, announced the discovery amongst the King's belongings of an iron chest filled with papers, apparently incriminating not just the King himself, but also some of the more moderate deputies. Those trying to defend the King were now on the defensive, fearful that they might in turn come under attack. A number chose to abandon Louis in order to protect themselves.

Early in December the Convention ended its discussion on the principle of trying the King and ordered an indictment to be prepared. On the eleventh Louis was brought before the Convention to answer the charge of fomenting counter-revolution. His replies, though dignified, were unconvincing.

Wordsworth had planned to be back in London during the month of October.[42] He had two poems ready for publication, and a woman in an advanced state of pregnancy who needed his support. But he lingered a month or more in Paris, no doubt fascinated to be on hand while the future of the world was being decided. It seems that he may have attended some of the debates in the Convention as a spectator. Two years earlier he had been unwilling to make a small detour to come to Paris; now he was unable to drag himself away. At last, he returned reluctantly to England,

> Compelled by nothing less than absolute want
> Of funds for my support.[43]

2

REACTION

Wordsworth arrived in England in December 1792 overflowing with love for humanity, only to find the majority of his fellow countrymen suspicious or even belligerent. Recent events in France had thoroughly alarmed conservative opinion in Britain. It was one thing to limit the powers of the monarchy: quite another to abolish the monarchy altogether. With each passing week came news of further excesses; émigrés arrived by the boatload on British shores, every one bringing stories of fresh outrages. In its anxiety to avoid war, Pitt's government had striven to remain neutral towards Revolutionary France, while stifling radical agitation at home. On 21 May 1792 a Royal Proclamation had been issued, encouraging magistrates to be more vigorous in controlling riotous meetings and seditious writings. Not much had ensued at the time, beyond a decision (perhaps taken beforehand) to prosecute Paine.

Meanwhile the victorious French armies had continued their advance, carrying all before them. The Prussians were driven back across the Rhine, and in November the French occupied Belgium, while in the south Savoy was annexed. On 19 November the Convention promised 'fraternity and assistance' to 'all those wishing to recover their liberty'. The war changed its character: it was no longer a defence of the Republic, but a war of liberation. In the Convention Brissot declared, 'We cannot relax until all Europe is in flames.'

The Convention's threat to export the Revolution prompted Pitt to act, beginning a succession of prosecutions of radical authors, printers and publishers. At the same time the government released a flood of crude anti-French, pro-monarchist propaganda. Stories spread of plots, of insurrection, of traitors in our midst. Spies, informers and *agents provocateurs* proliferated. Support for the Revolution was portrayed as unpatriotic. It was not difficult to stir up popular sentiment against France, nor against those who appeared to side with the Old Enemy. Dissenters were especially vulnerable. By this time religious dissent and political radicalism had become synonymous; it was easy to portray prominent dissenters as pro-French Revolutionary conspirators. There had already been an ominous indication of what could happen if the crude prejudices of the people were inflamed. Back in 1791, a dinner in Birmingham to celebrate the second anniversary of the fall of the Bastille had provoked three days of rioting. Though the mob chanted 'No Popery' (as well as the inevitable 'Church and King'), its victims were mainly prosperous dissenters with progressive views, most prominently Joseph Priestley, whose house (including his precious library) and laboratory were burned to the ground.

Britons were encouraged to draw up loyal addresses to George III. Those who declined to add their signatures were deemed to be suspect. Loyalists powdered their hair in the traditional style, while radicals let it hang loose in the 'French' fashion. Inns displayed gilt signs: 'NO JACOBINS ADMITTED HERE'. In November the MP John Reeves founded an anti-Jacobin association, and branches sprang up around the country, a counter-revolutionary equivalent to the Jacobin clubs. A month later Reeves founded an Association for Preserving Liberty and Property against Republicans and Levellers, which met fortnightly at the Crown and Anchor tavern in The Strand. Burke proposed the toast: 'Old England against new France'.

A further Royal Proclamation on 1 December 1792 summoned the militia to suppress 'seditious activities'. Parliament was recalled to combat the threat of insurrection. In the House of Commons, Fox attempted to calm exaggerated fears:

> An insurrection! Where is it? Where has it reared its head!
> Good God! An insurrection in Great Britain! No wonder
> the militia were called out, and parliament assembled in the
> extraordinary way in which they have been. But where is it?[1]

But his ironic words were scarcely heard in the storm of panic sweeping across the country. Fox's allies began to desert him, going over to the ministry one by one, until eventually he would be left with only a rump of loyal supporters, too small to be able to make any serious challenge in Parliament.

The case against Paine had come to court in June, only to be adjourned. It was widely rumoured that the Attorney-General was reluctant to proceed to trial because he did not approve of the prosecution (a charge he denied). But the government's own propaganda created pressure to make an example of Paine. He was dogged by government hirelings who hissed and hooted at him on every public occasion. Pillars of the community demonstrated their loyalty by burning his book in public.

Paine was among well-wishers at Joseph Johnson's house in St Paul's Churchyard one evening when another radical, the poet William Blake, warned him not to go home; a warrant had been issued for his arrest. Paine left that night for Dover. Within days he had taken up his seat in the Convention. On 18 December he was tried *in absentia*, and after being found guilty by a packed jury, was declared an outlaw.* Demonstrations against him were promoted around the country. His effigy was burned, shot at, hanged, and pounded to smithereens with a sledgehammer. According to the undergraduate Samuel Taylor Coleridge, then making a rare visit to his home town of Ottery St Mary, the locals were very disappointed that Paine had not been 'cut to pieces at Canterbury'.

Such was the atmosphere when Wordsworth returned to England: a dismaying contrast with the mood in France – and about to become much worse. On 21 January 1793 the former King of France went to the guillotine. The news horrified the British public. (In the Convention, Paine had tried to argue against the execution, only to be shouted down by Marat.) Radicals were already divided in their responses to the developing situation in France, and on the defensive against the new programme of government repression. Now public opinion

* Only days before he was condemned in the name of George III, Paine, as a deputy in the Convention, had been sitting in judgement on the former French King.

hardened against them. Just as the radical cause in Britain had been boosted by the outbreak of the Revolution, so it was undermined by the killing of the King.

John Frost, secretary of the Corresponding Society, was among the country's most prominent radicals. He had been one of the pair of delegates sent to Paris by the Society for Constitutional Information to assure the French Convention that the British people would never support a war against liberty. In this capacity he had been present at Louis XVI's trial, and as a result he had been denounced by Burke as 'the ambassador to the murderers'. Early in 1793 Frost was arrested on a charge of sedition, on the basis of an alleged conversation in Percy's coffee house, Marylebone; he was supposed to have declared that he wanted 'no king in England', and that 'the constitution of this country is a bad one'. (It seems that he was drunk at the time.) On these flimsy grounds Frost was struck off the attorney's roll, imprisoned for six months, required to provide £500 as a surety of good behaviour for five years or face prolonged imprisonment until he did so, and made to stand in the pillory for an hour. (The latter was no small punishment; men had been mutilated or even killed as a result of blows received in the pillory.) Frost's was one of a number of prosecutions for sedition promoted by the government in the spring of 1793 in an attempt to intimidate radicals.

On 29 January Wordsworth's poems 'An Evening Walk' and 'Descriptive Sketches' were published by Joseph Johnson in two quarto volumes. If not quite his first appearance in print – a poem of his had been published in the *European Magazine* – these were, at the very least, an attempt to prove himself: 'as I had done nothing by which to distinguish myself at the university, I thought these little things might shew that I could do something'.[2] But his hopes fell flat. Reviews were cool and sales were slow. Given the timing, that was hardly surprising. Three days after the poems were published, France declared war on Britain. 'Descriptive Sketches', which concluded in a hymn of praise to the new Republic, could scarcely have appeared at a less propitious moment.

The coming of war increased Wordsworth's sense of alienation. He loved his country deeply; and hated what his country was doing. For him, Revolutionary France was the hope of Mankind; now his own kin made war on her, in unholy alliance with the despotic emperors of central Europe. Even now these tyrants were carving up Poland between them, crudely annexing the territory of a free people. Wordsworth secretly rejoiced at news of British defeats, and in church sat silent among the congregation, 'like an uninvited guest', while prayers were offered up for British victories.

> Oh, much have they to account for, who could tear
> By violence at one decisive rent
> From the best youth in England their dear pride,
> Their joy, in England . . .[3]

In France, Wordsworth had come to feel himself a patriot; in England he was made to feel a traitor. Moreover, war with France divided him from his mistress and his daughter, born in December and baptised in the cathedral at Orléans. It was, as he recognised, a profound shock to his moral nature:

> . . . I felt
> The ravage of this most unnatural strife
> In my own heart; there lay it like a weight
> At enmity with all the tenderest springs
> Of my enjoyments. I, who with the breeze
> Had played, a green leaf on the blessed tree
> Of my beloved country – nor had wished
> For happier fortune than to wither there –
> Now from my pleasant station was cut off,
> And tossed about in whirlwinds . . .[4]

Since his return from France Wordsworth had been lodging with his elder brother Richard, a lawyer in Staple Inn.* According to De Quincey, his companions were forced to play cards with him every night, 'as the best mode of beguiling his sense of distress'. Disaffected and resentful, he was indignant to read the strictures on the French

---

* One of the now-defunct Inns of Chancery, then attached to Gray's Inn. The building still stands on High Holborn.

Revolution by Richard Watson, Bishop of Llandaff. The Bishop's remarks were written in response to the execution of Louis XVI, and rushed into print a few days afterwards as an appendix to a sermon delivered eight years earlier. The very title of the original sermon was provocative: 'The Wisdom and Goodness of God in having made both Rich and Poor'. It was hard to take such stuff from anyone, least of all from a man renowned for his venality. But it was the new appendix that especially infuriated Wordsworth. Watson commended the British government's measures against radicals, 'the flagitious dregs of a nation'. When the Revolution began, Watson had given his 'hearty approbation' to the French attempts to free themselves from arbitrary power, just as he had sided with the American colonists – but recent developments in France had caused him to 'fly with terror and abhorrence from the altar of liberty'. Pitt's administration was right not to tolerate the 'wild fancies and turbulent tempers of discontented or ill-informed individuals'. The British constitution might not be perfect, but it already provided as much liberty and equality as was desirable, and was far too excellent to be amended by 'peasants and mechanics'. British courts were impartial and incorrupt; parliamentary reform was unnecessary; provision for the poor in Britain was so liberal as to discourage industry. 'Look round the globe,' urged Watson complacently, 'and see if you can discover a single nation on all its surface so powerful, so rich, so beneficial, so free and happy as our own.'

Such opinions were not uncommon. The Scottish Lord Justice Clerk, Lord Braxfield, for example, held that the British constitution *was* perfect; and therefore that anyone proposing any change was *prima facie* guilty of sedition. But Watson's words particularly irritated Wordsworth. Maybe it was because he read them at an especially vulnerable moment. And maybe it was the author himself, as much as what he wrote, that irritated him. Wordsworth and Watson had much in common. Like Wordsworth, Watson came from the Lakes, and indeed lived there still, on the banks of Windermere (far from Llandaff). Like Wordsworth, Watson was a Cambridge man. Until now he had been known as a levelling prelate, the Bishop of dissenters

– which rendered his defection more grievous. He had risen from modest origins, a fact that made his condescending attitude to the poor even more unforgivable.

Wordsworth wrote a furious retort, which he entitled 'A Letter to the Bishop of Llandaff, on the Extraordinary Avowal of his Political Principles'. He defended the killings in France, including the execution of the King, as 'a convulsion from which is to spring a fairer order of things'. Contrasting the Bishop of Llandaff with the Bishop of Blois, he quoted Grégoire's words at the opening of the Convention, and repeatedly stressed the unanimity of twenty-five million Frenchmen as in itself legitimising acts carried out in their name. Declaring himself to be 'an advocate of republicanism', he argued the necessity of abolishing not just the monarchy, but the aristocracy too. This system of 'fictitious superiority' produced idleness, corruption, hypocrisy, sycophancy, pride and luxury. Poverty bred misery, promiscuity and prostitution. Britons were like slaves:

> We are taught from infancy that we were born in a state of inferiority to our oppressors, that they were sent into the world to scourge and we to be scourged. Accordingly we see the bulk of mankind actuated by these fatal prejudices, even more ready to lay themselves under the feet of *the great*, than the great are to trample upon them.

Wordsworth's use of the first person plural identified him with the oppressed, the 'swinish multitude' of Burke's notorious sneer. 'Redress is in our power' – but the popular mind had been 'debauched'.

> Left to the quiet exercise of their own judgment do you think the people would have thought it necessary to set fire to the house of the philosophic Priestley, and to hunt down his life like that of a traitor or a parricide; – that, deprived almost of the necessaries of existence by the burden of their taxes, they would cry out as with one voice for a war from which not a single ray of consolation can visit them to compensate for the additional keenness with which they are about to smart under the scourge of labour, of cold, and of hunger?

Wordsworth deplored the 'infatuation' with war, 'which is now giving up to the sword so large a portion of the poor and consigning the rest to the more slow and painful consumption of want'. Drawing on his own experience of the Lonsdale lawsuit, he condemned 'the thorny labyrinth of litigation', 'the consuming expense of our never-ending process, the verbosity of unintelligible statutes, and the perpetual contrariety in our judicial decisions'. In a bitterly sarcastic finale he thanked the Bishop for his 'desertion' from the friends of liberty, 'conscious that an enemy lurking in our ranks is ten times more formidable than when drawn out against us'.[5]*

Wordsworth's arguments were made with passionate fervour. In them one can trace the influence of the seventeenth-century Puritans, republican writers like Sidney, Marvell and Harrington, as well as that of Paine and the French orators whose debates he had heard so recently.[6] But primarily this was a very personal piece of writing, the fierce heat of the author's emotions blazing on the page. It is beyond question that Wordsworth wanted to blast Watson. Yet his diatribe was not published. Why not?

It is suggestive that the surviving manuscript of the 'Letter to the Bishop of Llandaff' is not in Wordsworth's hand. Perhaps he had a fair copy made as a first step towards publication, and then something prevented him from proceeding? It may have been difficult to find a publisher willing to risk publishing such an intemperate pamphlet in such a combustible climate. There was also a considerable risk to Wordsworth himself, even if he published it anonymously. To sign yourself 'a Republican' at such a moment, as Wordsworth had done, was provocative; it implied approval of Louis's execution. 'The very term is become one of the most opprobrious in the English Language,' Priestley was quoted as saying in February 1793. The author of such a pamphlet would be notorious if identified; he might well face prosecution, like Frost; he could certainly abandon any hopes he

---

* In fact Watson had not gone over to the other side. On 27 January 1795, for example, he was the only Bishop to vote against the continuance of the war with France, arguing in the House of Lords that there was no connection between 'the establishment of a Republic in France, and the subversion of the English constitution'.

might still cherish of preferment in the Church, or in any other profession. Some years later Gilbert Wakefield would be sentenced to two years' imprisonment for writing what was deemed to be a seditious pamphlet,* in response to another effusion of Watson's. Wordsworth's elder brother may have urged him to suppress the work. Perhaps prudence triumphed over passion.

Whatever happened, the letter to the Bishop did not appear in print. Wordsworth remained angry and frustrated.

If Wordsworth had been in any doubt about the risks of publishing his 'Letter to the Bishop of Llandaff' at such a time, he needed to look no further than his old university, where proceedings were beginning against William Frend, a Fellow of Jesus College, for publishing what was in most ways a much more innocuous pamphlet. Its title, *Peace and Union*,† does not sound particularly provocative. But early in 1793 'peace' was a dirty word.

Cambridge attitudes to the Revolution reflected those of the country as a whole. The university had welcomed its early manifestations; there had been a proposal to hold an annual dinner to mark the fall of the Bastille. The young men were encouraged to write on the subject. In September 1790 one of them delivered a prize-winning speech in Trinity College chapel in memory of William III, hero of the 'Glorious Revolution' of 1688, making an explicit comparison with recent events in France: 'Liberty has begun her progress, and hope tells us, that she has only begun.'[7]

Subsequent developments across the Channel had divided opinion in Cambridge, as they had divided opinion everywhere. Many of the older men recoiled from the violent disturbances that ensued as the French authorities lost control of events. In the summer of 1792 they signalled their feelings by sending a loyal address to King George. But not all of them concurred. Radicals and reformists sympathetic to

---

* Wakefield likened the possibility of a restoration of the monarchy in France to a dog returning to its vomit, a phrase Wordsworth would later use to characterise the coronation of Napoleon as Emperor of France in 1804. See pages 214n and 377.
† Its full title was *Peace and Union recommended to the associated Bodies of Republicans and Anti-Republicans.*

the revolutionaries constituted an intellectually active minority within the university, centred on Frend's college, Jesus. Many of these were more or less openly nonconformist (particularly Unitarian). Though in theory it was impossible to take a degree or to obtain a college Fellowship without subscribing to the Thirty-Nine Articles (the measure of conformity to the Church of England), in practice there was a degree of toleration. Nonconformists were not permitted to teach, but they were usually allowed to retain their Fellowships and to reside in college.

Among the undergraduates, the developing Revolution stimulated impassioned debate. Younger men were much more open to change, much less wary of turmoil. Some zealots relished Revolutionary violence as a necessary purge; others justified it in the service of a greater good. Revolutionary rhetoric made a compelling appeal to the young; the high ideals of the revolutionaries contrasted strongly with the cynical corruption omnipresent in British society. The Revolution stressed abstract virtues: liberty, fraternity and equality. Its reactionary opponents seemed negative in their reliance on tradition, caution and stability. The revolutionaries believed in the nobility of man – though not of course in that of certain criminal individuals – and what young person does not believe in the nobility of man? The Revolution was the future, or so it seemed. To the intellectually curious, this experiment in humanity could not but be fascinating.

Moreover, it was hard not to feel moved by the events in France. Who could fail to be stirred by the heroic defence of the Republic against seemingly insuperable odds? Professional armies of mercenaries had been beaten back by untrained boys. In Paris, barely-armed citizens, men and women alike, had prevailed time and again against the organised musketry of soldiers. The Convention itself was a theatre, its theme the fate of mankind, its principals men like Marat and Robespierre, distinguished not by the pedigree of their bloodlines but by their strength of character, their courage, their conviction, their purity.

As tension increased between Britain and France, so divisions at home became deeper and the debate more heated. In Cambridge, as in the rest of the country, positions were hardening. There were riots in the city that winter: a dissenters' meeting house and several shops were attacked. Tom Paine was burned in effigy on the last day of 1792. A hundred and twelve local publicans solemnly pledged to report to the magistrates treasonable or seditious conversations, books, or pamphlets. Nonetheless, 'pamphlets swarmed from the press'. Samuel Taylor Coleridge was then in his second year at Jesus, and according to his fellow undergraduate and former schoolmate Charles Valentine Le Grice, his room was 'the constant rendezvous of conversation-loving friends'. There was no need for the other undergraduates to read the latest pamphlets, because Coleridge had read them all on the morning they appeared; 'and in the evening, with our negus,* we had them *viva voce* gloriously'.[8]

One such pamphlet was Fox's *Letter to the Westminster Electors*, which followed the line he had taken in Parliament in attempting to soothe the 'false alarm' raging in the country. Fox believed the government to be deliberately stirring up animosity towards reformists and dissenters, using rumour and hearsay in support of its repressive policies. Evidently Coleridge was sympathetic to Fox's views. 'Have you read Mr Fox's letter to the Westminster Electors?' he wrote to his sweetheart, Mary Evans. 'It is quite the *political Go* at Cambridge, and has converted many souls to the Foxite faith.' He signed his letter 'with the ardour of fraternal friendship'.[9]

William Frend's *Peace and Union* appeared a few days later. Frend lamented the fact that Britain was on the brink of war, a war against the friends of mankind. He aimed to reconcile the 'contending parties', the advocates of a republic and the defenders of the constitution. Britain was split into two camps, he wrote: 'the minds of men are at present greatly agitated; and the utmost rigour of government, aided by the exertions of every lover of his country, is necessary to preserve us, from falling into all the horrors attendant on civil commotions'. As a prominent dissenter, Frend had good reason to fear public

---

* A mixture of fortified wine and hot water, sweetened and flavoured.

disorder. He had already suffered at the hands of the mob, when the manuscript of a book on which he had been collaborating with Joseph Priestley was burned during the 1791 Birmingham riots. He was horrified by the 'assassinations, murders, massacres, burning of houses, plundering of property, [and] open violations of justice' which had marked the progress of the French Revolution. For him, the moral to be drawn from these events was clear: that abuses and grievances should be corrected as soon as they were known. 'Had the French monarch seasonably given up some useless prerogatives, he might still have worn the crown; had the nobility consented to relinquish those noble privileges, which were designed only for barbarous ages, they might have retained their titles; could the clergy have submitted to be citizens, they might still have been in possession of wealth and influence.' To prevent similar upheaval here in Britain, argued Frend, parliamentary reform was essential.[10]

Though this might seem reasonable enough, the university authorities decided otherwise. The Master and Fellows of Jesus College passed resolutions condemning Frend, and initiated proceedings that would lead to his expulsion from the college and ultimate banishment from the city. The case provoked letters to the papers in Frend's defence, and he attracted plenty of undergraduate support: slogans such as 'Frend and Liberty!' or 'Frend for Ever!!' were chalked or daubed on college walls, and even etched in gunpowder on the lawn of Trinity College quadrangle.

Frend's prosecution could be explained only in terms of the polarised politics of the moment. Though his pamphlet expressed opinions that would have upset many of his colleagues – defending the execution of Louis XVI and opposing the war with France – these could hardly be described as seditious. The Vice-Chancellor virtually admitted that the trial had been a political one when he later asserted that the expulsion of Frend had been 'the ruin of the Jacobinical party as a *University thing*'. That this was no isolated event became obvious in the late summer, with the trials of several Scottish radicals. One of these, the Reverend Thomas Fyshe Palmer, a Unitarian minister and a former Fellow of Queen's College, was sentenced to seven years' transportation, his 'crime' being to have corrected the proofs of a handbill written by a Dundee weaver (deemed to be seditious). Things had come to a pretty pass when former Cambridge Fellows were being shipped off in fetters to Australia.

Frend's trial in the university court began on 3 May 1793, frequently interrupted by (in the Vice-Chancellor's words) 'noisy and tumultuous irregularities of conduct' from the undergraduates who filled the public gallery, applauding the defendant and heckling his accusers. The university authorities attempted to suppress the rowdiness, and after he had called the Vice-Chancellor's attention to one young man ostentatiously clapping, the Senior Proctor was given permission to make an arrest. The Proctor hurried into the gallery to seize the miscreant, but too late; the culprit had fled. The young protestor was later identified as 'S.T. Coleridge, of Jesus College'.

A contemporary report in the *Morning Chronicle* had the Proctor apprehend the wrong man, who, on being accused of clapping, demonstrated that a deformed arm made him incapable of doing so, producing a barrage of ironic applause from the other undergraduates. (Coleridge himself may have been the source of this anecdote. In an account he gave many years later, the young man arrested had an iron hook instead of a hand. This sounds like a story that improved with age.)

Coleridge escaped with a reprimand, though he seems to have been prominent (if not conspicuous) among Frend's undergraduate supporters. He had known and admired Frend for the past year and a half, and had absorbed many of his ideas. 'Mr Frend's company is by no means invidious,' he had written teasingly to his elder brother George[11] – a cautious, caring, respectable person, who had no doubt expressed some concern at Sam's association with such a prominent dissenter. George stood as unofficial guardian to his baby brother, and had done so since the death of their father in 1781. Coleridge often described George – the most scholarly of his siblings – as a kind of father, though George was only eight years his senior. 'You have always been a brother to me in kindness and a father in wisdom,' he wrote to George late in 1792.[12]

Coleridge was then just twenty (two years younger than Wordsworth), loose-limbed and scruffy, 'a very gentle Bear' with long curling black hair, fleshy lips, dark heavy eyebrows and large blue eyes,
sometimes distant, sometimes burning with impatient energy. (He
believed himself to be ugly, and referred to the 'fat vacuity' of his
face.[13]) He had gone up to Cambridge in October 1791, some ten
months after Wordsworth left. A child prodigy, Coleridge promised
greatness. At the age of three he could read a chapter in the Bible.
He read every book that came his way, and showed astonishing
retentive power, being able to recite large chunks of any work after
only one reading. At school he soon outstripped all the other boys.
The youngest of ten children (one of whom died in infancy), he was
the favourite of the family. 'My Father was very fond of me, and I
was my mother's darling,' he wrote in retrospect; 'in consequence, I
was very miserable.' His brother Frank, the next youngest, was jealous
of this attention. He had one sister, Anne (known as Nancy), five
years older, who petted him and became his confidante, listening to
his 'puny sorrows' and 'hidden maladies'. Maybe he was a spoiled
child; he certainly seems to have been wilful:

> . . . I became a *dreamer* – and acquired an indisposition to all
> bodily activity – and I was fretful, and inordinately passionate,
> and as I could not play at any thing, and was slothful, I was
> despised & hated by the boys; and because I could read &
> spell, & had, I may truly say, a memory & understanding
> forced into almost an unnatural ripeness, I was flattered &
> wondered at by all the old women – & so I became very vain,
> and despised most of the boys, that were at all near my own
> age – and before I was eight years old, I was a *character* . . .[14]

His father, the Reverend John Coleridge, was both vicar of the Devon
town where the family lived, Ottery St Mary, and headmaster of the
local school. He was a gentle and learned man, absent-minded and
unworldly, with several obscure publications to his name. Coleridge
remembered that his father 'used to take me on his knee, and hold
long conversations with me'.[15] But John Coleridge was already fifty-
three when his youngest child was born, and he died suddenly a few

weeks before Sam's ninth birthday. The family was now in difficult circumstances. Soon afterwards Coleridge was sent away to a charitable boarding school, Christ's Hospital in London, from which it seems that he rarely returned home to Ottery. This felt to him like a rejection, and afterwards he never showed any affection towards his mother. 'Boy! the School is your father! The School is your mother!' bellowed his headmaster William Bowyer as he flogged the tearful child.

Coleridge's brilliance earned him the status and privileges of a 'Grecian', a pupil destined for Oxford or Cambridge who wore a special uniform to distinguish him from the ordinary 'blue-coat boys'. He won his place at Jesus in a blaze of honours. It was assumed that he was headed for the Church. A glorious career was in prospect; he might become a bishop, or perhaps headmaster of one of the great public schools.*

He read voraciously; years later he told his first biographer, James Gillman, that at fourteen, 'My whole being was, with eyes closed to every object of present sense, to crumple myself up in a sunny corner and read, read, read.' When an older schoolboy gave him a volume of William Lisle Bowles's evocative and melancholy sonnets, Coleridge was so entranced that he painstakingly wrote out forty copies for distribution to friends. Bowles's verse became a model for his own work, and Bowles himself a master whom the young Coleridge revered. When he later happened to see Bowles crossing the market-place in Salisbury, Coleridge was too shy to speak to him.

Every schoolboy of this era was expected to write verse, both for its own sake and as an exercise in the study of Latin and Greek, translating classical originals into English. Coleridge's early poetry was conventional stuff. It followed the classical models predominant in eighteenth-century verse, written in a convoluted 'poetic' diction that would soon come to be seen as artificial, characterised by elaborate abstractions far removed from everyday experience. The effect was strained, even turgid. Tired metaphors and phrases clogged up

* Three of Coleridge's brothers became soldiers, one became a doctor, one a clergyman, and two became schoolmasters.

the lines. There was an excess of ornamentation, with too many double epithets. Bowyer tried to counter this tendency, to instil a bias towards the plainest form of words. He had a list of forbidden introductions, similes and expressions. *'Harp? Harp? Lyre? Pen and ink, boy, you mean! Muse, boy, Muse? Your Nurse's daughter, you mean! Pierian spring? Oh, aye the cloister-pump, I suppose!'*

One of Coleridge's earliest poems was his 'Monody on the Death of Chatterton'. Like Coleridge, Thomas Chatterton had been a blue-coat boy, the orphaned son of a Bristol schoolmaster, a precocious poet who at the age of sixteen claimed to have discovered a chestful of poems, letters and other documents written by a fifteenth-century monk, Thomas Rowley. Though these aroused interest and indeed excitement, Chatterton failed to prosper by them, and at the age of only eighteen, alone in a London garret, he committed suicide, driven by poverty to despair. The tragic story of neglected genius cut off at such an early age caught the imagination of young men everywhere, and Coleridge was one of many who identified powerfully with him, ominously heading his poem 'A Monody on Chatterton, who poisoned himself at the age of eighteen – written by the author at the age of sixteen'.

In his last year at school Coleridge was confined for long months to the Christ's Hospital sanatorium, lying in bed while hearing the boys outside laugh and play. He had become seriously ill after swimming fully clothed in the nearby New River, and afterwards wearing his wet clothes as they slowly dried on his back. Unsurprisingly he developed a fever, complicated by jaundice, no doubt as a result of the foul water in which he had immersed himself. His friend and first biographer James Gillman believed that all his future bodily sufferings could be dated from this episode.* Coleridge was a young man of enormous energy and robust vitality, yet he succumbed to recurrent attacks of illness. There was also a lasting psychological effect of this long period of convalescence. In the school sanatorium his nurse's

---

* Coleridge believed that he had succumbed to rheumatic fever, which would affect him periodically from this moment on; but the autopsy performed after his death does not support this diagnosis.

daughter, Jenny Edwards, helped to care for him, and he developed sentimental feelings for her; as he recovered he wrote a sonnet in her honour – which adds piquancy to Bowyer's reported jibe about his 'Muse':

> Fair as the bosom of the Swan
> That rises graceful o'er the wave,
> I've seen thy breast with pity heave,
> And therefore love I thee, sweet Genevieve!

Forever after, Coleridge would derive a perverse erotic satisfaction from being helpless in the care of a desirable woman.

While ill he was regularly dosed with laudanum,* then prescribed as a panacea. Not only did opium relieve pain; it prompted delicious dreams that soothed the mind of the fevered boy. In future he was to resort to its use whenever he felt ill, or under pressure.

During his last year at Christ's Hospital, Coleridge received news that his 'sweet sister' had died of consumption. By this time four of his brothers were already dead. Four remained, three of them much older than him. Frank (the nearest in age) had already gone away to sea, and subsequently joined the army in India. A year later he too would be dead, after receiving a wound during the siege of Seringapatam. This left the young Coleridge isolated, with no siblings near to him in age – but he found a surrogate family in the widowed mother and three sisters of a schoolmate, Tom Evans. They lived in Villiers Street, not far from the school, and Coleridge spent his Saturdays there. The Evans women provided substitute sisters and a substitute mother, whom he hoped would love him and be amused by his antics. By the time he left for Cambridge he believed himself in love with the eldest girl, Mary, though he was too shy to declare himself. Instead he wrote them all (including the mother) jokey, flirtatious letters. After his first university term he returned to them for Christmas in a poor state of health, and Mrs Evans nursed him tenderly.

---

* Alcoholic tincture of opium, a reddish-brown liquid, lighter or darker according to strength. De Quincey kept his in a decanter, where it was sometimes mistaken for port by the unwary.[16]

'Believe me, that You and my Sisters have the very first row in the front box of my Heart's little theatre,' he wrote to her afterwards, 'and – God knows! *you are not crowded*.'[17]

In his first year at Cambridge Coleridge distinguished himself by winning a prize for a Greek ode on the then topical subject of the slave trade.* At the end of 1792 he narrowly failed to win a university scholarship, reaching the shortlist of four. Perhaps it was not surprising that he failed, given that for the six weeks preceding the examination – so he later said – he was almost constantly intoxicated. By this time he had acquired a reputation within Cambridge for his excellent classical scholarship, poetical language, and 'a peculiar style of conversation' – perhaps a euphemism, since Coleridge was always more inclined to talk than to listen.[18] 'He was very studious,' recalled Valentine Le Grice, 'but his reading was desultory and capricious.'[19] Coleridge himself claimed to have been 'a proverb to the University for Idleness'.[20]

He was also hopeless with money. Perhaps this judgement is harsh, because he never had a lot to spend, and was disappointed by his failure to win a scholarship. An annual income of almost £100 from a Christ's Hospital exhibition and two university awards, together with the odd handout from his brothers, should have been enough to keep him, however. But he seemed incapable of living within his means. On his arrival at Cambridge he rashly gave an upholsterer *carte blanche* to redecorate his rooms, and was then 'stupefied' by the size of the bill. Soon he was drinking heavily, and he seems to have resumed taking opium, 'building magnificent edifices of happiness on some fleeting shadow of reality' in 'soul-enervating reveries'. He often stole away to London, where there were plenty of temptations to empty his purse. Early in 1793 he wrote to his brother George summarising the state of his finances. He outlined his plans for a book of translations of 'the best Lyric poems from the Greek, and the modern Latin writers' – the first of many unrealised schemes. By

* In 1792 William Wilberforce had introduced to Parliament a Bill to abolish the slave trade. It was passed by the House of Commons; but lacking government support, it was rejected by the Lords.

raising two hundred subscriptions to this work, he felt that he would be able to pay off his debts, 'which have corroded my Spirits greatly for some time Past'. He reckoned them at £58. Though George sent him some money, he was soon behind again. By the end of his second year at Cambridge he had somehow managed to run up further debts, which he now calculated, with misleading precision, at £148.17s.1¼d. He returned to Devon and presented himself before his older brothers with some trepidation. 'I am fearful, that your Silence proceeds from Displeasure – If so, what is left for me to do – but to grieve? The Past is not in my Power – for the follies, of which I may have been guilty, I have been greatly disquieted – and I trust, the Memory of them will operate to future consistency of Conduct.'[21]

Coleridge's brothers provided him with a sum to stave off his creditors, but he quickly frittered away much of this, loitering ten days in Tiverton to conduct a flirtation with Miss Fanny Nesbitt, 'a very pretty girl' he met on the coach. Rather than returning directly to Cambridge, he lingered in London in order to be near Mary Evans. While walking between a tavern and a shop where he went to purchase a lottery ticket, he composed a poem, 'To Fortune', which was pub-lished in the *Morning Chronicle*. On his arrival back in college he discovered further embarrassments, 'which in my wild carelessness I had forgotten, and many of which I had contracted almost without knowing it'. Desperate, he fled back to London at eleven o'clock at night, where for three days he lived in a 'tempest of pleasure'. He returned to Cambridge and stayed a week, then left again for London, by now in a state of delirium. 'When Vice has not annihilated Sensi-bility, there is little need of a Hell!'[22] There he seems to have contem-plated suicide – but after a night in 'a house of ill-fame', ruminating in a chair, and an agitated morning walk in the park, he sought refuge instead in the bosom of the army, enlisting in the 15th Light Dragoons under the name Silas Tomkyn Comberbache.

Little is known of Wordsworth's life in the period after his return from France at the end of 1792. For us this is a dark time – no letters of his survive written between September 1792, when he was still in

Blois, and February 1794. Almost all that can be deduced of his activities during these lost seventeen months derives from incidental remarks in Dorothy's letters to her friend Jane Pollard, or from *The Prelude*. Until the twentieth century only a handful of close family members knew of his involvement with Annette Vallon. But soon after the First World War, two letters from Annette that had been intercepted by the French police almost 130 years earlier surfaced in the Loir-et-Cher archives. Both were dated 20 March 1793. One was addressed to Dorothy, the other to 'Williams'. Emotion overflows from both; they lack punctuation; the spelling is idiosyncratic and inconsistent. They read like the letters of a naïve young girl, not a woman of nearly twenty-seven. The content is in each case repetitive and confused. She swings one way and then the other, longing for him, yet fearing that he may be taken prisoner if he returns. It would comfort her, she writes, if he could come and give her the 'glorious' title of his wife, even if 'cruel necessity' would compel him to leave immediately. 'Come, my love, my husband, and receive the tender embraces of your wife, of your daughter,' she urges, apparently expecting his imminent arrival. Their child, now three months old and baptised 'Anne-Caroline Wordswodsth', she tells him, 'grows more and more like you every day'. Holding her baby close enough to feel her heart beat, Annette imagines how it will stir when she says, 'Caroline, in a month, in a fortnight, in a week, you are going to see the most beloved of men, the most tender of men.' She ends by sending him a thousand kisses, *'sur la bouche, sur les yeux et mon petit* que j'aime toujours, que je recomande bien a tes soins'*. Mention of other letters shows that she and Wordsworth were in regular correspondence, and her letter to Dorothy (enclosed with the one to William) makes it obvious that he has confided in his sister; Annette has already received at least one welcoming letter from her, perhaps more. She writes of the time, a little further off, when the three of them will live together in *'notre petit ménage'*. As for Caroline, 'My dear sister, you will be her second mother.'[23]

* An intimate reference.

It is not impossible that Wordsworth might have returned to France in 1793. Provision existed for non-combatants to travel between warring countries. The scientist Humphry Davy, for example, was invited to lecture in France at the height of the struggle between the two nations. Of course, there would have been difficulties, and this was a particularly hazardous time, the rule of law in France being so uncertain. Annette hoped that Wordsworth would return to legitimise their union, while acknowledging that it could be only a short visit; they would make a home together once the war was over. There was a widespread belief (which Annette shared) that it would not last long, now that the might of Great Britain had been added to that of the Continental Allies. France appeared to be in chaos, without an effective government while at war with almost all of Europe. After their initial successes, French armies were everywhere in retreat. The security of the young Republic was undermined by uprisings in several parts of the country in the spring of 1793, including a serious revolt in the Vendée.

These letters of Annette's never reached Wordsworth or his sister, and there is no evidence to indicate whether Wordsworth did consider returning to France to marry her. According to Dorothy, he was then 'looking out and wishing for the opportunity of engaging himself as Tutor to some young Gentleman'.[24] Early in July he set off on a tour of the West Country in the company of William Calvert, a friend from their days as fellow pupils at Hawkshead School. Calvert had become a man of property on the death of his father, and he offered to pay all their travelling expenses; since Wordsworth had nothing else to do, he accepted. They passed a month of 'calm and glassy days' on the Isle of Wight. In the evenings Wordsworth walked along the seashore, the prospect of the Channel fleet at Spithead preparing for sea always before him; as the sun set he would hear the evening cannon. But this magnificent sight only deepened his sense of isolation, symbolising as it did the division in his heart. He was full of melancholy and foreboding. He did not share the general confidence that the war would swiftly be brought to a successful conclusion. He had witnessed the spirit prevailing in France, and foresaw a long struggle ahead, 'productive of distress and misery beyond all possible calculation'.[25]

The French were dealing with the crisis in their own ruthless fashion. A decree was proclaimed condemning all rebels to summary execution; watch committees were set up in communes throughout the country; a Revolutionary tribunal was established to try traitors. In April a Committee of Public Safety with extraordinary powers came into being, which soon began to aggrandise all the powers of the executive. Later that summer a *levée en masse* would be declared, requiring all unmarried men between the ages of eighteen and twenty-five to register for military service. The struggle for power between the Girondins and the Mountain reached its climax at the beginning of June: after the Convention was besieged by a huge and heavily armed mob, Brissot and the other Girondin leaders were expelled and placed under house arrest. One by one, the remaining uncommitted deputies fled Paris, leaving the Convention in the hands of the Mountain. The assassination of Marat on 13 July provided a pretext for further purges, consolidating the Jacobin hold on the machinery of government. A Law of Suspects ordered the immediate arrest of anybody against whom there was even a suspicion of political disloyalty. Emergency powers gave Revolutionary committees throughout France the power of life and death. The accused were tried and condemned in groups. Pity for the criminal was itself proof of treason. The pace of executions accelerated. The Terror had begun.

We can only speculate how much of this reached Wordsworth at the time, and how he reacted. Developments in France were reported in detail in the English newspapers; the war gave them added relevance. It is hard to imagine that he would not have followed the news from France closely. The eclipse of the Girondins must have affected him, especially as he was acquainted with some of those men now outlawed or imprisoned. On 13 July his Orléans landlord, M. Gellet-Duvivier, was guillotined; if Wordsworth heard about this, it would have seemed to him that the Terror was closing in. Annette's family were (regrettably) royalists; would they be safe?* Already torn

---

* Her brother Paul was implicated in a plot to assassinate a prominent Jacobin and forced to go into hiding.

by a conflict of loyalties, Wordsworth had more and more reason to be anxious about the direction events were taking. He had given his heart to the Revolution; now perhaps he was beginning to experience the torment of doubt. Meanwhile change at home seemed further away than ever. The harsh sentences dealt to those convicted of sedition silenced reformers and radicals alike. Fear of prosecution deterred Wordsworth from expressing the emotion raging within him. It was understandable that he should seek to escape from his thoughts, to find relief

> ... by the sides
> Of the deep rivers, and the lonely streams,
> Wherever nature led; more like a man
> Flying from something that he dreads, than one
> Who sought the thing he loved ...

Around the end of July Wordsworth and Calvert crossed from the Isle of Wight to the mainland, and continued in a whiskey (a form of open carriage) towards Salisbury, intending to go on in the same way towards Wales and then up along the border to Chester; but the horse drawing them 'began to caper in a most dreadful manner', and dragged them into a ditch, damaging the vehicle beyond repair. Though neither man was injured, a decision was taken not to continue together – most probably for practical reasons. Calvert may have given Wordsworth some money for his journey; he then mounted his horse and rode off into the north, leaving Wordsworth to proceed, as Dorothy put it, supported by his 'firm friends, a pair of stout legs'. This unexpected parting turned out to be serendipitous, because the impressions Wordsworth received during the rest of the tour proved inspirational. On foot, and alone with his thoughts, he was more responsive to the landscape, and more open to encounters along the way.

His path took him along chalk tracks across the vast plateau of Salisbury Plain, the wind whistling through unending dreary fields of corn, crows eddying in the sky. It was a desolate place, with few trees or hedges to break the monotony; barely inhabited then, but pockmarked with prehistoric remains. As he walked, Wordsworth meditated on the savage past, and on the 'calamities, principally consequent on war, to which, more than other classes of men, the poor are subject'. He imagined a vagrant ex-soldier, caught in the open as a storm began to sweep the Plain, seeking shelter from the driving rain and howling wind among the monoliths of Stonehenge. It is tempting to speculate that Wordsworth did the same, especially as contemporary records describe 'a storm of extraordinary intensity [that] lashed southern England with hailstones as big as six inches round'.[26] But perhaps the temptation should be resisted, because in a letter written many years afterwards, Wordsworth recalled how 'overcome with heat and fatigue I took my siesta among the Pillars of Stonehenge', and complained jokingly that he 'was not visited by the Muse in my Slumbers'.[27]

If the muse left him alone on this occasion, she cannot have been far off, because another vision came to Wordsworth on the Plain, where relics of the distant past – standing stones, barrows, ancient tracks, stone circles, mounds and hill forts – are more evident than anywhere else in Britain. In *The Prelude* he tells us that

> While through those vestiges of ancient times
> I ranged, and by the solitude o'ercome,
> I had a reverie and saw the past,
> Saw multitudes of men, and here and there
> A single Briton in his wolf-skin vest
> With shield and stone-ax, stride across the wold;
> The voice of spears was heard, the rattling spear
> Shaken by arms of mighty bone, in strength
> Long mouldered, of barbaric majesty.[28]

Wordsworth goes on to describe a nightmare of darkness descending (perhaps a lowering storm?), a sacrificial altar lit by dismal flames, and the groans of those waiting to die; followed by a more peaceful vision of bearded Druids pointing with white wands to the starry sky.

From Salisbury Plain Wordsworth made his way via Bath towards the Welsh border, crossing the Severn Estuary somewhere near Bristol and then ascending the Wye Valley. Today, the lower Wye is still lovely enough to stir the heart, especially when sunlight penetrates the woods that line the valley's steep sides, glinting on the fast-flowing river below. Brooding cliffs tower against the sky. Ruined castles perch high above the gorge. Celebrated for its picturesque qualities,* this was one of the first places in Britain to attract tourists, and pleasure boats plied up and down the river. Its appeal was marred by importunate beggars who haunted the ruins of Tintern Abbey, and a number of ironworks belching smoke into the air, but neither seems to have bothered Wordsworth. Poetic inspirations came to him one after another: the lovely valley itself, Tintern Abbey, a girl he met at Goodrich Castle who became the heroine of 'We are Seven', a tinker he met at Builth who served as a model for 'Peter Bell'. Above all, the river itself:

> . . . Oh! How oft –
> In darkness and amid the many shapes
> Of joyless daylight; when the fretful stir unprofitable
>   and the fever of the world
> Have hung upon the beatings of my heart –
> How oft, in spirit, have I turned to thee,
> O sylvan Wye! Thou wanderer through the woods,
> How often has my spirit turned to thee!

Wordsworth continued north, reaching his friend Robert Jones's cottage in north Wales towards the end of August. Here he seems to have paused, in anticipation of an onward journey to Halifax to rendezvous with Dorothy, whom he had not seen for almost three years. 'Oh my dear, dear sister,' he had written to her earlier that summer, 'with what transport shall I again meet you, with what rapture shall I again wear out the day in your sight. I assure you so eager is my desire to see you that all obstacles vanish. I see you in a moment running or rather flying to my arms.'[29]

William and Dorothy had spent most of their lives apart. After the death of their mother in 1778, Dorothy, then only six years old, had

* For example, in the Reverend William Gilpin's *Observations on the River Wye* (1782), which Wordsworth carried with him on his return to the Wye Valley with Dorothy in 1798.

been separated from her siblings and sent to live with her mother's cousin, Elizabeth Threlkeld, more than a hundred miles off in Halifax, while her four brothers – Richard, William, and her two younger brothers, John and Christopher – remained with their father in Cockermouth. She did not return for her father's funeral in 1784, and was reunited with her brothers only in the summer of 1787, after a gap of nine years. 'You know not how happy I am in their company,' she wrote at the time to her bosom friend, Jane Pollard. 'They are just the kind of boys I could wish them, they are so affectionate and kind to me as makes me love them more and more every day.' William, then seventeen and nearly two years Dorothy's senior, was due to go up to Cambridge in the autumn. 'William and Christopher are very clever boys at least so they appear in the partial eyes of a Sister.'[30]

The reunion between Dorothy and her brothers in 1787 was all too brief. After a few weeks the young family was once again dispersed: William to Cambridge,* her eldest brother Richard to London where he would train as a lawyer, her two younger brothers back to school in Hawkshead. Dorothy remained unhappily with her grandparents in Penrith until William returned from university the following summer. Later that year Dorothy's uncle, the Reverend William Cookson, married and took up a living in East Anglia. It was decided that Dorothy, by now sixteen, should accompany her uncle and aunt to the Norfolk village of Forncett St Peter, and live with them there. She would remain at the Forncett rectory for five years, helping her aunt with her burgeoning family and running a little school. It was a lonely life for Dorothy, isolated from the friends she had grown up alongside in Yorkshire. The Cooksons did not share her pursuits and pleasures, though they treated her kindly and affectionately. But Forncett was conveniently close to Cambridge,† and William was able to visit her there in the holidays.

There was a special sympathy between these two. Sensitive, passion-

---

* William was sent back with his younger brothers to Hawkshead in midsummer, though Dorothy had hoped that he might be permitted to stay with her until he went up to Cambridge in late October.
† Dorothy and the Cooksons called on William there *en route* to their new home.

ate and uninhibited, Dorothy acted as a lightning rod for her more reserved brother, showing him flashes of feeling. 'I have thought of you perpetually,' he wrote to her while on his walking tour in the Alps, 'and never have my eyes burst upon a scene of particular loveliness but I have almost instantly wished that you could for a moment be transported to the place where I stood to enjoy it.'[31] Wordsworth spent the Christmas vacation before his finals at Forncett; every morning brother and sister would walk in the garden for two hours, pacing backwards and forwards on the gravel arm in arm, even when the keenest north wind was whistling among the trees, and every evening they would walk another two hours or so, engaged in 'long, long conversations'.

'I never thought of the cold when he was with me,' wrote Dorothy to Jane Pollard, to whom she confessed that though she was fond of all her brothers, William was her favourite. In comparison to their youngest brother Christopher (now also at Cambridge), while each was 'steady and sincere in his attachments', William was more ardent, with 'a sort of violence of affection' towards those whom he loved, like Dorothy, manifest in 'a thousand almost imperceptible attentions' to her wishes daily, 'a sort of restless watchfulness which I know not how to describe, a tenderness that never sleeps, and at the same time such a delicacy of manners as I have observed in few men'. Looking back at the time William was with her at Forncett, Dorothy recalled how 'he was never tired of comforting his sister, he never left her in anger, he always met her with joy, he preferred her society to every other pleasure, or rather when we were so happy as to be within each other's reach he had no pleasure when we were compelled to be divided'.[32]

'I am sure you would be pleased with him,' she told Jane Pollard; 'he is certainly very agreeable in his manners and he is so amiable, so good, so fond of his Sister! Oh Jane the last time we were together he won my affection to a degree which I cannot describe; his Attentions to me were such as the most insensible of mortals must have been touched with, there was no Pleasure that he would not have given up with joy for half an hour's conversation with me.'[33] Dorothy wanted her best female friend to think well of her 'dearest male friend', but she warned Jane not to expect too much, at least not at the beginning:

> In the first place you must be with him more than once before he will be perfectly easy in conversation; in the second place his person is not in his favour, at least I should think not; but I soon ceased to discover this, nay I almost thought that the opinion which I first formed was erroneous. He is however, certainly rather plain than otherwise, has an extremely thoughtful countenance, but when he speaks it is often lighted up with a smile which *I* think very pleasing . . .[34]

The young Wordsworth was not handsome, but not ugly either: slightly taller than the average, and gaunt, with a solemn manner that occasionally collapsed in quiet mirth. His face was dominated by a prominent straight nose, and deep furrows that ran vertically up both cheeks; his eyes were serious, lit by the odd twinkle; his mouth was broad, with full lips; his short fine hair was already beginning to recede.

Dorothy seems to have regarded herself as plain too; she describes herself to Jane Pollard as being without accomplishments, 'your old friend Dolly Wordsworth', with 'nothing to recommend me to your regard but a warm honest and affectionate heart'.[35] At twenty she confessed that 'no man I have seen has appeared to regard me with any degree of partiality; nor has any one gained my affections'.[36] Nor was it likely that a dependent young woman with no parents and no inheritance would have found a suitor, unless she was remarkably pretty. For such women, the prospects were bleak: genteel poverty at best* – unless, as often happened, she found a home with a male relative.

Another long period of separation followed Wordsworth's departure from Forncett early in 1791. Dorothy consoled herself by anticipating 'the day of my felicity, the day in which I am once more to find a home under the same roof with my brother'. There seemed no

---

* An obvious comparison is Jane Fairfax's situation at the outset of *Emma*.

doubt in her mind that the day would come. While she still believed that William would take holy orders, she imagined their 'little parsonage': closing the shutters in the evening, setting out the tea table, brightening the fire. She pictured the scene when Jane Pollard would come to stay: 'When our refreshment is ended I produce our work, and William brings his book to our table and contributes at once to our instruction and amusement, and at intervals we lay aside the book and each hazard our observations upon what has been read without the fear of ridicule or censure . . . Oh Jane! With such romantic dreams as these I amuse my fancy during many an hour which would otherwise pass heavily along.'[37]

This idyll survived the revelation that Wordsworth had fathered a child in France – though the 'little parsonage' became 'our little cottage'. One immediate effect, however, was that Wordsworth was no longer welcome at Forncett. His uncle Cookson was already disappointed by his clever nephew's failure to follow the path he had laid, via a Cambridge Fellowship into the Church. From his point of view, Wordsworth had thrown away an excellent opportunity. No doubt he had heard something of Wordsworth's radical opinions. Early in 1792 Cookson had been appointed Canon of Windsor, a post that brought him into regular contact with the royal family. It must have been embarrassing for him to be connected to a young man who professed republicanism. This latest news decided him.[38]* A man who had fathered an illegitimate child – a French, Catholic child – could not be considered respectable company for his wife, and must be an unsuitable influence on Dorothy.

So matters stood after Wordsworth's return from France. He was excluded from Forncett; while Dorothy could not leave Forncett without her uncle's permission. In the middle of the year 1793, however, a new possibility opened. Since Dorothy's departure from Halifax, Elizabeth Threlkeld had become Mrs William Rawson; now she and

---

* Wordsworth's fathering of an illegitimate child seems not to have been a secret within the immediate family, nor was it kept from intimate friends such as Jane Pollard, though it remained hidden from the public until Annette's letters were discovered in the twentieth century.

her husband invited Dorothy to come and stay whenever she was free to do so. Dorothy was fond of Mrs Rawson, who in caring for her from the age of six until sixteen had treated her like a daughter, and she very much wanted to pay another visit to the place where she had spent much of her childhood – but she also had a secret reason for accepting the invitation. The Rawsons had seen Wordsworth in London, and had pressed him too to visit them next time he was in the north. Dorothy knew that her uncle Cookson might withhold his permission for her visit to Halifax if he suspected that she might meet her brother there. She and William therefore made a clandestine arrangement to visit the Rawsons at the same time, as if by accident. It was difficult to co-ordinate, because Dorothy could not travel until she could find an escort to chaperone her. Wordsworth had arrived in north Wales, poised to make the short onward journey to Halifax, towards the end of August – but then he had to wait for Dorothy. It would be midwinter before they met. And what he did for the remainder of the year is a mystery.

The next glimpse we have of Wordsworth is at Christmas time, when he is staying with one of his uncles in Whitehaven, on the Cumbrian coast. Again, there is a tantalising clue to suggest what he might have been doing in the interim. In a memoir written in 1867 and published posthumously in his *Reminiscences* (1881), Thomas Carlyle reported a conversation with Wordsworth held around 1840, a few years after the publication of Carlyle's history of the French Revolution. Wordsworth apparently told Carlyle that he had witnessed the execution of the journalist Gorsas – who was guillotined on 7 October 1793. Might he really have been in Paris then? Could he have tried to reach the Loire, to see Annette and his infant daughter? Did he plan to marry Annette, as she hoped he might?

It seems unlikely. For one thing, it clashed with his secret plan to meet Dorothy in Halifax. At last an opportunity for them to meet had presented itself: an opportunity that might be lost if he were not there to take it. Then there were numerous practical difficulties Wordsworth would have needed to overcome, including the expense.

Also, it was becoming much more dangerous; between 11 and 15 October 1793 all Englishmen remaining in Paris – even Tom Paine – were arrested and imprisoned. After this there would be no further possibility of going to France while the war persisted. Heads were rolling. Gorsas was the first deputy sent to the scaffold; Brissot and many of the remaining Girondin deputies would follow at the end of the month. Marie Antoinette, too, was guillotined on 16 October, a deed that provoked horror throughout Europe. An order went out from the Convention to repress counter-revolution ferociously: 'Terror will be the order of the day!' In Lyons, for example, men and women were forced to dig ditches and then stand beside them under cannon fire until they tumbled into their own mass graves. Meanwhile the Atlantic coast was in upheaval. Wordsworth believed – mistakenly, as it turned out – that his friend Beaupuy had been killed while fighting the Vendée rebels.

Even so, it is hard to dismiss altogether the possibility that Wordsworth might have made a visit to France at this time. As a historian of the French Revolution, Carlyle had been impressed by Wordsworth's strong testimony to the 'ominous feeling' which Gorsas's execution 'had produced in everybody', and quoted words that Wordsworth said (or thought) at the time: 'Where will it *end*, when you have set an example in *this* kind?' In all his reading Carlyle had not before found any trace of the public emotion excited by Gorsas's death, and he concluded, 'Wordsworth might be taken as a true supplement to my book, on this small point.' He seemed convinced that Wordsworth had indeed been there to see Gorsas die. And the implication that some have drawn from Wordsworth's reported comment is that this must have been the moment when he lost faith in the Revolution.

Any hypothesis that rests on Carlyle's *Reminiscences* has to take into account the fact that he was an old man when he wrote the memoir, shattered by the sudden death of his wife, and that he was recalling a conversation that had taken place nearly thirty years before, with another old man who was reminiscing about events that would have happened almost half a century before that. A certain degree of scepticism is legitimate, especially as Carlyle purports to quote from Wordsworth verbatim.

Apart from Carlyle's report, there is nothing of substance to support the speculation that Wordsworth returned to France in the autumn of 1793. In a volume in Wordsworth's library there is a marginal note where Gorsas is mentioned: 'I knew this man. W.W.' It is easy to imagine how Wordsworth might have known Gorsas while he was staying in Paris the previous winter; much harder to imagine how he could have got to know him immediately before his execution, while he was in hiding and then in prison. But the proof that Wordsworth had known Gorsas at some stage makes Carlyle's story a little more credible. For those who want to make a case for Wordsworth's visit to France at this time there is yet another sliver of evidence, in the form of a third-hand account published in 1884 of a meeting in Paris between Wordsworth and 'an old republican called Bailey' – but the story is so garbled and contradictory as to be worthless.

Nor is there any reference in *The Prelude* to another visit to France. It is plausible that Wordsworth might have wanted to hide any trace of a visit to Annette; but that would not explain why he should conceal a visit to Paris. The horror of witnessing the guillotine in action – in the execution of a man he knew – would have left a deep impression on him: an impression which the poet would surely have wanted to describe in the poem on the growth of his own mind, of which such impressions form the essence.

Perhaps Wordsworth did return to Paris in the autumn of 1793. It is not impossible. But the evidence is too flimsy to form conclusions from it – about Wordsworth's faith in the Revolution, his feelings for Annette Vallon, or anything else.[39]

By the middle of February 1794 Wordsworth was staying with the Rawsons in Halifax, together with Dorothy. One can be confident that their reunion was a very happy one. And it was extended when William Calvert offered Wordsworth the use of Windy Brow, a farm-house near Keswick, on a steep bank above the River Greta. The surrounding scenery was magnificent: there were views from a terrace above the house of the whole vale of Keswick, Derwent Water in one direction and Bassenthwaite in the other, with mountains towering all around. Dorothy was so happy to be there with her brother, living in frugal simplicity, that she prolonged her stay from a planned few days to several weeks.

To reach Windy Brow they travelled by coach from Halifax to Kendal, then continued on foot, a two-day ramble much disapproved of by another of their aunts, who sent Dorothy a letter of censure to which Dorothy wrote a spirited reply: 'So far from considering this as a matter of condemnation, I rather thought it would have given my friends pleasure to hear that I had courage to make use of the strength with which nature has endowed me, when it not only procured me infinitely more pleasure than I should have received from sitting in a post-chaise – but was also the means of saving me at least thirty shillings.' Her aunt had supposed that Dorothy was living in 'an unprotected situation'. 'I consider the character and virtues of my brother as a sufficient protection,' Dorothy declared defiantly. She defended her decision to prolong her stay at Windy Brow: 'I am now twenty-two years of age,' she pointed out, 'and such have been the circumstances of my life that I may be said to have enjoyed his company only for a *very few* months. An opportunity now presents itself of obtaining this satisfaction, an opportunity which I could not see pass from me without unspeakable pain. Besides I not only derive much pleasure but much improvement from my brother's society. I have regained all the knowledge I had of the French language some years ago, and have added considerably to it, and I have now begun reading Italian . . .'[40]

The walk itself would remain long in the memory of both. Its significance increased as the years passed. This was a return to the country of their childhood – but it also provided a glimpse of their future together, passing through places that would become sacred to them. 'I walked with my brother at my side, from Kendal to Grasmere, eighteen miles, and afterwards from Grasmere to Keswick, fifteen miles, through the most delightful country that was ever seen.'[41] It was early April when they set out, a day of mixed sun and showers. At their first stop, Staveley, they drank a basin of milk at a public house, and Dorothy washed her feet in a brook, afterwards putting on a pair of silk stockings at her brother's recommendation. A little further on they reached Windermere, and continued north on the road that runs along the east bank of the lake to Ambleside. They picnicked beside a beck below Wansfell. Towards sunset, as they approached Grasmere, they left the road and followed the footpath along the south side of Rydal Water. The slanting yellow light cast deep shadows before the surrounding mountains.

3

IDEALISM

'I am studying such a book!' gushed Robert Southey, a nineteen-year-old Oxford undergraduate, in a letter to a former schoolmate on 22 November 1793.[1] He was reading William Godwin's enormously influential *An Enquiry concerning Political Justice, and its Influence on General Virtue and Happiness*, published in two volumes earlier in the year, which he had borrowed from the Bristol Library. Southey's rapturous reaction typified that of thousands of English radicals. For Henry Crabb Robinson, for example, then a teenage articled clerk, *Political Justice* 'made me feel more *generously*', that the good of the community was his sole duty. Godwin, a former dissenting minister and self-taught philosopher, offered a solution to the problems of these troubling times. Humanity was perfectible, or at least susceptible to permanent improvement. Man was essentially a rational creature; since reason taught benevolence, it followed that men were capable of living in harmony without laws or institutions. In modern terms, Godwin was an anarchist. Society was nothing more than an aggregation of individuals. 'Efforts for improvement of society must therefore be aimed at the improvement of each individual in it. Until each individual is made more rational, and therefore more moral, social institutions will not become more just.' Vice resulted from injustice – but this injustice could be overcome only by changing individuals. Godwin rejected all forms of association, including organised political agitation for social reform.

Southey was excited by this new philosophy, which seemed to overturn conventional wisdom. 'We are born in sin and the children

of wrath – says the catechism. It is absolutely false. Sin is artificial –
it is the monstrous offspring of government and property. The origin
of both was in injustice.' In a rhetorical flourish, Southey asked any
man of feeling to survey the lobby at the theatres or to look at the
courtesans on the streets of London. Society was manifestly depraved,
he wrote primly. It was innately unjust; by aggrandising the few it
oppressed the many. 'Would man thieve did not want tempt him?
Poverty is the nurse of vice where she is dogged by disgrace.' He did
not ask much for himself. 'Every day's experience shews me how little
Man wants, and every hours reflection now tends to fix my wishes
on the grave' (he was still very young). But 'whilst Reason keeps the
balance I dare live'.[2]

He rejected the conventional title 'esquire'. A man who deplored
social distinctions could obviously have no truck with monarchy –
thus Southey repeatedly declared himself to be a republican, even
though to do so publicly might damage his prospects: 'Perish every
hope of life rather than that I should forfeit my integrity.' He had
been swept up in the first wave of enthusiasm for the Revolution; it
appeared to him as if the human race was being washed clean. Like
Wordsworth, he had fantasised about fighting on the frontier to
defend the young Republic. Though subsequently alarmed by the
September Massacres and repelled by the execution of the Queen, he
remained a determined radical: 'I can condemn the crimes of the
French & yet be a Republican.'[3]

Even before he discovered Godwin, Southey had imagined an ideal
community, an island populated by philosophers. There society could
begin anew, without rules or gradations. His imagination was fired
by reports of the tropical idyll that had lured the crew of the *Bounty*
into mutiny;* Tahiti had many inducements, he insisted, 'independant [*sic*] of its women' – not only for the sailor, but for the philosopher too. Perhaps Southey was taken with the example of Fletcher
Christian, a young rebel against tyrannical authority. Another of his
utopian visions was of an ideal city, Southeyopolis. In a letter describ-

---

* In 1792 Captain Bligh published his account of the mutiny, and in September of that
same year ten prisoners repatriated from Tahiti to England were tried by a naval court.

ing his grandiose scheme for Southeyopolis, Southey felt it necessary to protest that he had not been drinking.[4]

Increasingly, Southey began to talk of emigration to America.[5] There, in a state of nature, he would find contentment. To the democratic mind there was something attractive in the idea of clearing one's own land and living in a cottage one had built oneself. As the political outlook in Britain became bleaker, America began to look more attractive. The 1790s saw a new wave of emigrants to America,* many of them dissenters depressed by repeated failure to reform the laws that discriminated against them. Early in 1794 Joseph Priestley decided that he too had had enough of England and sailed across the Atlantic, where he settled in Pennsylvania, on the banks of Susquehanna River.

'I have been doing nothing and still continue to be doing nothing,' Wordsworth had admitted to his undergraduate friend William Mathews while he and Dorothy were staying with the Rawsons; 'what is to become of me I know not.' He could not face either of the two careers proposed to him, the law or the Church.[6] It was now more than three years since he had left Cambridge, and he was still drifting from place to place. His only obvious achievement in all this time had been to publish two poems, and though he had another (inspired by his walk across Salisbury Plain) ready for the press, the 'unmerited contempt' with which those had been treated by some of the periodicals made him reluctant to publish anything further unless he could hope to 'derive from it some pecuniary recompense'.[7] With no income, he was living as modestly as possible, relying on the hospitality of relatives and friends and the occasional subvention from his elder brother, who controlled what meagre resources remained to the young family.

When he confessed to doing nothing, Wordsworth did not mean that he was entirely idle; he was correcting and adding to the poems he had written, a process he continued throughout his career. For

* In 1795 the *Gentleman's Magazine* reported that a group of Girondin émigrés had settled at Frenchtown near the Susquehanna.

Wordsworth, a poem was never finished; as he changed, so he wanted the poem to change, to conform with the man he had become. He found it hard to let go of his work, and only reluctantly would he ever give it to the world. In revising these two poems it may be that he was responding to Dorothy's criticisms; certainly his later judgement of them closely resembles comments she had made in a letter to Jane Pollard soon after they were published.[8] New passages he added to 'An Evening Walk' anticipate ideas that Coleridge would later articulate to him more fully, and show that the two of them had been following the same tracks before they came into contact.[9]

Mathews urged Wordsworth to come to London. He and another young man were thinking about starting a monthly periodical, and wanted Wordsworth to join them. For his part, Wordsworth felt that he could not venture to London unless he were sure of a regular income – but he was attracted by the notion of a 'monthly miscellany', and saw no reason why he should not contribute while remaining in the country. In a succession of letters in the early summer of 1794 he set out his thoughts on the subject. He envisaged 'a vehicle of sound and exalted morality', provisionally entitled *The Philanthropist*. ('Philanthropist' was a term much used at the time, meaning progressive or reformer.) Wordsworth felt that the three of them should not be ignorant of each other's political views. 'You know perhaps already that I am of that odious class of men called democrats, and of that class I shall for ever continue,' he announced boldly.[10]

It was not a good moment to advertise radical sentiments. Parliament had just passed a declaration that 'a traitorous and detestable conspiracy had been formed for subverting the existing laws and constitution, and for introducing the system of anarchy and confusion which has so lately prevailed in France' – after ministers had presented intelligence to secret committees of both Houses. The Habeas Corpus Act (which protected the individual from detention without trial) was accordingly suspended. Twelve prominent radicals, including leaders of the London Corresponding Society and the Society for Constitutional Information, were arrested and imprisoned in the Tower, awaiting trial on charges of treason. Suspect letters were inter-

cepted and opened by the authorities. On the very day that Wordsworth wrote to Mathews, his elder brother Richard warned him to
'be cautious in writing or expressing your political opinions'. Dorothy
(who until very recently had been living with her brother at Windy
Brow) replied to Richard: 'I think I can answer for William's caution
about expressing his political opinions. He is very cautious and seems
well aware of the dangers of a contrary conduct.'[11]

The government's crackdown was the culmination of months of
less co-ordinated repression. In December 1793 a 'British Convention'
of reformers meeting in Edinburgh had been broken up by the authorities; the secretary, William Skirving, and two delegates from the
London Corresponding Society, Joseph Gerrald and Maurice Margarot, were found guilty of sedition and sentenced to fourteen years'
transportation. The dignified conduct of the prisoners during their
manifestly unfair trials made a powerful impression on the public,
and the widespread revulsion at the savagery of their sentences was
strong enough to counterbalance the prevalent horror at events in
France. In a separate Scottish case, Robert Watt and David Downie
were accused of planning an armed uprising and found guilty of
treason: both were sentenced to death, but Downie was pardoned.
Watt, who was executed, had been a government informer, and may
have been acting as an *agent provocateur*; the whole conspiracy was
probably a bungled attempt to entrap Downie and other radicals.
In England, several prosecutions for sedition collapsed in a mêlée
of disreputable witnesses and ridiculous charges. For example, the
London Corresponding Society was accused of plotting to assassinate
the King with a poisoned arrow fired from an airgun, a charge so
ludicrous that it immediately earned the name the 'Pop-Gun Plot'.

Dorothy was mistaken in her assurances to Richard, because a
week or so later Wordsworth wrote another letter to Mathews,
setting out his political views in greater detail: 'I disapprove of
monarchical and aristocratical governments, however modified.
Hereditary distinctions and privileged orders of every species I think
must necessarily counteract the progress of human improvement:
hence it follows that I am not amongst the admirers of the British

constitution.' He argued that the constitution was being subverted by two causes: the 'infatuation profligacy and extravagance of men in power', and the 'changes of opinion rapidly' taking place 'in the minds of speculative men'. He deplored 'the miserable situation of the French' – as well he might, because as he wrote these words the Terror was approaching its murderous climax – and believed that 'a more excellent system of civil policy' might still be established in Britain without a cataclysmic upheaval. Ministers, not radicals, were driving the country towards the precipice. 'I recoil from the bare idea of a revolution; yet, if our conduct with reference both to foreign and domestic policy continues such as it has been for the last two years how is that dreadful event to be averted?' Wordsworth was sure of the answer: 'gradual and constant reform of those abuses which, if left to themselves, may grow to such a height as to render, even a revolution desirable'. There was, he felt, 'a further duty incumbent upon every enlightened friend of mankind', namely to propagate principles of 'political justice'; these 'will guide the hand of reform, and if a revolution must afflict us, they alone can mitigate its horrors and establish freedom with tranquillity'.[12]

This is a Godwinian manifesto, punctuated with Godwinian ideas and terminology. Indeed the whole *Philanthropist* project reeks of Godwin. It is obvious from Wordsworth's letters in the spring of 1794 that he has read Godwin's *Political Justice*. He is moving away from a belief in direct action to achieve political change in Britain towards one of disseminating progressive ideas to bring about reform. 'I know that the multitude walk in darkness. I would put into each man's hand a lantern to guide him,' he wrote to Mathews – echoing Godwin's metaphor 'the illumination of our understanding'. Quite when Wordsworth read Godwin is not obvious. It is interesting to speculate how he might have obtained a copy of *Political Justice*, given that it was relatively expensive* and he was so short of money. Perhaps Calvert had a copy. (Pitt is supposed to have advised the Privy Council that there was no need to suppress *Political Justice*, as 'a three guinea

---

* Seventy-two times the price of *Rights of Man* (6d). By comparison, the average weekly income was around ten shillings.

book could never do much harm among those who had not three shillings to spare' – though the price of the first edition was in fact £1.16s.[13])

Coleridge's military career lasted little more than four months. He was an unsuitable dragoon, being 'a very indocile equestrian' and moreover saddle-sore. In a single week he was thrown from his horse three times, and 'run away with' almost every day: 'I ride a horse young, and as undisciplined as myself.' During a couple of months' basic training in the Home Counties Coleridge had evidently not impressed his commanding officers, because when the regiment moved on he was left behind in Henley-upon-Thames to care for a soldier suffering from smallpox. An anxious letter from his brother George caught up with him there. Coleridge's reply was hysterical with pious remorse and abject self-pity: 'O that without guilt I might ask of my Maker Annihilation!'[14] He did not attempt to explain his conduct: 'my mind is illegible to myself'. George tried to organise his release; his eldest surviving brother James, a professional soldier, made a direct appeal to the General in command. The General was too busy to reply, being fully occupied in raising a new regiment, but after three weeks' delay a response came from the new officer in command. Coleridge had received six and a half guineas' bounty to enlist; his brothers must pay twenty-five guineas to secure his discharge – on the basis that it would require such an amount to obtain a substitute. No substitute was forthcoming, so another pretext for his release had to be found. An entry in the muster roll of the regiment dated 10 April 1794 reads, 'discharged S.T. Comberbach/Insane'.

Coleridge returned to Cambridge, to receive another reprimand from the Master. His punishment was to be gated for a month, and to translate ninety pages from the Greek. He accepted his sentence humbly, conscious of his luck that the college had kept his place open. To complete his degree he would have to stay an extra year, to the end of 1795. His brothers had supplied him with cash for his immediate expenses, and raised a handsome sum towards liquidating his college debts; in return, Coleridge promised to reform. In fact, his mind was wandering. At the end of the Trinity term, after only a couple of months in Cambridge, he set out on a walking tour with a good-natured undergraduate called Joseph Hucks. They were destined for Wales – but first they made a stopover in Oxford, to visit Coleridge's earliest school friend, Robert Allen, who was studying medicine at University College. Allen, who in time would himself join the dragoons as a military surgeon, had sent Coleridge money and various small luxuries during his army ordeal, and twice visited him in his quarters. Allen was renowned for his charm, his intelligence and his good looks; after he had accidentally run into a barrow woman in the street one day, she started to swear at him until she saw his face: 'Where are you driving to, you great hulking, good-for-nothing – beautiful fellow, God bless you!'

Allen introduced them to another medical student, Robert Southey of Balliol, who coincidentally had made his own 'pedestrian scheme' to Cambridge and back the previous May,* when he had attended Frend's trial in the university court and admired Frend's oratory in his own defence. Southey and Coleridge took to each other immediately. Though very different characters, the two had much in common: politics, poetry, philosophy, anxiety about money, enthusiasm for walking. They began 'disputing on metaphysical subjects', arguing, debating, laughing in the sheer pleasure of having found a kindred spirit. Coleridge was so delighted with his discovery that he postponed his departure from Oxford by more than a fortnight. Hucks, who had accepted Coleridge's word that they would be stopping in Oxford no longer than three or four days, was compelled to wait while the two new friends talked incessantly.

Southey, still not quite twenty (two years younger than Coleridge), was the eldest son of a Bristol linen-draper who had fallen on hard times and died, leaving the young undergraduate responsible for his mother and three younger brothers. He had acquired polished manners at the home of his wealthy aunt, where he had spent much of his childhood and where he continued to be a favoured guest. Like

---

* The previous Easter he had made a three-week walking tour of the Midlands.

Wordsworth and so many others, he was depressed by the looming prospect of a career in the Church – 'starving in creditable celibacy upon 40 pounds a year' – not least because he found it impossible to stifle doubts, and disliked the thought of perjuring himself. At Westminster he had started a school magazine, *The Flagellant*; with such a title, it was inevitable that the publication should vigorously condemn the practice of corporal punishment in schools, the only surprise being that this attack was not launched until the fifth issue; Southey was expelled as a result. He arrived in Oxford with 'a heart full of poetry and feeling, a head full of Rousseau and Werther'.* As if in imitation of Werther, he became infatuated with a young woman before discovering that she was already attached – inspiring him to compose an 'Ode to Grief'. Southey wrote very fast, all the more impressive as poor eyesight prevented him from reading or writing by candlelight. Together with another young Bristol poet, the Quaker Robert Lovell, he was preparing a volume of poems. Furthermore, he was working on a long epic poem, *Joan of Arc*, and contemplating another, *Wat Tyler*. These historical epics rang with contemporary resonance. Southey's Joan addressed the common people as 'Citizens' and owed her position to their support. 'My Joan is a great democrat,' he wrote; and in his hands Tyler would become a revolutionary martyr, another Marat.† The story of the peasants' revolt seemed apposite at a time when *sans-culottes*‡ were escorting aristocrats to the scaffold, and indeed Southey was convinced that a revolutionary cataclysm was inevitable in Britain.

Southey freely expressed extreme political opinions, often adopting a posture of noble self-sacrifice. In another poem, 'The Exiled Patriots', he celebrated the reformers transported to the colonies:

---

* Goethe's novel *The Sorrows of Young Werther* (1774) influenced several generations of young men across Europe. 'Wertherism' became a recognisable syndrome. The novel's hero is a melancholic, an artist at odds with society and hopelessly in love with a girl engaged to another man. He eventually commits suicide as a result.
† An added attraction was the potential embarrassment to his conservative Aunt Tyler.
‡ Literally, 'without knee-breeches', since coarse long trousers were the habitual dress of the Parisian working class: used as shorthand for those political activists – mainly small shopkeepers, tradesmen and artisans – who constituted the foot-soldiers of the Revolution.

So shall your great examples fire each soul
So in each freeborn heart for ever dwell
'Till Man shall rise above the unjust controul
Stand where ye stood – & triumph where ye fell.

For Coleridge, this combination of politics and poetry was irresistible. 'Thy soaring is even unto heaven,' he wrote to Southey the day after they parted – 'Or let me add (for my Appetite for Similies is truly canine at this moment) that as the Italian Nobles their new-fashioned Doors, so thou dost make the adamantine Gate of Democracy turn on it's [*sic*]* golden Hinges to most sweet Music.'[15]

Tall and bony, Southey was reckoned handsome; in an attempt at dignity he held his chin high; he refused to let his 'mane' of dark curly hair be shorn by the college barber, boldly allowing it to hang free and unpowdered when he went into hall to dine; large, dark eyes framed a prominent, beakish nose, giving him 'a falcon glance'; long, curving eyebrows suggested a sardonic cast of mind. Generous, suave and stoical, stern, principled and dogmatic, he emanated self-satisfied rectitude. To Coleridge, Southey's combination of cool decisiveness and violent convictions was compelling. He admired his disciplined working habits, and was excited by his daring republican talk. Southey seemed to him to embody the admirably austere qualities of the ancients. 'He is truly a man of *perpendicular Virtue* – a *down-right upright Republican!*' wrote Coleridge, who could rarely resist a pun, in this case a *double entendre*; he had discovered that Southey was still a virgin.[16]

Southey was immediately impressed by Coleridge's volcanic intellect, hurling out ideas red hot from the bubbling tumult of his brain: 'He is of most uncommon merit – of the strongest genius, the clearest judgment, the best heart.'[17] Within a day or two of their meeting he was writing of his new friend as 'one whom I very much esteem and admire tho two thirds of our conversation be spent in disputing on metaphysical subjects'.[18] Coleridge's intellectual interests were encyclopaedic, nourished by voracious reading. In particular he was drawn

---

* Coleridge's spelling was haphazard, as was his grammar and use of capitals; in particular, he always wrote 'it's' when he meant 'its'.

towards philosophy – not the abstract philosophy of word games, but metaphysics, enquiry into the ultimate nature of reality. His arrival energised Southey, who had been languishing in a melancholic stupor.

It was inevitable that these two young idealists should discuss Southey's utopian dreams. Into the mixture went Rousseau and Godwin, republicanism and philanthropy, notions of pastoral simplicity and honest toil. Within three weeks they had sketched the outline of a scheme for an ideal community of a dozen young couples, isolated from the rest of the world, in which property should be held in common, labour should be contributed to the common good, and all (even women) should participate in government. Two or three hours' manual work each day should be enough, they calculated, and the rest of the time could be given up to 'study, liberal discussions, and the education of their children'. Coleridge, who made a habit of coining new words, came up with a name for this system of complete equality: 'Pantocracy', later amended to 'Pantisocracy'.* Some remote part of America seemed the obvious place to try this experiment; Southey proposed Kentucky, but they settled on the Susquehanna as the best possible destination – because, Coleridge later said, he liked the name. It was agreed that they should seek out others to join them. Another Balliol man, George Burnett, was quickly recruited; he and Southey were to travel to Bristol, where they hoped to persuade Robert Lovell to come too. More in hope than expectation, Southey invited his aristocratic friend Grosvenor Charles Bedford: 'When the storm burst[s] on England you may perhaps follow us to America.' As Pitt's government tightened the screw in England, the news from France was of more and more executions, and Southey seems to have envisaged Pantisocracy as a refuge from an impending Armageddon. He decided that his mother and siblings should accompany them. 'The storm is gathering, and must soon break,' he wrote to Bedford's brother Horace. He amused himself with the idea of seeing all his aristocratic friends 'come flying over for shelter' to America: 'You must all come when the fire and brimstone descend.'[19]

* From the Greek 'pant-', a root meaning 'all'; 'isos', meaning 'equal'; and 'krat', meaning 'power'.

At last, on 5 July, Coleridge was ready to continue his interrupted walking tour. To make up for lost time, he and Hucks caught the fly* to Gloucester, from where Coleridge wrote to Southey – whom he had left only the day before – saluting him 'Health and Republicanism!' Perhaps remembering Southey's horrifying story of a fifteen-year-old servant girl who had strangled her newborn baby, he parroted Hucks's reaction to an episode on the road:

> It is *wrong*, Southey! for a little Girl with a half-famished sickly Baby in her arms to put her head in at the window of an Inn – 'Pray give me a bit of Bread and Meat'! from a Party dining on Lamb, Green Pease, & Sallad – Why?? Because it is *impertinent* & *obtrusive*! – I am a Gentleman! – and wherefore should the clamorous Voice of Woe intrude upon mine Ear!?

'My companion is a Man of cultivated, tho' not vigorous, understanding,' he explained; 'his feelings are all on the side of humanity – yet such are the unfeeling remarks, which the lingering remains of Aristocracy occasionally prompt.' Coleridge was confident that their new system would put an end to such things. (But even so, there were limits – when, later in the tour, a horny-handed Welsh democrat shook his hand vigorously, Coleridge 'trembled' lest some parasite had 'emigrated'.) In high spirits he informed Southey that he had bought 'a little Blank Book, and a portable Ink horn – as I journey onward, I ever and anon pluck the wild Flowers of Poesy'. Thus began a lifelong habit of note-keeping.

He continued with an allegory of regicide: 'When Serpents *sting*, the only Remedy is – to *kill* the *Serpent* . . .' (These were dangerous ideas to express in a letter. Though Southey voiced extreme views in conversation, he was more circumspect about what he committed to paper.[20]) There followed an extract from a poem Coleridge was composing, entitled 'Perspiration, A Travelling Eclogue':

> The Dust flies smothering, as on clatt'ring Wheels
> Loath'd Aristocracy careers along.

* A one-horse hackney carriage, i.e. a taxi.

Coleridge ended his lively letter, 'Farewell, sturdy Republican!' and begged Southey to send 'Fraternity and civic Remembrances' to Lovell.[21]

Coleridge and Hucks walked north-west, through Ross and Hereford, and then turned north, following the Welsh border. On the road they met two other undergraduates from Coleridge's college, and 'laughed famously' because 'these rival *pedestrians* . . . were vigorously pursuing their tour – in a *post chaise!*' Their excuse for taking it easy thus was that one of them 'had got *clapped*'. A week after leaving Hereford, Coleridge arrived at Wrexham, where he wrote to Southey again: 'I have positively done nothing but dream of the System of no Property every step of the Way since I left you.'[22]

At Wrexham Church Coleridge was surprised to see Elizabeth, sister of his former girlfriend Mary Evans; he had forgotten that their grandmother lived there. Indeed, he had virtually forgotten Mary – but the chance encounter provided an opportunity for a good deal of posturing on both sides. Later, at the inn, he saw both Eliza and Mary hovering outside the window: 'I turned sick, and all but fainted away!' The young women passed by the window several times. 'I neither eat, or slept yesterday,' he wrote after he and Hucks had resumed their journey; 'but Love is a local Anguish – I am 16 miles distant, and am not half so miserable.' Coleridge plunged into an ecstasy of Wertherism, all the more delicious because he could expatiate to Southey:

> She lives, but lives not for me: as a loving bride, perhaps –
> ah, sadness! – she has thrown her arms around another man's
> neck. Farewell, ye deceitful dreams of a love-lorn mind; ye
> beloved shores, farewell; farewell, ah, beautiful Mary!*

He convinced himself that he had not pursued Mary because his prospects were so dim. 'I never durst in a whisper avow my passion, though I knew she loved me.'[23]

'For God's sake, Southey! enter not into the church.' Coleridge's abhorrence of Anglicanism was grounded in belief rather than doubt. He was a devout Christian, then tending towards Unitarianism, and his conscience would not allow him to accept the compromises

---

* These lines were encoded in Latin verse.

swallowed by many young men wanting to pursue a career in the established Church.

Coleridge and Hucks continued across north Wales to Anglesey, where they were reunited with the other two Cantabs, now back on their feet. Together they climbed some of the highest peaks in Wales, including Snowdon and Cader Idris, several of the ascents made during the midday summer heat. Coleridge, who thought nothing of walking forty miles in a single day, went so fast that Hucks found it difficult to keep up with him. Afterwards they made their way south again, parting company at Llandovery. Coleridge was headed for Bristol, and followed the Wye Valley downstream towards the sea via Tintern, taking the same route that Wordsworth had followed a year earlier, but in the opposite direction.

Arriving in Bristol, Coleridge immediately sought out Southey. He sent a message to Lovell – signing himself 'Your fellow Citizen' – asking where his friend was to be found. Southey happened to be dining that evening with Lovell and his new wife, the actress Mary Fricker, together with her pretty eldest sister, Sara.* These three had already heard much from Southey of Coleridge's genius, so they were intrigued when he appeared at the dinner table, brown as a berry, his clothes in tatters and his hair wild, weary of walking but certainly not of talking. He was in high good humour, exhilarated at seeing Southey again, animated and funny. Sara laughed at his jokes and made some sharp remarks of her own. As he held forth, he noticed her sparkling dark eyes, her brown curling hair and her full, inviting figure.

There were five Fricker girls (and one boy), as Coleridge rapidly discovered, daughters of a widow who kept a dress shop in Bristol. Lovell had just married one daughter, and Southey was courting another. George Burnett had his eye on a third. Obviously it was urgent for the Pantisocrats to find themselves mates. It seemed possible that the whole Fricker family, mother and all, might be joining them on the banks of the Susquehanna. How appropriate if Coleridge were to become united with one of the two remaining daughters! For

* Actually Sarah, but Coleridge almost always spelled it Sara, so I have used this throughout.

him, it was a similar set-up to the one he had enjoyed at Villiers Street. He had lost Mary Evans, and in doing so lost a family. Now, perhaps, he had found another.

Over the next few days, as they discussed and refined the Pantisocratic project, Southey introduced Coleridge to his Bristol friends and showed him around. Until recently Bristol had been England's second city after London, though it was rapidly being overhauled by the new industrial cities of the north. It remained an important port, with a busy quayside and clusters of masts poking up above the roofline, lurching at drunken angles when the tide fell and the ships settled on the mud. Also prominent on the skyline were many church steeples, and the chimneys of glassworks belching out black smoke. The city had spread right across the floodplain of the Avon, and extended up the adjoining hills to form the smart suburbs of Clifton and Kingsdown, where gracious terraces and crescents provided commanding views. The river curved behind the hills through a gorge, with hanging woods: 'a scene truly magnificent', wrote Southey, 'and wanting nothing but clearer water'.[24] Bristol was a centre of glass and china manufacture, with significant numbers of literate and politically sophisticated artisans. The radical sympathies of a prosperous nonconformist community confronted the conservatism of professional men and wealthy merchants, including those who had grown rich trading in slaves.[25] The issue of the war cut across this divide. Because Bristol was so dependent on commerce, it had been badly affected by mercantile failures consequent upon the war; there had been riots in the city for the past two years.

One of those whom Coleridge met in Bristol was Joseph Cottle, a young Baptist bookseller-publisher and would-be poet who kept a shop on the corner of Corn Street and High Street. Cottle had recently been thrown from a gig, an accident which left him lame for the rest of his life. Lovell had introduced Southey to Cottle, and now introduced Coleridge. Cottle immediately recognised Coleridge's 'intellectual character' – exhibiting, as he did, 'an eye, a brow, and a forehead, indicative of commanding genius' – and subsequent meetings 'increased the impression of respect'. The friendly manners of the

Pantisocrats, Cottle wrote many years later in his *Reminiscences*, 'infused into my heart a brotherly feeling, that more than identified their interests with my own'.[26] He agreed to publish the joint volume of poetry by Southey and Lovell, and offered a lavish fee of fifty guineas for Southey's *Joan of Arc*. As Southey wrote many years afterwards, 'it can rarely happen that a young author should meet with a publisher as inexperienced and ardent as himself'.

In mid-August Coleridge and Southey set out from Bristol on a walking tour into Somerset, where they were to seek more recruits to Pantisocracy. Both seem to have been in a state of high excitement, relishing each other's company. They walked first to Bath, to spend the night with Southey's mother, herself already drafted into the Pantisocratic regiment, as was Southey's brother Tom. At her house in Westgate Buildings they found Sara Fricker, whom Mrs Southey had invited to stay so that they could 'talk over the American affair'. Perhaps Southey connived in bringing Sara together with Coleridge again. By the time the two men left the next morning, accompanied by Southey's dog Rover, some kind of understanding seems to have been reached between Coleridge and the eldest Miss Fricker – though they had known each other little more than a week. (She would still be there when they returned a week later, drunk on the heady wine of Pantisocracy; and after another conversation, Coleridge seems to have committed himself further.)

Their route took them across the Mendip Hills, via Chilcompton and Wells. They spent their first night at Cheddar, sleeping in a garret, where they were locked in by a suspicious landlady who took these wild-looking young men for possible 'footpads'. There was only one bed. 'Coleridge is a vile bedfellow and I slept but ill,' complained Southey.[27] The next day they made for Huntspill, down on the Somerset Levels, to call on George Burnett, who was fired with fresh enthusiasm for Pantisocracy, much to the dismay of his father, a prosperous farmer who intended his son for the Church. Then the two missionaries headed for Shurton on the west Somerset coastline, to the home of Henry Poole, one of Coleridge's fellow undergraduates from Jesus. He proved more resistant to the new religion, but escorted the two visitors to see his cousin Thomas Poole, a known radical who lived not far away in the small town (really no more than a large village) of Nether Stowey, at the base of the Quantock Hills (this was familiar country for Southey, whose grandfather had farmed at nearby Holford). Poole was the son of a successful tanner, a stout, plain, sensible man of twenty-nine with a rubicund complexion and a noticeable West Country burr. Yet his prosaic exterior concealed a mind generous, liberal and well-read. An enlightened employer with a practical concern for the poor and downtrodden,* Poole was liked and admired even by those who detested his principles. His enthusiasm for revolutionary politics had earned him the label 'the most dangerous person in the county of Somerset' (perhaps not *such* a distinction), and some of his letters had been intercepted and opened on government instructions.

Coleridge talked freely, not just about Pantisocracy, but about his own 'aberrations from prudence', which he promised were now at an end. Poole was very impressed by this visitor, a 'shining scholar' whom he considered 'the Principal in the undertaking'. He was not so impressed by Southey, who seemed 'a mere boy' by comparison, lacking Coleridge's 'splendid abilities', though he was 'even more violent in his principles'. Poole, who had himself considered emigrating to America, listened sympathetically as they outlined their scheme; but he felt that however perfectible human nature might be, it was 'not yet perfect enough' for Pantisocracy.[28]

In France, Robespierre and his associates tightened their grip on power, eliminating their rivals without qualm. The purge of the Girondins was followed by further purges in the spring of 1794. Death followed death, and more deaths. Everyone was afraid, but no one dared show fear. Now the severed heads being displayed to the Paris crowds were those of prominent revolutionaries, men who themselves had until recently been demanding executions. 'Oh Liberty, what

---

* Poole was one of those who refused to allow the use of sugar in his household, insisting that cakes be made with honey instead. The anti-slavery campaigner Thomas Clarkson estimated that 300,000 people in England took part in a nationwide boycott of sugar, protesting at Parliament's failure to pass a Bill abolishing the slave trade.

crimes are committed in thy name!' cried the Girondin Madame Roland from the scaffold – though it was she who had declared that there must be blood to cement the Revolution. A macabre poster displayed a group of heads hanging horridly from a board, the leering faces still recognisable, with the legend, 'It is dreadful but it is necessary.' Robespierre himself possessed the certainty of a zealot. He was incorruptible; he spoke for the Republic; anyone who criticised him was an enemy of the people. The ideologue of the Revolution, he articulated the principles of the slaughter. He envisaged a Republic of virtue; he would make man better. The aims of the Revolution were the peaceful enjoyment of liberty and equality, and the reign of eternal justice. He exhorted his listeners to seal their work with blood, so that they might see the dawn of universal happiness. 'Terror is the only justice that is prompt, severe, and inflexible; it is thus an emanation of virtue . . .'[29]

For those ideologically committed to the young Republic, like Wordsworth, this was a time of torment. A believer could not relinquish his faith without a struggle. As the Revolution progressed, its fellow travellers had accepted one sacrifice after another in the cause of the greater good; accepted them, and then justified them to the world. They had swallowed so much blood already; now they were choking on it. Wordsworth confessed to nightmares that continued for years after the Terror had abated:

> I scarcely had one night of quiet sleep,
> Such ghastly visions had I of despair,
> And tyranny, and implements of death,
> And long orations which in dreams I pleaded
> Before unjust Tribunals, with a voice
> Labouring, a brain confounded, and a sense
> Of treachery and desertion in the place
> The holiest that I knew of – my own soul.[30]

Yet even now, Wordsworth did not lose faith. On the contrary, in the 'rage and dog-day heat' of the Revolution, he found 'something to glory in, as just and fit'. Like so many intellectuals since,

> I felt a kind of sympathy with power.[31]

In the confused period after the September Massacres, Wordsworth shared the general longing for a strong man to impose order, 'not doubting . . .'

> But that the virtue of one paramount mind
> Would have abashed those impious crests, have quelled
> Outrage and bloody power, and in despite
> Of what people were through ignorance
> And immaturity, and, in the teeth
> Of desperate opposition from without,
> Have cleared a passage for just government
> And left a solid birthright to the state,
> Redeemed according to example given
> By ancient lawgivers . . .[32]

But which ancient lawgivers? There was no question that the 'one paramount mind' was Robespierre – but was he a Brutus, or a Caesar? A Cato, or a Tarquin? Was the exemplar of civic virtue becoming a tyrant? Wordsworth's inner struggle was one of interpretation. Should Robespierre be seen as the apotheosis of the Revolution, to be defended, indeed admired, even though he was drenched in blood? Or was he rather, as Wordsworth began to perceive, an aberration, a perversion of the Revolutionary ideal? Arriving at the latter conclusion came as a huge relief to Wordsworth. All the horrors that had seemed concomitant with the Revolution could be ascribed to this deviation from its true path.

Wordsworth had refused to accept the taunts of scoffers, those who sneered that the chaos of the Terror was the inevitable result of democratic government. On the contrary, this was a legacy of the past:

> . . . it was a reservoir of guilt
> And ignorance, filled up from age to age,
> That could no longer hold its loathsome charge,
> But burst and spread in deluge through the land.[33]

He detested 'the execrable measures pursued in France', but equally insisted on holding up 'to the approbation of the world such of their regulations and decrees as are dictated by the spirit of Philosophy'.[34] For him, Terror was not intrinsic to the Revolution; it was a reaction to the threat from without, aided by the enemy within. As he saw it, the entry of Britain into the coalition against Revolutionary France had prompted the bloodshed:

> In France, the men who for their desperate ends
> Had pluck'd up mercy by the roots were glad
> Of this new enemy. Tyrants, strong before
> In devilish pleas, were ten times stronger now,
> And thus beset with foes on every side,
> The goaded land waxed mad . . .[35]

And when, in an astonishing turnaround, the new conscript army repelled the enemies of France, and once more surged across the borders, Wordsworth rejoiced – even when English troops fled the battlefield in shame and confusion:*

> . . . the invaders fared as they deserved:
> The Herculean Commonwealth had put forth her arms,
> And throttled with an infant Godhead's might
> The snakes about her cradle; that was well,
> And as it should be . . .[36]

The Terror reached a climax in the early summer. In response to a manufactured 'conspiracy' a new law was passed, granting the Revolutionary Tribunal absolute powers. Only by the most extreme measures would the enemy within be exterminated. The accused were permitted no defence; there were to be no witnesses; there would be only one sentence: death. Every day there were dozens of executions. A contemporary cartoon showed Robespierre, having ordered the execution of everyone else, guillotining the executioner. In fact, for much of the six-week period known as the Great Terror, Robespierre kept ominously aloof from both the Committee of Public Safety and

---

* *The Prelude*, X, 258–63. Most Wordsworth scholars follow De Selincourt in taking this passage to refer to the French victory at Hondeschoote on 6 September 1793; but the description seems to fit better the rout of the British army at Tourcoing on 18 May 1794, when their commander the Duke of York (the King's brother) was hunted across the country and escaped only thanks to the speed of his horse.

the Convention. Then, after a month, he returned to the Convention on 26 July, denouncing a new conspiracy and demanding yet another purge. This time his opponents were prepared. When Robespierre tried to address the Convention again the next day, he was shouted down. He was arrested, and after a bungled attempt at suicide he was hastily guillotined, together with Saint-Just and other close associates. It was the 10th of Thermidor, in Year II of the Republic (28 July 1794).

Wordsworth heard of Robespierre's downfall while he was staying with cousins at Rampside, near Barrow-in-Furness, the southernmost tip of the Lake District. Some months earlier he and Dorothy had left Windy Brow and gone in different directions, promising each other that they would soon be reunited in a more permanent home; since then he had remained in the Lakes, rotating around his relatives in the area. One morning he strolled to Cartmel, a village just across the estuary of the two little rivers that flow out of Windermere and Coniston. There, wandering through the churchyard, he had happened across the grave of his former schoolteacher, William Taylor. Now he was walking back to Rampside, across the miles of sand revealed by the receding tide. It was sunny, with magnificent prospects of the mountains to the north. At low tide it is easy to wade the shallow stream; the sands stretch far out into Morecambe Bay, and on this fine summer day they were spotted with coaches, carts, riders and walkers. While he paused on a rocky outcrop drinking in the view, a passer-by told him that Robespierre was dead. An exultant Wordsworth let forth a shout of triumph: 'Come now, ye golden times.'

> . . . few happier moments have been mine
> Through my whole life than that when first I heard
> That this foul tribe of Moloch was o'erthrown
> And their chief regent levelled with the dust.[37]

His wavering faith was renewed.

> . . . In the People was my trust,
> And in the virtues which mine eyes had seen,
> And to the ultimate repose of things
> I looked with unabated confidence.

I knew that wound external could not take
Life from the young Republic, that new foes
Would only follow in the path of shame
Their brethren, and her triumphs be in the end
Great, universal, irresistible.[38]

Coleridge and Southey heard of Robespierre's death while they were still with Poole in west Somerset. 'I had rather have heard of the death of my own father,' Southey declared solemnly – a declaration that loses some of its force when one reflects that his father had died several years before. But Poole's cousins in Over Stowey, whom he had taken the visitors to meet, were suitably indignant at such outrageous talk, and even more so when they heard one of the two young men say that Robespierre had been 'a ministering angel of mercy, sent to slay thousands that he might save millions'.[39]

There was no doubt in the minds of the Pantisocrats that Robespierre's fall was a 'tragedy'. For Southey, Robespierre was 'this great man', who had been 'sacrificed to the despair of fools and cowards'. For Coleridge he was a man 'whose great bad actions cast a disastrous lustre over his name'. They agreed that he had been 'the benefactor of mankind, and that we should lament his death as the greatest misfortune Europe could have sustained'.[40] To these young idealists, Robespierre's fanatical zealotry was preferable to Pitt's opportunistic pragmatism. They admired Robespierre's ardour, his oratory, his ferocity. He had aimed at human perfection, even if he had stumbled along the route. Like other British radicals, they explained away the Terror as a response to pressures from without. Robespierre and his associates had been provoked into violence. Indeed, the Terror was Pitt's responsibility.

On the walk back to Bristol the two young men decided to commemorate Robespierre's fall by writing a verse drama, to be published as quickly as possible. Coleridge was to write the first act, Southey the second, and Lovell the third (in the event Lovell dropped out). The money raised from this instant publication would be used to fund the Pantisocracy scheme. They began immediately, working around the clock. Southey's talent for speedy composition proved useful, as did taking in large chunks from newspaper reports of speeches in the Convention.

> . . . Never, never,
> Shall this regenerated country wear
> The despot yoke. Though myriads round assail
> And with worse fury urge this new crusade
> Than savages have known; though all the leagued despots
> Depopulate all Europe, so to pour
> The accumulated mass upon our coasts,
> Sublime amid the storm shall France arise
> And like the rock amid surrounding waves
> Repel the rushing ocean. – She shall wield
> The thunder-bolt of vengeance – She shall blast
> The despot's pride, and liberate the world.

These sentiments might just as easily have been expressed by Wordsworth. But having lived in France and having witnessed the Revolution at close quarters, Wordsworth was much more committed than either Coleridge or Southey; he struggled to interpret each bewildering development, like a believer trying to cling on to his failing faith. Coleridge, on the other hand, was excited by the Revolution, but not caught up in it, as is shown by his eccentric decision to enlist. Had he remained in the army he might well have found himself fighting against Beaupuy and those young volunteers so admired by Wordsworth. Indeed, had Wordsworth followed his impulse to join the Revolutionary cause, the two might have found themselves fighting on opposite sides.

Within a week *The Fall of Robespierre* was all but finished. Cottle prudently declined to publish it. Coleridge therefore took the manuscript with him to London, where he hoped to find a publisher while he sought new recruits to Pantisocracy. Before he left, the Pantisocrats finalised their scheme. The party would be made up of twelve men and their families. A total of £2,000 would be needed to fund the expedition, including the cost of their passage and the purchase of the land. Within twelve months (at most) they would be settled on the banks of the Susquehanna in Pennsylvania. During the course of the winter, Coleridge decided, 'those of us whose bodies, from habits of sedentary study or academic indolence, have not acquired their full tone and strength, intend to learn the theory and practice of agriculture and carpentry, according as situation and circumstances make one or the other convenient'.[41]

For Southey, parting from Coleridge was like 'losing a limb'. But he looked forward to 'sharing in the toil and in the glory of regenerating mankind ... Futurity opens a smiling prospect upon my view and I doubt not of enjoying the purest happiness Man can ever experience.'[42]

Once again Wordsworth declined Mathews's invitation to come to London. By chance an opportunity had presented itself to escape from the drudgery he dreaded. Raisley Calvert, younger brother of William, the school friend whom Wordsworth had accompanied to the Isle of Wight, offered Wordsworth a share of his income. This was a gentlemanly formula for helping Wordsworth with his essential expenses at a time when he was obviously struggling, while allowing him a degree of independence. Later, when it became clear that Raisley Calvert was dying of tuberculosis, he converted this into a legacy of £600, eventually increased to £900. Such a bequest was not unknown, but it was unusual enough for Richard Wordsworth to remark on Calvert's 'generous intentions towards you'. It was not as if Calvert was an old friend; he and Wordsworth had met only once before, when Calvert was passing through London early the previous year. Clearly this was a potential source of embarrassment, enough so for Wordsworth himself to want to inform William Calvert, who would otherwise have inherited the money along with the remainder of his brother's estate. 'It is at my request that this information is communicated to you, and I have no doubt but that you will do both him and myself the justice to hear this mark of his approbation of me without your good opinion of either of us being at all diminished by it.'[43] Why Raisley Calvert felt Wordsworth should benefit in this way is not certain. In later years Wordsworth claimed that Calvert had made the bequest 'entirely from a confidence on his part that I had powers and attainments which might be of use to mankind'.[44] If this is accurate, it is striking evidence of Wordsworth's sense of mission, and the way in which this could communicate itself to others – especially as his achievements to date were not especially impressive.

As Calvert's health deteriorated Wordsworth felt obliged to remain close to him, no doubt from a mixture of motives. Provided that his expenses were paid, he was willing to accompany Calvert to Portugal, and stay with him there until his health was re-established. On 9 October they set out from Keswick together, but had only reached Penrith when Calvert's condition forced them to return. 'He is so much reduced as to make it probable he cannot be on earth long,' Wordsworth reported to his brother Richard a week later.

Wordsworth feared that Calvert's legacy might be claimed by his aunt, as payment for the sums advanced for his education by her late husband. He therefore asked his brother Richard to indemnify him against such a claim. In his anxiety to secure Calvert's legacy, Wordsworth's request was made in a peremptory tone; Richard's reply showed his irritation at being addressed in such a manner by his younger brother:

> There is one Circumstance which I will mention to you at this time. I might have retired into the Country and I had almost said enjoyed the sweets of retirement and domestick life if I had only considered my own Interest. However as I have entered the busy scenes of a town life I shall I hope pursue them with comfort and credit. I am happy to inform you that my Business encreases daily and altho' our affairs have been peculiarly distressing I hope that from the Industry of ourselves at one time we will enjoy more ease and independence than we have yet experienced.[45]

If Wordsworth was stung by this implied criticism, he did not show it. Perhaps he accepted the rebuke as just. He had nothing to show for his expensive education. And since leaving Cambridge almost four years earlier, his only contribution to the family had been an illegitimate child by a French mistress.

4

SEDITION

Arriving in London at the beginning of September, Coleridge was too ashamed of his scruffy clothes to go to the coffee house where he had stayed in the past, so instead he lodged at the Angel Inn, down a lane off disreputable Newgate Street. Southey's aristocratic friend Grosvenor Charles Bedford received him politely – even though his appearance was 'so very anti-genteel' – and was civil enough not to stare at the address Coleridge gave him. As expected, he was not enthusiastic about Pantisocracy. A couple of days later Coleridge was introduced over breakfast to George Dyer, an eccentric middle-aged Unitarian, author of *Complaints of the Poor People of England*, who had been a pupil at Christ's Hospital and an undergraduate at Emmanuel College, Cambridge. By contrast with Bedford, Dyer was 'enraptured' with Pantisocracy, and 'pronounced it impregnable'. Coleridge told Southey complacently that Dyer was 'intimate with' Joseph Priestley (already settled on the Susquehanna), 'and doubts not, that the Doctor will join us'. On being shown part of the verse drama 'he liked it hugely' and opined that it was a 'Nail, that would drive'. Dyer offered to speak to Robinson, his 'Bookseller' (publisher), about it, and when Robinson proved to be away in the country, took it to two others, neither of whom seemed keen.[1] After this depressing reaction Coleridge decided that he and Southey should publish the drama themselves, printing five hundred copies; 'it will repay us amply'. It should be published under his name alone, he told Southey, because 'it would appear ridiculous to put two names to *such* a Work', and because his name would sell at least a hundred copies within

Cambridge.[2] *The Fall of Robespierre* duly appeared as the work of Samuel Taylor Coleridge at Jesus College at the end of September.

For the next fortnight or so, Coleridge spent every evening at another ale house in Newgate Street, the Salutation and Cat, where he preached Pantisocracy to two former Christ's Hospital schoolboys, both nineteen, Samuel Le Grice (younger brother of Coleridge's contemporary Valentine) and Samuel Favell. The three Sams made a comfortable party, talking and drinking porter and punch around a good fire. They were joined by another former Christ's Hospital pupil, who remembered Coleridge kindly, a young man who had spent the last five years in America. He advised that they could buy land a great deal cheaper over there, Coleridge informed Southey, and that 'twelve men may *easily* clear *three hundred* Acres in 4 or 5 months'; that the Susquehanna valley was to be recommended for its 'excessive Beauty, and it's security from hostile Indians'; that 'literary Characters make *money* there'; that 'he never saw a *Byson* in his Life – but has heard of them'; that 'the Musquitos are not so bad as our Gnats – and after you have been there a little while, they don't trouble you much'.[3] Altogether this was very encouraging.

Coleridge returned to Cambridge later than he had intended, to find that the undergraduates he had encountered on the road during his tour of Wales had 'spread my Opinions in mangled forms'. He soon set them right. There was some interest in Pantisocracy within the university, and some amusement too; Coleridge was a colourful character. But his eloquence trounced all opposition; within a month of his return, he boasted, Pantisocracy was the 'universal Topic' there. Meanwhile – notwithstanding his understanding with Sara Fricker – he flirted with Ann, sister of the celebrated actress Elizabeth Brunton and daughter of John Brunton, actor-manager of a company based in Norwich. He dedicated to her a poem on the French Revolution which he inscribed in a presentation copy of *The Fall of Robespierre*. He planned to visit the Bruntons in Norwich in the New Year. 'The young lady is said to be the most literary of the beautiful, and the most beautiful of the literatae,' he wrote provocatively to Southey – while almost in the same breath defending himself against the charge that he had written too seldom to Sara.

Southey had been having a difficult time. Once Coleridge had left, it seemed that 'all the prejudices of the human heart are in arms against me'. Neither his fiancée nor his mother was keen to leave England. His rich aunt turned him out of the house one wet night when she discovered his plan to emigrate from her servant Shadrach Weeks, whom Coleridge had recruited to Pantisocracy. She was equally disapproving of his plan to marry Edith Fricker, a milliner. Though Southey (parroting Godwin) preached disregarding '*individual* feelings' – towards one's mother or future wife, for example – he found this principle hard to practise. To Coleridge, Southey appeared to be backsliding, now saying that some of the emigrants might continue as servants, thereby freeing others of domestic chores. 'Let them dine with us and be treated with as much equality as they would wish – but perform that part of Labor for which their Education has fitted them,' he advocated. '*Southey* should not have written this Sentence,' insisted Coleridge, who suspected that his friend's resolve was being undermined by the women in the party.[4]

But while Coleridge strove to keep Southey to the founding principles of Pantisocracy, Southey chided him for neglecting Sara Fricker. Each sought the moral high ground. Southey was painfully aware that he had forfeited his aunt's favour, at least partly for Edith's sake. In self-righteous mood, he was intolerant of Coleridge's vacillating commitment to Sara. It is possible that Southey was under pressure from Edith to argue her sister's case with his friend. But it seems likely too that Southey was genuinely concerned about Sara. There is some evidence that he had been interested in her himself, before turning his attentions towards her more placid younger sister. In later life he continued to be solicitous for her welfare. Moreover, in encouraging Coleridge's relationship with Sara, he was binding Coleridge closer to himself – 'I shall then call Coleridge my brother in the real sense of the word.'[5] Conversely, Coleridge encouraged Southey's relationship with Edith. 'I am longing to be with you,' he wrote to Southey on his first morning in Cambridge: 'Make Edith my Sister – Surely, Southey! We shall be *frendotatoi meta frendous.*

Most friendly where all are friends. She must therefore be more emphatically my Sister.' In this overwrought dialogue, each man was goading the other to commit – to the woman certainly, but also to Pantisocracy, perhaps also to himself. For Coleridge, all three were bound up with each other: 'America! Southey! Miss Fricker!' He convinced himself that he was in love with her: 'Yes – Southey – you are right – Even Love is the creature of strong Motive – I certainly love her.'[6] Yet a week later he described himself as 'labouring under a waking Night-Mair of Spirits'[7] – not the expected state of mind for a young man in love. In the first letter he wrote to Sara from Cambridge, his own eloquence betrayed him into expressing emotions he did not fully feel. He later described this as 'the most criminal action of my Life . . . I had worked myself to such a pitch, that I scarcely knew I was writing like an hypocrite.' When it was too late, he recognised that he had 'mistaken the ebullience of *schematism* for affection, which a moment's reflection might have told me, is not a plant of so mushroom a growth'.[8]

'God forbid!' replied Southey, 'that the *Ebullience* of *Schematism* should be over. It is the Promethean Fire that animates my soul – and when *that* is gone, all *will be darkness*! I have DEVOTED myself!–"[9]

The night he arrived back in Cambridge, Coleridge wrote a strange, emotional letter to Edith, recalling his own dead sister Nancy.

> I *had* a Sister – an only Sister. Most tenderly did I love her! Yea, I have woke at midnight, and wept – because *she was not . . .*
> There is no attachment under heaven so pure, so endearing . . .
> My Sister, like you, was beautiful and accomplished . . . I know, and *feel*, that I am *your Brother* – I would, that you would say to me – 'I *will* be your sister – your *favourite* Sister in the Family of Soul.'[10]

A month later, Coleridge was thrown into deeper confusion by the arrival of an unsigned letter in a familiar hand: 'Is this handwriting altogether erased from your Memory? To whom am I addressing myself? For whom am I now violating the Rules of female Delicacy? Is it for the same Coleridge, whom I once regarded as a Sister her best-beloved Brother?' The writer urged him to abandon his 'absurd and extravagant' plan to leave England. 'I cannot easily forget those whom I once loved,' she wrote teasingly, and finished: 'Farewell – Coleridge – ! I shall always feel that I have been your *Sister*.' The writer, of course, was Mary Evans. She may have written at the request of George Coleridge, who was deeply distressed at the possibility that his youngest brother might emigrate. George had also written to him direct – a letter of 'remonstrance, and Anguish, & suggestions, that I am deranged!!'

Coleridge copied out Mary's letter for Southey:

> I loved her, Southey! almost to madness . . . I endeavoured to be perpetually with Miss Brunton – I even hoped, that her Exquisite Beauty and uncommon Accomplishments might have cured one passion by another. The latter I could easily have dissipated in her absence – and so have restored my affections to her, whom I do not love – but whom by every tie of Reason and Honour I ought to love. I am resolved – but wretched!

He was now in even more of a muddle. 'My thoughts are floating about in a most Chaotic State,' he confessed. 'What would I not give for a Day's conversation with you? So much, that I seriously think of Mail coaching it to Bath – altho' but for a Day.'[11]

His excitable state of mind is evident in a letter he wrote around this time to Francis Wrangham, formerly of Cambridge, now a Cobham curate, in which he sneered at the stock formula of sending 'compliments'.*

> *Compliments!* Cold aristocratic Inanities – ! I abjure their nothingness. If there be any whom I deem worthy of remembrance – I am their Brother. I call even my Cat Sister in the Fraternity of universal Nature. Owls I respect & Jack Asses I love: for Aldermen & Hogs, Bishops & Royston Crows I have

---

* In a letter to Southey of 17 December 1794, Coleridge asks his pardon for the 'aristocratic frigidity' of the expression 'I took the Liberty – '.[12]

not particular partiality –; they are my Cousins however, at
least by Courtesy. But Kings, Wolves, Tygers, Generals, Ministers, and Hyaenas, I renounce them all – or if they *must* be
my kinsmen, it shall be in the 50th Remove –

He ended this letter with the exhortation: 'May the Almighty Panti-
socratizer of Souls pantisocratize the Earth.'[13] A little later, he
addressed a poem 'To a Young Ass', which opened with the line 'Poor
Little Foal of an oppressed Race':

> Innocent Foal! Thou poor despis'd Forlorn! –
> I hail thee Brother, spite of Fool's Scorn!
> And fain I'd take thee with me in the Dell
> Of high-soul'd Pantisocracy to dwell;

Coleridge was much mocked for this poem after it was published.

He could not stop thinking about Mary Evans. 'She WAS VERY
lovely, Southey!' He wrote a poem about her, 'On a Discovery Made
Too Late'. Finally, he screwed up the courage to write to her: 'Too
long has my Heart been the torture house of Suspense.' He had heard
a rumour that she was engaged to be married to another man. Was
it true? In asking this, he had no other design or expectation, he said,
'than that of arming my fortitude by total hopelessness'. He saw that
she regarded him 'merely with the kindness of a Sister'. For four years,
he wrote, 'I have *endeavoured* to smother a very ardent attachment . . .
Happy were I, had it been with no more than a Brother's ardor!'[14]

He received another letter from George, now suggesting that he
should leave Cambridge and study law in the Temple – and in reply,
assured his brother that the views he had put into the mouths of his
characters in *The Fall of Robespierre* were not his own. 'Solemnly, my
Brother! I tell you – I am *not* a Democrat.'[15] (Thomas Poole had
described Coleridge as 'in politicks a Democrat, to the utmost extent
of the word'.[16])

Early in November Coleridge travelled up to London with his
friend Potter, an undergraduate at Emmanuel, a fellow poet, and
liberal in politics despite having £6,000 a year and his own phaeton.
The cases against the twelve prominent radicals charged with treason

had come to trial,* and Coleridge wanted to be on the spot. (He may have attended the trials themselves in the public gallery.) Robert Lovell was in town too; he visited one of the defendants, Godwin's close friend Thomas Holcroft, in Newgate prison, and attempted to convert him to Pantisocracy. He believed (mistakenly) that he had succeeded, and reported back to Southey that 'Gerrald,† Holcroft and Godwin – the three first men in England, perhaps in the world – highly approve our plan'.[17] Superbly represented in court by the brilliant advocate Thomas Erskine (who had defended Paine when he was tried *in absentia* in 1792), the accused had also been powerfully defended in print by Godwin, whose pamphlet *Cursory Strictures on the Charge delivered by Lord Chief Justice Eyre to the Grand Jury* dissected the treason charges, leaving them in tatters. (Coleridge may well have read Godwin's *Strictures*, which were reproduced in the *Morning Chronicle*.) Though the government had raided the homes of the radicals and seized their papers, the searches had failed to turn up incriminating evidence of a conspiracy. The Attorney-General, Sir John Scott (later Lord Eldon), resorted to petulant tears in his attempt to persuade the jury to convict – but in vain. As one after another of the defendants was acquitted, it became clear that the government had overreached itself. Pitt himself was subpoenaed by the defence and humiliated in the witness box. After several successive acquittals, charges against the remaining prisoners were dropped.

The verdicts were a triumph for the resurgent radical cause. On their release, the radicals – among them Thomas Hardy, founder of the London Corresponding Society, the orator and writer John Thelwall, and the pamphleteer John Horne Tooke – were greeted as heroes. Coleridge celebrated with a sonnet in honour of Erskine, the first of a sequence of eleven 'Sonnets on Eminent Characters' published in the *Morning Chronicle* from 1 December onwards. Most of his subjects were prominent liberal or radical figures, such as Priestley, Godwin

---

* See page 64.
† Gerrald, though sentenced some months before to transportation, was still being held in Newgate, in the hope that he might recant. Southey visited him there when he collected Coleridge from London.

and Sheridan,* but he also wrote a sonnet honouring William Lisle Bowles, the poet he had admired so much as a schoolboy, and even a sonnet to Southey. One sonnet was devoted to Tadeusz Kościuszko, the Polish patriot who had led the armed resistance to the partition of his country; another, unlike the others scathingly critical, to a subject who, though unnamed, was obviously ('foul apostate from his father's fame') the Prime Minister.

Coleridge had returned to Jesus after a week in the capital, but early in December he again left Cambridge for London, this time never to return. Once more he based himself at the Salutation and Cat, where, as one story has it, he attracted so many listeners that in recognition the landlord provided him with free lodging.† Here Coleridge was reunited with another former Christ's Hospital pupil, Charles Lamb, who was to become one of his closest friends. They had known each other at school – but not intimately, since Lamb was three years younger. Indeed Lamb had hero-worshipped Coleridge, whose schoolboy eloquence was such that it could make the casual passer-by pause in the cloisters and stand entranced. Lamb was a lovable figure, gentle and delicate. A severe stutter provoked indulgent affection rather than derision from his schoolmates. Slightly built, with spindly legs and a shambling gait, the legacy of childhood polio, Lamb habitually dressed in worn black clothes, giving him the appearance of a country curate recently arrived in town. The austerity of his dress was relieved by what Hazlitt (a painter) later described as his 'fine Titian head': his curly hair, his startling eyes, each a different colour, and his characteristic expression of droll amusement. Though nervous and shy, and prone to depression, Lamb had an independent mind, fine critical judgement, a strong sense of the ludicrous and a teasing wit. Like Coleridge, he had been a 'Grecian', but circumstances had not enabled him to attend university, and he now supported his parents and his elder sister Mary by working as a clerk in the East India Office. In the evenings he unwound in convivial conversation,

* Richard Brinsley Sheridan, now best remembered as a playwright, was a leading radical politician and a close ally of Fox.
† But see page 147. The story may be a legend, like so many associated with Coleridge.

smoking and drinking, sometimes heavily. After Coleridge had left London Lamb would cherish the memory of their comfortable evenings together by the fire in the Salutation and Cat, drinking 'egg-hot'* and smoking Oronoko.† Like Coleridge he was a sincere Christian, and at this time of his life was strongly drawn to Unitarianism. Coleridge particularly admired Lamb's devotion to his sister Mary, whose mind was 'elegantly stored' and her heart 'feeling'.[18]

On 16 December Coleridge dined with the two editor-proprietors of the *Morning Chronicle*. Also present was Thomas Holcroft, known for his dogmatism and fierce argumentativeness. It was immediately obvious that Holcroft had not been impressed when Lovell visited him in Newgate, and he launched into a violent attack on Pantisocracy. Coleridge was not overawed, at least not in the version he relayed to Southey:

> I had the honour of *working* H. a little – and by my great *coolness* and command of impressive Language certainly *did him over* – /Sir (said he) I never knew so much real wisdom – & so much rank Error meet in one mind before! Which (answered I) means, I suppose – that in some things, Sir! I agree with you and in others I do not.[19]

Holcroft invited Coleridge to dine at his house four days later. Among the other guests was Godwin himself, then at the zenith of his powers. 'No one was more talked about, more looked up to, more sought after,' wrote Hazlitt of this period many years afterwards, 'and wherever liberty, truth, justice was the theme, his name was not far off.' Though there is no detailed record of their conversation, Godwin noted in his diary afterwards that the talk was of 'self love & God'. One can be confident that Coleridge – only twenty-two years old – held his own against these two formidable middle-aged men, one an atheist, the other 'inclined to atheism'. In a letter to Southey some months earlier he had remarked of Godwin, 'I think not so highly of him as you do – and I have read him with the greatest attention.'[20]

---

* A drink of warm ale, mixed with a beaten egg, sweetened and spiced with nutmeg or ginger. Wine or brandy could be used as the base instead of ale.
† A tobacco mix, smoked in a pipe.

Coleridge rejected one of Godwin's essential tenets: of an antithesis between 'universal benevolence' and personal or private affections. In support of his argument Godwin cited the example of Brutus* – a cult figure in revolutionary thought – who *pro patria* sentenced his own sons to death, for plotting to restore the monarchy. Coleridge's thinking on this subject was the very opposite of Godwin's: 'The ardour of private Attachments makes Philanthropy a necessary *habit* of the soul. I love my *Friend* – such as he is, all mankind are or *might be!*'[21]

Just at this moment, Coleridge received a belated reply from Mary Evans. It is not clear what she wrote – but he decided that it was a brush-off. He was calm, he told Southey:

> To *love her* Habit has made unalterable. . . . To lose her! – I can rise above that selfish Pang. But to marry another – O Southey! bear with my weakness. Love makes all things pure and heavenly like itself: – but to marry a woman whom I do *not* love – to degrade her, whom I call my Wife, by making her the Instrument of low Desire – and on the removal of a desultory Appetite, to be perhaps not displeased with her Absence! . . . Mark you, Southey! – *I will do my Duty.*[22]

For seven weeks or more Southey had been 'in hourly expectation' of Coleridge. He renewed the pressure on his friend, who had been promising for at least three weeks to return to Bristol 'within a day or two'. Coleridge protested that he was 'all eagerness' to leave town, and resolved to be in Bath by the following Saturday (3 January 1795).[23] But on 2 January he wrote a frantic letter to Southey, full of excuses: the roads were dangerous, the inside of a coach unhealthy, the outside too cold, he had no money, he had a sore throat. Finally he offered to come by wagon, sharing it with four or five calves, wrapped up snugly in the hay. Southey and Lovell walked more than forty miles to Marlborough to meet the wagon – 'but *no S. T. Coleridge was therein!*' Southey wrote irritably to Sara Fricker: 'Why will he

---

* Not the Brutus who assassinated Caesar, but his ancestor who led the revolt against Tarquin, the last Roman King.

ever fix a day if he cannot abide by it?'[24] He decided to fetch Coleridge from London himself.

Mathews wrote to Wordsworth announcing the abandonment of the periodical scheme. He once again encouraged Wordsworth to come to London and earn a living writing for the newspapers. Wordsworth replied that he had decided to come when he could. But he would only feel happy working for an opposition paper, he told Mathews, 'for really I cannot in conscience and in principle, abet in the smallest degree the measures pursued by the present ministry. They are already so deeply advanced in iniquity that like Macbeth they cannot retreat.'[25] Wordsworth's bitterness against Pitt and his fellow ministers is remarkable, and lasted long after his radicalism had shrivelled – it was obvious even as he wrote *The Prelude*, a decade later:

> Our shepherds (this say merely) at that time
> Thirsted to make the guardian crook of law
> A tool of murder . . .

He believed them blind to the lesson of the Terror:

> Though with such awful proof before their eyes
> That he who would sow death, reaps death, or worse,
> And can reap nothing better, childlike longed
> To imitate – not wise enough to avoid,
> Giants in their impiety alone,
> But, in their weapons and their warfare base
> As vermin working out of reach, they leagued
> Their strength perfidiously to undermine
> Justice, and make an end of Liberty.[26]

Wordsworth joined Mathews in rejoicing at the verdicts in the treason trials: 'The late occurrences in every point of view are interesting to humanity. They will abate the insolence and presumption of the aristocracy by shewing it that neither the violence, nor the art, of power, can crush even an unfriended individual.' Wordsworth was further cheered by signs of a shift in opinion in favour of a negotiated peace with France.[27]

'I begin to wish much to be in town,' he informed Mathews; 'cataracts and mountains are good occasional society, but they will not do for constant companions.'[28] Like Coleridge, he was intrigued by developments in the capital.* While Raisley Calvert lingered on, Wordsworth felt unable to leave him; but he quit Penrith almost immediately after Calvert's death in early January 1795, and a few weeks later he was in London. Straight away, it seems, he found himself at the centre of radical discussion. On 27 February he took tea at the house of William Frend, who had moved to London after his expulsion from Cambridge and was now teaching pupils privately (among them the future social philosopher Thomas Malthus). Also present were eight others, all radicals, including Holcroft, Dyer and Godwin. This was a high-powered gathering of writers, lawyers and university Fellows. These radicals were closely interconnected through a multitude of personal and institutional links, shared interests and beliefs. A majority of those present were Cambridge men, at least two were Unitarians, and several were members of either the Society for Constitutional Information or the London Corresponding Society. Wordsworth, though new to this group, was not a stranger: he had known some of the younger men at Cambridge, George Dyer had been an old friend of his schoolmaster William Taylor, and Holcroft had reviewed his poems (unfavourably) in the *Monthly Review*. Another of those present, James Losh, a Cambridge friend of Wordsworth's, had been in Paris late in 1792, and the two of them may have met there, perhaps at the dinner of expatriate Englishmen at White's Hotel where a toast to Tom Paine had been drunk. Losh and Wordsworth had a further connection in that both came from Cumberland.

Wordsworth called on Godwin the very next day (probably by invitation), and then again ten days later, when he was invited to breakfast. For Wordsworth, to be able to converse *tête à tête* with the famous philosopher made an exhilarating change from hours spent at Raisley Calvert's bedside, unable to talk with or even read to the

---

* On the same day that Wordsworth wrote to Mathews, Coleridge was travelling to London from Cambridge.

dying young man. During the previous year he had been spouting Godwinian ideas; now he could drink them fresh from the source. This was the time when, according to Hazlitt, Wordsworth urged a young student, 'Throw aside your books of chemistry, and read Godwin on Necessity.' Over the coming months Wordsworth called on Godwin a number of times, usually alone, but twice with Mathews, and on one of these occasions also with Joseph Fawcett. Godwin paid Wordsworth the compliment of calling on him too, suggesting that he valued Wordsworth's company: further evidence, perhaps, of the favourable impression this young man made on others.

Wordsworth's poetry written in this period shows a strong Godwinian influence. In particular, drawing on Godwin's philosophical novel *The Adventures of Caleb Williams* (1794), he planned to rewrite his Salisbury Plain poem to show how 'the vices of the penal law and the calamities of war' could lead an otherwise innocent man to commit the most terrible of crimes.[29]

Southey bundled a protesting Coleridge onto the Bristol coach, and stood guard over him until they reached their destination. There the two founding Pantisocrats settled into cheap lodgings with George Burnett while they considered their next move. The scheme was not going to plan. There had been no further recruits, and they had not managed to raise anything like enough money to fund their emigration – barely any money at all, in fact (*The Fall of Robespierre* had not sold so well as hoped). Southey was now in favour of taking a farm in Wales, as a less ambitious venture. When he had first proposed this back in early December, Coleridge had dismissed it as 'nonsense'. Now, demoralised, he accepted the revised plan.

The immediate need was to earn some money. While in London Southey had tried to interest publishers in his *Wat Tyler*, but all had declined for fear of prosecution. Coleridge toyed with a number of alternatives, including returning to London to work as a reporter for the *Telegraph*, and going to Scotland to act as tutor to the sons of the Earl of Buchan. But both of these meant abandoning Sara, and now that they were together again Coleridge found that he did not want to leave her – indeed, very much the opposite. He discovered, too, that she had attracted the attentions of two other men, 'one of them of large Fortune', and that she was being pressed by her relatives to accept this suitor if Coleridge would not marry her first. Naturally this discovery increased Coleridge's interest.

Very quickly it was decided that Coleridge should give a series of public lectures in Bristol's Corn Market, capitalising on his qualities as an orator by charging a shilling a head in attendance money. The idea may have been inspired by the example of John Thelwall, who since his acquittal had been drawing large audiences – as many as eight hundred at a time – for his political lectures (though even so he found it hard to find a venue that would take him). Coleridge's first lecture was written at a single sitting, under Southey's super-vision, between midnight and breakfast time of the day on which it was to be delivered. The lectures blasted Pitt's repressive government and condemned its war against Revolutionary France, earning Cole-ridge a local reputation as a dangerous radical. He revelled in the notoriety: 'Mobs and Mayors, Blockheads and Brickbats, Placards and Press gangs have leagued in horrible Conspiracy against me.' Soon after delivering the first lecture he published this as a pamphlet, claiming he felt 'obliged' to do so, 'it having been confidently asserted that there was Treason in it'. He triumphed over hecklers, and proudly announced to Dyer that he had succeeded in provoking 'furious and determined' opposition from 'the Aristocrats', to the extent of hiring thugs – 'uncouth and unbrained Automata' – who threatened to attack him. After the second lecture it was felt necessary to move the third to a private address – and even then a crowd gathered outside could scarcely be restrained from attacking the house on Castle Green where the 'damn'd Jacobine was jawing away'.[30]

Coleridge was an amusing lecturer, and his talks were both well attended and enthusiastically received. He dealt cleverly with hecklers. On one occasion 'some gentlemen of the opposite party', disliking what they heard, began to hiss. Coleridge responded instantly: 'I am not at all surprised, when the red hot prejudices of aristocrats are suddenly plunged into the cool water of reason, that they should go off with a hiss!' His witty riposte was greeted with 'immense applause'. There was no more hissing after that.

The lectures were crafted to appeal to the sentiments of the dissenters who formed the majority of Bristol's radical population. Coleridge likened the People to the blinded Samson, standing between 'those two massy Pillars of Oppression's Temple, Monarchy and Aristocracy'; they needed guidance. While deploring revolutionary violence, he insisted on the need for reform to prevent such violence occurring. The 'great object in which we are anxiously engaged' was 'to place Liberty on her seat with bloodless hands'. All this was meat and drink to Bristol's radicals, who were further cheered by his second lecture, 'On the Present War', which referred to 'the distressful stagnation of Trade and Commerce', and its woeful effect on the poor in particular:

> War ruins our Manufactures; the ruin of our Manufactures throws Thousands out of employ; men cannot starve; they must either pick their countrymen's Pockets – or cut the throats of their fellow-creatures ... If they chuse ... the former, they are hung or transported to Botany Bay. And here we cannot but admire the deep and comprehensive Views of our Ministers, who having starved the wretch into Vice send him to the barren shores of New Holland to be starved back again into Virtue.

Soon afterwards, Southey began delivering a course of twelve historical lectures on the background to the French Revolution. Each lecturer helped the other; it was a joint endeavour in suitably Pantisocratic style. 'We live together and write together,' Southey reported happily. 'Coleridge is writing at the same table; our names are written in the book of destiny, on the same page.'[31]

In London Coleridge had tried to place a volume of his poems, but most of the booksellers would not even look at them, and the only offer he received was a derisory six guineas. Here in Bristol, Cottle generously offered him thirty guineas, to be paid in advance as required. 'The silence and the grasped hand, showed that at that moment one person was happy.'[32] Coleridge began collecting his poems and composing new ones for a volume to appear later in the year. Southey was still completing his long historical epic *Joan of Arc*, to which Coleridge contributed 255 lines and 'corrected' the rest. Cottle commissioned handsome portraits of both young authors by Peter Vandyke, a supposed descendant of the Flemish master.

Despite, or perhaps because of, the popularity of Coleridge's lectures, he was 'soon obliged by the persecutions of Darkness to discontinue them'.[33] Undeterred, a group of prominent Bristol dissenters commissioned him to deliver a fresh course of six lectures on revealed religion at the Assembly coffee house on the Quay.[34] Drawing on the ideas of Unitarian thinkers such as Frend and Priestley, Coleridge denounced the corruption of the Church of England. He ridiculed the dogma of the Trinity, and rejected the doctrine of the Redemption. For Coleridge, the teaching of Jesus Christ called for the complete abolition of private property – a measure too extreme for even the wildest Jacobins.* Indeed, passages from his sixth and final lecture sound like a manifesto for Pantisocracy:

> The necessaries of twenty men are raised by one man, who works ten hours a day exclusive of his meals. How then are the other nineteen employed? Some of them are mechanics and merchants who collect and prepare those things which urge this field Labourer to unnatural Toil by unnatural Luxuries – others are Princes and Nobles and Gentlemen who stimulate his exertions by exciting his envy, and others are Lawyers and Priests and Hangmen who seduce or terrify him into passive submission. Now if instead of this one man the whole twenty were to divide the labor and dismiss all unnecessary wants it is evident that none of us would work more than two hours a day of necessity, and that all of us might be learned from the advantages of opportunities, and innocent from the absence of Temptation.

The lectures demonstrate the central importance to Coleridge of Christian revelation, an emphasis that distinguished him from

---

* Thelwall, for example, often depicted as the most extreme of the English Jacobins, would not countenance any attack on the institution of private property.

radicals such as Thelwall. Indeed, Coleridge was repelled by the atheism and apparent immorality of many of the most prominent radicals, and appalled that such men might capture the leadership of the people. He was particularly concerned at the ubiquity of Godwin's ideas in the minds of radicals. In the process of writing these lectures Coleridge sought to develop a Christian alternative to Godwin's atheistic radicalism.[35] Much of his opposition to Godwin stemmed from his (brief) personal experience of the man, and of Godwin's close associate Holcroft. There is a pugnacious tone to his criticism of Godwin, which suggests rivalry: 'I set him at Defiance.'

Coleridge also delivered two stand-alone lectures, one, 'by particular desire', devoted to a subject particularly controversial in Bristol: a condemnation of the slave trade. Coleridge's final lecture was on Pitt's recently introduced hair-powder tax, a fine subject for his satirical wit, as democrats chose to wear their hair unpowdered anyway. Only 'aristocrats' would pay the guinea necessary for a licence to wear hair powder.

Meanwhile, all was not well in the Pantisocratic household. Coleridge exasperated Southey by his erratic working habits. Southey was by nature disciplined and organised, Coleridge wayward and chaotic. Even Coleridge's appearance irritated Southey: untidy, unkempt and sometimes not entirely clean.[36] The strain began to show. Coleridge had agreed to give the fourth of Southey's historical lectures – 'On the Rise, Progress, and Decline of the Roman Empire' – as it was a subject which he had particularly studied. At the end of Southey's third lecture, therefore, it was announced that Coleridge would be giving the next. When the time came, 'the room was thronged' – but the lecturer failed to appear. After waiting half an hour, the disgruntled crowd dispersed. Coleridge was eventually found in his lodgings, smoking a pipe, deep in thought.

The next day, on a ramble up the Wye Valley with Cottle and the two Fricker sisters, Southey remonstrated with Coleridge. The two friends quarrelled, embarrassing Cottle, especially when each of the sisters entered the argument in support of her suitor. Afterwards, in the woods above Tintern, they lost their way as darkness descended, with Coleridge riding ahead on Cottle's horse and shouting back encouragement, while Southey advanced supporting a sister on each arm, and the lame Cottle hobbled along behind, until at last they reached the inn.

Southey's zeal for Pantisocracy was cooling. His priorities had changed; marriage to Edith was now in the forefront of his mind, and other considerations subsidiary. He began to express reservations about aspects of the scheme. Coleridge perceived his diminishing enthusiasm, and strove to keep him true to the principles to which they had devoted themselves. Southey was caught in a trap of his own making. Having advertised his own integrity so freely, having laid such stress on principle, having insisted to Coleridge that Pantisocracy was a duty, he found it difficult to withdraw. A succession of impassioned arguments ensued, followed by partial reconciliations. Each man accused the other of behaving coldly towards him. Strong words were exchanged, and tears shed. One night, just before they went to bed, Southey confessed that he had acted wrongly. But soon his manners became cold and gloomy again. It was like the break-up of a marriage. Poor George Burnett was a spectator of this contest; he watched aghast.

Then a wealthy friend offered Southey an annuity of £160, to begin the following autumn. Now that he had the prospect of some property, Southey found himself less inclined to share it. He put forward a new proposal: everything in Wales should be owned separately, except five or six acres. Coleridge reacted with indignation and contempt; Southey's scheme amounted to rank apostasy: 'In short, we were to commence Partners in a petty Farming Trade. This was the Mouse of which the Mountain Pantisocracy was at last safely delivered!' From this time on, Coleridge kept up the appearance of a friendship with Southey – 'but I *locked up* my heart from you'.

In August, Southey's clergyman uncle Herbert Hill returned to England from Portugal. He had funded Southey's education at Westminster and Oxford in the expectation that his nephew would follow his example, and he now wrote urging Southey to take Holy Orders. Apparently Hill was intimate with a bishop, and a post worth £300 a year was Southey's for the asking. Southey informed his fellow lodgers of the offer one evening. 'What answer have you returned?' asked Coleridge. 'None – Nor do I know what Answer I shall return,' replied Southey, and retired to bed. Coleridge was incredulous; Southey had been as scathing as he was on the iniquity of the Church – indeed, had been so before they met (in December 1793, for example, Southey had written that to enter the Church 'I must become contemptible infamous and perjured'[37]). Burnett sat gaping, half-petrified at the possibility that his idol might abandon them. Coleridge wrote a letter to Southey that same night, frantically urging him not to '*perjure himself*'. The next morning he walked with Southey to Bath, insisting on the 'criminality' of such an action. Southey wavered, tempted by the prospect of a regular income that would at last allow him to marry Edith. After a struggle, he decided against the Church; but his uncle was determined to lure him away from Pantisocracy. Further inducements were placed in front of Southey to return to Oxford and study law – a course that Coleridge described as 'more opposite to your avowed principles, if possible, than even the Church'. The temptations were proving too great for Southey, whose scruples disappeared one by one. He was now talking of 'rejoining Pantisocracy in about 14 years', citing Coleridge's 'indolence'* as a reason for his quitting. On 22 August 1795 Coleridge wrote bitterly to Cottle that Southey 'leaves our Party'. On 1 September Southey quitted their shared lodgings in College Street. Their landlady was reduced to tears at his departure.

A week or two later Coleridge made his way back to west Somerset. On 19 September Poole's cousin Charlotte noted in her journal that Tom had with him a friend by the name of 'Coldridge: a young man of brilliant understanding, great eloquence, desperate fortune, democratick principle, and entirely led away by the feelings of the moment'. A poem by Poole (not known as a poet) addressed to 'Coldridge' – 'Hail to thee, Coldridge, youth of various powers!' – is dated seven days earlier. Presumably Coleridge stayed the intervening

---

* Perhaps a coded reference to opium-taking?

week with Poole at Nether Stowey. He may have visited Henry Poole at Shurton Court as well, because some time during September he composed a poem nearby, at Shurton Bars, where a murky, gently shelving sea recedes with the tide to reveal a shingle beach, broken by bars of exposed rock. 'Lines Written at Shurton Bars' was a response to a letter from Sara, in which she seems to have referred to chilly treatment from Southey and Edith. The growing estrangement from Southey was obviously prominent in Coleridge's thoughts at the time. Poole's poem refers to the same subject. On his return from Shurton to Bristol, Coleridge encountered Southey, who offered his usual handshake. Coleridge took Southey's outstretched hand, and shook it 'mechanically'. The significance of this handshake, or lack of it, subsequently became a point of contention between them.

In 'Lines Written at Shurton Bars' Coleridge quoted an expression borrowed from Wordsworth's 'An Evening Walk'. Such borrowing was a form of acknowledgement much practised at the time, and in fact Coleridge had already used another phrase of Wordsworth's else-where.[38] A note to the published version of Coleridge's poem would refer to 'Mr. Wordsworth' as 'a Poet whose versification is occasionally harsh, and his diction too frequently obscure; but whom I deem unrivalled among the writers of the present day in manly sentiment, novel imagery, and vivid colouring'.[39] Obviously Coleridge had read and admired Wordsworth's otherwise neglected poems published in 1793. What is striking about this note is that he should have rated Wordsworth so highly, on the evidence of so little.

Coleridge had decided to marry Sara. Though his addresses to her had at first been paid 'from Principle not Feeling', now his heart was engaged: 'I love and I am beloved, and I am happy!' He had found a cottage for them at Clevedon, a dozen or so miles west of the city, overlooking the Bristol Channel, for the modest rent of £5 per year. There they would live with George Burnett, the object of the Susque-hanna delayed but not yet wholly abandoned. There Coleridge set 'The Eolian Harp', the first of what have since become known as his 'conversation poems', written in blank verse and usually addressed to an intimate companion, in which contemplation of nature evokes associated feelings, and leads to the resolution of an emotional or psychological problem. It would be hard to overstate the influence of these poems on Wordsworth and the later Romantic poets, and indeed on lyric poets ever since.[40] Some critics have argued that they are not so original as has sometimes been claimed; that Coleridge drew on earlier poets such as Cowper and Thomson. But many great writers have plundered the past. And even if this new style of poetry did have its antecedents, it was Coleridge's conversation poems that shaped the future.

'The Eolian Harp' opens with Coleridge seated, Sara's cheek resting on his arm, outside the cottage which will be theirs when they are married, gazing up at the evening sky. The scent of flowering plants fills the air, while the sea murmurs in the distance. Sensuousness permeates the poem, suffusing it with tender eroticism. Everything is in harmony, and Coleridge meditates on the conceit of the Aeolian harp, a stringed instrument that plays as the wind blows though it. Coleridge was fascinated by Hartley's* belief that all sensation in the body takes place by means of vibrations along the nerves, like the strings of a musical instrument, and that each vibration leaves a trace that can be detected by the memory. Coleridge imagines 'all of animated Nature' as 'organic harps' that 'tremble into thought' as a divine 'intellectual breeze' blows through them. In the conclusion of the poem, Sara gently bursts the philosophical bubbles that arise within his 'unregenerate mind', and in doing so, lovingly leads this 'sinful and most miserable man' back to his maker. Thus erotic fulfilment is linked with redemption; the conflict between sacred and profane love is resolved.

On 4 October† they were married in Bristol's St Mary Redcliffe, the vast church where Chatterton had claimed to have found Rowley's manuscripts. Southey was not present at the wedding. He was still in

---

* David Hartley (1705–57), dissenting philosopher, physician and pioneering psychologist. Like many nonconformists, he believed that 'the Final Happiness of All Mankind' was imminent.

† Mary Evans married nine days later, on 13 October.

an agony of indecision. He could not face Coleridge; they passed each other in the street without acknowledgement. In a letter he accused Coleridge of having withdrawn his friendship – though to others he maintained that Coleridge was more his friend than ever. Tongues were wagging in Bristol; Southey charged Coleridge with 'gross misrepresentation and wicked and calumnious falsehoods'. He complained to Grosvenor Charles Bedford that Coleridge had 'behaved wickedly towards me'.[41] Cottle attempted to reconcile them, without success. Southey's uncle suggested an escape from his quandary: six months' stay in Lisbon while he pondered his future. He hoped to prise his nephew away from an unfortunate attachment. Edith nobly pressed him to go, as did Southey's mother. But he did not want it to be thought that he had abandoned Edith. Without telling his uncle, he married her 'with the utmost privacy' and left for Portugal a few days later.

Coleridge learned of this plan only a couple of days before. Wounded and angry, he sat down to denounce his former friend in a long, indignant, devastating letter:

> O Selfish, money-loving Man! what Principle have you not given up? – Tho' Death had been the consequence, I would have spit in that man's Face and called him Liar, who should have spoken the last sentence concerning *you*, 9 months ago. For blindly did I esteem you. O God! That *such a mind* should fall in love with that low, dirty, gutter-grubbing Trull, WORLDLY PRUDENCE!!

To Robert Lovell, Southey had cited Coleridge's indolence as his reason for quitting Pantisocracy, a thrust against a vulnerable part. 'I have exerted myself more than I could have supposed myself capable,' protested Coleridge – not just on his own behalf, but on Southey's too. He instanced his contribution to *Joan of Arc* and his exertions to improve the remainder: 'I corrected that and other Poems with greater interest, than I should have felt for my own.' He had devoted his 'whole mind and heart' to Southey's lectures: 'you must be conscious, that all the *Tug* of Brain was mine: and that your Share was little more than Transcription'. He conceded that Southey wrote more easily:

> The Truth is – You sate down and wrote – I used to saunter about and think what I should write. And we ought to appreciate our comparative Industry by the quantum of mental exertion, not by the particular mode of it: By the number of Thoughts collected, not by the number of Lines, thro' which these Thoughts are diffused.

He retraced the history of their 'connection': 'I did not only venerate you for your own Virtues, I prized you as the Sheet Anchor of mine!' He detailed the 'constant Nibblings' that had 'sloped your descent from Virtue'. Again and again, he said, he had been willing to give Southey the benefit of the doubt: 'My Heart was never bent from you but by violent strength – and Heaven knows, how it leapt back to esteem and love you.'

Once Southey had allowed himself to be tempted by the Church, Coleridge had ceased to confide in him: 'I studiously avoided all particular Subjects, I acquainted you with nothing relative to myself ... I considered you as one who had *fallen back into the Ranks* ... FRIEND is a very sacred appellation – You were become an Acquaintance, yet one for whom I felt no common tenderness.' But now everything between them was at an end: 'This will probably be the last time I shall have occasion to address you.' He never expected to meet another whom he would love and admire so much. 'You have left a large Void in my Heart – I know no man big enough to fill it.'[42]

Perhaps through Godwin, Wordsworth met Basil Montagu, a young lawyer who was reading for the Bar. Though near contemporaries at Cambridge, they seem not to have known each other then. Now they rapidly became friends. Montagu was the illegitimate son of the fourth Earl of Sandwich, then First Lord of the Admiralty, and his mistress, the singer Martha Ray; in 1779 she had been shot outside a theatre where she had been performing by a disappointed suitor, the Reverend James Hackman, vicar of Wiveton in Norfolk, who had been hanged as a result. The story of Montagu's mother's murder had been a sensational scandal, recently revived by James Boswell in his *Life of Johnson* (1791). Poor Montagu was dogged by tragedy; his wife, whom he married soon after quitting Cambridge – against the wishes of his father, who never spoke to him again* – had died in childbirth, leaving him with an infant son, also called Basil. In the wreck of his happiness Montagu was 'misled by passions wild and strong'; but his careful new friend gently but firmly led him away from these. 'I consider my having met Wm Wordsworth the most fortunate event of my life,' Montagu wrote in a memoir.

Montagu introduced Wordsworth to another recent Cambridge graduate, Francis Wrangham, who like Montagu was taking pupils in order to make ends meet. In 1793 – the year of Frend's trial – Wrangham had failed to obtain an expected Cambridge Fellowship because he was rumoured to be friendly to the French Revolution. Since then he had been 'vegetating on a curacy' in Cobham, Surrey, where Wordsworth and Montagu often visited him. Wrangham was another radical, and a would-be poet; he had been in correspondence about his poetry with Coleridge, whom he had known at Cambridge. Now he and Wordsworth began collaborating on a verse satire based on Juvenal a scholarly form of protest, which Wordsworth later abandoned.

By the summer of 1795, shortage of funds was becoming acute. After almost six months in London, nothing had come of Words-worth's plans to write for the newspapers, and none of the money from Raisley Calvert's legacy had yet materialised. Four and a half years after leaving Cambridge, Wordsworth still had no career, no income and no home of his own. Perhaps worst of all, he was not writing. As Dorothy put it, 'the unsettled way in which he has hitherto lived in London is altogether unfavourable to mental exertion'.[43] Meanwhile they still hoped to make a home together. Dorothy had not returned to Forncett, and was staying with friends in the north. There was an idea that she might come to London, and live by

* Montagu's timing was not ideal; by one account he married a week after the publication of the *Life of Johnson*. Lord Sandwich died the following year.

translating – a proposal which her Aunt Rawson dismissed as 'mad'.

Montagu and Wrangham had two young pupils, Azariah and John Frederick Pinney, whose father John Pretor Pinney was a wealthy 'West Indian', a Bristol merchant with extensive plantations on Nevis, a sugar-producing island in the Caribbean. As well as a handsome townhouse in Bristol, Pinney Senior owned Racedown Lodge, a large country house in north Dorset. This was not much used by the family, and had been advertised to let (at £42 per annum) as early as 1793, without finding a taker. The younger Pinney now suggested that Wordsworth might like to have it, rent free, with the proviso that he and his brother might come down for the occasional stay, principally to shoot.

Wordsworth seized the offer. Here was a chance to escape from the city, where things had not turned out as he had hoped. In the country, free from temptation or distraction, he could settle down to work. Moreover, it was an opportunity to live with Dorothy; Racedown would be 'our little cottage'. There they could live simply and frugally, keeping a cow and growing vegetables in the kitchen garden. Dorothy would attend to most of the domestic chores, with the help of only one maidservant (she hoped for 'a strong girl'). Together they would care for young Basil Montagu, whose father would pay £50 a year for his keep. There was a prospect of at least one other child, a little girl, and perhaps another boy as well, one of the younger Pinney brothers, then in his early teens. Dorothy was fond of children and had experience of looking after them. For her, this was a chance at last to 'be *doing something*':

> . . . it is a painful idea that one's existence is of very little use which *I* really have always been obliged to feel; above all it is painful when one is living upon the bounty of one's friends, a resource of which misfortune may deprive one and then how irksome and difficult it is to find out other means of support, the mind is then unfitted, perhaps, for any new exertions, and continues always in a state of dependence, perhaps attended with poverty.[44]

Outlining the arguments in favour of the Racedown 'scheme' to her friend Jane Pollard (who had recently married John Marshall, a linen manufacturer), Dorothy argued that it would give her brother 'such opportunities of studying as I hope will be not only advantageous to his mind but his purse'. She hoped that it 'may put William into a way of getting a more permanent establishment'.[45]

With the money for the two children, and interest on the capital from Raisley Calvert's legacy (which was at last beginning to trickle through), Dorothy was confident of an annual income of at least £170 or £180. This should be enough to enable them to live comfortably, and even to make some provision for the future.* There was the prospect of a further £200 a year if her brother's 'great hopes' of having the Pinney boy entrusted to him as tutor were realised.

It was agreed that Wordsworth would travel to Bristol, where he would stay at the Pinneys' house in Great George Street until Dorothy was able to join him and they could journey on together to Racedown. No doubt John Pretor Pinney wanted to take a good look at this young man who would be occupying his country house. For Wordsworth, there was the added benefit of an opportunity to make new contacts in a city with its own flourishing intellectual life. Among those he met in Bristol, almost in passing, was a young man who had been making a good deal of noise, and whose name he had almost certainly heard already.†

Nobody knows for certain where or when Wordsworth and Coleridge first met, what the circumstances were, or what was said. There are three contradictory stories, each based on reminiscences long after the event. The confusion is not altogether surprising; it is often hard to remember how we met someone who afterwards becomes familiar. Though these two would later become so important to each other, they could scarcely have anticipated this at their first encounter.

---

* For comparison, a skilled worker such as a printer earned approximately £90 a year, while a gentleman with a small household and a servant could live modestly in London on £200 a year.[46]
† In a letter to Mathews written around this time, Wordsworth refers to 'Coleridge' without further explanation, as if he expects Mathews to be familiar with the name.

What is known is that they met in Bristol during Wordsworth's five-week stay in the city from around 21 August until 26 September 1795. The proof is in a letter Wordsworth wrote to Mathews from Racedown in October: 'Coleridge was at Bristol part of the time I was there. I saw but little of him. I wished indeed to have seen more – his talent appears to me very great.'[47] There is a tradition that the two met at John Pretor Pinney's house, where Wordsworth was staying, but this may be no more than a guess. One reason for doubting it is the awkwardness of Coleridge's being received at the house of a prominent 'West Indian' only a few months after delivering a public lecture condemning the slave trade. The Bristol *Observer* had commented on the lecture as 'proof of the detestation in which he [Coleridge] holds that infamous traffic'. It is hard to imagine Coleridge comfortable as the guest of one of the largest slave-owners in the city, or that Pinney would have welcomed him into his home.

Fifteen years later, the painter Joseph Farington noted in his diary that the two poets had met at a political debating society, 'where on one occasion Wordsworth spoke with so much force & eloquence that Coleridge was captivated by it & sought to know Him'.[48] His note was based on a conversation with Lady Beaumont, a woman who had come to know both men well (but who had not known them at the time); though one might suspect that in being told to her, and then by her, the story had become garbled, and that Coleridge rather than Wordsworth had been the speaker. Another cause for doubt is the explanation of *how* they became acquainted. Coleridge was on record as an admirer of Wordsworth's poetry; he would not have needed to hear Wordsworth speak in order to want to know him.

Half a century afterwards, Wordsworth tried to recall the circumstances of the meeting for Coleridge's daughter Sara. Confessing that he did not have 'as distinct a remembrance as he could wish', he told her 'the impression upon his mind' was that he had seen her father and her mother together with her uncle Southey and her aunt Edith 'in a lodging in Bristol'.[49] If Wordsworth's memory can be relied upon, the Frickers' home in Redcliffe Hill seems the most likely location for the meeting – though why Wordsworth should have been there remains unexplained. One should remember that at this stage neither of the couples was married. The Fricker sisters had attracted plenty of unpleasant comment because of their association with the Pantisocrats; they would surely not have wanted to risk their reputations further by visiting the young men's cramped bachelor lodgings in College Street.[50]

There is another difficulty with the story. 'I met with Southey also,' Wordsworth continued his letter to Mathews – which makes it sound as if this happened on a different occasion. By now relations between Coleridge and Southey were strained; Coleridge later claimed to have used the 'most scrupulous care' to avoid Southey after his return from Shurton in mid-September. Wordsworth went on to describe Southey's qualities: 'his manners pleased me exceedingly and I have every reason to think very highly of his powers of mind . . . I recollect your mentioning you had met Southey and thought him a coxcomb. This surprises me much, as I never saw a young man who seemed to me to have less of that character . . .' At Southey's invitation Wordsworth read some passages of *Joan of Arc*, then in press; and Southey contributed a couple of lines to Wordsworth's Juvenalian satire – which Wordsworth later told Wrangham were the two best verses in it.[51] This sounds like a relaxed encounter, more relaxed than one might have expected had Coleridge been there at the same time. Perhaps, then, Wordsworth's memory should not be relied upon, and in fact he met Coleridge and Southey separately.

Despite so much uncertainty, the available fragments of evidence make it possible to date their meeting to within the space of only a few days.

In a continuation of the note to 'Lines Written at Shurton Bars' deleted in manuscript, Coleridge observed that reviewers had spoken with contempt of Wordsworth's 'Descriptive Sketches', but indicated that for him, such abuse was a recommendation: 'A gentleman near Bristol* makes it an invariable rule to purchase every work that is

---

* Poole? Possibly Coleridge had been rereading Wordsworth's poems in Poole's library, and this prompted him to borrow from 'An Evening Walk' in his 'Lines Written at Shurton Bars'.

violently abused by the Reviewers: and with a very few exceptions I never saw a more judicious selection of recent Compositions, both in prose and verse.' Years later, Coleridge scribbled on a printed version of the poem that this had been written before he had ever seen Wordsworth, and then added bitterly in Latin, 'and would that I had known only his works'.[52]

If Coleridge's marginalium is accurate, it follows that he and Wordsworth cannot have met until after Coleridge's return from Shurton, probably during Wordsworth's last week in Bristol. Dorothy arrived on the night of 22 September, and it is difficult to imagine brother and sister being parted afterwards, yet it is clear that she had never seen Coleridge until he came leaping across the field towards her in the garden at Racedown almost two years later. As it seems from Charlotte Poole's journal entry* that Coleridge was still in west Somerset on 19 September, and as even by coach it would have taken him the best part of a day to return to Bristol, the most likely dates for his first meeting with Wordsworth are therefore 21 or 22 September 1795, more probably the latter.

It must have been quite a coincidence for Coleridge. One moment he had been meditating on an expression coined by a poet whom he admired but had never met; the next moment the same poet stood before him, as if he had stepped off the page. No doubt he took the opportunity to mention his borrowing to Wordsworth, and this led to a wider discussion of the poem from which it came, and indeed the other poem Wordsworth had published more than two years before. Coleridge would have been intrigued to hear the revisions that Wordsworth had since made, exhibiting very similar ideas about 'animated nature' to those he himself had articulated in 'The Eolian Harp'. He was bound to ask if Wordsworth had written anything since. Hearing that Wordsworth was working on a long, as yet unpublished poem, Coleridge encouraged him to recite it (this was the poem inspired by his journey across Salisbury Plain). More than twenty years later, in his *Biographia Literaria*, Coleridge would recall

* See page 104.

'the sudden effect produced on my mind, by his recitation'. He recognised immediately that this poem represented a great advance on the earlier work: gone were the 'occasional obscurities' and the 'hackneyed and fantastic' phrases which, for him, rendered most eighteenth-century verse so stultifying.

> It was not however the freedom from false taste, whether as to common defects or to those more properly his own, which made so unusual an impression on my feelings immediately, and subsequently on my judgement. It was the union of deep feeling with profound thought; the fine balance of truth in observing with the imaginative faculty in modifying the objects observed; and above all the original gift of spreading the tone, the *atmosphere* and with it the depth and height of the ideal world, around forms, incidents and situations of which, for the common view, custom had bedimmed all the lustre, had dried up the sparkle and the dewdrops.

It is possible that Coleridge recited some of his 'Eolian Harp' to Wordsworth; somehow he impressed him. But even a brief conversation would have revealed Coleridge's ebullient genius. It was often said of him (as it was of Dr Johnson) that his conversation might have been taken down and published without alteration – though this did not mean that he was always comprehensible. Towards the end of his life Wordsworth compared Coleridge's talk to

> a majestic river, the sound or sight of whose course you caught at intervals, which was sometimes concealed by forests, sometimes lost in sand, then came flashing out broad and distinct, then again took a turn which your eye could not follow, yet you knew and felt that it was the same river: so there was always a train, a stream, in Coleridge's discourse, always a connection between its parts in his own mind, though one not always perceptible to the minds of others.[53]

Everyone who met Coleridge in those days was impressed by him: by his energy, his enthusiasm and his erudition, as well as his obvious talent. He was a young man of whom wonders were expected. On

10 October Poole wrote to congratulate him on his recent marriage: 'The world is all before you,* your road seems yet to choose.' Reviewing the schemes that Coleridge had outlined over the past few months, he dismissed the idea of going back to Cambridge and resuming the imitations:† '*original* works of genius are your forte. Think not I wish to damp for a moment your extending your literary knowledge, or your improving yourself by the most profound speculations. No – what I mean is, that you should set yourself about some work of consequence, which may give you a reputation, whether it be in poetry or prose.' Poole's letter made clear his belief that Coleridge had the creative power to advance the social and political causes in which they both believed.[54]

Despite making such an impression on each other at their first encounter, Wordsworth and Coleridge were not to meet again for another eighteen months. Wordsworth was on the brink of departing for the Pinneys' house in Dorset, and by the time he next visited Bristol, Coleridge had left. In the interim it seems that they were in touch by letter, though since none of the correspondence has survived it is difficult to estimate how much or how often. It is a tantalising thought that they might have been in contact with each other much earlier. Had Wordsworth decided to go back to Cambridge to study oriental literature in the autumn of 1791, as his family wanted, rather than embarking for France, he would have returned there just as Coleridge arrived. With so much in common, they would surely have met sooner or later. But then, had Wordsworth not gone to France, he would have been different; he might never have become the man that Coleridge would afterwards value so highly.

The two had another near-miss eighteen months or so later. Early in 1793 Dorothy Wordsworth wrote to her friend Jane Pollard, criticising her brother's recently published poems, 'An Evening Walk' and 'Descriptive Sketches'. While they contained 'many Passages exquis-

---

* 'The world was all before them' (*Paradise Lost*, XII, 646). Later Wordsworth was to provide another echo of Milton's phrase: 'The earth is all before me . . .' (*Prelude*, I, 14).
† The translations of Greek and Latin lyric poems, a project first mooted in January 1793.

itely beautiful', she felt, they also contained many faults: 'the chief of which are Obscurity, and a too frequent use of some particular expressions and uncommon words' (others felt the same). 'I regret exceedingly that he did not submit the works to the Inspection of some Friend before their Publication, and he also joins with me in this Regret' (perhaps Wordsworth had been chastened by some of the reviews). She noted that she and her brother Kit (Christopher) had prepared 'a very bulky Criticism, which he was to transmit to William as soon as he should have added to it the remarks of his Cambridge Friends'.[55]

One of these Cambridge friends could have been Coleridge. At the time he and Christopher Wordsworth were fellow undergraduates (though not at the same college or in the same year), with a common interest in literature. We do not know when they became acquainted, beyond the fact that later in the year they were among a handful of founder members of a small literary society. In a diary fragment for Trinity term 1793, Christopher recorded a meeting of the society on 4 November, at which his older brother's two poems were discussed.[56] Coleridge was evidently aware of them, because Christopher noted that he 'spoke of the esteem in which my brother was holden by a society at Exeter'.

Coleridge's own account in *Biographia Literaria* shows that he was greatly impressed by 'Descriptive Sketches', and it is certain that had he been given the opportunity to inspect Wordsworth's poems before publication, his critique must have been interesting and constructive. Wordsworth did not usually respond well to criticism from those whose opinion he did not respect, but in later life he always valued Coleridge's advice highly. Had he received Coleridge's remarks in a package from his brother Christopher, he could well have written back via the same route – and who knows what might then have followed? Two young men with so much to talk about would surely have wanted to meet. Perhaps Coleridge would have steeled Wordsworth to publish his angry polemic 'A Letter to the Bishop of Llandaff', with consequences heaven knows what? Perhaps Wordsworth might have been tried for sedition, found guilty and transported to the colonies? Or Coleridge might have fired Wordsworth with enthusiasm for Pantisocracy, and the two of them would have emigrated to the banks of the Susquehanna River? Instead of the brooding Victorian with the great domed forehead, there might have been an alternative legend of unfulfilled promise, like that of Chatterton: a young Wordsworth lying dead in the woods, an arrow through his heart.

And what of Coleridge? Had he met Wordsworth earlier, perhaps he might not have been so drawn to Southey, and thus not have become entangled with Sara Fricker? In which case he would have been free for his beloved Asra. One can imagine an alternative past, in which Wordsworth and Coleridge married sisters and the four lived in domestic harmony. The lonely sage of Highgate vanishes, to be replaced by a cheerful Coleridge, perhaps completing the often-contemplated but never-realised *magnum opus*. (Or perhaps not.)

Wordsworth pre-empted these possibilities by deciding to publish his poems soon after his return from Paris, before his brother had the chance to consult his Cambridge friends. Yet another missed opportunity came at the beginning of 1795. Had Southey not been so insistent in retrieving Coleridge from London, or had Raisley Calvert not hung on so long before expiring, Wordsworth and Coleridge would have been in London at the same time, mixing in the same small society, and would surely have quickly discovered one another.

Years later, Wordsworth expressed the same sense of a lost opportunity. In 1804, as he worked on the sixth book of *The Prelude*, after Coleridge (as he thought) had set sail for Malta, he lamented that the two of them had not met earlier:

> . . . Oh, it is a pang that calls
> For utterance, to think how small a change
> Of circumstances might to thee have spared
> A world of pain, ripened ten thousand hopes
> For ever withered . . .

He imagined Coleridge as an undergraduate:

... I have thought
Of thee, thy learning, gorgeous eloquence,
And all the strength and plumage of thy youth,
Thy subtle speculations, toils abstruse
Among the schoolmen ...

And then he speculated on what might have happened had they been
at Cambridge together:

... Not alone,
Ah, surely not in singleness of heart
Should I have seen the light of evening fade
Upon the silent Cam, if we had met,
Even at that early time: I needs must hope,
Must feel, must trust, that my maturer age
And temperature less willing to be moved,
My calmer habits, and more steady voice,
Would with an influence benign have soothed
Or chased away the airy wretchedness
That battened on thy youth ...[57]

PART II

Friends

'The flames of two Candles joined give a much stronger Light
than both of them separate'[1]

5

CONTACT

Racedown Lodge is said to have been the model for Kellynch Hall, the seat of Sir Walter Elliot in Jane Austen's *Persuasion*. If not quite a 'mansion' (as Coleridge later described it), it is nevertheless a stately Georgian house of three storeys, obviously the property of a man of substance. Built on the side of a hill, it stands a few miles inland, within walking distance of the coast, near the point where the three counties of Dorset, Somerset and Devon meet. The surrounding hills restrict the views from the house itself, but the sea is usually visible from a high point only 150 yards or so off.

The Wordsworths arrived at Racedown around midnight on 26 September 1795. They found the house in good order, having recently undergone four years of renovation. It was well furnished, with marble chimneypieces, mahogany chairs, tables and bookcases, a leather sofa, a pianoforte, a good Axminster carpet in the best parlour, and a well-stocked library of some four hundred volumes. There were two parlours, one more formal and a smaller breakfast room, a kitchen, scullery, pantry and butler's pantry, two cellars, four excellent bedrooms on the first floor, and a further four bedrooms on the attic floor. Outside were a wash house, a brewhouse, stabling and two 'necessaries'. There was also a walled kitchen garden. Dorothy was pleased to find Racedown well equipped with 'household conveniences', so much so that she did not need to spend as much as ten shillings setting it to rights. The house was under the care of Joseph Gill, a ne'er-do-well cousin of the Pinneys who also managed the farm and acted as overseer of the local brickyard. There was a gardener, who attended only erratically, as gardeners are wont to do. Dorothy had plenty to keep her busy, cooking, washing, making shirts and repairing clothes, as well as working with her brother in the kitchen garden. At first she had no help in the house, but after a month she found a servant girl, Peggie Marsh, 'one of the nicest girls I ever saw'. They employed a washerwoman for three days every month. Altogether it was a very substantial establishment for a pair of orphans who had never before had a home they could call their own. Nevertheless, they were only guests in the house. The wine glasses, decanters and tumblers were kept locked up, and distributed to the Wordsworths only when the young Pinneys came down for a visit.

The other member of the household was young Basil Montagu, then not quite three, 'a shivering half-starved plant', indulged and neglected by his widower father. (The little girl who it had been hoped would join them never came.) Over the next few years William and Dorothy would act as his surrogate parents. Dorothy in particular found Basil 'a perpetual pleasure'. She took the fretful boy in hand, instilling regular habits, helping him to curb his temper, encouraging him in self-control. 'Our grand study has been to make him *happy*,' she wrote. 'We teach him nothing at present but what he learns from the evidence of his senses. He has an insatiable curiosity which we are always careful to satisfy to the best of our ability.' Within months Basil was transformed into 'a lusty, blooming fearless boy', interested in everything around him, who played by himself happily for hours.[1]

'We are now at Racedown,' Wordsworth reported to his friend William Mathews after he and Dorothy had been there a month, 'and both as happy as people can be who live in perfect solitude.'[2] There was no congenial society locally, but they had each other. At last they were together, and indeed they would never again be parted. 'I think Racedown is the place dearest to my recollections upon the whole surface of the island,' Dorothy wrote several years afterwards. 'It was the first home I had.'[3] They walked together for about two hours every morning, and soon discovered plenty of pleasant walks from the house, with lovely meadows above the combes, and fine views from the hilltops. Some of these were left wild, and covered with gorse and broom, reminding Dorothy of landscapes she had known as a girl. Though they were seven miles* from Crewkerne, the nearest town, they could obtain almost all their immediate needs locally; their greatest inconvenience was living so far from a post office.

Dorothy had the precious gift of silence, knowing when to speak to her brother and when to keep quiet, which allowed him to compose in her company. This he generally did outside, keeping step with the rhythm of his verse, his head down and mumbling to himself. Often he would pace back and forth along the same route until a poem 'kindled' in his mind. He held the poem there, rarely committing it to paper until it was near complete. One reason for this was that paper was expensive; another was his aversion to the physical process of writing. Often Dorothy would transcribe to his dictation. Another of Wordsworth's practices was to recite his new poems as they walked, allowing him to modify and improve them if they did not sound right, perhaps too responding to comments from Dorothy. Thus she was able to offer her brother practical help with his poetry, as well as providing a home in which he could work comfortably and undisturbed.

At Racedown Wordsworth revised his Salisbury Plain poem, perhaps encouraged by Coleridge's enthusiasm for his recital. Within a couple of months he had added and altered so much 'that it may be looked on almost as another work'.[4] His revisions were to make 'Adventures on Salisbury Plain' a parable of Godwinian principles, a story of hardship and its consequences, very much in evidence in the neighbourhood. 'The country people are wretchedly poor,' Wordsworth informed Mathews; 'ignorant and overwhelmed with every vice that usually attends ignorance in that class – lying and picking and stealing &c &c.' Dorothy was less judgemental. 'The peasants are miserably poor,' she wrote to Jane Marshall: 'their cottages are shapeless structures (I may almost say) of wood and clay – indeed they are not at all beyond what might be expected in savage life.'[5]

* Dorothy arrived at this figure by pushing a perambulator (a device for measuring distance) there and back.

In the same letter Dorothy mentioned that her brother had received 'a letter from France', i.e. from Annette Vallon. Apparently Annette referred to half a dozen previous letters she had sent, none of which had reached him. The possibility of their being reunited seemed more remote than ever. And perhaps he was no longer so keen for this to happen, if indeed he ever had been.

After the Wordsworths had been at Racedown three months, the Pinney brothers arrived for the first of several visits. (They tactfully insisted on paying for food and drink while they were there.) The four of them enjoyed each other's company, relishing the pleasures of the fireside in the evenings and outdoor exercise in the mornings. When the weather was fine they would all go walking, or the three young men would spend the morning riding, hunting, shooting, hare-coursing, or chopping wood – the last much approved of by Dorothy, because the activity both kept them warm and supplied the house with fuel, in an area of the country where coal was very expensive.

The Pinneys brought with them a present for Wordsworth from Joseph Cottle: a presentation copy of Southey's *Joan of Arc*. Cottle evidently showed interest in Wordsworth's Salisbury Plain poem. It is possible that Wordsworth had met Cottle while he was in Bristol the previous summer, but equally possible that Coleridge had recommended him to Cottle since then. Wordsworth was keen for the poem to be published if he could make some money from it, but he had to admit in his letter of acknowledgement to Cottle that it was not yet ready. He promised to send it in a few days' time, and added a postscript: 'Best compts to Coleridge, and say I wish much to hear from him.'[6]

On 26 October 1795 a vast crowd, estimated at over 100,000 strong, assembled in Copenhagen Fields in Islington to hear speeches from leaders of the London Corresponding Society. Since the collapse of the treason trials radicals had been expectant of progress. Speakers demanded universal suffrage and annual Parliaments. But the priority was to stop the disastrous war. In March the remnant of the British army had been evacuated from Bremen after French troops rampaged through the Low Countries, annexing Belgium. Now the French controlled the whole Channel coast; preparations began for an invasion. Meanwhile the balance of power shifted decisively: first Prussia, then Holland and Spain made peace with France. Pitt was reduced to subsidising his only remaining ally, Austria, with British gold. Taxes were increased to pay for the war, while the resulting disruption of trade damaged commerce. Several successive harvest failures had pushed up food prices to record levels; famine now threatened. There were food riots that year in London, Birmingham and other British cities. The squeeze pinched tightest those least able to pay. The roads of Britain were littered with the dispossessed, discharged soldiers and sailors (often crippled) and vagrants driven from their homes. Able-bodied men were pressed into service, or forced to accept the bounties offered as incentives to recruitment. 'Philanthropists' tried to alleviate the distress of the local poor.* Hardship fuelled the radical engine. In Copenhagen Fields, speaker after speaker protested at the cost of the war.

Three days after the meeting in Copenhagen Fields, the King was hissed and hooted while on his way to open a new session of Parliament. There were cries of 'Bread! Peace! No Pitt!' A missile of some kind – probably only a stone – shattered a window of his carriage. Construed as an attempted assassination, this sufficed as a pretext for the introduction of two 'gagging' Bills – the Seditious Meetings Bill, which banned meetings (including lectures, except in universities and schools) of more than fifty people unless under the strict control of local magistrates; and the Treasonable Practices Bill, which redefined the law of treason, in an attempt to close the 'loophole' through which Thelwall and his co-defendants had escaped conviction. Fox's supporters complained that if the proposed new law had been in force ten years earlier, Pitt himself would have been liable to transportation to the colonies, for criticising the constitution in his failed attempt to introduce an electoral reform Bill. At this moment Godwin

* Poole, for example, experimented with methods of producing bread more cheaply by using barley, beans, potatoes and even turnips instead of wheat.

chose to publish a pamphlet under the name 'A Lover of Order', in which he attempted to stand above the increasingly polarised argument. He attacked the two proposed Bills for curtailing freedom of speech, but condemned the incendiary tactics of the radicals, which, he believed, were encouraging partisanship, hatred and violence. It seemed to many that Godwin had deserted his friends at a moment of crisis. Thelwall, who until this moment had been one of Godwin's disciples, angrily turned on his former mentor.

Before the Acts became law, another huge crowd, perhaps the largest yet assembled for a political cause, gathered once again in Copenhagen Fields to hear Thelwall, Frend and others condemn the government's repressive legislation. Though the protests so far had been orderly, many feared this could not continue: measures to bottle up the people's anger would only cause it to explode with even greater fury. 'You may prevent men from complaining,' warned Fox, 'but you cannot prevent them from feeling.' A petition against the Bills attracted 130,000 signatures. In Bristol, a loyalist meeting held at the Guildhall to deplore the 'attack' on the King and to congratulate him on his 'providential escape' was disrupted by an organised group who put forward a motion imploring His Majesty to relieve the distresses of the people by restoring peace. A newspaper reported that in the ensuing kerfuffle one particular member of the audience was heard calling '*Mr Mayor! Mr Mayor!*', at first fruitlessly, and having at last attracted the attention of the chairman, 'Mr Coleridge began the most elegant, the most pathetic, and the most sublime Address that was ever heard, perhaps, within the walls of that building.' The attack on the King would never have happened, he argued, 'if the people had not been rendered outrageous by their sufferings under the present cruel, sanguinary, and calamitous war'. Though the war might take much from the property of the rich, Coleridge continued, 'it left them much; but a PENNY taken from the pocket of a poor man might deprive him of a dinner'. At this point the horrified Tory Mayor stopped him from saying anything further.[7]

Coleridge was in the thick of the Bristol anti-war group, which met again three days later to approve a petition to Parliament against the two Bills. (Azariah Pinney wrote to Wordsworth at Racedown telling him about the meetings, and mentioned Coleridge's role in them.) With so much happening, Coleridge felt that he could not remain isolated in Clevedon; Bristol was too far away to walk there and back every day. He missed the stimulation provided by his Bristol friends, and the easy access to the Bristol Library. Now that winter was coming on, a rural idyll no longer seemed so attractive. The pleasures of the countryside shrank, while the lure of the city grew. Perhaps married life seemed more claustrophobic than expected. After only six weeks in his new home Coleridge moved back to Bristol, leaving Sara alone in the cottage, to be plagued by neighbours who were 'a little too tattling and inquisitive'. In his poem 'Reflections on Having Left a Place of Retirement', he idealised 'the Valley of Seclusion' as 'a Blessed Place'. He portrayed himself as summoned by duty to quit 'our pretty Cot':

> . . . Was it right,
> While my unnumber'd brethren toil'd and bled,
> That I should dream away the entrusted hours
> On rose-leaf beds, pampering the coward heart
> With feelings all too delicate for use?

Of course not:

> I therefore go, and join head, heart, and hand,
> Active and firm, to fight the bloodless fight
> Of Science, Freedom, and the Truth in Christ.

On 26 November, at the Pelican Inn in Thomas Street, Coleridge delivered a lecture condemning the gagging Bills. This was published in pamphlet form a few days later as *The Plot Discovered; or an Address to the People against Ministerial Treason*. He also repackaged as one pamphlet the first two lectures he had given at the beginning of the year, under the title *Conciones ad Populum, or Addresses to the People*. These concluded in a diatribe against the war.

Coleridge was now a figure of some prominence in the radical movement, respected by some, notorious to others. His activities had made him conspicuous; he had shown himself to the enemy.

Early in December the Acts passed into law, but radicals remained hopeful of their speedy repeal. The ministry seemed in retreat: recognising the unpopularity of the war, the government began peace overtures to France. Pitt announced to Parliament that the King was ready to treat for peace. In Bristol, a group of friends met at the Rummer Tavern and encouraged Coleridge to start a new radical periodical, promoting the causes of peace and reform, to be published every eight days (thereby avoiding tax). This would be a miscellany containing news, parliamentary reports, essays and poetry, thus (so the handbills claimed) supplying 'at once the places of a Review, Newspaper and Annual Register!!!' The formula was identical to that of Wordsworth's planned but never published *Philanthropist*. Indeed, before the breakdown in their friendship Coleridge and Southey had contemplated starting a similar journal, entitled the *Provincial Magazine*. There was a dearth of liberal journals in the provinces; journals published outside London tended to rely for their content on official handouts, and were therefore unlikely to criticise the government. Coleridge's new publication would be sold in the cities of the English regions, where many of those sympathetic to progressive ideas were clustered. A high proportion of his expected readers would be politically-minded dissenters. Coleridge decided to call this new publication *The Watchman* – perhaps taking his cue from Thomas Erskine, who in an address to the Whig Club had rallied 'every friend of freedom' to act as 'a species of watchman on the outworks of the Constitution'. The name resonated with biblical associations; printed below the title was the epigraph 'That all may know the truth; and that the truth may make us free!!' Coleridge produced a 'flaming prospectus', announcing as his chief objects the repeal of the two Acts and obtaining the 'Right of Suffrage general and frequent'. Each issue would be thirty-two pages, in large octavo size, and priced at fourpence. He would combine the roles of editor, publisher and chief contributor, and promised to dedicate himself 'entirely' to *The Watchman*.[8]

Those who knew Coleridge of old were sceptical of this new venture. 'Of all men, Mr Coleridge was the least qualified to display periodical industry,' sighed Cottle in his *Reminiscences*, and although this observation was made with the benefit of hindsight, it represented a common view among Coleridge's acquaintants at the time.[9] One of his Cambridge contemporaries, noting 'how subject Coleridge is to fits of idleness', forecast to another that after three or four numbers *The Watchman* would contain 'nothing but Parliamentary debates'; he imagined Coleridge adding a note at the bottom of the page: 'I should think myself deficient in my duty to the Public if I did not give these *interesting* Debates at *full* length.'[10]

The Watchman quickly attracted almost four hundred subscribers in and around Bristol, but Coleridge reckoned that he needed around a thousand to make it pay, so early in January 1796 he set out on a tour of the Midlands to solicit further subscriptions. He took with him letters of introduction from his Bristol friends and supporters, who also funded his expenses. While on tour he publicised *The Watchman* by preaching to congregations of dissenters, who gathered in large numbers to hear this charismatic young speaker. Unlike their ministers, who wore drab black clothing, Coleridge's usual dress was a blue coat and white waistcoat, the radical uniform worn by Thelwall, Frend and others. 'My *Sermons* spread a sort of sanctity over my *Sedition*,' he wrote – though he admitted that the sermon he delivered to a huge Birmingham congregation of around fourteen hundred was '*precociously peppered with Politics*'.[11] In Nottingham he was invited to a fashionable ball, where an 'Aristocrat' cast a sneering glance over his prospectus. Referring to the epigraph, he remarked, 'A *Seditious* beginning!' On being informed that it was a quotation 'from another Author', he replied, 'Poo! – what Odds is it whether he wrote it himself or quoted it from any *other seditious Dog*?' At which point the 'aristocrat' was advised to look into the Gospel of St John, where he would find that the '*seditious Dog* was – JESUS CHRIST!'[12]

In Birmingham, Coleridge passed a 'delightful' evening with the local dissenting minister and his friends. Earlier in the afternoon he had been persuaded to smoke a pipe, which left him feeling so ill that on arriving at the minister's house pale and sweating profusely, he sank back on the sofa in a sort of swoon. At length he 'awoke from insensibility' and looked around the room, blinking in the light of the candles that had been lit in the interim. One of the gentlemen present asked him if he had read a newspaper that day. 'Sir,' he replied, rubbing his eyes, 'I am far from convinced that a Christian is permitted to read either newspapers or any other works of merely political and temporary interest.' The ludicrous incongruity of this remark produced a general burst of laughter, and during the remainder of the evening those present joined in attempting to convince Coleridge 'in the most friendly and yet most flattering expressions that the employment was neither fit for me, nor I fit for the employment'.*

In five weeks Coleridge visited Worcester, Birmingham, Derby, Nottingham, Sheffield, Manchester and Lichfield, and would have gone on to collect further subscriptions in Liverpool and then in the capital itself had he not been summoned back home by Sara, who, pregnant and fearing a miscarriage, had left the cottage in Clevedon and moved back to her mother's house in Bristol. Coleridge had been in high spirits for most of the tour, but lapsed into a depression towards the end. He was obviously under stress, worrying about everything that needed to be done; collecting subscriptions clashed with preparation of the content, and he had been forced to postpone the launch of *The Watchman* by almost four weeks. It was already clear that he could not expect to make much money from the publication, while practical difficulties of various kinds threatened to overwhelm him. Terms had to be negotiated individually with booksellers in each city, including how the copies would be delivered and how and when remittances would be paid. This was not the kind of detail at which Coleridge excelled. His mind bubbled over with fear, doubts and difficulties. He unburdened himself in a letter to Josiah Wade, a Bristol merchant who was one of the principal supporters of *The Watchman*, ending his list of woes in verse: 'My past life seems to me like a dream, a feverish dream! all one gloomy huddle of strange

---

* Hazlitt (who of course was not present) gives another account of what seems to have been the same occasion, in which Coleridge awoke on a sofa and then 'launched into a three hours' description of the third heaven, of which he had had a dream'.

actions, and dim-discovered motives! Friendships lost by indolence, and happiness murdered by mismanaged sensibility!'

> Oh, Nature! cruel step-mother, and hard,
> To thy poor, naked, fenceless child the Bard!
> No Horns but those by luckless Hymen worn,
> And those, (alas! alas!) not Plenty's Horn!
> With naked feelings, and with aching pride,
> He bears th'unbroken blast on every side!
> Vampire Booksellers drain him to the heart,
> And Scorpion Critics cureless venom dart![13]

On Coleridge's return to Bristol Cottle began pressing him for the preface to his poems, which had been standing in type some months. The result was an explosion from Coleridge: 'I am writing as fast as I can – depend on it, you shall not be out of pocket for me!' He should have been more thankful, he told Cottle, if God had made him 'a journeyman Shoemaker, instead of an "Author by Trade"!'

> I have left my friends, I have left plenty – I have left that ease which would have enabled me to secure a literary immortality at the price of pleasure, and to have given the public works conceived in moments of inspiration, and polished with leisurely solicitude: and alas! for what have [I] left them – for a specious rascal who deserted me in the hour of distress, and for a scheme of Virtue impracticable and romantic. – So I am forced to write for bread – write the high flights of poetic enthusiasm, when every minute I am hearing a groan of pain from my Wife – groans, and complaints & sickness! – The present hour, I am in a quickset hedge of embarrass-ments, and whichever way I turn, a thorn runs into me – . The Future is cloud & thick darkness – Poverty perhaps, and the thin faces of them that want bread looking up to me! – Nor is this all – my happiest moments for composition are broken in on by the recollection of – I *must* make haste – I am too late – I am already months behind! I have received my *pay* beforehand! – O way-ward and desultory Spirit of Genius! ill canst thou brook a task-master! The tenderest

touch from the hand of *Obligation* wounds thee, like a scourge
of Scorpions!

This 'astonishing' outburst was in response to an unopened note from
Cottle – 'I have not seen it; but I guess its contents.' In fact Cottle
had sent him an invitation to dinner.[14]

Harassed by his publisher, anxious about his wife's health, worried
about money, Coleridge might have abandoned his commitment to
The Watchman. But he felt a duty to persist. Southey had quit; he
was not going to do the same. He and Sara moved out of his mother-
in-law's house to a new address in Kingsdown, a Bristol suburb on a
hill overlooking the city. On 1 March 1796 the first number of *The
Watchman* appeared.

Coleridge's *Poems on Various Subjects* was now printed, though not
bound; as well as the preface and the notes, he had yet to complete
the last poem in the volume, the ambitious 'Religious Musings', which
he considered his most important work to date. The previous October
he had confessed that 'it has cost me much labour in polishing, more
than any poem I ever wrote – and, I believe, deserves it more'.[15] Early
in March he sent a note to Cottle to say that 'The Religious Musings
are finished, and you shall have them on Thursday.' A week or so
later he adopted a delaying tactic: 'My eye is so inflamed that I cannot
stir out.'[16] Excuse followed excuse. Eventually Cottle sent him 'a severe
reproof', which Coleridge admitted that he deserved on account of
his 'indolence and frequent breach of promise' – though 'my present
brain-crazing circumstances made this an improper time for it'.[17] The
pressure was telling; he wrote to one of his contributors that he had
been 'tottering on the edge of madness', so much so that he had been
obliged to take laudanum almost every night to relieve his distress.[18]
In his agitation he allowed his pen to run away with him, beginning
the second number of *The Watchman* with an article on fasts, headed
by a quotation from Isaiah: 'Wherefore my Bowels shall sound like a
Harp'. More than a month afterwards he was still apologising for this
lapse, which had given great offence to his pious readers. He later

estimated that this light-hearted treatment of a solemn subject 'lost me near five hundred of my subscribers at one blow'.

'It is one of the disadvantages attendant on my undertaking, that I am obliged to *publish* extempore as well as compose.'[19] One reason why he was so pressed was that he found it hard to attract other contributors, especially as he could not afford to pay them. George Burnett, who was living with the Coleridges in Kingsdown, was supposed to provide editorial assistance, but he proved so incompetent as to be more hindrance than help. Meanwhile Coleridge believed that Sara had miscarried, though it later became obvious that he had been mistaken. He remained very anxious about money, conscious of the fact that his wife, her little brother, his mother-in-law and Burnett all depended on him for support: 'five mouths opening & shutting as I pull the string!' *The Watchman* (so he believed) yielded 'a *bread-and-cheesish* profit', but he was forced to work flat out: 'Formerly I could select a fine morning, chuse my road, and take an airing upon my Pegasus right leisurely – but now I am in stirrups all day, yea, and sleep in my Spurs.'[20]

Towards the end of March, Coleridge arranged to go round to Cottle's shop at half past six one evening to write the preface and the notes to his poems. He promised to work late into the night. 'If you will give me a dish of tea,' he wrote, 'I give you leave to turn the lock & key on me.'[21] Unsurprisingly, the notes betrayed signs of haste, and in the second edition of the poems he would feel obliged to apologise for a note alleging that Samuel Rogers had been guilty of plagiarism in his popular poem 'The Pleasures of Memory'; Rogers was said to have been 'sorely hurt' by the allegation.

An essay on 'Modern Patriotism' in the third number of *The Watchman* satirised those followers of Godwin who seemed to think 'filial affection folly, gratitude a crime, marriage injustice, and the promiscuous intercourse of the sexes right and wise'. Rightly or wrongly, this was construed as a gibe at democrats such as Thelwall. After a challenge in the *Bristol Gazette*,[22] Coleridge renewed his attack in the fifth number, stating that he considered Godwin's principles 'vicious' and his *Political Justice* 'a Pander to Sensuality'. It was perhaps not good business to offend his readers in so forthright a manner. In a mere six weeks he had contrived to alienate the sympathies of dissenters, democrats and Godwinites. Small wonder that he received 'many abusive letters'.[23]

By the time the seventh number of *The Watchman* was published, Coleridge had the mortification of seeing preceding numbers on sale 'in sundry old iron shops for a penny a piece'. A subsequent incident provided further evidence of the unsaleable nature of his writings, as he ruefully related in his *Biographia Literaria*. Coming downstairs one morning after he had risen earlier than usual, he noticed the servant girl putting 'an extravagant quantity of paper' into the grate in order to light the fire, and 'mildly checked her' for her wastefulness. 'La, Sir!' she replied, 'why, it is only *Watchmen*.'

At last he finished his 'Religious Musings', begun on Christmas Eve fifteen months before, a few days after his fierce debate with Holcroft, which may have provided the initial stimulus. On this work, as he said on several occasions, 'I build all my poetic pretensions'.[24] It was a long poem, written in blank verse, and represented a significant step forward for Coleridge. 'Religious Musings' was packed with ideas – too packed, in the view of its critics. As Coleridge himself had written to Southey a fortnight before he began the poem, 'I cannot write without a *body* of *thought* – hence my *Poetry* is crowded and sweats beneath a heavy burthen of Ideas and Imagery!'[25] He found it necessary to add much explanatory annotation to 'Religious Musings'. Among the ideas jostling for position within the poem is Coleridge's concept of a universe vibrating in harmony with the mind of God, a development of Hartley's notion of 'vibrations' (a notion admirably suited to an age of sensibility). Nature broadcasts the music of the creator; it follows that human beings can receive this music through the medium of all things natural, great or small. Thus delight in natural splendour is itself a form of religious fervour:

> But lo! the bursting Sun!
> Touched by th'enchantment of that sudden beam
> Straight the black vapour melteth, and in globes
> Of dewy glitter gems each plant and tree;

On every leaf, on every blade it hangs!
Dance glad the new-born intermingling rays,
And wide around the landscape streams with glory!

There is one Mind, one omnipresent Mind,
Omnific . . .

More generally, 'Religious Musings' was Coleridge's attempt to make sense of the cataclysmic events of the past few years in terms of revealed religion. He was excited by the millenarian ideas swirling around in the backwash of the French Revolution. As one of his footnotes shows, he was inspired by reading a sermon preached by Priestley before his departure to America, which had interpreted the Revolution as the fulfilment of the biblical prophecy of the Second Coming and the rule of the millennium:

Yet is the day of Retribution nigh:
The Lamb of God hath open'd the fifth seal;
And upward rush on swiftest wings of fire
Th'innumerable multitude of Wrongs
By man on man inflicted! Rest awhile,
Children of Wretchedness! The hour is nigh:
And lo! The Great, the Rich, the Mighty Men,
The Kings and the Chief Captains of the World,
With all that fix'd on high like stars of Heaven
Shot baleful influence, shall be cast to earth,
Vile and down-trodden, as the untimely fruit
Shook from the fig-tree by a sudden storm.

After the poem was published, Coleridge received a complaint from Poole's brother Richard that it was too metaphysical for common readers. 'I answer – the Poem was not written for common Readers.'[26]
But the reviews, when they came, were 'wonderful':

The Monthly has *cataracted* panegyric on my poems; the Critical has *cascaded* it; and the Analytical has *dribbled* it with very tolerable civility. The Monthly has at least done justice to my Religious Musings – They place it 'on the very top of the scale of Sublimity' – ! – ! – !'[27]

It was true that the *Monthly Review* praised Coleridge's genius, energy and sublimity, but it also criticised his metres, coined words and double epithets.

Some of Coleridge's poetry had appeared in *The Watchman*, eliciting this favourable response from a reader.

> Sir! I detest your principles, your prose I think very so so – ; but your poetry is so exquisitely beautiful, so gorgeously sublime, that I take in your Watchman solely on account of it.

The correspondent entreated him: 'more verse & less democratic scurrility'.[28]

Coleridge sent a presentation copy of his *Poems on Various Subjects* to Charles Lamb, as well he might, since the volume included four 'effusions' of Lamb's, albeit heavily revised. There seems not to have been much contact between the two men since those comfortable winter evenings in the Salutation and Cat more than a year before. Lamb confessed that he had felt bereft after Southey had dragged Coleridge away from London. 'You are the only correspondent and I might add the only friend I have in the world,' he wrote. 'I have never met with any one, never shall meet with any one, who could or can compensate me for the loss of your society – I have no one to talk all these matters about to.'[29] Towards the end of the previous year, Lamb cheerfully explained, he had spent six weeks 'very agreeably' in a madhouse, following some form of breakdown (possibly connected with an unrequited passion). 'I am got somewhat rational now, and don't bite any one.' But he looked back on this period

> with a gloomy kind of Envy. For while it lasted I had many many hours of pure happiness. Dream not Coleridge, of having tasted all the grandeur and wildness of Fancy, till you have gone mad. All now seems to me vapid; comparatively so.[30]

Lamb revealed that his elder brother had blamed Coleridge for his breakdown – 'you and your damned foolish sensibility and melancholy'.[31] Perhaps there was some truth in this; Coleridge was to prove a dangerous companion for the highly-strung. 'My head ran on you in my madness,' Lamb confessed, 'as much almost as on another person, who I am inclined to think was the more immediate cause of my temporary frenzy.' He later revealed that he had been reluctant to introduce his sister to Coleridge for this very reason.[32] But the affectionate correspondence that now began between the two men seems to have benefited them both. Coleridge's letters provided Lamb with much-needed intellectual stimulation, while Lamb offered Coleridge sound advice and detailed criticism of his poems, often made more palatable by being framed in his gentle teasing wit. Though praising 'Religious Musings' as 'sublime', Lamb criticised the 'Gigantic hyperbole by which you describe the Evils of existing society'.[33] He liked 'the simple, tender, heart-flowing lines with which you conclude your last, and in my eyes, best, sonnet', and this preference led him to urge: 'Cultivate simplicity, Coleridge, or rather, I should say, banish elaborateness; for simplicity springs spontaneous from the heart.'[34]

Coleridge sent another copy of his newly bound poems to John Thelwall, who like Coleridge edited his own journal, *The Tribune*, and who had published his *Poems written in Close Confinement in the Tower and Newgate* the previous year. His earlier work, *The Peripatetic; or, Sketches of the Heart, of Nature and Society* (1793), was a three-volume excursion through multiple genres, exploring in both prose and verse such subjects as the rights of women, social injustice, slavery and patriotism. Its very title suggested that the author was a wanderer, something of an outcast. Self-educated, Thelwall had emerged from the 'swinish multitude'; he had been a tailor and then an attorney's clerk before his enthusiasm for the Revolution swept him into writing and lecturing. He had proved his mettle when defiantly facing a possible death sentence during the treason trials. A man of outstanding ability, an intellectual and a political theorist as well as a thrilling orator, Thelwall had a strong claim to be the leading radical in the country. Coleridge had respectfully described him as 'the voice of tens of thousands'. Nonetheless he felt able to address Thelwall as an equal: 'Pursuing the same end by the same means we ought not to be strangers to each other.' Coleridge assured Thelwall that a reference to him as an 'unsupported malcontent' in his pamphlet *The Plot Discovered* had been meant sardonically (he made no mention of his *Watchman* essay 'Modern Patriotism'). Indeed, wrote Coleridge, only 'a fit of modesty' had prevented him from bracketing himself with Thelwall under the same heading.[35]

Coleridge had written (but not published) a 'Sonnet to John Thelwall' in which he gratefully acknowledged his debt to 'Citizen John': Thelwall's 'fair example', he wrote, first taught him to 'glow/With patriot zeal'. The poem contrasted his 'ill-adventur'd youth by Cam's slow stream', when he had 'Pin'd for a woman's love in slothful woe', with his years of manhood, which henceforth would be dedicated to 'Thy stern simplicity and vigorous Song'. This sonnet was not printed in the volume he sent to Thelwall, but there is some reason for believing that it may have been inscribed therein.[36] Coleridge's letter solicited Thelwall's opinion of his poems, 'which you will read with a POET'S EYE'. He was sure that Thelwall would 'find much to blame in them – much effeminacy of sentiment, much faulty glitter of expression'. He drew Thelwall's particular attention to his 'Religious Musings'.

Thelwall's reply was startlingly frank. The most religious passages in 'Religious Musings' were 'the very acme of abstruse, metaphysical, mystical rant'; the whole poem was 'infected with inflation and turgidity'. Nor was this all: Coleridge's phrase 'th'imbrothelled atheist's heart' was 'one of those illiberal and unfounded calumnies with which Christian meekness never yet disdained to supply the want of argument'. Thelwall was equally unsparing of Coleridge's conventional pieties: the line '*Lovely* was the *death* of him whose life was love' was enough 'to make any man sick'.

> Before I wipe the gall from my pen, I must notice an affecta-
> tion of the Della Cruscan school* which blurs almost every

---

* The 'Della Cruscan' poets, followers of Robert Merry, were very much in vogue in the late 1780s and the 1790s. Their writings were characterised by a mannered, sentimental and ornamental style. Coleridge's early work was embellished with many Della Cruscan flourishes. *Lyrical Ballads* was a reaction against the artificiality of the Della Cruscans.

one of your poems – I mean the frequent accent upon the adjectives and weak words . . .[37]

Perhaps Thelwall, who was eight years older than Coleridge and much more experienced both as a writer and as a political activist, felt that Coleridge's approach to him had been presumptuous, and that he might benefit from being knocked down. But Coleridge enjoyed robust debate; he was not intimidated by reputation, as he had shown in his clash with Holcroft; and he was sensible enough to acknowledge that Thelwall's uninhibited remarks on his poems were 'just in general'. They began to correspond regularly. Thelwall's criticism, like Lamb's, played a part in freeing Coleridge to find his own poetical voice, helping to liberate him from both the sub-Miltonic bombast of 'Religious Musings' and the tired conventions of eighteenth-century verse. Within the next year these influences would disappear from his work. 'The Eolian Harp' pointed the way forward.

Of course, it was wounding for Coleridge to take such broadsides against the poem of which he was so proud. He was keen to assert that the appeal of 'Religious Musings' was not restricted to the devout. In its defence he could not resist citing to Thelwall Wordsworth's opinion (though he did not name Wordsworth) that passages from 'Religious Musings' were the best in the volume – 'and this man is a Republican & at least a *Semi*-atheist'.[38]

In their exchanges, Thelwall tried to induce Coleridge to shake himself free of 'illiberal dogmatism' and 'intolerant prejudices', while Coleridge renewed his attack on what he saw as Godwin's 'immorality', particularly his attitude to marriage.

> *Marriage is indissoluble* . . . Marriage, that confines the appe-
> tites to one object, gradually causes them to be swallowed up
> in *affection* . . . The real source of inconstancy, depravity, &
> prostitution, is *Property*, which mixes with & poisons every
> thing good – & is beyond doubt the Origin of all Evil.

The quarrel between Thelwall and Godwin over the opposition to the gagging Acts freed Coleridge of any inhibitions about expressing his disapprobation of the latter, now bordering on active dislike: 'He appeared to me to possess neither the strength of intellect that discovers truth, or the powers of imagination that decorate falsehood – he talked futile sophisms in jejune language – I like Holcroft a thousand times better, & think him a man of much greater ability.'[39]

In his letters to Thelwall, Coleridge could work through his ideas about political engagement and religious belief. Thelwall provided an articulate antagonist, one against whom he could test his evolving opinions. Their political sympathies were similar, even if their philosophical background was not: 'We run on the same ground, but we drive different Horses.' And alongside this continuing philosophical argument there was the opportunity 'for a little sparring about poetry'. Though vigorously argued, these were friendly exchanges: Coleridge offered Thelwall a bed any time he came to Bristol.[40]

Coleridge was intrigued by Thelwall, a man of indubitable courage and integrity, 'wrong-headed but good-hearted',[41] an atheist apparently exemplary in his private life. It was one of Coleridge's assumptions that religious belief was a necessary guard against sensuality, but Thelwall seemed an exception to this rule. After they had been corresponding six months or so, Coleridge asked Thelwall to describe himself: 'I should like to know all things *about* you – for *you*, I am confident, I know already.' After Thelwall sent him a self-portrait in words, Coleridge responded in kind:

> As to me, my face, unless when animated by immediate eloquence, expresses great Sloth, & great, indeed almost idiotic, good nature. 'Tis a mere carcase of a face: fat, flabby, & expressive chiefly of inexpression . . . As to my shape, 'tis a good shape enough, if measured – but my gait is awkward, & the walk, & the *Whole man* indicates *indolence capable of energies.* – I am, & ever have been, a great reader – & have read almost every thing – a library-cormorant – I am *deep* in all out of the way books, whether of the monkish times, or the puritanical era . . . Metaphysics, & Poetry, & 'Facts of mind' – (i.e. Accounts of all the strange phantasms that ever possessed your philosophy-dreamers . . .) are my darling Studies. – In short, I seldom read except to amuse myself –

& I am almost always reading. – Of useful knowledge, I am a so-so chemist . . . all else is *blank* . . .

I cannot breathe thro' my nose – so my mouth, with sensual thick lips, is almost always open. In conversation I am impassioned, and oppose what I deem [error] with an eagerness, which is often mistaken for personal asperity – but I am ever so swallowed up in the *thing*, that I perfectly forget my *opponent*. Such am I.[42]

The radical cause was suffering. In April 1796 Thelwall was harassed into leaving London, and abandoning *The Tribune*. He attempted 'to revive discussion' by lecturing in East Anglia and the Midlands, but he was hounded by hired mobs, almost pressed into the navy, and at Stockport escaped being thrown into the canal only by backing against a wall and drawing his pistol. Defeated and disheartened, he was almost ready to give up the struggle. The gagging Acts, though rarely enforced, intimidated many radicals into silence. There were no more mass meetings. After his acquittal Thomas Hardy, founder of the London Corresponding Society, had resigned; this was for personal reasons – his wife had died during his internment and his business had failed – but the Society was left divided and its effectiveness diminished. Government propaganda succeeded in isolating the radicals, making them appear at best deluded, at worst venal. Even Coleridge was naïve enough to believe slanderous stories spread about poor Gerrald, to Thelwall's dismay.* In Parliament, Fox and his much-diminished band of followers raged impotently against the ministry. After the defeat of another attempt to extend the franchise and reform some of the more blatant electoral abuses, the disheartened Foxite Whigs 'seceded', staying away from Parliament altogether for the next few years.

Meanwhile the continuing belligerence of France made it difficult to criticise the ministry's war policy. It was one thing to oppose a war against a brave, beleaguered enemy; quite another to maintain such opposition when a triumphant enemy threatened invasion. Moreover, France itself had changed. A turbulent year had followed the fall

---

* Gerrald died later that year in the penal colony.

of Robespierre, culminating in cannon being used to defend the Convention, the artillery under the command of the young General Bonaparte. After this the Convention had been dissolved, replaced by a toothless assembly under the strict control of a five-man Directory. The new authorities had introduced restrictions on the right of assembly and censorship of political news – an uncomfortable echo of the gagging Acts. In the spring Bonaparte began an aggressive campaign of conquest in northern Italy. *The Watchman* published a 'Remonstrance to the French legislators', lamenting the bellicose policy of the Directory and deploring the fact that British peace initiatives had been spurned. Once, wrote Coleridge, 'we heard with transport of the victories of Frenchmen, as the victories of Human Nature'. But now the unnecessary prolonging of the war put at risk all their achievements, and made possible the return of tyranny; even, perhaps, a royalist revival. 'I am out of heart with the French,' a disillusioned Coleridge would write later that year.[43]

Wordsworth too was dismayed by the turn of events. Like Coleridge, he had celebrated the heroic defence of the young Republic; now he too deplored the Directory's expansion of the war:

> . . . become oppressors in their turn,
> Frenchmen had changed a war of self-defence
> For one of conquest, losing sight of all
> Which they had struggled for . . .[44]

In such a changed atmosphere, much of the radical impetus behind *The Watchman* was lost. As the subscribers fell away, so the drudgery of editing and coping with the many associated complications weighed more heavily on Coleridge. He had worked hard, and persisted longer than many predicted, but he was losing hope. After the ninth number was published, he poured out his feelings to Poole:

> It is not pleasant, Thomas Poole! to have worked 14 weeks for nothing – *for nothing* – nay – to have given to the Public in addition to that toil five and 40 pounds![45]

Sara had by now recovered, but her mother seemed on the brink of death, and to make matters even worse for the family Coleridge's brother-in-law Robert Lovell died of a fever, leaving a young widow and infant child. In Lovell's last hours Coleridge sat up until morning with his sister-in-law, praying beside her in the kitchen. It was a stormy night, and whenever the howling wind dropped her husband's deep groans could be heard from his bedroom across the courtyard, sending the poor young woman frantic. Meanwhile *The Watchman* expired also. The tenth number, published on 13 May 1796, was the last.* In a final 'Address to Readers', Coleridge explained why: 'The reason is short and satisfactory – the Work does not pay its expenses.' He concluded on a suitably biblical note: '*O Watchman! thou hast watched in vain!*'

In March, Wordsworth had sent his finished Salisbury Plain poem to Cottle, with the request that Coleridge should inspect it and note down anything he thought worthy of comment. He seems not to have doubted that Cottle would take it. 'I mean to publish volume-wise,' he wrote confidently to Wrangham, while Dorothy informed Jane Marshall that 'Wm. is going to publish a poem.'[46] Azariah Pinney delivered 'Adventures on Salisbury Plain' to Cottle on Wordsworth's behalf, and a fortnight later he reported back that Coleridge had interleaved the manuscript with pages of his own annotation: 'He feels so lively an interest to bring forward so valuable a Poem (as he terms it) that he assures me his Bookseller will assist him in such a manner in the publication that he can secure you from every expense, without risk to himself, and you will receive the profits that may arise after the expenses are paid.'[47] Coleridge suggested printing 500 copies, rather than the 250 Wordsworth had been contemplating. He forwarded the manuscript to Lamb for further comments.

In mid-April Azariah Pinney mentioned 'Adventures on Salisbury Plain' in a letter to a friend in London: 'It is now at Coleridge's, by whom it has been attentively read and pronounced a very fine poem.' He predicted that it would be in print 'within the duration of a few Weeks'.[48] In fact 'Adventures on Salisbury Plain' was to remain in

* Within a fortnight of its death Coleridge thought of reviving *The Watchman*, but this plan came to nothing.

manuscript almost two centuries.* Cottle may have found the poem too bleak, or he may have been reluctant to take on a new commitment when his affairs were already complicated by his involvement with *The Watchman*.

Coleridge had been too optimistic, as was often the case. Nevertheless, it was remarkable that he should have devoted such 'considerable attention' to another man's work when he had so much else to occupy him. It was indicative of the high value he placed on Wordsworth's poetry. In a letter to Thelwall, Coleridge described Wordsworth as 'the best poet of the age' – a surprising verdict on a man whose only two published poems had appeared three years earlier, leaving little impression on either critics or public. Many years later, in his *Biographia Literaria*, Coleridge would describe the effect on him of these two poems: 'Seldom, if ever, was the emergence of an original poetic genius above the literary horizon more evidently announced.' But this was far from being the general view at the time.

In the same letter to Thelwall, Coleridge referred to Wordsworth in passing as 'a very dear friend of mine'.[49]† This too seems a startling description of a man he had met only briefly eight months before.[50] (He had no need to exaggerate to Thelwall; on the contrary, describing Wordsworth in such terms rather undermined the point he was trying to make.) The most likely explanation is that they had been in correspondence in the interim; various indications suggest that they were in regular contact. Coleridge often cultivated friendships by letter, as indeed he was doing with Thelwall. Yet the expression seems remarkable all the same. 'Friend' was not a term Coleridge used lightly. Perhaps in some way he already sensed what Wordsworth would come to mean to him.

Coleridge had lost money on *The Watchman*,‡ but allies rushed to

---

* 'Guilt and Sorrow', a poem adapted from the Salisbury Plain manuscripts, was published in 1842.
† Coleridge used the same expression of Poole in a letter to Charles Lloyd, Sr, on 15 October 1796 – but with much more obvious reason for so doing.
‡ Expenses on *The Watchman* exceeded income by £5. In addition, Coleridge had received but not paid for paper worth £40, and Cottle had laid out considerable sums to the printer which he never recovered.

his aid. Poole organised a group of seven or eight well-wishers who each contributed five guineas to a fund on his behalf, and pledged to do so annually. Dyer also sent him some money. Lamb paid a bill at the Salutation and Cat, outstanding since Coleridge had been dragged off to Bristol sixteen months earlier. A group of ladies subscribed to his poems at a guinea each, to compensate the author 'for his disappointment in The Watchman'. The Royal Literary Fund sent him ten guineas after hearing that he was 'in extreme difficulties'. Some months afterwards Dr Edward Long Fox, a philanthropist who kept a private asylum in Bristol, presented Coleridge with a handsome gift of £50.

Thrashing around for some form of income as *The Watchman* failed, Coleridge had written to Poole outlining two possibilities, 'the first impracticable – the second not likely to succeed'. The first scheme was for him to obtain a commission from a London bookseller to translate the complete works of Schiller. The bookseller would pay him two guineas per quarto page, say, and fund the Coleridges to travel to the University of Jena, where Schiller lived. There he proposed to study chemistry and anatomy, and on his return start a school of advanced study for young men at a hundred guineas each, drawing on the knowledge he had acquired in Germany. It only remained to learn German, but Coleridge was confident of being able to read the language 'with tolerable fluency' within six weeks. The other scheme was to become a dissenting parson; though it was contrary to his principles to earn money by preaching, the alternative, of remaining in need, was worse.

A pattern was emerging: whenever Coleridge was in trouble, he would cast around helplessly for advice and support. At the beginning of July he received an offer to write for the *Morning Chronicle*. This would mean moving to London. Those he consulted in Bristol advised him to accept. 'My heart is very heavy,' he wrote to John Prior Estlin, the local Unitarian minister, then on holiday with his wife in Bridgend, 'for I love Bristol & I do not love London . . . But there are two Giants leagued together whose most imperious commands I must obey however reluctant – their names are, BREAD & CHEESE.' He used the same expression in a letter to Poole written the same day. 'I must do something,' he continued: 'If I go, farewell Philosophy! Farewell, the Muse! Farewell, my literary Fame!'[51]

Coleridge did not take up the offer from the *Morning Chronicle*. Another possibility had arisen: a rich Derbyshire widow offered him a salary of £150 per year to act as tutor to her children. Coleridge took Sara up to Derbyshire to discuss the plan. The widow, obviously smitten by Coleridge, was nevertheless persuaded by the children's less impressionable guardians to withdraw the offer, but she gave him a very generous £95 in compensation, while loading up Sara with baby clothes. Yet another scheme, for him to start a school in the neighbourhood, came to nothing. 'My dearest friend,' wrote Lamb, 'I grieve from my very soul to observe you in your plans of life, veering about from this hope to the other, & settling no where.'[52]

But on his journey back from Derby Coleridge found a disciple, Charles Lloyd, a sensitive, self-conscious, delicate young man (three years younger than Coleridge) from a family of wealthy Birmingham Quakers. Lloyd wanted to attach himself to Coleridge as a pupil, and after he had taken Sara back to Bristol, Coleridge returned to Birmingham to settle the business. Lloyd's grateful father agreed to pay £80 a year for his board, lodging and tuition. While Coleridge was in Birmingham, news came from Bristol that Sara had given birth to a boy, three weeks earlier than expected. He hurried home, taking Lloyd with him. On seeing his son for the first time, he did not feel the expected thrill, but two hours later, when he saw the infant at Sara's breast, he melted, and gave the child 'the Kiss of a FATHER'. The boy was named David Hartley Coleridge, 'in honour of the great Master of Christian Philosophy'.[53]

Lamb had planned to visit the Coleridges in Bristol as soon as he could arrange leave from his employers. Before this, however, a tragedy intervened. Lamb's sister Mary had been showing increasing signs of mental instability. She was then working as a dressmaker, and shared cramped lodgings in the Temple with her two brothers, their by-now senile father, invalid mother and indolent aunt. It seems that fatigue brought about a crisis: the strain of caring for her elderly relatives on a modest income, combined with the long hours she worked, brought Mary to the point of exhaustion. Whatever the cause, by the morning of 22 September 1796 her symptoms had become alarming enough to induce Charles to leave their lodgings early in search of a doctor. He returned in mid-afternoon to a scene of horror. The parlour was in disarray, the furniture overturned, and the floor littered with food, broken crockery, and cutlery that had been hurled around the room. His father, bleeding from a head wound, bent sobbing. His aunt sat motionless, white with shock. His sister stood with a carving knife in her hand, her eyes wild, her face and clothes spattered with blood – and her mother's corpse at her feet.

Mary was taken to an asylum, where Lamb visited her regularly, and she quickly recovered her sanity. In his distress Lamb had written to Coleridge seeking comfort – 'Write, as religious a letter as possible' – and Coleridge had immediately obliged, with what Lamb described as 'an inestimable treasure of a letter'. Within a few weeks Lamb was again writing playfully to Coleridge. 'Have you made it up with Southey yet? Surely one of you two must have been a very silly fellow, and the other not much better, to fall out like boarding-school misses; kiss, shake hands, and make it up.'[54]

Southey had returned from Portugal in May, and in September, perhaps prompted by Edith, he took the first step towards a reconciliation, sending Coleridge a slip of paper on which he had written a translation from Schiller: 'Fiesco! Fiesco! thou leavest a void in my bosom, which the human race, thrice told, will never fill up.' But Coleridge would not easily be won over. A month or so later Southey sent him a copy of his new volume of poems, prompting this response:

> I thank you, Robert Southey! for your poems; and by way of
> return present you with a collection of (what appear to me)
> the faults.

After some wounding comments – 'the four last lines appear to drag excrementitiously' – Coleridge concluded: 'I have animadverted on those poems only which are my particular favourites.'[55]

Cottle tried to reconcile the brothers-in-law, and he was delighted when the two men called on him, arm in arm, after a pleasant walk in the country. Apparently they had met at the house of a relation – Mrs Fricker? – and 'the relentings of nature threw them silently into each other's arms'.[56]

Even so, they were not as they had been, as Coleridge explained to Thelwall:

> Between ourselves, the *Enthusiasm* of Friendship is not with S & me. We quarrelled – & the quarrel lasted for a twelvemonth – We are now reconciled; but the cause of the Difference was solemn – & 'the blasted oak puts not forth its buds anew' – we are *acquaintances* – & feel *kindliness* towards each other; but I do not *esteem*, or Love Southey, as I must esteem & love the man whom I dared call by the holy name of Friend![57]

6

RETREAT

Soon after his son was born, Coleridge took Charles Lloyd to see Poole at Nether Stowey. Coleridge's correspondence with Poole in the latter half of 1796 shows a deepening emotional involvement with the older man. He began his letters 'My very dear Poole', 'My beloved Friend', 'My dear, very dear Poole', 'My beloved Poole', or 'My dearest Poole', while Poole addressed him as 'My dear, my very dear Coleridge', and 'My dear, dear boy'.[1] To Poole, Coleridge confessed his schemes, his hopes and his disappointments, while demanding affection, approval and admiration.

After the visit to Poole, Coleridge wrote to Lloyd's father announcing a new plan:* he had decided 'to retire once for all and utterly from cities and towns', and to take a cottage with half a dozen acres of land at Adscombe, a mile or two above Nether Stowey, in the foothills of the Quantocks. There were various reasons, but above all he was anxious that his children should be brought up 'in the simplicity of peasants, their food, dress, and habits completely rustic'. Like Wordsworth, Coleridge would live a simple life and cultivate vegetables, labouring with hand in the morning and brain in the afternoon. This, of course, was a variant on the Pantisocratic ideal. It was only twelve months since he had quit his rural retreat at Clevedon, drawn back to the city by the call of politics; but now, promised Coleridge, he had 'snapped my squeaking baby-trumpet of sedition, and have hung up its fragments in the chamber of

* E.V. Lucas describes this as an 'almost Micawberesque' letter.[2]

Penitences'.[3] He liked this expression so much that he used it in another letter more than a year later.

'I doubt not, that the time will come when all our Utilities will be directed in one simple path,' he wrote to Thelwall, defending his decision to withdraw from active participation in politics. 'I am not *fit* for *public* Life; yet the Light shall stream to a far distance from the taper in my cottage window. Meantime,' he exhorted, 'do *you* uplift the *torch* dreadlessly, and shew to mankind the face of that Idol, which they have worshipped in Darkness!'[4]

Coleridge evoked a rural idyll in his poem addressed to Charles Lloyd, 'To a Young Friend, On His Proposing to Domesticate with the Author', imagining the two of them climbing a hill together, sharing the soothing delights of the natural beauty around them.

> Such a green mountain, 'twere most sweet to climb,
> E'en while the bosom ach'd with loneliness –
> How much more than sweet, if some dear friend should bless
> The adventurous toil, and up the path sublime
> Now lead, now follow . . .

Escape to the innocence of the country, away from the corruption of the city, was a recurrent theme in Coleridge's thought. 'Man was not made to live in Great Cities!' he had exclaimed to George Dyer back in March 1795. 'The pleasures, which we received from rural beauties, are of little Consequence compared with the Moral Effect of these pleasures – beholding constantly the Best possible we at last become ourselves the best possible.'[5]

Coleridge became obsessed with this idea as a solution to all his difficulties, and his letters to Poole on the subject became hysterical:

> To live in a beautiful country & to inure myself as much as possible to the labors of the field, have been for this year past my dream of the day, my Sigh at midnight – but to enjoy these blessings *near you*, to see you daily, to tell you all my thoughts in their first birth, and to hear your's, to be mingling identities with you, as it were; – the vision-weaving *Fancy* has indeed often pictured such things, but *Hope* never dared whisper a promise!

Two days afterwards he insisted that this '*flighty*' letter, though 'written under the immediate inspiration of Laudanum', was nonetheless 'most accurately descriptive both of facts & feelings'.[6] He had taken between sixty and seventy drops of laudanum – a very large amount – to obtain relief from what sounds like migraine, running about the house naked in an attempt to divert his mind from the pain. The doctor had diagnosed nervous disorder, 'originating in *mental* causes', anxiety perhaps, or overwork. Lloyd too was suffering from some form of psychological illness, and possibly the two were connected in some way. Coleridge's extreme sensibility and lack of emotional restraint made him dangerous to know. Lloyd's 'Lines Addressed to S.T. Coleridge'* provides some idea of the intensity of his feelings for his mentor:

> My Coleridge! take the wanderer to thy breast
> The youth that loves thee, and who, faint, would rest
> (Oft rack'd by hopes that frenzy and expire)
> In the long Sabbath of subdued desire!

Lloyd succumbed just as Lamb had done; he fell into a kind of waking nightmare, with delirious fits. Coleridge warned Lloyd's father that he could no longer continue to act as his tutor, and that henceforth Lloyd might stay with him only as lodger and friend, paying half a guinea a week for his board and lodging. Lloyd left the household soon afterwards.

Perhaps Poole was beginning to be alarmed at the prospect of such a neurotic household nearby. He wrote to say that the cottage in Adscombe was not going to be available after all. But the Coleridge family urgently needed somewhere to live, as the lease on the Kingsdown house was due to expire at the end of the year. There had been a plan for them to rent an unprepossessing thatched cottage on the edge of Nether Stowey itself until the one at Adscombe was ready; Coleridge now proposed that they should take this for an indefinite

---

* Several years later Coleridge commented on this poem in an annotation to the volume in which it appeared: 'Too loving by Half! Am obliged to C. Ll for his kind *wishes*, but would rather not!'

period. Poole wrote to discourage the idea, on the grounds that the cottage was small, damp and uncomfortable. Coleridge reacted violently, demanding to know if there was an unspoken reason for Poole's 'heart-chilling Letter'. He suspected that Poole's family objected to his living so close. The very next day he wrote again, countering every objection to the scheme that Poole had raised, in a frenzy of self-pity. 'O my God! my God! when am I to find rest!'[7]

Faced with this avalanche of emotion, Poole's resistance was swept away. On the last day of the year, Coleridge, Sara and Hartley moved to Nether Stowey.

The year 1796 had been a lean one for Wordsworth. Raisley Calvert's legacy was being paid to him in portions, as it were grudgingly; it would be another two years before the last of the money was made over. By the beginning of the year he had received £525, of which he lent £300 to Montagu and £200 to a friend of Montagu's, Charles Douglas, on the promise of interest at 10 per cent (Montagu later took over some of Douglas's debt). As it turned out, Montagu was able to pay the interest only sporadically, and then not always in full; the capital appeared in jeopardy, and Wordsworth felt obliged to take out an expensive insurance policy on Montagu's life. The Wordsworths were left considerably short of their expected income. Wordsworth had counted on annual interest of £70 or £80 on Calvert's legacy of £900, and a further £50 each from the fathers of the two children they had expected to have in their care: only one of these had materialised, young Basil, and Montagu had difficulty paying for his board. It is not clear quite how much the Wordsworths received in their first year, but it was certainly a lot less than expected. Richard Wordsworth was alarmed at his younger brother's imprudence. More than half of Calvert's legacy had been risked on insecure loans that failed to produce the expected return. Richard urged William to keep tighter control of his accounts.

The effect of this shortfall was enforced economy. There was no money for books or newspapers. Dorothy's letters to her friend Jane Marshall complained about the high prices of coal and meat; they were forced to rely instead on the resources of the garden and the surrounding countryside. Wordsworth spent many hours outside chopping wood, rooting up hedges and tending the vegetable garden. They ate so many cabbages, he joked, that 'into cabbages we shall be transformed' – as one of his London friends had indeed prophesied. Only when the Pinney brothers came down for a visit was this austerity relaxed, and then Wordsworth ate heartily. But for most of the time they subsisted on a very frugal diet. 'I have lately been living upon air and the essence of carrots cabbages turnips and other esculent vegetables, not excluding parsley the produce of my garden,' he complained early in 1797, and begged Wrangham (who had recently been awarded a lucrative living in Yorkshire) to frank his next letter, 'else ten to one I shall not be able to release [it] from the post office'.[8]* To make matters still worse, his cousin Robinson Wordsworth announced that he was getting married, and pressed William for cash in order to help him set up house. He wanted £250, in consideration of the money his father had advanced for William's education. Wordsworth acknowledged the claim as just, but was at a loss to meet it.

He was reduced to borrowing money from Richard in order to get by, and even the odd sovereign from the caretaker Joseph Gill. He and Dorothy might have suffered real hardship had they not been living rent-free – an arrangement that could easily have been terminated in the spring of 1796, when John Pretor Pinney discovered it. Pinney was angry at being deceived by his sons, and no doubt irritated too. For a self-made merchant and aspiring gentleman, the thought that his beautiful country home was being enjoyed by a young man of no profession and modest means, whom he no doubt considered to be an idle scribbler, must have been hard to bear. He threatened to call on Wordsworth for the missing rent, but was eventually persuaded not to do so by his sons. Nevertheless it was obvious that the Wordsworths remained at Racedown only on sufferance.

In the early summer Wordsworth spent a month in London, where

---

* In those times postal charges were paid by the recipient, not the sender. Holders of privileged offices were permitted to 'frank' their letters, allowing them to be sent free of charge. This system was widely abused.

he and one of the Pinney brothers called on Godwin, and then ate supper with Godwin at Montagu's later that evening. Subsequently he saw Godwin a number of times during his stay, and seems to have mixed with a group of young men his own age – including Montagu and Coleridge's old friend Robert Allen – who were all admirers of Godwin. Yet Wordsworth was uneasy. He sensed something wrong about Godwin's thought that he was not yet able to articulate. In trying to reconcile himself to Godwin's philosophy, Wordsworth began a painful self-examination, in which nothing was hidden, nothing sacrosanct:

> Thus strangely did I war against myself;
> A Bigot to a new Idolatry
> Did like a Monk who hath forsworn the world
> Zealously labour to cut off my heart
> From all the sources of her former strength[9]

While in London Wordsworth collected the manuscript of 'Adventures on Salisbury Plain' from Lamb, who did not share in the general idolatry of 'Professor Godwin'. Wordsworth may have tried to interest London publishers in the poem; if so, he had no success. It is of course possible that he changed his mind about the desirability of publishing it, but more likely that he simply failed to find a publisher prepared to take the risk. 'As to writing it is out of the question,' he wrote gloomily to Mathews.[10] He tried his hand at a few satires in a desultory way, but without application. He never completed the imitation of Juvenal.

After the rejection of 'Adventures on Salisbury Plain' Wordsworth was once again forced to confront the value of what he was doing. It was more than five years since he had left Cambridge; more than three since he had published 'Descriptive Sketches' and 'An Evening Walk'. Since then he had published nothing. From his university days he had carried a strong conviction that he was destined to be a great poet – but what was the point of writing poems that nobody read? His contemporaries were getting on with their lives; even his fellow radicals were making progress in their careers. Wordsworth had been lucky enough to receive an unexpected windfall – only to have invested the bulk of it unwisely, maybe even squandered it. In the eyes of the world he was a failure, a rash failure at that.

This was the very nadir of his fortunes, when Wordsworth needed all his considerable stock of self-belief to sustain him. To persist might lead him deeper into the mire; to abandon his chosen course would mean admitting that he had wasted his opportunities. He could not be oblivious to continuing criticism from within his family. Rejection damaged his self-respect; isolation deprived him of stimulus; poverty exposed him to humiliation. It would have been easy to lose heart.

Instead, towards the end of the year Wordsworth began writing again. In late October Dorothy reported that her brother was 'ardent in the composition of a tragedy'. This was *The Borderers*, a play written in blank verse which would occupy Wordsworth for the next six months. He felt his creative strength returning to him, like a warm breeze stirring. Since the winter the house had been sweetened by the presence of Dorothy's friend Mary Hutchinson. 'She is one of the best girls in the world,' wrote Dorothy, 'and we are as happy as human beings can be.' By March 1797 her brother was 'as cheerful as any body can be', 'the life of the whole house'.[11]

Underlying Wordsworth's practical problems during his stay at Racedown had been a deeper moral crisis. He had reached a philosophical impasse. He had lost faith in the Revolution, and now he lost faith in Godwin too. The effect was to sever him from the sources of his creativity. For years he had been trying to find a means to write honestly and directly about human experience. But he could not see which way to proceed; his vision was obscured. He had strayed from his path, and around him all seemed dark.

The Prelude describes this great crisis in Wordsworth's life, when (as he put it) his imagination was impaired, and then restored. The poem traces the growth of his mind, and the uninterrupted development of his powers, to the time of his stay in France when, overcome by enthusiasm for the young Republic, he surrendered all doubts to embrace a new faith. Then, after his return to England at the end of 1792, his loyalties became confused between old and new allegiances, as his own country made war (as it seemed to him) on Liberty:

> This threw me first out of the pale of love,
> Soured and corrupted upwards to the source,
> My sentiments; was not, as hitherto,
> A swallowing up of lesser things in great,
> But change of them into their opposites,
> And thus a way was opened for mistakes
> And false conclusions of the intellect,
> As gross in their degree and in their kind
> Far, far more dangerous. What had been a pride
> Was now my shame; my likings and my loves
> Ran in new channels, leaving old ones dry;[12]

And when the Terror caused him to recoil from revolutionary politics he found refuge in Godwinism, as did so many other idealistic young Britons. For perhaps two years Wordsworth subscribed to

> . . . the Philosophy
> That promised to abstract the hopes of man
> Out of his feelings . . .

Godwin pictured a world governed by Reason, in which men would be happy and free – the same utopia offered by the revolutionaries, but without the politics.

> . . . the dream
> Was flattering to the young ingenuous mind
> Pleased with extremes, and not the least with that
> Which makes the human reason's naked self
> The object of its fervour. What delight!
> How glorious! In self-knowledge and self-rule,
> To look though all the frailties of the world,
> And, with a resolute mastery shaking off
> The accidents of nature, time, and place,
> That make up the weak being of the past,
> Build social freedom on its only basis,
> The freedom of the individual mind,

> Which, to the blind restraints of general laws
> Superior, magisterially adopts
> One guide, the light of circumstances, flashed
> Upon an independent intellect.[13]

Yet Wordsworth was never wholly at ease with Godwin's ideas. His heart rebelled against them. Instinct told him that they were wrong. Even the behaviour of little Basil fed his growing disenchantment.

The Pinney brothers brought down with them to Racedown new books by those who had played a part in the Revolution or who had witnessed the events at close hand, including a volume of memoirs by Louvet, the Girondin journalist who denounced Robespierre in the Convention while Wordsworth was in Paris. Reading these caused Wordsworth to reflect that men may commit the most hideous of crimes from the most noble of motives. As he later observed in a note to *The Borderers*, the study of human nature suggests that just as 'sin and crime are apt to start from their very opposite qualities, so are there no limits to the hardening of the heart, and the perversion of the understanding'.

Wordsworth did not see this at first. But doubts arose repeatedly in his mind. How had the noble principles of the Revolution been so perverted? The more he looked into this question, the deeper the problem seemed to lie. There was a sickness somewhere, something rotten within. Like a surgeon searching for a tumour,

> . . . I took the knife in hand
> And stopping not at parts less sensitive,
> Endeavoured with my best of skill to probe
> The living body of society
> Even to the heart; I pushed without remorse
> My speculations forward; yea, set foot
> On Nature's holiest places . . .[14]

The Terror was the apotheosis of the Revolution, but it was only the hideous sprouting of a seed planted much earlier, when legitimate government had been abandoned and violence had been allowed to prevail. As Wordsworth looked back over the history of the Revolution, he was forced to abandon cherished positions one after another. He still longed for a better world, but it was no longer obvious to him how such a world could be made.

Another of the books Wordsworth received at Racedown was Burke's *Letters on a Regicide Peace*. This was Burke in his final stage of complete disillusion with radical politics, an old man who had turned his back on youthful folly. He deplored the acquittals at the treason trials, and condemned Pitt's peace overtures. No compromise could be made with a government that had killed its king. Such a reactionary diatribe could scarcely be expected to appeal to the young Wordsworth, still clinging to the shreds of his idealism; yet it had an influence on him all the same. For one thing, it was superbly written. For another, it displayed an alternative vision of nationhood, of continuity between past and present, of unity, of loyalty, of nation as a 'moral essence'. As the years passed, Burke's vision would become embedded deeper and deeper in Wordsworth's mind.[15]

It was one of Godwin's precepts that no premise should be admitted as certain unless proven so. Accordingly Wordsworth tried to reason his route to the truth, like a prosecutor arguing a case:

> ... Thus I fared,
> Dragging all passions, notions, shapes of faith,
> Like culprits to the bar, suspiciously
> Calling the mind to establish in plain day
> Her titles and her honours, now believing,
> Now disbelieving, endlessly perplexed
> With impulse, motive, right and wrong, the ground
> Of moral obligation, what the rule
> And what the sanction, till, demanding proof,
> And seeking it in every thing, I lost
> All feeling of conviction, and, in fine,
> Sick, wearied out with contrarieties,
> Yielded up moral questions in despair.[16]

This was the philosophical dead end in which Wordsworth found himself. He could not advance; he could not retreat. He had discarded the old beliefs without being able to accept the new. He could not write, because he did not know what to write. His whole future as a poet seemed threatened. His heart was at war with his head. He was prostrate,

> . . . inwardly oppressed
> With sorrow, disappointment, vexing thoughts,
> Confusion of opinion, Zeal decayed,
> And lastly, utter loss of hope itself,
> And things to hope for . . .[17]

For a respite from his despondency he turned for a while to the study of mathematics, as a subject solid and clear.

Many scholars have tried to track the course of Wordsworth's moral crisis, identifying particular events and dates with the stages described in *The Prelude*. Yet perhaps the effort is fruitless. Wordsworth himself was writing in retrospect, retracing his course several years afterwards, making sense of changes that might at the time have seemed confusing. Such a revolution in a man's thinking is not susceptible to minute documentation.

Early in 1796, for example, he received from Montagu a copy of the second and much revised edition of Godwin's *Political Justice*. After perusing the new preface, he commented disparagingly on it to Mathews. But this was not enough in itself to show Wordsworth moving away from Godwinism. It was the style, rather than the content, to which he objected in his letter to Mathews: 'such a piece of barbarous writing I have not often seen'.[18] That summer, when he was in London for a month, Wordsworth twice called on Godwin, and saw him on two other occasions, in company with like-minded friends such as Montagu. The fact that he chose to do so suggests that he had not yet rejected Godwin's ideas. It would have been out of character for Wordsworth to seek out Godwin in order to debate with him; unlike Coleridge, he did not relish confrontations; his argument with Godwin was an internal one.

On the other hand, it is indisputable that while at Racedown Wordsworth turned his back on both Godwinism and the Revolution, and in this more general sense *The Prelude* can be relied upon as providing an authentic record of the crisis in his inner life up to the time when, his imagination restored, he stood prepared for the great tasks that lay ahead.

Just as 'Adventures on Salisbury Plain' shows Wordsworth in Godwin's camp, *The Borderers* reveals him in full retreat from Godwinism. The tragedy's most interesting character, Rivers,* has cast off the constraints of conventional morality. Iago-like, he tries to trick his young leader Mortimer into killing an innocent man, hoping thereby to 'liberate' the younger man from conscience, compassion, remorse and other such weaknesses. Through this crime Mortimer will be initiated into a higher state of being. In fact he does not succumb, and Rivers receives the comeuppance due to villains, his story a warning of what can result when Reason is not moderated by kinder feelings. To drive the point home, Wordsworth paraphrased these lines from Rivers in *The Prelude*, in describing the superficial allure of Godwinism:

> You have obeyed the only law that wisdom
> Can ever recognise; the immediate law,
> Flashed from the light of circumstances
> Upon an independent Intellect.[19]†

How did Wordsworth find his way forward? How was his imagination restored? Many years later, he referred to Coleridge and Dorothy as 'the two Beings to whom my intellect is most indebted'.[20] In *The Prelude* he ascribed his gradual recovery principally to his sister,

> . . . the belovèd Woman, in whose sight
> Those days were passed, now speaking in a voice
> Of sudden admonition, like a brook
> That did but cross a lonely road, and now
> Seen, heard and felt, and caught at every turn,
> Companion never lost through many a league,

---

* Changed to Oswald in the final, most-often-read version. Mortimer's name is changed to Marmaduke.
† See page 159.

Maintained for me a saving intercourse
With my true self; for though impaired and changed
Much, as it seemed, I was no further changed
Than as a clouded, not a waning moon:
She, in the midst of all, preserved me still
A Poet, made me seek beneath that name
My office upon earth . . .[21]

Dorothy's passionate devotion to her brother, and her unhesitating belief in his calling, strengthened him when he needed strength most. She continued to believe in him when he scarcely believed in himself. When his hopes of social reform collapsed, she gently drew him back to the sources of his inspiration. As a child, Wordsworth had experienced the external world with extraordinary intensity; he had been drunk on natural beauty, lost in a universe of sensation. 'I was often unable to think of external things as having external existence,' he remembered in old age, 'and I communed with all that I saw as something not apart from, but inherent in, my own immaterial nature. Many times while going to school have I grasped at a wall or tree to recall myself from this abyss of idealism to the reality.'[22] That time was gone, but still the memory of 'that dream-like vividness and splendour' lingered in his mind, an echo of his boyhood and a source of future power. His sister was inherently associated with those childhood days:

The Blessing of my later years
Was with me when a boy[23]

And even in adulthood she retained a miraculous sensitivity to natural beauty, through which he could feel what he could otherwise no longer reach:

. . . in thy voice I catch
The language of my former heart, and read
My former pleasures in the shooting lights
Of thy wild eyes. Oh! Yet a little while
May I behold in thee what I was once,
My dear, dear Sister![24]

Dorothy's journals reveal a habit of minute observation of light and cloud, the ever-changing bounty of natural forms, the subtle variations in familiar landscapes; this fed her brother's imagination, and much of it became the subject of his poetry.* Like a scout, she went before him; she showed him what he might otherwise have overlooked:

> She gave me eyes, she gave me ears.[25]

Together at Racedown they walked every day, and slowly, nature's influence 'revived the feelings of my earlier life', leading him back towards half-forgotten truths.

It was when Wordsworth had turned to the study of mathematics, having 'yielded up moral questions in despair', that Coleridge, 'most precious friend',

> . . . didst lend a living help
> To regulate my Soul . . .[26]

This is all Wordsworth says in *The Prelude* about his intellectual debt to Coleridge, and even this little was removed when he revised the poem in 1816–19. Some critics, aware that the two men had barely met until Wordsworth's last few weeks at Racedown, have suggested that in his first draft of the poem Wordsworth cast Coleridge in a role that he was not to play until later.[27] But that may be to underestimate the impact on Wordsworth of Coleridge's letters. These have not survived, yet his letters to Thelwall offer some hint of what they may have been like. Indeed Coleridge often used the same phrases, sentences and examples in letters addressed to different people. To Thelwall (a man he had never even seen) he wrote long, lively, combative but affectionate letters, in which (*inter alia*) he consistently attacked Godwin and his followers. 'I write freely, Thelwall! For tho'

---

* A famous example is Wordsworth's poem 'I wandered lonely as a cloud' ('Daffodils'), which draws on Dorothy's journal for 15 April 1802, when the two of them were walking beside Ullswater. The poem was not written until at least two years afterwards, maybe longer. Thus Wordsworth used Dorothy's journal to recapture experiences they had shared together – though excluding her from the poem itself.

personally unknown, I really love you, and can count but few human beings, whose hand I would welcome with a more hearty Grasp of friendship.'[28]

Coleridge's letters fizzed with ideas, illustrated with vivid and startling images. He coloured his thoughts with emotion, radiating warmth as well as misery. For Wordsworth, whose own letters were somewhat staid, their effect must have been exhilarating. Moreover, Coleridge provided what his sister could not. Dorothy was no intellectual. She could not follow her brother through the maze of Godwinism, while Coleridge was just the man to show him the exit. Armed with a powerful and original mind, he had made it his task to vanquish Godwin, as it were in single combat. Coleridge was a published poet, a critic whose opinion commanded respect. While Wordsworth might dismiss Dorothy's good opinion of his work as mere sisterly devotion, he could hardly think the same of praise from Coleridge.

Dorothy was wholly uninterested in politics. She had little sympathy for her brother's radicalism. Even as Wordsworth had thrilled to the republican rhetoric of Grégoire, his sister had been simpering in the presence of royalty, testifying that it was 'impossible to see the King and his Family at Windsor without loving them'. Indeed, she was so much dazzled by the royal presence as to assert that she 'never saw so handsome a Family'. While Wordsworth solemnly declared himself to be a democrat, Dorothy confessed to being 'too much of an aristocrate' not to revere the King.[29] By contrast, Coleridge had been immersed in radical politics and had certainly flirted with republicanism. His political opinions were very like Wordsworth's; they had traced a similar course, and reached a similar point. This was a side of Wordsworth's experience that he understood well, and Dorothy did not.

Late in 1796 Wordsworth's poem 'Address to the Ocean' appeared in the *Weekly Entertainer*, with a note that its first line, 'How long will ye be round me roaring', was borrowed from Coleridge. Both men had now published poems quoting from the other's verse, a conventional means of mutual acknowledgement, but nevertheless an indication of their growing closeness.

*

In the last few days of 1796 Coleridge published a new poem, his 'Ode on the Departing Year', with a dedication to Poole. In the grandiose Miltonic style of 'Religious Musings', the 'Ode' was a grim survey of the state of the nation, prophesying its imminent defeat:

> O doomed to fall, enslaved and vile,
> O ALBION! O my mother Isle!

In October Spain had declared war on Britain. The position was the reverse of what it had been at the beginning of the war, when France had been encircled by enemies; now Britain was menaced from all sides. The navy was outnumbered, facing threats from the Dutch and Spanish fleets as well as the French; a decision was taken in principle to withdraw the British fleet from the Mediterranean. In December a French invasion fleet set sail for Ireland (the 'back door' into Britain for more than a century), and only bad weather and poor seamanship prevented a landing. Unrest simmered there, while mutinies in both the Channel fleet and the North Sea fleet left the nation temporarily defenceless. In February a French squadron of four vessels anchored off Ilfracombe on the north Devon coast. Their orders were to raid Bristol, destroying the valuable shipping at harbour there, laying waste to the docks and setting fire to the town. Afterwards they were to re-embark and attack Cardiff, then other west-facing ports, Chester and Liverpool. Adverse weather once again thwarted the French plans: they sailed on to land 1,200 troops at Fishguard in Wales, where this small force was easily rounded up by the militia. But the expedition had demonstrated the danger to British ports. No stretch of the coastline was safe; afterwards the West Country stood on alert. Fortunately the Royal Navy began a succession of glorious victories. In February 1797 the British Mediterranean fleet defeated a Spanish fleet twice its size at Cape St Vincent, off the southern coast of Portugal, an action in which the most prominent part was played by a brilliant naval officer, Horatio Nelson; and in October the Dutch invasion fleet would be destroyed at Camperdown, off northern Holland. Nevertheless the threat of invasion remained. The object of the raids upon the western ports had been to strike at British commerce and to spread panic throughout the country, perhaps even to stimulate a revolutionary insurrection. In writing of his own humble antecedents, Coleridge joked that 'the time may come when it will be useful to be able to prove myself a genuine Sans culotte, my veins uncontaminated with one drop of Gentility'.[30]

Poole had tried to make the cottage at Nether Stowey 'an abode of comparative comfort', but there was only so much that could be done with such a tiny and dilapidated building. It remained damp, dark and draughty. One compensation for its small size was that it warmed up quickly, once the chimney began to draw. Downstairs were two small parlours on either side of a hallway, plus a rudimentary kitchen (with no proper oven) extending at the back. Upstairs were three small bedrooms. The cottage was overrun with mice, which Coleridge was too soft-hearted to trap. Outside the front door ran a small stream, which occasionally flooded into the house, and beyond that a busy road. At the back was a long, narrow kitchen garden, ending in a small orchard of fruit trees. In later years Coleridge would describe the cottage as 'our little hovel', but at first he was full of enthusiasm for his new home, for which he paid a rent of eight guineas* per annum, in quarterly instalments.

'I am already an expert Gardener,' he boasted after he had been in Nether Stowey only a few weeks – in January, not the most demanding month for horticulturists.[31] But the calluses on his hands testified to his hard work. 'I raise potatoes & all manner of vegetables; have an Orchard; and shall raise Corn with the spade enough for my family,' he wrote proudly to Thelwall, who was perhaps more familiar with manual labour. 'We have two pigs, & Ducks & Geese.' He described a typical day. 'From seven to half past eight I work in my garden; from breakfast till twelve I read & compose; then work again – feed the pigs, poultry &c, till two o'clock – after dinner work again till Tea – from Tea till supper *review*. So jogs the day.' He urged Thelwall to think of doing the same: 'You will find country Life a happy one; and you might live comfortably with an hundred a year.'[32]

---

* See footnote on page 286.

'Is it a farm you have got?' asked Lamb, 'and what does your worship know about farming?' He asked about little Hartley: 'you don't mean to make an actual ploughman of him?'[33] 'We are *very* happy,' insisted Coleridge. 'I have society – my *friend*, T. Poole and as many acquaintances as I can dispense with – there are a number of very pretty young women in Stowey, all musical – & I am an immense favourite; for I pun, conundrumize, *listen*, & dance. The last is a recent acquirement.' He wrote enthusiastically about his little boy. 'You would smile to see my eye rolling up to the ceiling in a Lyric fury, and on my knee a *Diaper* pinned, to keep warm.'[34]

Nevertheless, with the three Coleridges and a live-in servant the cottage was crowded, even more so when Charles Lloyd rejoined them after a period of convalescence in Birmingham and then in London, where he had become friendly with Lamb. To escape the crush Coleridge often left the house and walked through the fruit trees to the end of his strip of garden, then passed through the specially installed gate that led directly into Poole's garden, where a jasmine-draped arbour had been created beneath the shelter of a lime tree. If he did not find sanctuary there, he could continue past Poole's tannery to the back door of his comfortable sandstone house, which seemed particularly spacious after the cramped cottage, and where he was always a welcome guest. And if he did not feel like company, he could climb the external steps that led from the garden directly to Poole's library, which was available to him at all hours.

Another escape, which became increasingly attractive as the exceptionally cold winter burst into spring, was up onto the Quantock Hills. These were only a short walk from Nether Stowey, and provided a variety of delightful routes, along stream-cut combes and through woods sprinkled with wildflowers up onto the bare moorland plateau, offering panoramic views over the sea from the northern ridge and across the Somerset Levels to the east, huge skies overhead and magnificent sunsets over Exmoor in the west. Coleridge began to make almost daily walks up onto the hills, frequently taking his notebook and pencil out of his coat pocket to begin 'making studies, as the artists call them, and often moulding my thoughts into verse, with the objects and imagery immediately before my senses'. He was contemplating a long philosophical poem called 'The Brook', following the course of an imaginary stream from its source up in the hills down to the sea, past villages, towns and ports, along which he hoped to find 'equal room and freedom for description, incident and impassioned reflection on men, nature and society, yet supply in itself a natural connection to the parts, and unity to the whole'.

On Sundays Coleridge would sometimes walk over to Bridgwater (eight miles) or Taunton (ten miles) to preach in the local Unitarian chapels at the invitation of the ministers. He never prepared before he set out, confident that a text would come to him as he walked, and refused payment for preaching. Word of this fiery speaker quickly spread, attracting some of the best families to his sermons. Members of the congregation would shake the preacher's hand afterwards. They admired his mesmerising oratory, but deplored his uncombed hair and shabby coat.

In February 1797 he wrote the first of several autobiographical letters to Poole. The intention was to write his life in instalments, to be delivered every Monday morning. As it turned out, he wrote only five such letters intermittently over the year that followed, and then stopped. Nevertheless the process caused him to reflect more deeply on his childhood, on his feelings of estrangement from home and rejection by his family. Coleridge treated Poole like a dependable elder brother – a figure whose love and loyalty were assured, and whose status commanded authority. Often he would cite Poole's opinions in support of his own.

Coleridge worked late into the night, reading by candlelight in one of the parlours while his wife and child slept upstairs. He read very widely, books of travel and exploration as well as science and philosophy, and he had begun to review books for the *Critical Review*. And for some time now he had been contemplating a counterblast to Godwin. 'I shall shortly be delivered of an Examination of Godwin's Political Justice,' he had written early the previous November, and in the middle of that month he had informed Thelwall that it 'will appear now in a few weeks'. By mid-December the publishing details had apparently been settled. 'My answer to Godwin will be a six shilling Octavo,' designed to show 'the absurdities and wickedness of *his* System,' he announced. 'Many things have fallen out to retard the work; but I hope, that it will appear shortly after Christmas, at the farthest.' He mentioned the book on several further occasions – but each time the references became less and less specific.[35]

He was preparing a second edition of his poems, discarding some, revising others and writing a few new poems as well – 'my choicest fish, pick'd, gutted, and clean'd'.[36] He told Cottle that he wanted time to consult both Wordsworth and Lamb, 'whose *taste & judgement* I see reason to think more correct & philosophical than my own, which yet I place pretty high'.[37] Lamb's letters prove that he took great care to scrutinise Coleridge's poems and suggest changes or improvements. The new edition was to contain a supplement of poems by Lamb and Lloyd, which Coleridge believed would widen its sale. 'I want you to write an Epic poem,' Lamb had urged soon after Coleridge's move to the country. 'Nothing short of it can satisfy the vast capacity of true poetic genius. Having one great End to direct all your poetical faculties to, & on which to lay out your hopes, your ambition, will shew you to what you are equal.' Lamb urged him to attempt 'something more ample' than the 'occasional brief ode or sonnet', something to 'make yourself for ever known', like one of the great poets: Milton, say, or Spenser. 'When you are exalted among the Lords of Epic fame,' wrote Lamb, 'I shall recall with pleasure, & exultingly, the days of your humility,' when Coleridge had not been too proud to include his own 'promising first fruits . . . in the same volume with mine'. In urging Coleridge to be more ambitious, Lamb drew an analogy with Pantisocracy: 'You have learning, you have fancy, you have enthusiasm – you have strength & amplitude of wing enow for flights like those I recommend. In the vast & unexplored regions of fairyland, there is ground enough unfound and uncultivated; search there, and realize your favourite Susquehanna scheme.' He reminded his friend that during their congenial evenings at the Salutation and Cat, 'you were talking of the Origin of Evil as a most prolific subject for a long poem'. Why not adopt it now? Coleridge added 'The Origin of Evil, an Epic Poem' to his list of projected works.[38]

A new possibility opened when Coleridge received a letter via William Lisle Bowles (with whom he had established contact) indicating that Sheridan – who as well as being a politician and playwright was manager of the Drury Lane Theatre – wished him to write a tragedy 'on some popular subject'. It is not clear how seriously Sheridan had meant this suggestion, or even that he did make it (the letter originated from his brother-in-law, a neighbour of Bowles's); if he did, he may have been influenced by the laudatory sonnet Coleridge had published two years before in the *Morning Chronicle*, which had likened Sheridan to the archangel Michael, vanquishing the satanic 'apostate' William Pitt. Coleridge wrote to him for clarification, and Sheridan replied asking to see an outline in the first instance. Coleridge took this as a form of commission and set about writing diligently, though as he admitted to Cottle, 'I have no genius that way.'[39] Within a few weeks he had sketched a plan 'romantic & wild & somewhat terrible'. He confessed to being influenced by the Gothic novels he had been reviewing. 'Dungeons, and old castles, & solitary Houses by the Sea Side, & Caverns, & Woods, & extraordinary characters, & all the tribe of Horror & Mystery, have crowded on me – even to surfeiting.'[40]

Meanwhile there was drama at home, as Lloyd was once again seized with fits. One night he remained in 'one *continued* state of *agoniz'd Delirium*'.[41] Coleridge sat up with him from midnight to five o'clock in the morning, trying to repress his frantic struggles. Soon afterwards Lloyd left Nether Stowey to return home to Birmingham, from where he was removed to a Lichfield sanatorium, under the care of Dr Erasmus Darwin, physician, poet, naturalist and 'lunar man'.*

Coleridge was again suffering from stress, late with his reviews and under pressure from a 'clamorous' Cottle to finalise the corrections for the second edition of his poems, which required his presence in Bristol. The problems with Lloyd may have tipped him over the edge.

---

* A member of the society of Midlands scientists, inventors, engineers, industrialists and entrepreneurs who met in Birmingham every full moon.

He dropped into 'a depression too terrible to be described'. He wrote to Cottle apologising for his absence on a day they had planned to spend together: 'I am not the man I have been – and I think never shall. A sort of calm hopelessness diffuses itself over my heart.'[42]

Wordsworth was buoyant, full of energy and enthusiasm now that he was emerging from the torpor that had afflicted him for a year or more. He had almost finished *The Borderers*, and had begun working on a new poem, 'The Ruined Cottage'. Dorothy was pleasantly surprised by the change in him.

'The Ruined Cottage' is a tragic tale of domestic hardship, drawing on the evidence of rural poverty and distress the Wordsworths witnessed in the countryside around Racedown, and influenced by Coleridge's contributions to Southey's epic *Joan of Arc*. It tells of a young family, stricken by failed crops and illness which erode their meagre savings until at last the husband is compelled to enlist in the army for the sake of the bounty, leaving his wife Margaret to cope alone; years pass, their cottage decays, their baby dies, she receives news that her husband has been killed, and eventually she too dies, so that the cottage falls into ruin. Though the poem demonstrates very clearly Wordsworth's sympathy for Margaret's plight, there is no Godwinian moral; the stark story speaks for itself. Margaret is an individual, not a social stereotype; Wordsworth has abandoned the poetry of protest for the poetry of the heart.

One morning in mid-March 1797 Basil Montagu arrived at Racedown unexpectedly early, before anybody was up. He stayed only a few days, but made himself amiable to Dorothy and to Mary Hutchinson, so that the four of them seem to have had a very jolly time together. Montagu could see how well his son was developing under Dorothy's care. He returned to London via Bristol, and Wordsworth accompanied him there for a stay of about a week. In Bristol, Montagu took Wordsworth to dinner at Cote House, home of John Wedgwood, eldest son of the late Josiah, wealthy potter and philanthropist. The next morning they breakfasted with James Losh, a fellow radical who had been among the group at Frend's house when Wordsworth met

Godwin back in February 1795. Losh had just sent Wordsworth a parcel of books and pamphlets, including Coleridge's 'Ode on the Departing Year' and *Conciones ad Populum*. The three passed some hours walking about the city and paying calls. After Montagu had left for London, Wordsworth took the opportunity to call on Cottle. On the walk back to Racedown, he made a diversion to Nether Stowey for a brief visit to Coleridge. Possibly he met Coleridge in Bristol and they walked back to Stowey together.

This was (so far as anybody knows) only the second encounter between the two men, but each had already developed a high regard for the other, and each was interested in what the other was doing. If they had not discovered before that both were working on blank-verse tragedies, they must have been amused by the coincidence. It seems probable that they discussed *The Borderers* together, because a couple of months later Dorothy reported that her brother had 'good hopes' of getting it shown to Sheridan. Naturally Coleridge took Wordsworth to see Poole, who told him several tales of rural life that later re-appeared in his poems. According to Coleridge, Poole shared his high opinion of their guest. 'T. Poole's opinion of Wordsworth is – that he is the greatest man, he ever knew – I coincide.'[43]

As well as their own work, the two men discussed Southey's recently published poems. Wordsworth had been irritated by Southey's preface to his *Joan of Arc*, which he described to Mathews as 'a very conceited performance'.[44] He complained to Coleridge that Southey wrote '*too much at his ease*' – a sentiment with which Coleridge could not disagree, since he had long resented Southey's comparative fluency. 'I think, that an admirable Poet might be made by *amalgamating him & me*,' Coleridge had written to Thelwall on the last day of 1796. 'I *think* too much for a *Poet*; he too little for a *great* Poet. But he abjures *thinking* – & lays the whole stress of excellence – on *feeling*. Now (as you say) they must go together.'[45]

Writing to Cottle after Wordsworth's departure, Coleridge conceded that Southey's fluency would certainly make literature '*profitable*'. But his poetry was too uneven:

... his exquisite beauties will lose half their effect from the bad company they keep. Besides I am fearful that he will begin to rely too much on *story* and *event* in his poems, to the neglect of those *lofty imaginings*, that are peculiar to, and definitive of, the poet.

Warming to his theme, Coleridge outlined the way that *he* would approach the writing of an epic poem. His description sounds more like his planned philosophical work than a poem on the Origin of Evil:

Observe the march of Milton – his severe application, his laborious polish, his deep metaphysical researches, his prayers to God before he began his great poem, all that could lift and swell his intellect, became his daily food. I should not think of devoting less than 20 years to an Epic Poem. Ten to collect materials and warm my mind with universal science. I would be a tolerable Mathematician, I would thoroughly know Mechanics, Hydrostatics, Optics, and Astronomy, Botany, Metallurgy, Fossilism, Chemistry, Geology, Anatomy, Medicine – then the *mind of man* – then the *minds of men* – in all Travels, Voyages and Histories. So I would spend ten years – the next five to the composition of the poem – and the five last to the correction of it.[46]

This was not a programme likely to appeal to a practical publisher.

Invigorated by Wordsworth's visit, Coleridge worked with renewed energy after his departure. By 10 May he had written 1,500 lines of his tragedy, now called *Osorio*. Poole was 'in extacies with it', he informed Cottle.[47] Before submitting it to Sheridan, however, he wanted Bowles's criticisms. He planned to visit Bowles and read the tragedy aloud to him. Towards the end of May he sent the preface to the new edition of his poems to Cottle, along with one more new poem, addressed to his brother George, to whom the volume was dedicated, at Cottle's suggestion. (The Reverend George Coleridge was 'displeased and thought his character endangered' by this dedication.) In his preface Coleridge addressed the criticisms that had been made of the first edition. 'I have pruned the double-epithets with no sparing hand; and used my best efforts to tame the swell and glitter both of thought and diction.' But he defended himself robustly against the charge of obscurity: 'if any man expects from my poems the same easiness of style which he admires in a drinking-song, for him I have not written'.

One morning early in June he left Stowey on foot, intending to visit the Wordsworths on his way to see Bowles, who lived at Down-head, near Shaftesbury, on the far side of Dorset. *Osorio* was not quite complete, but Coleridge seemed confident that he could finish it 'in a day or two', while staying with the Wordsworths.[48] At the Unitarian chapel in Bridgwater he preached a sermon on 'The contemptibleness and evil of lukewarmness'. The next morning he breakfasted with Josiah Toulmin, the Unitarian minister in Taunton, before beginning to walk the twenty-odd miles to Racedown. As he neared his destination the landscape began to change, with hills rising to either side of the narrow, winding lanes and swift streams flowing along broad valleys. This was a remote part of the country, with few landmarks to help the traveller. Some time in the afternoon he reached a field-gate, and paused, gazing down towards a house about 150 yards away, where two figures could be seen working in the kitchen garden.

7

COMMUNION

Dorothy first glimpsed Coleridge as he hurtled down towards her, bounding through the corn. It was an image that caught the restless energy of the man himself; in retrospect it would suggest his impatience to be in their company. A moment later he and William were greeting each other joyfully. The next moment she was being introduced to Coleridge, of whom she had of course heard a great deal already. But the reality was much more vivid; like so many others, Dorothy was dazzled by this brilliant young man, whose shining genius was reflected in his sparkling conversation, one minute highlighting some minute detail and the next illuminating some grand philosophical conception. She described her first impressions of Coleridge in a letter to her friend Mary Hutchinson, who had left Racedown only the day before his arrival, after a stay of more than six months:

> You had a great loss in not seeing Coleridge. He is a wonderful man. His conversation teems with soul, mind, and spirit. Then he is so benevolent, so good tempered and cheerful, and, like William, interests himself so much about every little trifle. At first I thought him very plain, that is, for about three minutes: he is pale and thin, has a wide mouth, thick lips, and not very good teeth, longish loose-growing half-curling rough black hair. But if you hear him speak for five minutes you think no more of them. His eye is large and full, not dark but grey; such an eye as would receive from a heavy soul the dullest expression; but it speaks every emotion of his

animated mind; it has more of the 'poet's eye in a fine frenzy rolling'* than I ever witnessed. He has fine dark eyebrows, and an overhanging forehead.[1]

Almost immediately, it seems, the two young men began to discuss their writing: reading their latest works to each other, criticising, and excitedly putting forward suggestions. Within hours – perhaps even minutes – of Coleridge's arrival, Wordsworth was reading aloud his new poem 'The Ruined Cottage' (with which Coleridge seemed 'much delighted'), and after tea Coleridge recited two and a half acts of his tragedy *Osorio*. 'Wordsworth, who is a strict & almost severe critic, thinks *very* highly of it – which gives me great hopes.'[2]

The next morning Wordsworth read Coleridge *The Borderers*. 'His Drama is absolutely wonderful,' Coleridge reported to Cottle; he detected in it 'those *profound* touches of the human heart' found sometimes in Schiller, and often in Shakespeare. 'I speak with heart-felt sincerity & (I think) unblinded judgement, when I tell you, that I feel myself a *little man by his* side; & yet do not think myself the less man, than I formerly thought myself.'[3]

Coleridge's enthusiasm for his work would have been gratifying to Wordsworth, who had not enjoyed much encouragement over the past few years – except, of course, from Dorothy. At Racedown he was isolated; though he invited his friends to visit, very few came. Bereft of intellectual stimulation and lacking like-minded company (apart from that of his sister), he had already leant heavily on the support he received from Coleridge's letters. Now Coleridge was here in his exhilarating person.

Coleridge's gifts were obvious, Wordsworth's less so. He spoke more slowly and less fluently, though with conviction and authority. 'His genius is most *apparent* in poetry,' commented Coleridge after he had lived in close proximity to Wordsworth almost a year, 'and rarely, except to me in *tête à tête*, breaks forth in conversational excellence.'[4] Coleridge recognised Wordsworth's strength of purpose, his single-mindedness and his ambition. Just as he had admired Southey, so he

* *A Midsummer Night's Dream*, V, i.

admired Wordsworth for those qualities in which he felt himself lacking. And Wordsworth's emotional restraint must have been a relief for Coleridge after his experiences with Lloyd.

The two men were still discovering each other, each delighting in what he found. Though very different in character, they had much in common. Both came from respectable families in the middle ranks of society. Both had lost their fathers in boyhood, with catastrophic effects on the family fortune. Both had shown promise at school (Coleridge especially), both had gone to Cambridge with great expectations and failed to live up to them. Neither had settled to a profession. Both were radicals, excited by the Revolution in France and appalled by its aftermath, and both had written passionate political polemics. Neither had much money, nor much prospect of earning any. Both had published poems, and both believed that poetry could have a profound influence on the general culture of the nation. Neither saw any limit to what he might achieve; they thought constantly of the great poets, of Milton in particular. Both, though still young, had decided to withdraw from the world to a place of retirement – in Wordsworth's case Racedown, in Coleridge's Nether Stowey – in order to study, to reflect and to write.

Of course, there were differences between them. One of these was in their attitudes to France. Coleridge was not very interested in France: he never visited the country, and often expressed the prejudices against anything French – 'French morals', for example – typical of Englishmen of the time. Wordsworth, on the other hand, had lived there; he knew the people and had shared in their excitement; he had become emotionally entangled in Revolutionary France – and unravelling this commitment would be a long and painful process for him. Perhaps a more significant difference was religion. 'On one subject we are habitually silent,' wrote Coleridge in May 1798; 'we found our data dissimilar, & never renewed the subject.'[5] Coleridge's Christianity was central to his thinking; while Wordsworth, if not an out-and-out atheist, was certainly not at this stage an orthodox Christian.

From the start Coleridge acknowledged Wordsworth's greater

genius. No praise was too extravagant; within a day or two Coleridge was writing of Wordsworth as 'a great man'. In later years, remembering the impact on him of hearing 'The Ruined Cottage' at this time, he would describe it as 'the finest Poem in our Language' by comparison with any of the same or similar length.[6] Comparing their two tragedies, he saw that Wordsworth's was much superior. Though confident of his own towering talent, Coleridge was content to accept a subsidiary role to Wordsworth, devoting innumerable hours to the correction and improvement of his friend's work. In a way it was odd that he should so readily defer to Wordsworth; although he was more than two years younger, Coleridge was much better known and had achieved much more. Wordsworth was then twenty-seven; Coleridge was still only twenty-four, but he was already a public figure, a radical polemicist and a recognised poet whose work was about to appear in a second edition. By comparison, Wordsworth was a nobody. But Coleridge saw what Wordsworth was capable of, and decided that his calling was to help.

Later that summer Coleridge advised a young man about to meet Wordsworth that he was entering the presence of greatness. 'He has certainly the physiognomical traits of genius,' the young man conceded in a letter to his family: 'a high manly forehead, a full and comprehensive eye, a strong nose to support the superstructure.'[7]

As for Dorothy, Coleridge found her 'exquisite'. It was not that she was pretty, he informed Cottle – but in mind and heart 'she is a woman indeed!' Here was the 'sister' for whom he had always been searching. Her manners were 'simple, ardent, impressive'. He quickly appreciated how her sensibility fed his friend's work, 'her eye watchful in minutest observation of nature – and her taste a perfect electrometer* – it bends, protrudes, and draws in, at subtlest beauties & most recondite faults'.[8] Years later, Thomas De Quincey would

---

* A device for measuring electricity, usually consisting of two delicate gold leaves attached to a metal plate, which bend when an electric current is passed through it. The first true electrometer was created by de Saussure in 1766. There was much research into the nature of electricity in the late eighteenth and early nineteenth centuries; until the destruction of his laboratory, Priestley had been among the most active of English scientists in this area.

describe Dorothy – her gipsy tan, her wild and startling eyes, the glancing quickness of her motions, the powerful feelings that would sometimes cause her to stammer as distressingly as Charles Lamb himself – and remark on the 'exceeding sympathy, always ready and always profound, by which she made all that one could tell her, all that one could describe, all that one could quote from a foreign author, reverberate as it were, *à plusieurs reprises*, to one's own feelings, by the manifest impression it made upon her'. Such intense attention from a young woman was something any man might enjoy. Though 'her knowledge of literature was irregular', continued De Quincey, 'she was a person of very remarkable endowments intellectually'. In this respect she was 'very much superior' to Sara Coleridge, who was unable to appreciate or even to comprehend her husband's genius.[9]

'I am sojourning for a few days at Racedown, the mansion of our friend Wordsworth,' Coleridge wrote complacently to Cottle. Indeed it was idyllic for these three young people to be together in such an elegant house, surrounded by lovely countryside (bursting with life in those early summer days), with nothing to do but talk about those subjects which interested them most deeply. Coleridge found the company so compelling that he repeatedly prolonged his stay. Despite his original intention, he does not seem to have done much work on *Osorio*; it was still unfinished when he left, meaning that the visit to Bowles had to be postponed. He did keep on correcting and adding to his poems, though the sheets of the new volume were already printed and bound. The obliging Cottle patiently printed a list of errata – but even after this Coleridge came up with a dozen or so further changes, which Dorothy wrote out for him. He proposed that Cottle should employ a boy to go through the printed volumes and make the changes by hand, 'with a fine pen, and dainty ink'.[10] Cottle did not take up this suggestion.

Eventually, after more than three weeks had passed, Coleridge decided that he must go back to Nether Stowey. Even now he and Wordsworth could not be parted, so it was agreed that Wordsworth should accompany him. Coleridge promised to return for Dorothy. At the cottage he found a letter from Lamb, who had at last been permitted to take time off from his work at the East India Office and proposed coming down to Stowey the following week. Coleridge was delighted at the thought of seeing his old friend again after such a long time, and excited by the thought of bringing him together with the Wordsworths – though his wife may have been less enthusiastic about the prospect of accommodating three guests in such a small cottage. Nor was this the limit, for Thelwall was expected imminently, and Coleridge decided to invite Cottle too to join the party. 'Could you not contrive to put yourself in a Bridgwater Coach – & T. Poole would fetch you in a one horse chair* to Stowey,' he wrote to Cottle. 'What delight would it not give us.' Cottle did not come, perhaps a relief to Sara. A few days later Coleridge returned to Racedown in a cart – almost certainly lent by Poole – to collect Dorothy, priding himself on driving her expertly over 'forty miles of execrable road'.

Dorothy responded immediately to the Quantocks:

> There is everything here; sea, woods wild as fancy ever painted, brooks clear and pebbly as in Cumberland, villages so romantic; and William and I, in a wander by ourselves, found out a sequestered waterfall in a dell formed by steep hills covered with full-grown trees. The woods are as fine as those at Lowther, and the country more romantic; it has the character of the less grand parts of the Lakes . . .[11]

The waterfall quickly became a favourite spot, where Wordsworth later composed his 'Lines Written in Early Spring'. Nearly half a century afterwards, he recalled it as 'a chosen resort of mine':

> The brook fell down a sloping rock so as to make a waterfall considerable for that country, and across the pool below had fallen a tree, an ash, if I rightly remember, from which rose perpendicularly boughs in search of the light intercepted by the deep shade above. The boughs bore leaves of green that for want of sunshine had faded into almost lily-white; and from the underside of this natural sylvan bridge depended long and beautiful tresses of ivy which waved gently in the breeze that might poetically speaking be called the breath of

* A simple cart.

the waterfall. This motion varied of course in proportion to the power of water in the brook.[12]

Very soon Dorothy and her brother began to dream of living in the area, perhaps in the 'little cottage' they had so long imagined.

Lamb arrived soon after Dorothy, having travelled from London to Bridgwater on the outside of a coach. In such a crowded and no doubt noisy household he was a little tongue-tied, but he afterwards claimed to have enjoyed his visit, even if he did not show it at the time. Coleridge wanted very much to show his friends around, and took them to meet Poole – but he was prevented from joining them on their rambles into the countryside by an accident: Sara, perhaps struggling with the demands of this influx of guests as well as those of her own husband and infant, spilt boiling milk on his foot, so scalding him that he was unable to hobble more than a couple of hundred yards. The injury confined him to the environs of the cottage the whole week that Lamb was there. One evening, while the three visitors were out on a walk, a frustrated Coleridge sat in the bower at the end of Poole's garden and composed another 'conversation poem', picturing in powerful images what 'my Sister and my Friends' might be seeing, and in the process overcoming his desire to be with them. 'This Lime-Tree Bower My Prison' was a further development of the new style he had initiated in 'The Eolian Harp'. It was full of characteristic verbal inventiveness – the 'overwooded' dell, the 'unsunn'd' ash, 'those fronting elms' – now used to accompany detailed description of natural forms, in a manner surely influenced by Dorothy. Underlying the poem was a philosophical acceptance of the unity of all nature: the idea that Coleridge would come to describe as the 'One Life'.

Cottle visited Nether Stowey soon after Lamb's departure. Coleridge proudly showed him around the house and garden. 'Mr C. took peculiar delight in assuring me (at least, at that time) how happy he was,' Cottle recorded. Afterwards they sat with Poole in the arbour, where a table had been laid with 'delicious' bread and cheese, accompanied by a jug of 'true Taunton ale'. With blue sky overhead, dappled sunlight beneath the canopy, and birdsong filling the air, it was an idyllic scene. The friends talked happily, and when Sara Coleridge approached with her infant son, 'the father's eye beamed transcendental joy'.[13]

Another visitor, a young man of means who may have been sizing up Coleridge as a possible tutor, was equally impressed. 'I have seen domestic life in all its beauty and simplicity,' he wrote to his brother, 'affection founded on a much stronger basis than wealth – on esteem.' He was taken with Mrs Coleridge, whom he thought 'sensible, affable and good natured, thrifty and industrious, and always neat and prettily dressed'. She was 'indeed a pretty woman'.[14]

Coleridge's domestic happiness and his delight in his new friends may have encouraged him to try to cut back on his opium use, with distressing side-effects. Wordsworth was a witness to the violent attacks of internal pain that 'sometimes caused him, when we walked together in Somersetshire, to throw himself down and writhe like a worm upon the ground'.[15]

Their walks onto the Quantocks often took the Wordsworths by a small village called Holford, about three miles from Nether Stowey, at the mouth of two combes formed by streams trickling down from the hills. A track led up from the village onto the ridge through an avenue of ancient beech trees. And above the waterfall the Wordsworths followed a drive leading through a deer park towards an apparently unoccupied mansion nestling on the northern slopes of the Quantocks and overlooking the sea, only two miles away. It was a fine house, with a pediment above the central of three bays and a Tuscan porch overhanging the front door. Poole identified the building as Alfoxden* Park, until recently the home of the Reverend Lancelot St Albyn, who had died childless. His widow let the estate to a local farmer, who confirmed that the house was available to rent; and Wordsworth, acting with uncharacteristic impetuousness, decided to take it. On the face of it this was a surprising decision. Alfoxden was

---

* Or so the Wordsworths usually spelt it, but the correct spelling is Alfoxton.

a spacious house, in a beautiful setting – but then so was Racedown. Why should the Wordsworths, dependent on a small and uncertain income, give up a house where they were living rent-free in favour of one for which they had to pay, indeed one that provided far more than they needed? The cost of Alfoxden was comparatively low, considering what they had for it, but nonetheless it was almost half their annual income, and nearly three times as much as Coleridge paid for his cottage. If, as has been suggested, the Wordsworths had been given notice that they would soon need to quit Racedown, why not look for somewhere more modest? In fact they would contemplate returning to Racedown once their year's lease on Alfoxden had expired,[16] indicating their belief that they might have continued to live there had they so wished. Lamb, who had left their company only a day or two before, maybe only hours before Wordsworth signed the lease, seems to have been quite unaware that they might stay in the area. 'Are Wordsworth and his sister gone yet?' he enquired from London on his return.[17]

In a letter to Mary Hutchinson, Dorothy explained the reason for their sudden decision: 'Our principal inducement was Coleridge's society.'[18] The importance of this eclipsed all other considerations. Both men were in a state of high excitement; both felt it essential not to be parted.

The Wordsworths moved into Alfoxden on 16 July, having been a fortnight at Nether Stowey. Plans were made for a celebratory dinner the following Sunday. A few days afterwards Wordsworth returned to Racedown to collect Basil and their servant Peggy. Coleridge and his wife stayed with the Wordsworths on their first night in the new home, while little Hartley remained at the cottage under the care of their servant. Sara returned to Stowey the next morning to superintend the washing, leaving Coleridge behind 'for change of air'. From Alfoxden he wrote exultantly to Southey:

> I had been on a visit to Wordsworth's at Racedown near Crewkherne – and I brought him & his Sister back with me & here I have *settled them* – . By a combination of curious circumstances a gentleman's seat, with a park & woods,

elegantly & completely *furnished* – with 9 *lodging rooms*, three parlours & a Hall – in a most beautiful & romantic situation by the sea side – 4 miles from Stowey – this we have got for Wordsworth at the rent of £23 *a year, taxes included*!!

Alfoxden's size meant that it could accommodate plenty of guests, and over the coming months a succession of visitors would arrive to stay. Coleridge himself was in and out of the house. On Wordsworth's behalf he issued an invitation to Southey and Edith, offering them a suite of rooms and even promising to collect them from where they were living, near Ringwood in Hampshire. It would provide an opportunity for Edith and Sara to see each other, suggested Coleridge, '& Wordsworth is very solicitous to know you'. It would be good for Southey's poetry, too: 'so divine and wild is the country that I am sure it would increase your stock of images'. Coleridge was undoubtedly sincere in wanting Southey to join them, yet in praising his new friend he could not avoid a glancing blow at the old one. 'Wordsworth is a very great man,' he wrote to Southey, 'the only man, to whom *at all times* & in *all modes of excellence* I feel myself inferior – the only one, I mean, whom I *have yet met with.*'[19]

In the year that followed Wordsworth and Coleridge would meet almost daily, and were frequently together for weeks without parting. This was their *annus mirabilis,* when each man's talent would ripen into maturity, and bear marvellous fruit; the year when they 'together wantoned in wild Poesy'. Wordsworth's phrase* catches the sense in which roaming and writing were intertwined, the one supplying energy to the other; and the careless rapture of this time of discovery, each man relishing the other's company. It was, perhaps, a kind of love.

The affectionate friendship between these two in those idyllic Quantock months might seem as perfect as any that could be conceived. In this period of communion, each found in the other qualities that he had been searching for. The solitariness of the creative

* From the revised version of the poem. The original phrase was 'wandered in wild Poesy'.

individual was relieved, for a while; in the euphoria of sharing, doubts disappeared and insecurities faded. The barriers of rivalry and reserve were removed, allowing thought and feeling to flow freely. Often they wrote at the same table. They read their work to each other, and exchanged criticism and advice. Several of the poems later claimed by one of them contained lines or even whole stanzas written by the other. Regular scrutiny quickened the resolve. Words raced across the paper. They jokingly referred to themselves as 'the Concern', a 'commercial or manufacturing establishment' for the production of verse.

Their conversations turned frequently on the nature of poetry, as they sought new forms with which to express ideas and impressions. In Coleridge, Wordsworth encountered a mind of apparently limitless capabilities, interested in every aspect of human enquiry: a mind moreover nourished by encyclopaedic reading. Wordsworth too possessed a powerful mind, one less analytical than Coleridge's but nonetheless perpetually probing the sublime, a disciplined mind that fed on a rich hinterland of experience.

In the last book of *The Prelude*, Wordsworth would look back towards the sweet memory of

> That summer, under whose indulgent skies,
> Upon smooth Quantock's airy ridge we roved
> Unchecked, or loitered 'mid her sylvan coombs[20]

These two spent much of the time outside, rambling with Dorothy and glorying in the natural beauty of their surroundings, which itself became the subject of so much of what they wrote. Often they walked out after dark, attracting suspicion from the locals. Philosophical discussion was interrupted by the need to take note of clouds, of light, of the moon, of leaves, or flowers: images that embellished their work.

Such sharing drew these three young people closer together. Their hearts and minds were opened to each other. Coleridge has been quoted as saying of this time that they were 'three people, but one soul',* and though the occasion of this Spenserian echo has not been traced, it seems an accurate description of how they felt.† Each was intensely interested to understand the other two, and each luxuriated in the happiness of being understood. Laughter punctuated their conversations. Coleridge was sensitive to the tender feeling that existed between William and Dorothy. He referred to her as 'our sister', and indeed he and Wordsworth were as brothers. Following the convention of their time, the two men usually addressed each other by their surnames, but this did not imply any distance between them – on the contrary, Coleridge detested his two Christian names and disliked their use. Dorothy too addressed him as 'Coleridge', while other intimate male friends such as Lamb and Poole addressed him as 'Col'.‡ Sara was one of the few to call him 'Samuel'.

Dorothy's keen observation delighted Coleridge, and he began to draw on it just as her brother did. He developed a respect for her taste, and sought her approval of his work. Indeed, he was so chastened by her response to one of his reviews (which he had assumed would amuse her) that he burnt them all.[22] For her part, Dorothy was captivated by Coleridge's company. She was content to share her brother with one who seemed to admire him as much as she did herself, recognising that as a fellow poet Coleridge offered him something she could not provide. Only Coleridge's wife was a discordant presence, and she was hardly ever included in their rambles.

'Is the Patriot come yet?' asked Lamb from London. 'I was looking out for John Thelwall all the way from Bridgwater, and had I met

* These three did loue each other dearely well,
And with so firme affection were allyde,
As if but one soule in them all did dwell,
Which did her powre into three parts diuyde;
Like three faire branches budding farre and wide,
That from one roote deriu'd their vitall sap.
Spenser, The Faerie Queene, IV, ii, 43, ll.1–6
† 'Tho' we were three persons, it was but one God,' he wrote a few years afterwards.[21] This remark was made at least partly in jest.
‡ At school Coleridge had been known as 'Colly'. Possibly his name was pronounced by his friends with a short 'o' rather than the long one conventionally used by posterity.

him, I think it would have moved almost me to tears.'[23] Poor Thelwall was been persecuted wherever he went; he would write later that he had been 'hunted from society'.[24] Like Coleridge he was in retreat from active participation in politics,* and now was seeking a refuge where he and his family might live quietly.

He appeared at Nether Stowey around nine o'clock in the evening of 17 July 1797, having walked from London. The Wordsworths had moved into Alfoxden the day before; Coleridge was still there, but Sara had returned to the cottage to oversee the washing, and she allowed the exhausted Thelwall to sleep that night in Coleridge's 'cot'. Early the next morning he and Sara strolled over to Alfoxden, arriving in time for breakfast.

Though they had been in correspondence for more than a year, this was Coleridge's first glimpse of Thelwall, who proved to be a stout little man with dark cropped hair, merry and energetic. Immediately they resumed the good-humoured banter that had marked their correspondence. When Thelwall teased him about the weeds in his garden, Coleridge responded by likening them to children, in a sly dig at Thelwall's liberal beliefs about the education of children. 'John Thelwall is a very warm hearted honest man,' Coleridge wrote to a friend in Bristol, 'and disagreeing, as we do, on almost every point of religion, of morals, of politics, and of philosophy; we like each other uncommonly well.'[25]

Thelwall was full of enthusiasm for 'the Academus of Stowey', as he described it in a letter to his wife written soon after his arrival. He informed her that he was seriously thinking of settling in this 'friendly retreat':

> We have been having a delightful ramble today among the plantations, and along a wild, romantic dell in these grounds, through which a foaming, rushing, murmuring torrent of water winds its long artless course. There have we ... a literary and political triumvirate, passed sentence on the productions and characters of the age, burst forth in poetical

---

* Though, as E.P. Thompson has pointed out, he had not retreated altogether; see below.

flights of enthusiasm, and philosophised our minds into a state of tranquillity, which the leaders of nations might envy, and the residents of cities can never know . . . Faith, we are a most philosophical party.

While the three of them sat together on the grass overlooking the now-favourite glen, with the sound of rushing water ringing in their ears, Coleridge addressed his newfound friend. 'Citizen John!' he declared, 'this is a fine place to talk treason in!' – 'Nay! Citizen Samuel!' replied Thelwall, 'it is rather a place to make a man forget that there is any necessity for treason!'[26]

They stayed three days at Alfoxden, and then walked back as a group to Nether Stowey, talking of many things – among them the moral character of democrats and of aristocrats, and the 'pursuits proper for literary men', who, it was generally agreed, were 'unfit for management of pecuniary affairs'.[27]

Coleridge's excitement is obvious in a short note he sent Poole, soliciting a redundant coat and some half-silk stockings: 'You shall be my Elijah,' he wrote, '& I will most reverentially catch the Mantle, which you have cast off.'

Why should not a Bard go tight & have a few neat things on his back? Ey? – Eh! – Eh![28]

On the Sunday fourteen people sat down to dinner at Alfoxden, to feast on lamb provided by Poole. Guests had been invited to a reading of The Borderers under the trees beforehand. After dinner Thelwall stood up to make an impromptu speech, and 'he talked so loud and was in such a passion' that a local man hired to wait at table was frightened; his account of goings-on at Alfoxden spread quickly from servant to servant, and confirmed stories of the alarming behaviour of its new occupants. That very same day Poole's cousin Charlotte registered in her journal how she and her family were 'shocked to hear that Mr Thelwall has spent some time at Stowey this week with Mr Coleridge, and consequently with Tom'. She noted that Alfoxden had been taken by 'one of the fraternity', and asked herself: 'To what are we coming?'[29]

Thelwall stayed a few more days before setting off to Bristol, hoping to return soon with his family. He seems to have asked Coleridge to find a house for him in the area. On his journey to Bristol he put his hopes into verse; his 'Lines written at Bridgwater, in Somersetshire, on the 27th of July, 1797; During a Long Excursion, in Quest of a Peaceful Retreat' were addressed to 'My Samuel',

> . . . best-belov'd of friends!
> Long-loved ere known: for kindred sympathies
> Link'd, tho far distant, our congenial souls.

In the poem Thelwall imagined how life would be if they were neighbours:

> Ah! 'twould be sweet, beneath the neighb'ring thatch,
> In philosophic amity to dwell,
> Inditing moral verse, or tale, or theme,
> Gay or instructive; and it would be sweet,
> With kindly interchange of mutual aid,
> To delve our little garden plots, the while
> Sweet converse flow'd, suspending oft the arm
> And half-driven spade, while, eager, one propounds,
> And listens one, weighing each pregnant word,
> And pondering fit reply . . .

When their daily toil was over, he pictured them seated 'alternate, in each other's bowers' in summer and by a 'blazing hearth' in winter, sharing 'frugal viands' and 'home-brew'd beverage', their wives by their sides,

> . . . and, perchance,
> Allfoxden's musing tenant, and the maid
> Of ardent eye, who, with fraternal love,
> Sweetens his solitude . . .

This was a Pantisocratic vision indeed, and one that Coleridge encouraged – but it was soon expunged. News of the 'very suspicious business' at Alfoxden reached Bath, where the loyal Dr Daniel Lysons heard of it from his cook and promptly despatched a letter on the subject to the Duke of Portland, the Home Secretary. In a follow-up letter, Lysons informed the Duke that 'the master of the House has no wife with him, but only a woman who passes for his Sister'; that they went on excursions day and night, carrying camp-stools and a portfolio in which they entered observations; they had been overheard to say that these were 'almost finished' and that 'they should be rewarded for them'; and that they had been 'very attentive to a River near them'. This 'emigrant family' spoke in a strange accent; it was thought that they might be French. One incriminating detail was their habit of 'washing and Mending their Cloaths all Sunday'. An agent was ordered to Somerset to investigate.

Coleridge soon learned of the agent's presence from a local inn-keeper. In *Biographia Literaria* twenty years later he gave a satirical account of this ludicrous episode, depicting the 'truly Indian persever-ance' of the spy (as he called him), who lurked for hours behind a bank to eavesdrop on his conversations with Wordsworth. According to Coleridge, the spy feared that he had been discovered when he overheard mention of the philosopher Spinoza – which he interpreted as 'Spy Nozy'. The inquisitive agent's 'Bardolph nose' added colour to the story.

Coleridge imagined the landlord's interrogation by 'Sir Dogberry', a local bigwig:

> D. Has he not been seen wandering on the hills towards the Channel, with books and papers in his hand, taking charts and maps of the country? L. Why, as to that, your honour! I own, I have heard; I am sure I would not wish to say ill of anybody; but it is certain that I have heard – D. Speak out, man! Don't be afraid; you are doing your duty to your King and government. What have you heard? L. Why, folks do say, your honour! As how he is a Poet . . .

At the time, however, it did not seem so amusing as it did in retro-spect. In reality the agent was a good deal more sophisticated than the caricature Coleridge had drawn, and he swiftly identified the Alfoxden 'gang' as 'a Sett of violent Democrats' rather than French-men or French spies. One of them was 'the famous Thelwall' – though he had since left the vicinity, as the Duke knew from the Mayor of Bristol, who reported to him that Thelwall had attempted to convene a meeting of the Corresponding Society in the city at the end of July.[30]

It seems to have been decided at an official level that no further surveillance of 'those Rascalls from Alfoxton' was necessary. But the agent's visit had brought out local opposition to the presence of these 'Jacobins' in the neighbourhood. Coleridge became anxious that they might be driven out of the area: 'the Aristocrats seem determined to persecute, *even Wordsworth*'.[31] To the unsophisticated mind, 'French' politics implied 'French' morals, and scandalous rumours spread about the strange tenants of Alfoxden. It was suspected that they might not be brother and sister, as they pretended; the presence among them of an apparently parentless child (Basil Montagu) increased the speculation. 'There was nothing too bad for the rustics to believe,' observed a newcomer to the area (who arrived long after the Wordsworths had departed, but while there were still some around who remembered them).[32] Alarmed by what she heard, Mrs St Albyn made it known that the lease would not be renewed when it fell due the following summer. Though Poole intervened with her on Wordsworth's behalf, she would prove implacable. Poole's letter was by no means completely frank about the circumstances of Thelwall's visit; it may have been drafted by Coleridge.

After consulting both Poole and John Chubb, a prosperous Bridgwater merchant and former Mayor who was a close friend of Charles James Fox, Coleridge wrote to retract his invitation to Thelwall:

> Very great odium T. Poole incurred by bringing *me* here –
> my peaceable manners & known attachment to Christianity
> had almost worn it away – when Wordsworth came & he
> likewise by T. Poole's agency settled here – You cannot con-
> ceive the tumult, calumnies, & apparatus of threatened per-
> secutions which this event has occasioned round about us. If
> *you* too should come, I am afraid, that even riots & dangerous
> riots might be the consequence . . .[33]

Coleridge was ready to sacrifice Thelwall's company to safeguard Wordsworth's continuing presence in the neighbourhood.[34]

Thelwall eventually found a refuge at Llyswen, in the Wye Valley. He does not seem to have resented Coleridge's withdrawal of sanctuary – at least not obviously so, because he did not break off their correspondence, but on the contrary continued their philosophical debate. In a letter now lost, written about six weeks after Coleridge had urged him not to come back to Stowey, Thelwall appears to have evoked the splendours of natural beauty and the majesty of the universe. Responding, Coleridge expressed his yearning for the sublime:

> I can *at times* feel strongly the beauties, you describe, in themselves, & for themselves – but more frequently *all things* appear to me little – all the knowledge, that can be acquired, child's play – the universe itself – what but an immense heap of *little* things? – I can contemplate nothing but parts, & parts are all *little–*! – My mind feels as if it ached to behold & know something *great* – something *one & indivisible* – and it is only in the faith of this that rocks or waterfalls, mountains or caverns give me the sense of sublimity or majesty! – But in this faith *all things* counterfeit infinity![35]

Mystery surrounds 'Kubla Khan'. No one can be sure exactly when it was written; such evidence as exists points to several different dates. The confusion is exacerbated by the fact that it was not published until almost twenty years afterwards. Indeed, it may not have been 'written' in the same way as most poems; Coleridge referred to it as 'a vision in a dream', as if it came to him without any effort of composition. No one even knows whether it is complete; Coleridge describes it as a 'fragment', but there is a case for doubting this. Maybe it is not a poem at all. Hazlitt called it 'a musical composition'; Lamb described to Wordsworth the enchanting effect of hearing Coleridge 'while he sings or says it'. Though literary detectives have uncovered some of its sources, it remains difficult to say what the poem is about. Lamb feared 'lest it should be discovered by the lantern of typography and clear reducing to letters, no better than nonsense or no sense'.[36]

Coleridge provided some background in a note to the printed

poem. 'In the summer of the year 1797,' he began, 'the Author, then in ill-health, had retired to a lonely farmhouse between Porlock and Linton, on the Exmoor confines of Somerset and Devonshire.' This was (and still is) a very quiet part of the country, about a day's walk west of the Quantocks. Here the land rises so steeply from the sea that no road can follow the coastline; a path winds up from Porlock Weir to the smallest parish church in England, mysteriously isolated in woodland. Further inland, a few scattered farms are linked by sunken lanes, fringed by high hedges. Coleridge may have called at one of these for food and shelter on one of his exploratory walks along the coast.

In another note to a manuscript copy of the poem (probably written at an earlier date), Coleridge recorded that it was written 'at a Farm House between Porlock & Linton, a quarter of a mile from Culbone Church, in the fall of the year, 1797'. Such statements of Coleridge's have to be considered sceptically, since he was often maddeningly inaccurate about dates. But given these two notes, and in the absence of definite evidence to the contrary, it seems reasonable to assume that the poem was written during the latter half of 1797. From what is known of his activities then, it is possible to identify a gap when 'Kubla Khan' could have been written in the circumstances Coleridge describes.

Early in September Coleridge made his postponed visit to Bowles, taking with him the manuscript of *Osorio*, not quite complete even then. On his return to Stowey he was anxious to finish the tragedy and revise it as Bowles had suggested. He admitted that he had 'fagged so long at the work', and now saw so many imperfections in the plot, that he was sick of it; but he 'could not avoid attaching a pecuniary importance to the business'. It was difficult to find somewhere to work, however, because Charles Lloyd had returned to the cottage, and there were visitors staying at Alfoxden. Some time early in October Coleridge was away from home for a few days, and it may have been then that he 'retired' to the lonely farmhouse, seeking a quiet retreat where he could finish *Osorio* undisturbed. A few days after his return he was at last able to send Bowles the tragedy 'complete & neatly transcribed' for onward transmission to Sheridan.[37]

Coleridge's letter to Thelwall in mid-October refers to a recent absence from home, and contains images similar to those used in the poem, tending to corroborate this as the time when 'Kubla Khan' was written. He expressed a desire to 'float about along an infinite ocean cradled in the flower of a lotos', waking 'once in a million years for a few minutes – just to know that I was going to sleep a million years more'. This imagery strongly suggests the recent use of opium.

In the manuscript note Coleridge claimed that the poem had been composed 'in a sort of Reverie brought on by two grains of Opium, taken to check a dysentery'. In the published note he describes this reverie in more detail.

> The Author continued for about three hours in a profound sleep, at least of the external senses, during which time he has the most vivid confidence, that he could not have composed less than from two to three hundred lines; if that indeed can be called composition in which all the images rose up before him as *things*, with a parallel production of the correspondent expressions, without any sensation of consciousness or effort.

This metaphor of composition (if it can be so described) develops the idea of the Aeolian harp, of the poet as the passive recipient of the divine breeze.

What happened next is one of the most famous stories in the history of literature. On awakening, Coleridge took pen and paper and began to write down the lines that had so miraculously formed in his mind – until he was unfortunately interrupted 'by a person on business from Porlock', who detained him for more than a hour. When eventually free of this distraction, he found that the remaining lines were gone, leaving only 'a vague and dim memory of the general purport of the vision', and 'some eight or ten scattered lines or images'. He had fifty-four lines on paper; the rest was lost.

Whether or not this story is true is a subject that has been endlessly debated, and can never be resolved, unless new evidence emerges. But of course that does not really matter. The poem stands for itself: beautiful, sensuous and enigmatic.

One Thursday in mid-September, after Coleridge's return from seeing Bowles, Charles Lloyd went over to Alfoxden to hear Wordsworth read *The Borderers*. Coleridge remained behind at the cottage with a sore throat. Wordsworth too was ill, but nevertheless he and Dorothy pressed Lloyd to stay, as they were expecting an imminent visit from John Wedgwood and his younger brother Tom, a friend of Basil Montagu. 'This, as you may suppose was no great inducement,' Lloyd confided to Southey, 'but not having any important reason to alledge, for not accepting his invitation I intend staying till Monday.'[38] Lloyd's comment suggests he thought the Wedgwoods bores.

They were sons of the famous Staffordshire potter, who had died in 1795, leaving his children a fortune of more than half a million pounds. John, the eldest brother, was a banker who lived at Cote House, on the outskirts of Bristol; the next, Josiah, succeeded his father in managing the family business; the youngest, Tom,* was a chemist, an inventor, an early pioneer of photography, and a philanthropist who gave generously to individuals and institutions he thought worthy of support. Tom Wedgwood had a keen interest in metaphysics and a perilous fascination with psychotropic drugs. He suffered from a chronic intestinal disease, and was under the long-term care of Coleridge's friend Dr Beddoes in Bristol, often staying with his elder brother at Cote House. Their father, who had been a close associate of Joseph Priestley and Erasmus Darwin,† was thought radical enough to have been in danger of arrest at the time of the treason trials,[39] and the brothers too were 'French' in politics: Tom had spent some time in Paris in the summer of 1792, during the jittery period when the Assembly had declared '*la patrie en danger*'. Subsequently he had met Godwin in London and become interested in Godwin's ideas about education. Godwin and Montagu had

---

* Midway in age between Wordsworth and Coleridge.
† All three were 'lunar men'.

recently visited Tom in Staffordshire; Montagu was hoping to marry one of his sisters. In a letter to Godwin written after they had met, Tom Wedgwood envisaged a new school for genius, where the future leaders of mankind would be raised. 'I have been endeavouring some masterstroke which should anticipate a century or two upon the lazy-paced progress of human improvement,' he wrote boldly. The 'chaos of perceptions' would be simplified, 'unproductive occupation' eliminated, and the environment strictly regulated to encourage earnest thought. 'Romping, tickling and fooling' would be forbidden, and no time allowed for 'solitary musing'. The nursery would have plain grey walls so as not to distract the children, and would be hung with hard objects 'so as continually to irritate their palms'. They would never be permitted to go out of doors or leave their apartment. The school would be governed by a committee of philosophers, including Godwin, Beddoes, Holcroft, Horne Tooke and Wedgwood himself, and run by one or two superintendents – 'the only persons that I know of as at all likely for this purpose, are Wordsworth and Coleridge'. He had not then met either, but from what he had been told he believed that Wordsworth had many of the requisite qualities, and would 'come forward with alacrity' once he was convinced that this was 'the most promising mode of benefiting society'. As for Coleridge, he was said to have considerable talents, 'like Wordsworth's, quite disengaged' – though he might be 'too much a poet and religionist to suit our views'.[40]

It seems that Wedgwood had come down from Bristol to discuss this ambitious scheme with his suggested superintendents. Two years before, while he was still under the influence of Godwin, Wordsworth might have considered such a proposition; but now it was anathema to him. To coop up a child indoors, to attempt to limit his sensory experience, not to allow him time for reflection – this was the very antithesis of the method William and Dorothy had adopted with such success for young Basil Montagu. As for Coleridge, he was even less likely to sympathise with such a scheme.

The Wedgwood brothers spent several days in the Quantocks, visiting Nether Stowey as well as Alfoxden, where Tom Wedgwood formed a strong friendship with Tom Poole. At some stage when Coleridge was present, Wedgwood made a disparaging remark about Wordsworth. Coleridge retorted fiercely, 'He strides on so far before you, that he dwindles in the distance!'

Cottle drove down to Nether Stowey in a gig, bringing with him Wordsworth, who had been visiting Bristol for a few days.[41] They called at the cottage, then drove on to Alfoxden, while Coleridge, Dorothy and a servant girl followed on foot. The visitors had brought with them 'philosophers' viands', on which (supplemented by lettuces from the garden) they proposed to dine: a bottle of brandy, a loaf and 'a stout piece of cheese'. A little before the gig drove into the courtyard, they discovered that the cheese had gone – taken, Cottle had no doubt, 'while we were gazing at the magnificent clouds', by a beggar to whom they had given a lift. 'Mr Coleridge bore the loss with great fortitude, observing that we should never starve with a loaf of bread, and a bottle of brandy.' The brave poet unbuckled the horse 'with the dexterity of an adept'; and as the released shafts of the gig dropped, the bottle of brandy that had been placed carefully on the seat behind the passengers rolled forward, fell to the ground and smashed to pieces. Everyone stood around in horror, sniffing the spilled brandy. Cottle led the horse to the stables, where 'a fresh perplexity arose'. He was able to remove the harness without difficulty, but he could not remove the collar. Coleridge next tried his hand, but he was no more successful, declaring that the horse's head must have grown since the collar was put on. The servant girl then showed them how it was done, upending the collar so that it slipped off easily.

They were summoned in to dinner. At the top of the table stood 'a superb brown loaf', and in the centre a pile of Kos lettuces. At the other end, an empty plate indicated where the missing cheese would have been placed. Instead of the brandy, the hosts had broken out a supply of sparkling Castilian champagne. One of those present suggested that salt might render the lettuces a little more palatable. 'Indeed, sir,' replied the servant girl, 'I quite forgot to buy salt.' A 'general laugh' followed this announcement, and the meal cheerfully com-

menced, those present pitying 'the far worse condition of those, per-
chance as hungry as ourselves, who were forced to dine, off ether alone'.

'Kubla Khan' was anomalous in being written in isolation. Most of
Wordsworth and Coleridge's poems dating from this period were
composed by one poet under the critical eye of the other. One can
only surmise at the extent of their co-operation from the odd anecdote, and from influences scholars have detected in the texts themselves. Often a poem written by one alludes to a poem by the other;
thus in 'Tintern Abbey' Wordsworth uses a phrase from 'This Lime-
Tree Bower My Prison', a mark of how much his poem owed to the
style of poetry developed by Coleridge. This was a type of dialogue,
or perhaps a duet, in which one musician picks up and develops a
theme from the other. It was a subtle exchange, not always obvious
to the reader, or even subsequently to the scholar with access to the
original manuscripts. Both poets seem to have drawn on the same
commonplace books, and on the journal that Dorothy began to keep
early in 1798, recording details noticed by any of the three of them
while these were still fresh.*

A single anecdote exemplifies the kind of co-operation that must
surely have happened in other, unrecorded cases. Wordsworth's 'We
are Seven' was largely composed while he was walking to and fro 'in
the Grove' at Alfoxden, and many years later he gave an account of
how it was completed.

> When it was all but finished, I came in and recited it to Mr.
> Coleridge and my Sister, and said, 'A prefatory stanza must
> be added, and I should sit down to our little tea-meal with
> greater pleasure if my task was finished.'
> I mentioned in substance what I wished to be expressed, and
> Coleridge immediately threw off the stanza . . .[42]

As a further twist, Coleridge would later allude to the opening line
of this stanza in the conclusion to the second part of 'Christabel'.

* Possibly the degree to which the poets drew on Dorothy's journal has been exaggerated.
Coincidences are to be expected, since they spent so much time walking together, and
shared their observations as they walked.

Thus in one of his own poems Coleridge alluded to a line he had contributed to one of Wordsworth's.

In several instances the two men attempted closer collaboration. For example, soon after arriving at Alfoxden, Wordsworth abandoned 'The Three Graves', a projected ballad-drama of spurned love and a terrible curse. He had already written at least a hundred lines before giving these to Coleridge, who wrote a further four hundred or so lines before abandoning the poem in turn.

Early in November, Coleridge and the two Wordsworths returned after several days exploring the coast west as far as Lynmouth and beyond, into the Valley of the Rocks, a desolate place of scattered boulders and towering peaks of stone. At one end a gap in the cliff provides a view of the sea below. The streamless valley seems incongruous, more like the Highlands of Scotland than the English West Country. Coleridge was inspired by this strange, prehistoric landscape to propose a collaborative work in three cantos, 'The Wanderings of Cain'. It was to be written in a single night; the plan was for the two men to write separately and simultaneously: whoever was first to complete a canto was to set about the third. Having written his canto 'at finger-speed', Coleridge hastened to see how his friend had progressed, only to see a look of humorous despondency on Wordsworth's face, and an almost blank sheet of paper on his table. The experiment broke up in a laugh, and 'a sense of the exceeding ridiculousness of the whole scheme'. Thirty years afterwards, Coleridge reflected that it was impracticable 'for a mind so eminently original to compose another man's thoughts and fancies'.

At the time, however, he and Wordsworth were certainly open to further collaborative schemes. A week or so after their return from the Valley of the Rocks, the three walkers again set out along the coast westwards. They hoped to defray the expense of the tour by together writing a poem for the recently established *Monthly Magazine*. This was a liberal miscellany edited by the Unitarian physician Dr John Aikin, a friend of Priestley's; like *The Watchman*, it was intended to appeal to 'persons of free enquiry'. Its first number had lamented that the 'grand, the sublime, the Shakespearian, and the Miltonic, seem beyond the grasp of modern bards' – a challenge to ambitious young poets. In August Coleridge had travelled to Bristol to meet Aikin's sister, the writer Mrs Barbauld, who was herself involved with the magazine; and it seems that this meeting* left Coleridge with the expectation that the publishers might pay £5 for a ballad on a super-natural theme. A Stowey friend described to Coleridge a disturbing dream of a spectral ship, and it is possible that he floated this idea past Mrs Barbauld. Tales of the supernatural were certainly very popular at the time. 'Monk' Lewis's† play *The Castle Spectre*, which received its first performance at the Drury Lane Theatre in London towards the end of the year, is said to have earned a remarkable £18,000 in the first three months of its run. Coleridge had been 'devilishly severe' on the Gothic novels he had reviewed, and had enjoyed poking fun at their excesses, but he was not too fastidious to indulge such tastes if this was what the public wanted.

The three set out at half past four in the afternoon, just as it was getting dark. 'The evening was dark and cloudy,' wrote Dorothy to Mary Hutchinson; 'we went eight miles, William and Coleridge employing themselves in laying the plan of a ballad . . .' As they made their way across the Quantocks and then down towards the sea, the two men sketched the outline of the poem that would become known as 'The Rime of the Ancient Mariner'. Like 'The Wanderings of Cain', the poem would tell the story of an unnatural crime and its expiation, and like 'The Three Graves' it would relate the working-out of a terrible curse. Wordsworth, who had been reading George Shelvocke's *A Voyage round the World, by way of the Great South Sea* (1726), supplied some of the essential images and narrative ideas, including the fateful killing of the albatross, and the navigation of the ship by the dead sailors. They began composing the lines together, and Words-worth contributed two couplets, but as he later confessed, 'I soon found that the style of Coleridge and myself would not assimilate.'‡ That

---

* Following the meeting Mrs Barbauld addressed a poem to Coleridge, in which she advised him to abandon 'metaphysic lore'.
† Matthew 'Monk' Lewis had been a contemporary of Southey's at Westminster.
‡ 'We tried the poem conjointly,' he recalled years later, 'but we pulled different ways.'

same evening he withdrew 'from an undertaking upon which I could only have been a clog'. But Coleridge was on a roll, and within a week he had written about three hundred lines, almost half of the finished poem.[43] Much of this must have been written while he was still walking with the Wordsworths. At some point, probably at Dunster, they cut inland and walked southwards towards Dulverton, returning over the Brendon Hills and down into the Vale of Taunton Deane before once more crossing the Quantocks. Wordsworth later wrote that it had been 'a delightful tour, of which I have many pleasant, and some of them droll-enough, recollections'. It seems odd that such a haunting work should have originated in what was evidently a jolly party.

In deciding to write a ballad – a narrative poem in short stanzas, with simple diction and frequent repetition or refrains – the two poets hoped to catch the tide of popular taste, just as they hoped to do in choosing a supernatural theme. There was a new enthusiasm for the simple forms of ancient English poetry, a reaction against the perceived artificiality of much eighteenth-century verse. Researchers such as Percy and Ritson had dug deep into the medieval past and retrieved primitive nuggets for popular admiration; in Scotland, Burns had adapted old ballads into modern language and revived the form in new works;* and various writers had written imitations of antique ballads. The 'Ancient Mariner' was one of these: self-consciously archaic, particularly as originally published, with anti-quated spelling and forms of speech, even in the title – 'The Rime of the Ancyent Marinere' – suggesting that this was a recovered relic rather than a new work. The archaisms exploited the contemporary fascination with finds from the medieval past, which had encouraged the forgeries of 'Ossian' Macpherson and Thomas Chatterton, among others. The 'Ancient Mariner' was not one of these, of course, but the presentation conveyed a sense of events that might have occurred hundreds of years earlier. As the Advertisement to the published

---

* And in 1802 Walter Scott would publish his *Minstrelsy of the Scottish Border*, consisting of 'Historical and Romantic ballads collected in the Southern Counties of Scotland, with a few of the modern date, founded upon local tradition'.

poem stated, 'The Rime of the Ancyent Marinere was professedly written in imitation of the *style*, as well as of the spirit of the elder poets'. The brilliant device of the wedding guest, preserving a narrative tension in the present while the past unfolds in the mariner's telling, distinguishes the 'Ancient Mariner' from the mass of ballads it purports to imitate.

By the time the walkers returned home, the 'Ancient Mariner' had become too substantial to waste on the *Monthly Magazine*. What had begun as a cynical money-making exercise was changing into something wholly different. A spooky story concocted to appeal to the tastes of the moment had metamorphosed into a timeless allegory of human guilt and suffering, drawing on lessons Coleridge had learned from Wordsworth's treatment of such issues in his work, particularly *The Borderers*. Without intending to do so, Coleridge had written the epic on the Origin of Evil, the idea that he' had outlined to Lamb in the Salutation and Cat three years before. Though the crime of the mariner, his punishment and redemption could be interpreted as a Christian parable, other elements in the story defied doctrinal limitations. The mariner's fate was universal. Yet curiously, this was also an autobiographical poem; as the years passed Coleridge would increasingly come to identify with his own creation.

As Wordsworth explained many years afterwards, the poem 'grew and grew till it became too important for our first object, which was limited to our expectation of five pounds, and we began to talk of a Volume, which was to consist, as Mr. Coleridge has told the world,* of poems chiefly on supernatural subjects taken from common life, but looked at, as much as might be, through an imaginative medium'.

Instead of the 'Ancient Mariner', Coleridge sent three short poems to the *Monthly Magazine*, to be published as 'Sonnets Attempted in the Manner of Contemporary Writers' under the pseudonym

---

* i.e. in *Biographia Literaria*.

'Nehemiah Higginbottom'. As he freely admitted to Cottle, these ridiculed the characteristics of Lamb's and Lloyd's verse, as well as his own. 'I think they may do good to our young Bards,' he concluded.[44]

One of the sonnets lampooned his own 'indiscriminate use of elaborate and swelling language and imagery', using phrases borrowed from his earlier poems. It was Coleridge's way of moving on. Perhaps he imagined that such self-mockery would draw the sting of any offence given to his friends by these parodies. If so, this was a serious misjudgement. Lloyd in particular was not the sort of person who found it easy to laugh at himself. He may have felt especially targeted, as he had an uncle called Nehemiah. He was sensitive, with 'an exquisiteness of feeling' that, as Lamb commented, 'must border on derangement'.[45] What he wanted above all was something he eventually realised to be a chimera: a friend to whom he could pour out his feelings without restraint, someone who would understand him, a confidant of equal sensibility and similar experience who would listen without interruption.[46] Lloyd demanded regular attention, and became petulant or even hostile if he did not get it.[47] Coleridge's preoccupation with Wordsworth made this impossible. Moreover Lloyd was in emotional turmoil, passionately attached to a young woman whose wealthy parents disapproved of the match,* and contemplating an elopement. Lamb had warned Coleridge in September, not for the first time, that he should write to Lloyd more frequently: 'his is not a mind with which you should play tricks. He deserves more tenderness from you.'[48] As a consequence of what he interpreted as neglect, Lloyd's idolatry of Coleridge had been replaced by very different feelings. He wrote a letter to Dorothy in which he labelled Coleridge 'a villain', and cited a conversation between the two of them (in which he may have repeated comments about her made by Coleridge) as proof that she concurred; in tears, she brought the letter over to Nether Stowey from Alfoxden, but Coleridge laughed it off.[49] Lloyd inveigled himself into the homes of Coleridge's friends Lamb

* Sophia Pemberton, of Birmingham, whom he married, apparently with her parents' consent, in 1799.

and Southey,* and worked to turn them against him. He read Lamb extracts from Coleridge's letters that referred to Lamb in less than flattering terms. He repeated to Southey what Coleridge had told him in confidence about their quarrel in Bristol two years earlier, reopening the old wound. The effect was to deter Southey from accepting the invitation to Alfoxden, though he had been looking forward to seeing Wordsworth again, and Edith had wanted to see her sister.[50] Southey began to talk ominously of the need to defend his character. Stung by what he heard from Lloyd, Southey retaliated by telling him stories of Coleridge's past, from which Lloyd was able to make more mischief.

Perhaps stirred up by Lloyd, Southey convinced himself that he was one of the objects of Coleridge's ridicule. He apparently believed that one of the 'Nehemiah Higginbottom' poems, the sonnet 'To Simplicity', parodied his style, and that one line in particular – 'Now of my false friend plaining plaintively' – was directed at him. Coleridge felt obliged to write to Southey firmly denying any such intention:

> I am sorry, Southey! very sorry that I wrote or published those Sonnets – but 'sorry' would be a tame word to express my feelings, if I had written them with the motives which you have attributed to me. – I have not been in the habit of treating our separation with levity – nor ever since the first moment thought of it without deep emotion – and how you could apply to yourself a Sonnet written to ridicule infantine simplicity, vulgar colloquialisms, and lady-like Friendships – I have no conception.

He felt 'wounded' by Southey's readiness to 'believe evil of me', and to teach others (meaning Lloyd in particular) to believe the same (Coleridge was still unaware of the extent of Lloyd's malice towards him).[51] Southey seems to have accepted Coleridge's explanation, albeit grudgingly; he overcame his feelings of resentment by publishing his own parodies under the similar pseudonym 'Abel Shufflebottom'.

* Lloyd was 'an unexpected visitor' to Southey, as he had been to Lamb. It seems that he made a habit of arriving unannounced and perhaps uninvited.

In fact Coleridge's sonnet 'To Simplicity' satirised Lamb rather than Southey. When he protested that Southey was above such 'low, creeping language and thoughts', Coleridge condemned Lamb by implication. His reference to 'lady-like friendships' seemed to refer to Lamb and Lloyd. Moreover, the sonnet seemed to mock not just Lamb's style, but his manner too:

> *So* sad I am! – but should a friend and I
> Grow cool and *miff*, O! I am very sad!

Lamb was not quick to take offence. If he was upset by the parody, there was no sign of it in an affectionate letter he wrote to Coleridge towards the end of January 1798. But further trouble lay ahead.

Why should Coleridge have jeopardised several of his closest friendships by publishing the 'Nehemiah Higginbottom' poems? Exuberance drove much of his behaviour, and often propelled him to act rashly – which may be sufficient to explain what happened here. Perhaps too there was an element of irritation towards Lloyd, whose presence in his household had proved a trial. Their relationship was founded on a fiction: both chose to ignore that it had been essentially a commercial arrangement for Lloyd to be living with Coleridge. Instead they professed their friendship in exaggerated language; and when there was no longer any financial benefit to Coleridge, he found Lloyd's company increasingly irksome.

No doubt Coleridge relished the technical challenge of producing accurate parodies. Indeed, he claimed, so successful was the poem lampooning 'the characteristic vices' of his own style, that his friend Dr Thomas Beddoes (unaware that Coleridge had written it himself) warned a gentleman who was about to meet Coleridge at a dinner party not to mention it, adding that 'I was sore as a boil about that sonnet.'

'I have heard nothing about my tragedy, except some silly remarks of Kemble's,'* Coleridge reported to Cottle late in November 1797; 'it does not appear to me that there is a shadow of probability that it

---

* John Philip Kemble (1757–1823), actor and leading light of the Drury Lane Theatre.

will be accepted.'[52] He was annoyed not to have heard anything from Sheridan, who, he believed, owed him a prompt response after encouraging him to write the play. In the weeks before submitting the final text of *Osorio*, Coleridge had blown hot and cold about its prospects, telling Thelwall that he had 'no hopes' of its being staged, while to Southey he reckoned the likely profits at £500 or £600. He had already planned how he would spend the money.[53] Around the beginning of December, however, he learned that Sheridan had rejected it: 'his *sole* objection is – the obscurity of the three last acts'.[54]

Coleridge had obtained for Wordsworth an introduction to Thomas Harris, manager of the rival Covent Garden Theatre. *The Borderers* was despatched to Harris, though, as Dorothy confided to a friend, 'we have not the faintest expectation that it will be accepted'. Nevertheless, the initial response from Harris was encouraging enough to induce Wordsworth to travel to London to discuss certain alterations. Harris promised a 'prodigious run' if the play were accepted. Dorothy decided to accompany her brother, and they spent a week in town together. They called on Southey, who was then living at Red Lion Square while reading for the Bar, and dined three times at his house. 'He is a young man of the most rigidly virtuous habits,' wrote Dorothy a little while later, 'but though his talents are certainly very remarkable for his years (as far as I can judge) I think them much inferior to the talents of Coleridge.'[55] She wrote excitedly to relatives that the tragedy had been 'universally admir'd by all who read it'. She and William had planned 'many schemes' if the play was successful, including a pedestrian tour through Wales and by York-shire into Cumberland. 'This would *by many* be thought rather a *wildish* scheme,' commented one of their cousins, 'but by them it was thought very practicable and would certainly have been put into execution, had not the play been unfortunately rejected.' The reason given was 'the metaphysical obscurity of one character'.[56]

This negative decision strengthened Wordsworth's already-existing contempt for public taste. He attributed the failure of his tragedy to 'the deprav'd State of the Stage at present', and sneered at the success of 'Monk' Lewis's *The Castle Spectre*. This setback was the latest in a long line. Since the publication of his first two poems five years earlier, his work had gone completely unrecognised. So much rejection had embittered him; he had been able to maintain his self-belief only by disparaging the judgement of those unable to share his vision. The one reinforced the other: the surer he became of his own genius, the more dismissive he would be towards those who failed to recognise it. Criticism was unacceptable; praise was what he craved.

Following the rejection of *Osorio*, Coleridge was again very anxious about money. He 'began to feel the necessity of gaining a regular income by a regular occupation'.[57] There had been a possibility of another lodger-pupil, on a similar basis to Charles Lloyd, but nothing had come of this. For some months he had been discussing with Basil Montagu 'a project of Tuition', a programme of systematic study of all aspects of knowledge, for which eight students would pay £100 a year, plus board and lodging, while Coleridge and Montagu would act not as teachers, but only as 'Managing Students'. Perhaps not surprisingly, nothing came of this either. Through the Wedgwoods he gained an introduction to Daniel Stuart, editor and proprietor of the *Morning Post*, who offered a stipend of a guinea a week for a minimum level of contributions, whether in verse or in prose. Coleridge accepted the offer and began supplying copy to the *Morning Post* towards the end of the year. To help meet the demand Wordsworth gave Coleridge access to his notebooks, from which Coleridge extracted drafts, unfinished or juvenile poems and reworked these to his purpose; a handful were printed seemingly unchanged. However, the pay was not enough to meet his needs, which he reckoned at £100 a year, plus the £20 he set aside for Sara's mother. Some of his friends had subscribed to a fund on his behalf for a second year, but there was doubt as to whether they would continue. Coleridge had always opposed the principle of preaching for hire, but he was now forced to reconsider the idea of becoming a dissenting minister, 'as a less evil than starvation'.[58] This was very likely to mean moving to a different part of the country, and away from Wordsworth, but Wordsworth was going to have to leave Alfoxden anyway once his lease ran out, and perhaps he could follow where Coleridge led.

At the end of the year everything came to a head. Coleridge received a contingent offer to take up the post of Unitarian minister in Shrewsbury, and in the same post came a draft for £100 from Thomas and Josiah Wedgwood. The money was a gift, offered 'to enable you to defer entering into an engagement, we understand you are about to form, from the most urgent of motives'.

How this offer came about is not absolutely clear. Possibly Poole played a part in it. Among their common acquaintances there were plenty of people who could tell the Wedgwoods of Coleridge's financial difficulties, of which he made little secret.

Coleridge was now faced with a choice. He could not in all conscience accept the gift and take the job. But he was nearly £20 in debt. He feared that he would be forced to sell the 'Ancient Mariner' to the *Monthly Magazine* for £5 after all. He sought advice from all quarters. Poole advised him 'strenuously' to keep the money and stay in Stowey. Equally strenuously, Estlin (the Unitarian minister in Bristol) advised the opposite course of action. After 'much & very painful hesitation', and sleepless nights, Coleridge decided to return the draft, with a long covering letter setting out his reasons in great detail. 'I do not wish to conceal from you that I have suffered more from fluctuation of mind on this than any former occasion,' he wrote to Josiah Wedgwood, 'and even now I have scarcely courage to decide absolutely.' He did not fail to point out that the post in Shrewsbury was worth £120 a year, and came with a house worth a further £30 a year.[59]

In mid-January 1798, after borrowing money from friends in 'anticipation' of their annual subscriptions to pay off his urgent debts, Coleridge travelled up to Shrewsbury. Sara, by now heavily pregnant with their second child, and little Hartley remained behind in Nether Stowey. Coleridge arrived late one Saturday; the following day he preached two sermons, one in the morning and another in the afternoon. Among the morning congregation was young William Hazlitt,* still not twenty years old, the shy and impressionable son of the

---

* William Hazlitt (1778–1830), critic and essayist. After struggling to make a living as a painter he took up writing full time. A passionate admirer of Coleridge, he later became his bitter enemy.

Unitarian minister in Wem, a small town to the north of Shrewsbury. Hazlitt had trained for the ministry himself, and had only recently decided not to continue, hoping instead to become a painter. On this cold, raw January morning he had risen before daylight and walked ten miles through the mud to hear the celebrated Coleridge preach the gospel, which he saw as 'a romance, a sort of revival of the primitive spirit of Christianity, which was not to be resisted'. Indeed, Coleridge in those days seemed a sort of prophet. A quarter of a century afterwards the impression he made was still fresh in Hazlitt's memory. He had arrived at the chapel while the organ was still playing the psalm. As the notes died away

> Mr. Coleridge rose and gave out his text, 'And he went up into the mountain to pray, HIMSELF, ALONE.' As he gave out this text, his voice 'rose like a steam of rich distilled perfumes', and when he came to the two last words, which he pronounced loud, deep, and distinct, it seemed to me, who was then young, as if the sounds had echoed from the bottom of the human heart, and as if that prayer might have floated in solemn silence through the universe . . .
>
> In the dim light there was a 'strange wildness' in his aspect, 'a dusky obscurity'. The preacher then launched into his subject, like an eagle dallying with the wind. The sermon was upon peace and war; upon church and state – not their alliance, but their separation – on the spirit of the world and the spirit of Christianity, not as the same, but as opposed to one another. He talked of those who had 'inscribed the cross of Christ on banners dripping with human gore.' He made a poetical and pastoral excursion – and to show the fatal effects of war, drew a striking contrast between the simple shepherd-boy, driving his team afield, or sitting under the hawthorn, piping to his flock, 'as though he should never be old' and the same poor country lad, crimped, kidnapped, brought into town, made drunk at an alehouse, turned into a wretched drummer-boy, with his hair sticking on end with powder and pomatum, a long cue at his back, and tricked out in the loathsome finery of the profession of blood . . .

Hazlitt was entranced; 'the light of his genius shone into my soul',

> And for myself, I could not have been more delighted if I had heard the music of the spheres. Poetry and Philosophy had met together. Truth and Genius had embraced, under the eye and with the sanction of Religion. This was even beyond my hopes. I returned home well satisfied. The sun that was still labouring pale and wan through the sky, obscured by thick mists, seemed an emblem of the good cause; and the cold dank drops of dew, that hung half melted on the beard of the thistle, had something genial and refreshing in them; for there was a spirit of hope and youth in all nature, that turned everything into good.

It was the custom for dissenting ministers to exchange visits with their neighbours; accordingly, two days later Coleridge arrived at the house of Hazlitt's father. The young man was called down to meet him, and he sat in silence, listening to the visitor talk for two hours. Many years later, he recalled that morning:

> I had heard a great deal of his powers of conversation and was not disappointed. In fact, I never met with anything at all like them, either before or since. I could easily credit the accounts which were circulated of his holding forth to a large party of ladies and gentlemen, an evening or two before, on the Berkeleian Theory, when he made the whole material universe look like a transparency of fine words . . .

Hazlitt described Coleridge as he then appeared:

> His forehead was broad and high, light as if built of ivory, with large projecting eyebrows, and his eyes rolling beneath them, like a sea with darkened lustre . . . His mouth was gross, voluptuous, open, eloquent; his chin good-humoured and round; but his nose, the rudder of the face, the index of the will, was small, feeble, nothing . . . Coleridge, in his person, was rather above the common size, inclining to the corpulent . . . His hair (now, alas! grey) was then black and glossy as the raven's, and fell in smooth masses over his forehead.

At dinner their guest became more animated, and when he spoke of Burke, Hazlitt ventured his first comment, saying that he had always entertained a great opinion of Burke, and that speaking of him with contempt might be made the test of a vulgar, democratical mind. Coleridge remarked that this was a very just and striking observation. Hazlitt glowed with satisfaction. 'I remember the leg of Welsh mutton and the turnips on the table that day had the finest flavour imaginable.'

The next morning Coleridge was due to return to Shrewsbury. When Hazlitt came down to breakfast, he found that Coleridge had just received a letter from Tom and Josiah Wedgwood, offering him an annuity of £150 a year for life, free of any conditions whatsoever. The letter had been forwarded from Nether Stowey by Poole, who in a covering letter urged him not to hesitate, but to accept the offer, renounce his present pursuit, and return home. Hazlitt watched in dismay as 'Coleridge seemed to make up his mind to close with this proposal in the act of tying on one of his shoes.'

8

COLLABORATION

'I am not certain that I am not dreaming,' Coleridge wrote happily to Poole. He quit Shrewsbury at the end of January, leaving behind a disappointed congregation, much increased since his arrival – 'the people here absolutely *consume* me'. He had arranged to meet Tom Wedgwood in Bristol before returning to Nether Stowey, and after calling at Cottle's, he spent a few days with his new patron at Cote House. He had already settled in his own mind that he was to repay the Wedgwoods 'thro' the medium of Mankind', i.e. by producing work that would benefit mankind as a whole.[1] Coleridge contrived to give the impression that he was doing a favour to the Wedgwood brothers in accepting their money; they had given him the power of 'unanxious seclusion' to produce 'some work of some importance'. On one of his subsequent visits Wedgwood's sister Kitty complained that he made 'too great a parade of superior feeling'.

The Wedgwood annuity stirred some comment from Coleridge's friends and acquaintances. 'I hope the fruit will be good as the seed is noble,' Wordsworth remarked – perhaps a little grudgingly, given that he had himself benefited from a legacy.[2] It was not unusual for a struggling writer to be helped by a rich patron; Southey, for example, received an annuity of £160 from his friend Wynn, £10 more than Coleridge.

Thelwall described the circumstances of the gift to a mutual acquaintance in Liverpool, quoting from a letter Coleridge had sent him:

This letter was written in a great hurry at Cottle's shop in Bristol . . . & you will perceive that it has a dash of the obscure not uncommon to the rapid genius of C. Whether he did or did not accept the cure* of Unitarian Souls, it is difficult from this acct. to make out – I suppose he did not – for I know his aversion to preaching God's holy word for hire, & which is seconded a little I suspect by his repugnance to all regular routine & application – I also hope he did not – for I know he cannot preach very often without travelling from the pulpit to the Tower – Mount him upon his darling hobby horse 'the republic of God's own making', & away he goes like hey go mad, spattering & splashing thro thick & thin & scattering more levelling sedition, & constructive treason, than poor Gilly,† or myself ever dreamt of. He promised [*sic*] to write to me again in a few days; but tho' I ansrd. his letter directly, I have not heard from him since.[3]

Coleridge was mounted on his hobby horse (albeit disguised under a pseudonym) in the *Morning Post* of 8 January 1798, which printed his 'Fire, Famine, and Slaughter: A War Eclogue',‡ set in a desolate tract of the Vendée. Three sisters representing the three scourges of mankind were depicted in a dramatised conversation reminiscent of the witches' scenes in *Macbeth*. A much-repeated refrain hinted who set them loose: 'Letters four do form his name.' It was not difficult for readers to identify the Prime Minister.

But even Coleridge was finding it harder to portray ministers as warmongers. At the end of 1797 the French spurned British peace

---

* Possibly a misreading of 'care'?
† Gilbert Wakefield, scholar and radical, a Unitarian and former Fellow of Jesus College, Cambridge, who was notorious for his intemperate writings, though gentle and amiable in private. He maintained that the poor and labouring classes had nothing to lose from a French invasion. In 1798 he published a *Reply* to an anodyne pamphlet by Richard Watson, Bishop of Llandaff. Wakefield's *Reply* contained charges of corruption against the authorities and numerous accusations against Watson personally. A prosecution for seditious libel inevitably followed. Thomas Erskine offered his services for the defence, but Wakefield was convicted and sentenced to two years' imprisonment. It was for selling this pamphlet that Joseph Johnson was sentenced to six months' imprisonment and fined £50.
‡ Coleridge's subsequent comments about this poem were dismissive, and when it was republished many years later under his own name, he added a long 'Apologetic Preface' (perversely, he took particular pleasure in the style of the preface).

feelers for the third time. It was becoming impossible to maintain that France was continuing the war in self-defence, and increasingly obvious that the French intended to dominate Continental Europe. In January France attacked Switzerland, long regarded as a haven of liberty and independence, and after a short campaign established a puppet republic there. For many, this was the parting of the ways; in later years both Wordsworth and Coleridge identified it as the moment when they lost sympathy with Revolutionary France. At the end of 1797 there had been a general thanksgiving throughout Britain for the naval victories that had kept the nation safe from invasion; but the threat remained, and the outbreak of rebellion in Ireland again exposed the vulnerability of the British archipelago. In this situation radicals were further isolated, and hounded in particular by a new publication, the *Anti-Jacobin*, the brainchild of an ambitious young politician, George Canning, and a journalist, John Hookham Frere,* a Cambridge contemporary of both Wordsworth and Coleridge. The second issue of the *Anti-Jacobin* contained an attack on 'Jacobin poetry', accompanied by a clever parody of Southey's poem 'The Widow'. A few weeks later the *Anti-Jacobin* had a crack at another Southey poem (for which Coleridge had written the last stanza), 'The Soldier's Wife'. The thrust of these attacks was that 'Jacobin poets' affected sympathy for the poor merely to make a political point; they had no interest in relieving distress. The *Anti-Jacobin* might just as easily have attacked Wordsworth's Salisbury Plain poem, or even more, his 'Ruined Cottage'; but neither had yet been published.

Although, as Thelwall observed, Coleridge was still occasionally prepared to mount his hobby horse and go spattering and splashing and scattering sedition, his interests were turning away from politics. Early in March he replied to a letter from his brother George, seeking to reassure him that 'our opinions and feelings on political subjects are more nearly alike, than you imagine them to be'. He protested

---

* In 1816 Hookham Frere was introduced to Coleridge by the publisher John Murray, and subsequently he arranged for Coleridge to meet Canning. Afterwards he was a regular visitor to Coleridge in Highgate. He contributed £300 towards the cost of Derwent Coleridge's Cambridge education.

that his own opinions were 'utterly untainted' by 'French Metaphysics, French Politics, French Ethics, & French Theology', and recycled the phrase he had used to Charles Lloyd's father more than a year before, declaring again that he had 'snapped my squeaking baby-trumpet of Sedition'. George had apparently given his opinion that at this time of national crisis, one must be either for the government or against the government. Coleridge demurred; he thought the present ministry 'weak & perhaps unprincipled men; but I could not with a safe conscience vote for their removal' (this despite the Armageddon spread by Pitt). 'I am no Whig, no Reformist, no Republican,' claimed Coleridge; 'I am of no party.' Characteristically, he was harder on those with whom he had been allied than those whom he had opposed: 'The Opposition & the Democrats are not only vicious – they wear the *filthy garments* of vice.' He was now arguing that individuals should act as 'kind neighbours and good Christians, rather than as citizens & electors', and that it was a 'pernicious' error to attribute to governments 'a talismanic influence over our virtues & our happiness' (this was a line of argument that one would not have been surprised to have heard from the lips of Dr Johnson). In seeking to deny any beneficial effects of revolutionary change, Coleridge showed himself susceptible to the most tendentious arguments: 'In America (I have received my information from unquestionable authority) the morals & domestic habits of the people are daily deteriorating.'[4]

None of this would have been a surprise to Thelwall, who knew better than to expect consistency from Coleridge. Hazlitt described how, 'In digressing, in dilating, in passing from subject to subject, he appeared to me to float in air, to slide on ice.' While walking back together from Wem to Shrewsbury, Hazlitt had noticed that Coleridge continually crossed from one side of the footpath to the other: 'he seemed unable to keep on in a straight line'. This motion struck the young man as odd, but only later did he connect it with instability of purpose or involuntary change of principle.

The *Morning Post* was avowedly independent, critical of Pitt's ministry and sympathetic to France. In January the paper had dismissed attacks by the *Anti-Jacobin* as 'too contemptible for notice'.

But early in March the editor, Daniel Stuart, was summoned before the Privy Council and interrogated; after this chastening experience it suited him to trim to the government line, at least for a while. In April the *Morning Post* published with considerable fanfare Coleridge's 'The Recantation' (later republished under its better-known title 'France: An Ode'). The 'Argument' provided a convenient summary of the contents: 'The exultation of the Poet at the commencement of the French Revolution, and his unqualified abhorrence of the alliance against the Republic ... The blasphemies and horrors during the domination of the Terrorists, regarded by the Poet as a transient storm ... many apprehensions, yet still the poet struggled ... Switzerland, and the Poet's recantation ...'

Coleridge had begun his long letter to his brother by explaining why he had not replied earlier: he had been ill. An infection in his gum over the stump of a tooth (perhaps a wisdom tooth) had affected his eye, then his stomach, then his head, and resulted in a fever, and the pain was made worse by the efforts of a surgeon to remove 'the offending stump'. Laudanum had provided repose, not sleep: 'but You, I believe, know how divine that repose is – what a spot of enchantment, a green spot of fountains, & flowers & trees, in the very heart of a waste of Sands ... Sands!' (It is revealing that Coleridge expected his conservative and respectable elder brother to be familiar with the pleasurable effects of opium.) He was now 'recovering a pace', and enjoying 'that *newness* of sensation from the fields, the air, & the Sun, which makes convalescence almost repay one for disease'.

'I have for some time past withdrawn myself almost totally from consideration of *immediate* causes, which are infinitely complex & uncertain,' Coleridge announced to his brother, 'to muse on fundamental & general causes.' Through poetry he would strive to 'elevate the imagination & set the affections in right tune by the beauty of the inanimate impregnated, as with a living soul, by the presence of Life'. Nature would do what politics could not; the poet would withdraw from society, to meditate on eternal truths. 'I love fields & woods & mountains with almost a visionary fondness – and because I have found benevolence & quietness growing within me as that fondness [has] increased, therefore I should wish to be the means of implanting it in others.' Coleridge illustrated his meaning by quoting lines of as yet unpublished philosophic verse – not his own, but Wordsworth's.*

It might seem strange that in his letter to his brother Coleridge should utilise Wordsworth's poetry rather than his own to explain his change of heart. But it was indicative of a dynamic process going on at the time. Coleridge was struggling to articulate a philosophy that was to inspire much of Wordsworth's work.

Coleridge had expressed his concept of the 'One Life' (though he did not then call it that) in 'The Eolian Harp', and in his 'Religious Musings':

> . . . 'Tis the sublime of Man,
> Our noontide Majesty, to know ourselves
> Part and proportions of one wond'rous whole:
> This fraternizes man, this constitutes
> Our charities and bearings. But 'tis God
> Diffus'd thro' all, that doth make all one whole;

Within the next year or so he was to fall under the spell of Spinoza, whose philosophy he summarised as follows: 'each thing has a life of its own, and we are all one life'.⁵ This concept formed a persistent part of Coleridge's thinking, despite many changes in the decades that followed. Lines added some years later† to 'The Eolian Harp' provide his most mature statement of this idea:

> O the one life within us and abroad,
> Which meets all motion and becomes its soul,
> A light in sound, a sound-like power in light,
> Rhythm in all thought, and joyance every where –
> Methinks, it should have been impossible
> Not to love all things in a world so filled . . .

---

* The lines originally formed part of 'The Ruined Cottage'. They were eventually incorporated into the fourth book of *The Excursion*.
† These first appeared in print in 1817, though they may have been written long before.

For Coleridge, the 'One Life' philosophy was a means of reconciling reason and religion, a sensual appetite for nature and a spiritual yearning for God. But the 'One Life' also made a bridge between Coleridge's religious convictions and Wordsworth's vague pantheistic instincts. In their appreciation of the sanctity of all living things, in the sublime, in the transcendent value of the mind's response to Nature, the two men were as one.

The 'One Life' idea is also evident in 'Frost at Midnight', perhaps the most beautiful of Coleridge's 'conversation poems', written a few weeks after his return from Shrewsbury. His infant child slumbers next to him in front of the dying fire, while the rest of the house sleeps; outside the air is still following a snowstorm, and frost is forming. Coleridge remembers his own grim boyhood at boarding school, isolated from home 'in the great city'; there he 'saw nought lovely but the sky and stars'. He contrasts this with what his son may expect:

> But thou, my babe! shalt wander like a breeze
> By lakes and sandy shores, beneath the crags
> Of ancient mountain, and beneath the clouds,
> Which image in their bulk both lakes and shores
> And mountain crags: so shalt thou see and hear
> The lovely shapes and sounds intelligible
> Of that eternal language, which thy God
> Utters, who from eternity doth teach
> Himself in all, and all things in himself.

Coleridge is imagining a life for his child in Wordsworth's country.

The figure of Hartley would recur through both men's poetry in the years to come. For them he epitomised the child of Nature, a boy reared wild and free, his upbringing a complete contrast to the artificial and controlled schemes put forward by Godwinians such as Wedgwood.

In the first few months of 1798 Wordsworth revised 'The Ruined Cottage', distancing himself from the story, turning it into a tale told by a pedlar in conversation with the poet. Perhaps Wordsworth was influenced by Coleridge's use of the mariner in conversation with the wedding guest. The device provided Wordsworth with a context for philosophical reflection, and once again Coleridge's central idea surfaced in the pedlar's resigned acceptance of things as they are:

> . . . in all things
> He saw one life, & felt that it was joy.*

Wordsworth was now hitting his stride. 'His faculties seem to expand every day,' wrote Dorothy; 'he composes with much more facility than he did, as to the *mechanism* of poetry, and his ideas flow faster than he can express them.'[6]

Coleridge had made little progress with his poem 'The Brook': perhaps no more than a few fragmentary studies in his notebooks. His ideas about how it should be done changed periodically, becoming ever more ambitious. He had envisaged a poem that would articulate a coherent system of philosophy, an answer to godless Godwinism: 'the *first* and *only* true Phil. Poem in existence'.[7] But exposition was easier than composition. Now, exposed almost daily to the presence of what he increasingly perceived to be Wordsworth's superior gifts, Coleridge was struck by a revelation: surely Wordsworth was the man to write this masterwork? His revision of 'The Ruined Cottage' proved him to be a philosopher-poet in the making. His work showed a profound understanding of the human mind – what we now label psychology. Under Coleridge's guidance there was no limit to what Wordsworth might achieve. Coleridge would be the brain, Wordsworth the hands. An excited Coleridge imagined a poem greater than any yet written, greater even than *Paradise Lost* – indeed the poem itself would show the way to man's redemption. This masterpiece would reconcile Man to Nature, resolving all philosophical problems; love of Nature would lead to love of one's fellow man; universal brotherhood would inaugurate the millennium.[8]

To modern readers such an idea seems lunacy. But it was not anomalous in the atmosphere breathed by these two young men. The French Revolution had shattered all preconceptions, making anything

---

* These lines were later incorporated into *The Prelude*.

seem possible. The past was no more, the future would obviously be different; the world trembled on the brink of change. For believers in revealed religion, this appeared to be the moment when prophecies would be fulfilled. Among dissenters it was commonplace to argue that the millennium was at hand. Coleridge's 'Religious Musings' showed that he shared this vision. His own creative energies would increasingly be devoted to prose, to the philosophical *magnum opus* made possible by the Wedgwood annuity.* Both he and Wordsworth would work towards the same end, but in different ways.

There was no reason to hesitate; he would pass the cherished project to his friend. Wordsworth accepted the gift gratefully. Since early manhood he had sensed that he was destined for something great. Here was the task for which he had been waiting, one by which he could measure his genius. He would prove himself worthy of Coleridge's confidence. It was a vast undertaking, of course, which he estimated would take him at least eighteen months to complete: 'I know not of any thing which will not come within the scope of my plan.'

By March 1798 he could boast that he had been 'tolerably industrious': he had written 1,300 lines 'of a poem in which I contrive to convey most of the knowledge of which I am possessed'. This total was not quite so impressive as it seemed, however, since as well as the hundred or so lines later published as the 'Prospectus' to the work, it incorporated several poems that Wordsworth had already written, 'The Ruined Cottage' (nine hundred lines) and 'The Old Cumberland Beggar' (two hundred lines).[10] Wordsworth believed that these and other lesser poems would gradually coalesce into one great work. The plan was so vast and so vague that it could absorb almost anything.

Coleridge could see no limit to his friend's capabilities. 'My admiration, I might say, my awe of his intellectual powers has increased even to this hour,'† he wrote to Estlin in May;[11] he told Cottle that

---

* Asked later in the year what kind of man he was, Coleridge replied, 'Simply, *un Philosophe*.'[9]

† Coleridge's frequent references to Wordsworth's 'intellect' or his 'intellectual powers' may seem incongruous. Possibly he is using the terms in an older sense, somewhere between 'sanity' and 'penetration', rather than in the more modern meaning of analytical or reasoning power.

what 'The Giant Wordsworth' had produced so far was superior 'to any thing in our language which any way resembles it'.[12] He was perceptive in his assessment of Wordsworth's great gifts, but blind to his limitations; he could not see that Wordsworth was a poet of feeling rather than thought, of the heart rather than of the mind. As he later explained, Coleridge expected his friend to 'assume the station of a man in mental repose, one whose principles were made up, and so prepared to deliver upon authority a system of philosophy'.[13] But to elaborate a comprehensive system of philosophy within a poetic framework was not a project suited to Wordsworth's abilities – or indeed to anyone else's, except perhaps Coleridge himself.

Poole apparently believed this great work 'likely to benefit mankind much more than any thing, Wordsworth has yet written'.[14] Wordsworth himself hoped to make the poem 'of considerable utility'.[15] He now had a title, *The Recluse*, signifying the newly defined position of the poet as withdrawn from society; and a subtitle, *Views of Nature, Man, and Society*, perhaps inspired by Coleridge's description of his projected philosophical poem: 'impassioned reflection on men, nature and society'.

On 9 March the Coleridges arrived at Alfoxden for a stay that would last ten days. The departure of the Wordsworths was looming; it was now certain that new tenants would be moving into the house when the lease expired. 'Wordsworth has been caballed against *so long and so loudly*,'* Coleridge reported to Cottle,

> that he has found it impossible to prevail on the tenant of the Allfoxden estate, to let him the house, after their first agreement is expired, so he must quit it at Midsummer; whether we shall be able to procure him a house and furniture near Stowey, we know not, and yet we must: for the hills, and the woods, and the streams, and the sea, and the shores, would break forth into reproaches against us, if we did not

---

* Many years later, when Wordsworth's radical past had become an embarrassment, he denied that he had been compelled to leave Alfoxden. But the contemporary evidence suggests otherwise.

strain every nerve, to keep their Poet among them. Without joking, and in serious sadness, Poole and I cannot endure to think of losing him.[16]

The Wordsworths themselves were in a quandary. There seemed little prospect of finding another house nearby. 'We have no other very strong inducement to stay but Coleridge's society,' Dorothy wrote to Mary Hutchinson, 'but that is so important an object that we have it much at heart.'[17] Wordsworth was characteristically cooler: 'We have no particular reason to be attached to the neighbourhood of Stowey, but the society of Coleridge, and the friendship of Poole.'[18]

But if they could not stay in the area, where should they go? One possibility was to go back to Racedown. Another thought was that they might make a tour through Wales into the north of England – but pleasant though that might be, it was no solution; they would still be homeless, back in the same position as they had been three years before. Coleridge was very unwilling to lose them; if they were forced to leave, perhaps he should follow. Wordsworth reported on the outcome of their discussions to his Cambridge friend James Losh. A 'delightful scheme' had arisen: all four of them, the Wordsworths and the Coleridges, would go to Germany for perhaps two years, 'to acquire the German language, and to furnish ourselves with a tolerable stock of information in natural science'. They planned to settle in a village near a university town, so that once they had mastered the language they would be able to study there. Others could come too; Wordsworth suggested to the newly married Losh that he and his wife might like to join 'this little colony'.[19]

Two years earlier, before he moved to Nether Stowey, Coleridge had sketched a plan to go and live in Germany with his wife and child, intending to study chemistry, anatomy, theology and philosophy. Germany was where all the most exciting developments in philosophy were taking place. Coleridge was particularly intrigued by the work of the metaphysician Immanuel Kant, whose 'near incomprehensible' writings, his instinct told him, held the answer to the atheism of Locke and Hume. Though the Wedgwood annuity had been given without conditions, Coleridge nevertheless felt that he had been presented with a rare opportunity; it was incumbent on him to make the most of it. The attraction of Germany for Wordsworth was less obvious – but he knew now what he wanted to do, and he needed somewhere to go, so Germany was as good as anywhere. If the state of Europe allowed, they might get into Switzerland, and Wordsworth would then be able to show his sister scenes he had longed to share with her during his walking tour eight years earlier. Dorothy believed that they could live more cheaply in Germany than in England. It would mean leaving Basil behind; but then, Dorothy reasoned, he had reached an age (five) when he needed the company of other children 'whose minds were upon *the same level with his own*'.[20]

Moreover, Germany was outside the war zone. There were few other places in western Europe safe for an Englishman. France, Holland and Spain were all at war with Britain; Belgium overrun; Switzerland a puppet of France; northern Italy under French occupation; Austria threatened. Meanwhile the gloomy outlook for radicals led many to contemplate emigration. Southey told James Losh that he would leave the country if his *Joan of Arc* was suppressed, as then seemed possible. To counter the threat of invasion, volunteer corps were founded for the defence of the coast; it seemed conceivable that some form of military service might become compulsory, as it had become in France. And for those living near the coast there was the ever-present danger of impressment into the navy. In choosing to go to Germany, therefore, the two young men would be escaping the possibility of the draft.

The immediate requirement was to raise money. The trip to Germany would be expensive, and of course they would need funds for their living expenses abroad. Coleridge had his annuity, but the Wordsworths were very short of money. Wordsworth had so far received less than £600 of Raisley Calvert's legacy, of which he had lent more than half and spent some of the remainder. Coleridge wrote to Cottle asking what he would pay for two possible volumes: their two tragedies, packaged together, or a volume of Wordsworth's verse, consisting principally of the Salisbury Plain poem and 'The Ruined

Cottage', with a few other, smaller poems. In response, Cottle appears to have made a modest offer for the tragedies, which was not taken up. 'It is not impossible but that in happier times, they may be brought on the stage,' Coleridge wrote in reply, 'and to throw away this chance for a mere trifle, would be to make the present moment act fraudulently and usuriously towards the future time.' As for Wordsworth's poems, he continued, Cottle might have them for thirty guineas. He urged Cottle to come down to west Somerset 'as soon as you can', holding out the prospect of a roam along the coast to Lynton and Lynmouth, which in May 'will be in all their pride of woods and waterfalls, not to speak of its august cliffs, and the green ocean, and the vast valley of stones'.[21]

A few weeks later Coleridge visited his family in Ottery St Mary. The West Country was once again in a state of high alert, with fears of invasion fanned by rumours and reports of sightings of French ships. The militia was called out; Coleridge's brother James was Major-Commandant of the Exmouth and Sidmouth volunteers. On his return to Nether Stowey Coleridge wrote to inform George that he had written a poem 'which I think even the Major (who is no admirer of the art) would like'.[22] 'Fears in Solitude, written in April 1798, during the Alarm of an Invasion' opens with an evocative description of the poet's love for the hills above his home, silent and peaceful, and widens into his alarm for the safety of his fellow countrymen, though they have sinned grievously; nonetheless, as 'a son, a brother, and a friend/A husband and a father', he prays for deliverance from the threat; and the poem concludes with him walking home at sunset, the air once more quiet and still, looking down from the hills towards his cottage, 'where my babe/And my babe's mother dwell in peace'. His love for home and family symbolises his feelings for the nation.

But Coleridge's feelings for his family were ambiguous, as perhaps were his feelings for his country. However much he loved them, he found it easy to leave them. Sara Coleridge had become accustomed to his absences, sometimes for a few days, sometimes for weeks at a time. She did not share his intellectual interests; her concerns were more practical. She strove to make a home in difficult circumstances. It was hard for her to understand why, if her husband was so well thought of, he was not more prosperous. Knowing his habits as well as anyone, it was natural for her to ascribe his lack of success to his 'indolence' – particularly since this was a term Coleridge increasingly used of himself. In general she seems to have borne her lot cheerfully enough, but it must have been trying for her to find her husband prostrate in an opium-induced stupor, or to see him embark on yet another long walk when there was so little money to pay for everyday essentials. Sometimes, perhaps, her frustration erupted, and harsh words were exchanged. So Coleridge later claimed, and such outbursts would surely have been understandable enough.

Sara was not an empty-headed girl like *Middlemarch*'s Rosamond Vincy, though she came from a similar genteel, comfortable background, with plenty of servants to do the hard work. She was the daughter of a man who derived his income from trade but who considered himself too much of a gentleman to concentrate on the business. Her childhood had been divided between a smart Bath townhouse and a villa outside Bristol. She and her sisters had been educated better than most girls of their class, in a progressive household; they all read Mary Wollstonecraft's *A Vindication of the Rights of Woman* (1792) soon after it was published.[23] But her aspirations had been shaped by her experience. When she was sixteen her father had been declared bankrupt, and he died soon afterwards, leaving his wife and daughters homeless and virtually penniless, dependent on the charity of relatives and what they could earn with their own hands. Mrs Fricker moved into lodgings in Bristol, where she first of all ran a school, and then a dress shop. Sara and her sisters were forced to work as needlewomen. Young women in this trade were vulnerable, as the example of Kate Nickleby shows. Years afterwards, Byron sneered that Southey and Coleridge had married 'two milliners from Bath'; as De Quincey commented, 'everybody knows what is *meant* to be conveyed in that expression'. Coleridge often complained that his wife cared too much about appearances, but the Fricker sisters had every reason to be sensitive to the world's opinion; respectability was valuable to them.

Sara was the eldest child, and thus the one most affected by the decline in the family status. She was quick-tempered and sensitive to slights. It was difficult for her to share her husband's enthusiasm for the company of the shabby, unconventional Wordsworths. His admiration for Dorothy was particularly mortifying. He and Dorothy saw each other almost daily, usually in the company of Wordsworth, but not always by any means, often walking out after dark together and sometimes making tours that took them away for days. Her own maidservant and others of the same class began to drop expressions which alternately implied pity for Sara 'as an injured woman, or sneered at her as a very tame one'. It is unlikely that Sara suspected her husband of any impropriety with Dorothy. But it was galling for her to witness almost daily the preference that he showed for another woman's company. Dorothy bore no ill will towards Sara, and there are signs that she did try to ease the tension between them. But temperamentally they were very different; Dorothy was instinctive, passionate, spontaneous, almost wild. When the three walkers arrived at the cottage drenched and laughing, she unceremoniously ran upstairs and dressed herself with dry clothes from Sara's wardrobe. In doing so she was unconscious that her actions might be unwelcome; she took no liberty that she would not gladly have granted in return. But Sara was not glad about it at all, and the fact that her husband had allowed or even encouraged another woman to make free with her clothes only made it worse. He treated her complaints as symptoms of narrow-mindedness, which very likely infuriated her further. Sara considered Dorothy 'rustic', a term which implied a lack of polish, and unladylike in her willingness to venture outside for long walks in the dark and the mud. Coleridge made no secret of the fact that he regarded Wordsworth's sister as intellectually 'very much superior' to his wife, while Sara began comparing her husband unfavourably with her more disciplined brother-in-law.[24]

*

While still in Shrewsbury, Coleridge had read 'Monk' Lewis's play *The Castle Spectre*. He outlined his mixed response in a letter to Wordsworth. He praised in particular 'a pretty little Ballad-song' which formed part of the play: 'Lewis, I think, has great & peculiar excellence in these compositions.' The ballad's 'simplicity and naturalness' was the writer's own, not imitated; it was expressed in 'a language perfectly modern – the language of his own times, in the same way that the language of the writer of "Sir Cauline" was the language of *his* times' ('Sir Cauline' was a medieval ballad published by Thomas Percy in his *Reliques of Ancient English Poetry*, from which Coleridge had drawn archaic words and phrases used in his 'Ancient Mariner'). Coleridge was impressed: 'I find, *I* cannot attain this innocent nakedness, except by *assumption* – I resemble the Duchess of Kingston, who masqueraded in the character of "Eve before the Fall" in flesh-coloured silk.'[25]

'Sir Cauline' provided Coleridge with the name 'Christabel', the title of his next poem on a supernatural theme. Like the 'Ancient Mariner', 'Christabel' mimics the style and the language of much earlier verse. There is a dreamlike quality to the tale; a lurking sense of dread erupts into nightmare as the witch Geraldine lets fall her robe:

> Beneath the lamp the lady bowed,
> And slowly rolled her eyes around;
> Then drawing in her breath aloud,
> Like one that shuddered, she unbound
> The cincture from beneath her breast:
> Her silken robe, and inner vest,
> Dropt to her feet, and full in view,
> Behold! her bosom, and half her side –
> A sight to dream of, not to tell!
> O shield her! shield sweet Christabel!*

The pure maiden Christabel is apparently seduced by Geraldine, and then silenced by a spell. This is a story of innocence and corruption,

* This line is a later substitution. As first written, it read, 'And she is to sleep by Christabel'.

with a strong sexual flavour. It contains much of the standard apparatus of the Gothic romance: the seemingly unpopulated castle, the hooting owl, the clock tolling, the full moon, the ghost, the beautiful enchantress, and so on – but with an especially compelling quality, as the reader is drawn in to share Coleridge's mingled fascination and revulsion, echoing that of his heroine, Christabel herself. The first part, which Coleridge seems to have finished in the early spring of 1798, ends with tears of shame forming in Christabel's eyes.

More than two years later, and after much difficulty, Coleridge completed a second part, which ends inconclusively. Long afterwards he gave his biographer James Gillman an outline of a third part, which would have concluded the story, ending in the exposure of the witch. Various explanations, psychological and circumstantial, have been advanced to explain why Coleridge failed to finish 'Christabel'. But the fundamental problem may have been an artistic one. Perhaps his original conception never extended further than the first part; perhaps he conceived it as a fragment, like 'Kubla Khan'. Certainly there are fundamental differences between the two parts, and the first part satisfies in a way that the two parts together do not. In retrospect, Wordsworth seems to have felt that it had been a mistake for Coleridge to have gone beyond the first part,[26] and Lamb certainly thought so. After Coleridge's death, Lamb told Gillman, 'I was very angry with Coleridge, when I first heard that he had written a second canto, and intended to finish it.'[27] In a letter to Cottle written on 18 February 1798 Coleridge wrote as follows: 'I have finished my ballad – it is 340 lines.' This has usually been taken to refer to the 'Ancient Mariner', which in its first published form consisted of 658 lines. But Coleridge could have been referring to the first part of 'Christabel', which has somewhere between 319 and 331 lines (several versions exist in manuscript). If he considered the poem finished in 1798, and only later decided to continue with it, this may help to explain his subsequent difficulties.

It was noticed long ago that there are several coincidences between descriptions of weather and scenery in the first part of 'Christabel' and observations in Dorothy Wordsworth's journal for the first few months of 1798.[28] One problem with the suggestion that Coleridge was referring to 'Christabel' in his letter to Cottle is that at least one of these coincidences occurs after the date of the letter. But there are several possible explanations. It would not have been the first time that Coleridge had told Cottle a poem was finished when it was not; or observations may have been added as revisions to the first draft, perhaps in response to comments from the Wordsworths. Dorothy's journal for 23 March records that 'Coleridge dined with us. He brought his ballad finished.' This too has usually been identified as a reference to the 'Ancient Mariner'; but it may refer to 'Christabel'.

'The Three Graves' was another poem on a supernatural theme, and in March Coleridge began 'The Ballad of the Dark Ladiè', a companion piece to 'Christabel', though much less successfully realised, and never completed. In a completely different idiom he wrote another of his 'conversation poems', addressed to Wordsworth and his sister, since it turned on one of the subjects they had been discussing: the need to escape from the tired formulae in which so much contemporary verse was written. It was the same lesson that Bowyer had tried to flog into the boys at Christ's Hospital. 'The Nightingale' satirised the poetical cliché of the 'melancholy Bird', and in the process parodied Coleridge's own earlier 'To the Nightingale' (1795). He ridiculed the 'youths and maidens most poetical' who 'heave their sighs/O'er Philomela's* pity-pleading strains'.

> My Friend, and thou, our Sister! We have learnt
> A different lore . . .

Early in May he sent a copy of the poem over to Alfoxden, accompanied by a light-hearted piece of doggerel:

> In stale blank verse a subject stale
> I send *per post* my *Nightingale*;
> And like an honest bard, dear Wordsworth
> You'll tell me what you think, my Bird's worth.

---

* An Athenian princess who turned into a nightingale after being raped – another stale classical allusion, like the 'Pierian spring'.

Wordsworth had turned aside from *The Recluse* to concentrate on shorter poems, composed in a deliberately plain style, free from 'the gaudiness and inane phraseology' that both he and Coleridge so deplored. These were 'experiments', he explained, 'written chiefly with a view to ascertain how far the language of conversation in the middle and lower classes of society is adapted to the purposes of poetic pleasure'. And poems such as 'The Last of the Flock', 'Goody Blake and Harry Gill', 'The Idiot Boy' and 'The Convict' displayed Wordsworth's sympathy for the poor, the homeless, the despised and the condemned, presenting their thoughts and feelings as legitimate matter for poetry. Doing so was itself a form of social protest, an attempt to shake the complacency of the poetry-reading public. These are people like you and me, Wordsworth was saying to his readers; they think and feel as we do.

Though not obviously didactic, several of the poems seemed written to refute Godwinian doctrines. 'The Last of the Flock', for example, takes Godwin's idea that property causes vice and turns it on its head. Wordsworth began to revise his Salisbury Plain poem again, sifting out the Godwinian lumps.

Like 'The Three Graves' (one of the poems begun by Wordsworth and continued by Coleridge), 'Goody Blake and Harry Gill' was apparently based on a well-authenticated story of a curse and its terrible effects. Perhaps, too, it was inspired by Wordsworth's experiences at Racedown, where the hedges were repeatedly raided for firewood by the scavenging poor. When a farmer catches an old woman in the act of pilfering, she curses him, and from that moment on he can never again be warm. 'I wished to draw attention to the truth that the power of the human imagination is sufficient to produce such changes even in our physical nature as might appear almost miraculous,' wrote Wordsworth afterwards, echoing what Coleridge had written about 'The Three Graves' in his preface to the poem.*

---

* 'I was not led to chuse this story from any partiality for tragic, much less to monstrous events . . . but from finding in it a striking proof of the possible effect on the imagination, from an Idea violently and suddenly imprest on it.'

Towards the end of April Wordsworth began a much longer narrative poem in a similar or arguably even plainer style, 'Peter Bell', which in its final form reached a length of more than a thousand lines. The tale was inspired by a story Wordsworth happened to read in a newspaper, of a donkey found hanging his head wretchedly beside a canal over his master's floating dead body. In the woods at Alfoxden Wordsworth took great delight in watching donkeys. The figure of Peter Bell himself was based on a 'wild rover' who had walked with Wordsworth along the Wye, from Builth almost as far as Hay, back in the summer of 1793. 'He told me strange stories,' Wordsworth remembered half a century afterwards. 'It has always been a pleasure to me through life to catch at every opportunity that has occurred in my rambles of becoming acquainted with this class of people.'[29] 'Peter Bell' is Wordsworth's response to the 'Ancient Mariner', the story of a bad man eventually frightened into good, not through the agency of the supernatural, but through a series of natural events, in particular the actions of his abused beast, the donkey. Thus the story evokes the redemptive power of nature. Wordsworth wrote fast, and within a month the poem was ready to read to visitors.

'You will be pleased to hear that I have gone on very rapidly adding to my stock of poetry,' Wordsworth informed Cottle. 'Do come and let me read it to you, under the old trees in the park.' A month later he wrote to Cottle again: 'We look for you with great impatience, we will never forgive you if you do not come.' He explained that he was determined to finish the Salisbury Plain poem, and equally determined that Cottle should publish it. 'I have lately been busy about another plan, which I do not wish to mention till I see you,' he continued; 'let this be *very, very* soon.'[30]

The 'plan' was for a volume of poems by both men, to be published anonymously, as if by a single poet. This was the book that became known as *Lyrical Ballads*. It had been mooted at least six months before; something of the sort was certainly discussed on the walk to Lynton when Coleridge began the 'Ancient Mariner'.[31] The notion of a joint volume was the culmination of their experiments in various kinds of co-operation.

It is unclear how this plan related to the volume of Wordsworth's poems that Coleridge offered to Cottle for thirty guineas, or to a possible third edition of Coleridge's poems that was also under consideration. Coleridge's description of how *Lyrical Ballads* came about in his *Biographia Literaria* was written nearly twenty years afterwards, and rationalised a process that seems to have been much more haphazard. Moreover, the two men's ideas about what the volume should contain changed as time passed and circumstances altered, and the original scheme may or may not have been more coherent than the final result. As Coleridge admitted, the make-up of the first edition of *Lyrical Ballads* was a compromise rather than an ideal.

> During the first year that Mr. Wordsworth and I were neighbours, our conversations turned frequently on the two cardinal points of poetry, the power of exciting the sympathy of the reader by a faithful adherence to the truth of nature, and the power of giving the interest of novelty by the modifying colours of imagination. The sudden charm, which accidents of light and shade, which moon-light or sun-set diffused over a known and familiar landscape, appeared to represent the practicability of combining both. These are the poetry of nature. The thought suggested itself (to which of us I do not recollect) that a series of poems might be composed of two sorts. In the one, the incidents and agents were to be, in part at least, supernatural; and the excellence aimed at was to consist in the interesting of the affections by the dramatic truth of such emotions as would naturally accompany such situations, supposing them real. And real in this sense they have been to every human being who, from whatever source of delusion, has at any time believed himself under supernatural agency. For the second class, subjects were to be chosen from ordinary life; the characters and incidents were to be such, as will be found in every village and its vicinity, where there is a meditative and feeling mind to seek after them, or to notice them, when they present themselves.

In this idea originated the plan of the 'Lyrical Ballads'; in which it was agreed, that my endeavours should be directed to persons and characters supernatural, or at least romantic, yet so as to transfer from our inward nature a human interest and a semblance of truth sufficient to procure for these shadows of imagination that willing suspension of disbelief for the moment, which constitutes poetic faith. Mr. Wordsworth, on the other hand, was to propose to himself as his object, to give the charm of novelty to things of every day, and to excite a feeling analogous to the supernatural, by awakening the mind's attention from the lethargy of custom, and directing it to the loveliness and the wonders of the world before us; an inexhaustible treasure, but for which in consequence of the film of familiarity and selfish solicitude we have eyes, yet see not, ears that hear not, and hearts that neither feel nor understand.

With this view I wrote the 'Ancient Mariner,' and was preparing among other poems, the 'Dark Ladie,' and the 'Christabel,' in which I should have more nearly realized my ideal, than I had done in my first attempt. But Mr. Wordsworth's industry had proved so much more successful, and the number of his poems so much greater, that my compositions, instead of forming a balance, appeared rather an interpolation of heterogeneous matter.

Cottle came down from Bristol in May, and spent a week at Alfoxden, with Coleridge also present most if not all of the time. As promised, Wordsworth read many of his new poems to Cottle, who immediately perceived their 'extraordinary merit' and advised him to publish them, expressing a belief that they would be well received. The discussions continued during a jaunt with Coleridge along the coast to the Valley of the Rocks, Cottle on horseback because of his lameness. The publisher was not taken with the plan for a joint volume, nor with the idea of anonymous publication. His preference would have been to publish Wordsworth's poems in two volumes, under his own name, by implication omitting Coleridge's 'Ancient Mariner', which perhaps he hoped to bring out separately. 'It would be a gratifying circumstance to me,' Cottle remarked, 'to have been the publisher of the first volumes of three such poets, as Southey, Coleridge, and Wordsworth; such a distinction might never again occur to a Provincial bookseller.'[32]

In all of these dealings it was Coleridge who conducted the negotiations, while Wordsworth was content to remain in the background. Coleridge had known Cottle longer, of course, but it was also a question of temperament. Wordsworth confessed to being 'a stranger to matters of business'.[33] The notion of Coleridge as a man of business might have seemed comical to those who knew him; nevertheless, that is the role he played. After Cottle's departure, Coleridge wrote to say that he and Wordsworth had 'weighed' his proposal, and decided against. Wordsworth, he continued, 'would not object to the publishing of Peter Bell *or* the Salisbury Plain singly; but to the publishing of *his poems* in two volumes he is decisively repugnant & oppugnant – He deems that they would want variety &c. &c.'

This is an odd argument: on the face of it, Wordsworth is saying that he prefers the new volume to be less than coherent. In fact there was plenty of variety in his poetry. Indeed it could well be argued that the resulting volume suffered from too much variety, rather than too little. The reference to 'Peter Bell' and the Salisbury Plain poem at this late stage tends to confirm the view that plans for *Lyrical Ballads* were still much less fixed than Coleridge's later description suggested. Many years afterwards Wordsworth stated that he had intended 'Peter Bell' to be included in the volume.[34]

Coleridge continued:

> We deem that the volumes offered to you are to a certain degree *one work*, in *kind tho' not in degree*, as an Ode is one work – & that our different poems are as stanzas, good relatively rather than absolutely: – Mark you, I say *in kind* tho' not in degree.

It is difficult to know what Coleridge meant by this, beyond the general sense that the poetry written by both men during the

Quantock period benefited from their constant interaction. It is noticeable that he refers to 'volumes', in the plural.

Cottle had argued that anonymous publications were more difficult to sell. But on this point too his advice was rejected. Coleridge pointed out that many popular works had been published anonymously, including Pope's *Essay on Man*, Erasmus Darwin's *The Botanic Garden* and Samuel Rogers's *The Pleasures of Memory*. Besides, he added, 'Wordsworth's name is nothing – to a large number of persons mine *stinks*.'[35] He may have been influenced by the attacks on him and other 'Jacobin poets' in the *Anti-Jacobin*, which continued throughout the summer.

There was both a negative and a positive reason for the line taken by the two poets. Wordsworth knew that some people would ridicule his poems; he was extremely reluctant to expose himself to public attack by publishing them under his own name, 'a thing which I dread as much as death itself'. He was sensitive to criticism; he hated notoriety: 'privacy and quiet are my delight'.[36] On the more positive side, a joint volume would be a fitting product of a year in which the two men had worked so closely together, 'writing at the same table'.

That Coleridge's letter to Cottle represented the views of both men was demonstrated by the fact that a line in Wordsworth's handwriting, emphasising a point that Coleridge was making about the appearance of the new volume, was interpolated mid-sentence.

Since the middle of February Coleridge had also been in correspondence with Cottle about a possible third edition of his work. He was planning to add 'three blank verse poems' (presumably 'This Lime-Tree Bower, My Prison', 'Frost at Midnight' and another of the 'conversation poems'), though not, it seems, the 'Ancient Mariner' or 'Christabel'. An embarrassed Cottle asked if Coleridge might be 'persuaded to resign' Lloyd's poems.* It was curious, Coleridge

---

* It has generally been assumed that Cottle was acting on instructions from Lloyd. But Coleridge's subsequent letters make more sense if Cottle was acting on his own initiative, and then had to withdraw; this interpretation also helps to explain Lamb's reference to 'some ungracious bookseller' as 'author of the separation' in dedicating his *Works* to Coleridge in 1818.[37]

replied, that his consent should be asked to 'give up' poems originally included 'at the earnest request of the author'. He had no objection to any disposal of Lloyd's poems, he said, 'except that of their being republished with mine'. Then Cottle appears to have backtracked, perhaps after discovering that he had misunderstood Lloyd's wishes. 'Let all things be as before,' Coleridge responded indulgently: 'I have no wish respecting those poems, either before or against their republication with mine.' He wished to avoid a face-to-face confrontation with Lloyd, 'that might disturb that evenness of benevolent feeling which I wish to cultivate'.[38]

What Cottle knew, but as yet Coleridge did not, was that the eponymous hero of Lloyd's epistolary novel *Edmund Oliver*, which Cottle was about to publish, closely resembled his former mentor. As soon as he read the novel Coleridge had no difficulty in recognising a ludicrous version of himself: a man with a fickle and 'passion-troubled mind', childish and impetuous, given to extravagant and often absurd behaviour. The physical description tallied: 'his large glistening eye – his dark eyebrows . . . and the dark hair'. Edmund Oliver's story had plenty in common with his own; indeed, Coleridge identified in the novel incidents that he had confided to Lloyd at his own fireside. There were plenty more similarities, including a predilection for laudanum: Edmund was said always to carry a bottle of the stuff in his greatcoat pocket. Even Edmund's epistolary style – a succession of short sentences punctuated by dashes – seemed a parody of Coleridge's more agitated prose. One especially low blow was to put into Edmund's mouth arguments for the sacredness of marriage, even when 'a man of extraordinary intellect, of the acutest sensibilities' is linked 'to a woman of the foulest dispositions, and of a temper that is the torment of his life'. At the conclusion of the novel, Edmund, his sister and his friend Charles are living together, sharing their property in 'a little society of love and virtue' and proclaiming Pantisocratic-like tenets.

Coleridge was lacerated by his portrayal in *Edmund Oliver*, and it is easy to see why. In fact the central character is not wholly unsympathetic, and shares some characteristics with Lloyd himself as well as with Coleridge.[39] It is possible that a misguided Lloyd saw the allusions to Coleridge as some form of homage to their friendship. Nevertheless Coleridge felt betrayed, by a man he had trusted and invited into his home, and his feeling of betrayal was exacerbated by the suspicion that Southey and perhaps Lamb (to whom the novel was dedicated) had contributed their own brush-strokes to the portrait.* His closest friends had been laughing at him, and conspiring at his public humiliation. Cottle too was part of the conspiracy. There was even the possibility that the Wordsworths were in the plot, if only to put pressure on Lloyd to leave out something or other. It emerged that Dorothy and perhaps William too had seen Lloyd in London while they were there in December 1797. In January Southey had told Cottle 'how *very unhandsome* I think the conduct of Wordsworth and his sister to Charles Lloyd respecting the passage which he has omitted'. It was 'mean and overbearing', Southey continued, 'an act of vanity'.[40]

Perhaps the Wordsworths had persuaded Lloyd to omit a passage they considered particularly hurtful to Coleridge – though Southey's letter makes it sound as if the passage was something to do with Wordsworth himself. If indeed they had seen the manuscript, neither seems to have understood how hurt Coleridge would feel by its publication. Even if not, they were still slow to appreciate the viciousness of Lloyd's attack. On 9 May, for example, Wordsworth wrote to Cottle thanking him for a copy of the novel. He confessed that he had not yet read it. 'Dorothy has read it through,' he went on; 'she thinks it contains a great deal a *very* great deal of excellent matter but bears the marks of a too hasty composition.'[41]

Lloyd tried to justify himself in letters to Coleridge, but he had gone too far to be easily forgiven. Coleridge felt besieged, trying to fend off 'a series of wicked calumnies & irritations', returning 'patience, gentleness and good for evil'.[42] He was further grieved that instead of being sympathetic, Lamb took Lloyd's side in the quarrel. There seems to have been considerable correspondence between the

---

* Lloyd wrote in the preface to *Edmund Oliver* that 'the incidents relative to the army were given me by an intimate friend, who was himself eye-witness to one of them, and can produce testimony to the truth of the other two'.

three of them, all now lost. Coleridge discovered that Lamb and Lloyd were planning a volume of blank-verse poems together. Then Dorothy told him what she had heard from Lloyd, that Lamb no longer intended to correspond with him. Perhaps Coleridge should not have believed this information, given its source; but he wrote a letter of regret and remonstrance to Lamb, when he might have done better to let things lie. He asked Lamb to press upon Lloyd 'the propriety, nay the necessity of his giving me a meeting either *tête à tête* or in the presence of all whose esteem I value'. Just as Southey had done, Coleridge was now speaking of his duty to defend his own character, in the type of language a gentleman might have used in the run-up to a duel. 'Coleridge has written a very odd letter to Lamb,' Lloyd reported to Southey. 'I don't know what may be his sentiments with regard to our conduct, but I can perceive that he is bent on disassociating himself from us – particularly Lamb, I think he has used unkindly.' Coming from Lloyd, this was a bit rich.

Lloyd was again staying with Southey, who was now living in Bristol. Coleridge suspected that Southey was behind the attacks from 'poor Lloyd, whose infirmities have been made the instruments of another man's darker passions'.[43] In mid-May, a few days after the birth of his second son (whom he named Berkeley, after the philosopher-bishop), Coleridge set off with the Wordsworths to walk to Cheddar, spending a night at Bridgwater *en route*. They toured the Gorge and the caves, which Coleridge had explored with Southey four years earlier. Wordsworth's main business was to fetch Lloyd from Southey's house, and to bring him back to Stowey. Wordsworth had belatedly realised how much his friend had been hurt, and had decided to take the initiative in trying to resolve the quarrel before matters deteriorated further. On the road, however, they received word that Lloyd – possibly wanting to avoid a confrontation – was leaving for Birmingham. Wordsworth pressed on to Bristol, in the hope of catching Lloyd before he left, but in vain.

'I have lately had some sorrows that have cut more deeply into my heart than they ought to have done,' wrote Coleridge in an attempt to console Poole, whose brother Richard was on his deathbed. It may have seemed insensitive for Coleridge to compare his grief to Poole's at such a time. But it was a mark of his unhappiness that he should make such a comparison at all. To his friend Estlin, Coleridge fulminated against 'calumny & ingratitude from men who have been fostered in the bosom of my confidence!'[44] A year later, while in Germany, Coleridge would refer to 'those that hate me' – by which he almost certainly meant Lloyd and Southey, and perhaps Lamb too.[45] In later years he would write that the effort to remain calm in the face of Lloyd's attack had preyed on his mind and his body, and prevented him from finishing 'Christabel'. After the death of Richard Poole, Coleridge wrote to his grieving friend that 'so many unpleasant & shocking circumstances have happened to me or to my immediate knowledge within the last fortnight,* that I am in a nervous state & the most trifling thing makes me weep'.[46]

Cottle, perhaps feeling partially responsible, attempted to mend the breach by writing to urge Lloyd to visit Coleridge. 'I love Coleridge, and can easily forget all that has happened,' replied Lloyd – but added that he could not go to Stowey at present, having only just arrived at his parents' house in Birmingham, where he was to receive a visit from Lamb. Lloyd would continue to make trouble between the two old friends. Coleridge had compared himself to Lamb, Lloyd told him, as examples of genius and talent respectively. It is impossible to know whether Lloyd was telling the truth, but it was the kind of thing that Coleridge might have done; he did not try very hard to conceal from his friends that he was cleverer than they were. Lloyd also told Lamb that Coleridge had said (or written): 'Poor Lamb, if he wants any *knowledge* he may apply to me.'

As Lloyd was aware, such a patronising comment from Coleridge – taken, of course, out of context – must have been infuriating to Lamb, who would recognise it as characteristic. And so it proved. Lamb's response was to send Coleridge a catechism, a series of eight mock theological questions headed 'Theses Quaedam Theologicae', beginning as follows:

* Another of these was the drowning of his friend Dr Toulmin's daughter, who 'in a melancholy derangement' apparently walked into the sea near Sidmouth.

I Whether God loves a lying Angel better than a true Man?

II Whether the Archangel* *Uriel* could *affirm an untruth? And if he could* whether he *would*?

III Whether Honesty be an angelic virtue? etc

The form of the document, which may have been drawn up with Lloyd while Lamb was staying with him in Birmingham, was a parody of a set of queries that had appeared in *The Watchman* no. 3, and that Coleridge had recently republished in the *Morning Post*.[48] A bitterly sarcastic Lamb continued as follows:

> Learned Sir, my Friend,
> Presuming on our long habits of friendship & emboldened further by your late liberal permission to avail myself of your correspondence, in case I want any knowledge (which I intend to do when I have no Encyclopaedia, or Lady's Magazine at hand to refer to in any matter of science), I now submit to your enquiries the above Theological Propositions . . .

Coleridge had ended his last letter to Lamb 'God bless you'; Lamb chose to end his, 'I remain, Your friend and docile Pupil to instruct'. There was no mistaking Lamb's resentment. Handing Cottle this letter, Coleridge remarked sadly, 'These young visionaries will do each other no good.'[49]

Coleridge's precious friendship with Lamb had been damaged, possibly (so it seemed at the time) beyond repair. Twenty years later the subject of the quarrel resurfaced in a letter from Lamb to Coleridge. He referred to Lloyd as 'a sad tattler', who had caused an estrangement from one (unnamed) friend which he had been regretting ever since. 'He almost alienated you (also) from me, or me from you, I don't know which. But that breach is closed.'[50]

A day or two after Coleridge and Dorothy returned from Cheddar, William Hazlitt arrived at Nether Stowey, having walked from Shropshire to Somerset, a distance of 150 miles. Back in January, on the

---

* These satirical references to Coleridge as an angel or archangel anticipate by eighteen years Lamb's famous (and affectionate) description of him as 'an Archangel a little damaged'.[47]

morning when Coleridge had received the offer of an annuity from the Wedgwood brothers at Hazlitt's father's house in Wem, he had given the awestruck young man a piece of card on which he had written his address,* and had said that he should be glad to see him at Nether Stowey. 'I was not less surprised than the shepherd-boy,' Hazlitt wrote afterwards, 'when he sees a thunderbolt fall close at his feet. I stammered out my acknowledgments and acceptance of this offer.'

Hazlitt was well received by his hero, who took him over to Alfoxden in the afternoon, where the visitor was allowed to dip into Wordsworth's manuscript poems. 'I slept that night in an old room with blue hangings, and covered with the round-faced family portraits of the age of George I and II, and from the wooded declivity of the adjoining park that overlooked my window, at the dawn of day, could "hear the loud stag speak".'

In the morning the two men strolled out into the park, and when both were seated on the trunk of a fallen ash tree, Coleridge read aloud Wordsworth's ballads. As Hazlitt listened, 'the sense of a new style and a new spirit in poetry came over me. It had to me something of the effect that arises from the turning up of the fresh soil, or of the first welcome breath of Spring . . .'

That evening Hazlitt and Coleridge walked back to Nether Stowey in the moonlight. Coleridge lamented that Wordsworth was not more inclined to believe in the traditional superstitions of the place, and that 'there was a something corporeal, a *matter-of-fact-ness*, a clinging to the palpable, or often to the petty, in his poetry, in consequence. His genius was not a spirit that descended to him through the air; it sprung out of the ground like a flower, or unfolded itself from a green spray, on which the goldfinch sang.' Coleridge's criticism was confined to Wordsworth's descriptive pieces: 'his philosophic poetry had a grand and comprehensive spirit in it, so that his soul seemed to inhabit the universe like a palace, and to discover truth by intuition, rather than by deduction'.

* This card was recently rediscovered by Tom Mayberry, Archivist at the Somerset Record Office. It seems that Hazlitt had preserved it as a relic.

The next day Wordsworth arrived at Coleridge's cottage on his way back from Bristol, where he had been trying in vain to find Charles Lloyd. Hazlitt found him 'more gaunt and Don Quixote-like' than he had been led by Coleridge to expect:

> He was quaintly dressed (according to the *costume* of that unconstrained period) in a brown fustian jacket and striped pantaloons. There was something of a roll, a lounge in his gait, not unlike his own 'Peter Bell'. There was a severe, worn pressure of thought about his temples, a fire in his eye (as if he saw something in objects more than the outward appearance), an intense, high, narrow forehead, a Roman nose, cheeks furrowed by strong purpose and feeling, and a convulsive inclination to laughter about the mouth, a good deal at variance with the solemn, stately expression of the rest of his face.

Wordsworth sat down and began to 'make havoc' of the half of a Cheshire cheese on the table. 'He talked very naturally and freely, with a mixture of clear, gushing accents in his voice, a deep guttural intonation, and a strong tincture of the northern *burr.*' While in Bristol he had been to see 'Monk' Lewis's *The Castle Spectre*, which, he said contemptuously, 'fitted the taste of the audience like a glove'.* Looking out of the low, latticed window, Wordsworth remarked, 'How beautifully the sun sets on that yellow bank!' and Hazlitt thought, 'with what eyes these poets see nature!'

They walked over to Alfoxden again the next day, where Wordsworth read them his 'Peter Bell' in the open air. Hazlitt noticed that there was 'a *chaunt* in the recitation both of Coleridge and Wordsworth, which acts as a spell upon the hearer, and disarms the judgment'. He was fascinated to compare the styles of the two, which he ascribed partly to their different methods of composition:

> Coleridge's manner is more full, animated, and varied; Wordsworth's more equable, sustained, and internal. The one

---

* Before seeing it performed he had already read the play, probably the printed copy that Coleridge had with him in Shrewsbury and had promised in a letter to Wordsworth to bring back to Somerset.

might be termed more *dramatic*, the other more *lyrical*. Coleridge has told me that he himself liked to compose in walking over uneven ground, or breaking through the straggling branches of a copse-wood; whereas Wordsworth always wrote (if he could) walking up and down a straight gravel walk, or in some spot where the continuity of his verse met with no collateral interruption.

Returning that same evening to Nether Stowey, Hazlitt got into a metaphysical argument with Wordsworth,[51] while Coleridge was explaining the different notes of the nightingale to Dorothy. Hazlitt appears to have stressed the importance of learning and progress, while Wordsworth extolled the virtues of contemplation and 'wise passiveness'. Hazlitt had tried to explain his ideas to Coleridge back in January, while they were walking together from Wem to Shrewsbury, without much success. Now, in discussion with Wordsworth, 'neither of us succeeded in making ourselves perfectly clear and intelligible'. Wordsworth thought the young Hazlitt 'somewhat unreasonably attached to modern books of moral philosophy', and urged him to 'let Nature be your teacher'. He afterwards dramatised their argument in two short poems. 'Expostulation and Reply' was a defence against a charge of indolence, arguing for 'wise passiveness' in the contemplation of Nature; in 'The Tables Turned' Wordsworth counterattacked:

> One impulse from a vernal wood
> May teach you more of man,
> Of moral evil and of good,
> Than all the sages can.
>
> Sweet is the lore which Nature brings;
> Our meddling intellect
> Misshapes the beauteous forms of things;
> – We murder to dissect.
>
> Enough of science and of art;
> Close up those barren leaves;
> Come forth, and bring with you a heart
> That watches and receives.

Hazlitt spent three weeks at Nether Stowey, 'generally devoting the afternoons to a delightful chat in an arbour made of bark by the poet's friend Tom Poole, sitting under two fine elm trees, and listening to the bees humming round us, while we quaffed our *flip*'.* Towards the end of his stay Coleridge took him on their favourite walk, along the coast to Lynton. Accompanying them was a local man named John Chester:

> This Chester was a native of Nether Stowey, one of those who were attracted to Coleridge's discourse as flies are to honey, or bees in swarming-time to the sound of a brass pan. He 'followed in the chase like a dog who hunts, not like one that made up the cry'. He had on a brown cloth coat, boots, and corduroy breeches, was low in stature, bow-legged, had a drag in his walk like a drover, which he assisted by a hazel switch, and kept on a sort of trot by the side of Coleridge, like a running footman by a state coach, that he might not lose a syllable or sound that fell from Coleridge's lips. He told me his private opinion that Coleridge was a wonderful man. He scarcely opened his lips, much less offered an opinion the whole way.

It was a long day's march, past Dunster, which Hazlitt eyed wistfully, and through Minehead, descending into little sheltered valleys and then ascending conical hills up paths that ran through coppiced woodland to a barren top, like a monk's shaven crown. They reached Lynton around midnight. There they had some difficulty in knocking up people of the house where they meant to stay, but were rewarded at last with fried bacon and eggs. The next morning they explored the Valley of the Rocks. A thunderstorm broke while they were at the inn, and Coleridge ran out bareheaded to enjoy the commotion of the elements in the valley, but 'as if in spite, the clouds only muttered a few angry sounds, and let fall a few refreshing drops'. On the third morning they returned, and Coleridge remarked on the silent smoke curling up the valleys from the cottage chimneys where, a few evenings before, they had seen the lights gleaming through the dark.

*

* A mixture of beer and spirits, sweetened with sugar and heated with a hot iron.

The Wordsworths left Alfoxden towards the end of June, and stayed about a week at the Coleridges' cottage in Nether Stowey, where they left most of their possessions in store. As the Coleridges were unlikely to be ready to go abroad before the autumn, Dorothy and her brother arranged to spend the intervening months in Bristol, where William could supervise the printing of *Lyrical Ballads*. Early in July they left Nether Stowey on foot. In Bristol they spent their first few days at Cottle's house in Wine Street. By now it was clear that Wordsworth's poems would form the bulk of the joint volume; aside from the 'Ancient Mariner' and 'The Nightingale', Coleridge's only other contributions were two extracts from *Osorio*. Thus of the twenty-three poems in the first edition of *Lyrical Ballads*, only four were Coleridge's; though because the 'Ancient Mariner' was by far the longest poem in the collection, his contribution amounted to almost one-third of the total.

Why Coleridge did not supply any of the several other unpublished poems he had on hand is unclear. Originally the volume had been intended to include his 'Lewti, or, the Circassian Love-Chant', a sub-stantial poem of more than a hundred lines developed from a frag-ment of Wordsworth's and published in the *Morning Post*. This was omitted at the last moment, perhaps in an attempt to preserve the anonymity of the volume – though Wordsworth's 'The Convict', another poem published in the *Morning Post*, was included, and both had appeared anonymously. The same consideration was probably the reason for omitting 'France: An Ode' ('The Recantation'), which unlike the other *Morning Post* poems had been published under Coleridge's name. But he had available three further unpublished 'conversation poems', all of the highest quality, not to mention 'Kubla Khan' and 'Christabel', plus a number of lesser poems. Indeed, it would have been possible to compile a volume consisting solely of Coleridge's unpublished verse. Perhaps he was holding back some or all of these for the third edition of his own work. But there is little evidence that he was doing so, nor (if that were the case) any obvious reason why he should not feel the same about the 'Ancient Mariner', the most substantial of all his poems.

Though *Lyrical Ballads* was conceived as a joint volume, there was from an early stage a tendency to refer to it as the work of one man – as 'Wordsworth's poems', 'William's poems', 'my poems' – to dispose of as he thought fit, without even consulting his co-author. The imbalance between their respective contributions exacerbated, though it did not initiate, this tendency. It also lent credence to the myth, perversely encouraged by Coleridge, that Wordsworth had been far more productive in their year together. Wordsworth's 'industry' contrasted with Coleridge's 'indolence'. Years before, in his letter of remonstrance to Southey, Coleridge had rejected the idea that comparative industry could be assessed by the number of lines written.* But even by such a measure, Coleridge was not far behind Wordsworth, despite the fact that he had to cope with many more distractions. On a rough count, Wordsworth wrote 3,500 lines of poetry during his Quantock year, and in the same period Coleridge wrote about 2,500 lines, plus the last two acts of *Osorio*.

In general, the selection of poems for the volume seems much less systematic than the plan described by Coleridge in *Biographia Literaria*. During Cottle's visit to west Somerset it had been decided that the volume should be published under the title of *Lyrical Ballads*, though fewer than half of the poems included could accurately be described as ballads. Nor were the ballads of the type that most readers would describe as 'lyrical'; indeed, to use the term 'lyrical' of such poems seemed like an act of defiance, a form of challenge to the conventional reader. A decision was taken to modify the title to *Lyrical Ballads, with a few other poems*, but it might have been more accurate to call the volume *A Few Ballads, with many other poems*.[52]

Most of Wordsworth's poems in the volume were written in the plain style referred to in the 'Advertisement', though at least one of them – 'The Female Vagrant', extracted from the Salisbury Plain poem – was written in the type of language condemned there; thus the vagrant's sheep are 'my fleecy store', her father's cottage 'his old hereditary nook', and so on. Why he should have included this poem

* See pages 107–8.

and not 'Peter Bell', which was written in the plainer style of the other poems, is again unclear; perhaps he wanted to keep it back for separate publication.*

Moreover, there was also to be an unpremeditated addition, completely different from his other poems. After a week or so in Bristol, the Wordsworths set out for a ramble. They crossed the Severn Estuary by ferry and then walked up the Wye from Chepstow, passing the ruined abbey at Tintern, and continued on by Monmouth as far as Goodrich Castle. When he first followed this route five years before, Wordsworth had been alone; now he was there with his 'dearest Friend', his sister Dorothy, the companion who shared his life and his hopes. Seeing it again, remembering how it had appeared to him before, and seeing it afresh through his sister's eyes, led him to muse on his experience of natural beauty. The sights he once again beheld had nourished his mind since last he was there:

> . . . These beauteous forms,
> Through a long absence, have not been to me
> As is a landscape to a blind man's eye:
> But oft, in lonely rooms, and 'mid the din
> Of towns and cities, I have owed to them
> In hours of weariness, sensations sweet,
> Felt in the blood, and felt along the heart . . .

As they would do in the future:

> And now, with gleams of half-extinguished thought,
> With many recognitions dim and faint,
> And somewhat of a sad perplexity,
> The picture of the mind revives again:
> While here I stand, not only with the sense
> Of present pleasure, but with pleasing thoughts
> That in this moment there is life and food
> For future years . . .

Wordsworth developed ideas about the enriching and healing powers of Nature expressed in Coleridge's 'Frost at Midnight'. Though he

* 'Peter Bell' was eventually published on its own in 1819.

could no longer feel the 'aching joys' and 'dizzy raptures' of his boyhood, he had found 'abundant recompense' elsewhere; he had learned (from Coleridge) a reverence for all of creation, not least 'the still, sad music of humanity':

> ... And I have felt
> A presence that disturbs me with the joy
> Of elevated thoughts; a sense sublime
> Of something far more deeply interfused,
> Whose dwelling is the light of setting suns,
> And the round ocean and the living air,
> And the blue sky, and in the mind of man;
> A motion and a spirit, that impels
> All thinking things, all objects of all thought,
> And rolls through all things.

From Coleridge too he had learned a new type of poetry, the intimate, autobiographical style of the conversation poems, a fact that he acknowledged by allusions to both 'This Lime-Tree Bower My Prison' and 'Frost at Midnight'.* The result was his first fully realised masterpiece, both a philosophical poem and a triumphant assertion of powerful feeling:

> ... Therefore am I still
> A lover of the meadows and the woods,
> And mountains; and of all that we behold
> From this green earth; of all the mighty world
> Of eye and ear, both what they half create,
> And what perceive; well pleased to recognise
> In nature and the language of the sense,
> The anchor of my purest thoughts, the nurse,
> The guide, the guardian of my heart, and soul
> Of all my moral being.

---

* e.g. from 'This Lime-Tree Bower My Prison':
  '... Henceforth I shall know
  That Nature ne'er deserts the wise and pure.'

From 'Tintern Abbey':
  'Knowing that Nature never did betray
  The heart that loved her...'

In this, the most personal of Wordsworth's poems to date, he employed Coleridge's technique to express Coleridge's ideas.

The poem's full title is 'Lines, Written a Few Miles Above Tintern Abbey, On Revisiting the Banks of the Wye During a Tour, July 13, 1798'. Addressed to Dorothy, it was concluded in the evening, just as Wordsworth and his sister were walking down the hill from Clifton into the centre of Bristol, after a tour of four or five days. The whole poem was carried in his mind; not a word of it was written down before they reached Bristol, and not a line altered afterwards.

The Wordsworths went into lodgings while they waited to depart for Germany. About three weeks later they were joined by Coleridge, who had been visiting his patron Josiah Wedgwood in Surrey. No doubt the Wordsworths enthused to their guest about their tour of the Wye Valley; perhaps Coleridge felt a little jealous not to have been present. At any rate, one evening he proposed another 'dart into Wales', and at six o'clock the next morning they set out together, this time travelling far enough upriver to visit Thelwall at Llyswen, above Hay.

Before darting into Wales, Coleridge had written to Poole proposing a new arrangement: instead of taking Sara and the two boys to Germany, with all the concomitant expense and other inconveniences, he would accompany the Wordsworths alone. Within three or four months he would have learned the language; he would then decide whether to return, or to 'fetch over my family'. Characteristically he left it up to Poole: 'make up your mind on my scheme'.[53] In the event it was decided that Sara and the children would stay behind, while John Chester made a late addition to their party.

By mid-September they were ready to leave. The four travellers assembled in London, where Coleridge had been for several days, dining with Mrs Barbauld and visiting her publisher Joseph Johnson, by now regarded as the father of the book trade.* Johnson was nervously awaiting sentence following his conviction on a charge of

* For some reason Coleridge did not take the opportunity to call on the *Morning Post*'s Daniel Stuart, who expressed the fear in a letter to Sara that he might somehow have offended his contributor.

sedition merely for selling Gilbert Wakefield's pamphlet, and was understandably anxious to placate the authorities; Coleridge needed cash, and Johnson's payment of £30 for three poems, one of which he had been paid for already, was very acceptable. No doubt too Coleridge was keen to unburden himself of his Jacobin associations, which clung to him despite his withdrawal from radical activism. The two men's needs coincided; it was quickly arranged that Johnson would publish a quarto pamphlet of poems expressing loyalist sentiments at this time of national emergency. As Coleridge put it, Johnson 'received me civilly the first time, cordially the second, affectionately the third – & finally took leave of me with tears in his eyes'.[54] The title-poem was 'Fears in Solitude', to which was added 'Frost at Midnight' and the poem formerly known as 'The Recantation', now retitled 'France: An Ode'.* Furthermore, Johnson agreed to take over the publication of *Lyrical Ballads* – an agreement that may have been brokered by Coleridge. Cottle was in financial difficulty, and was believed (mistakenly, as it turned out) to want to free himself from this commitment. Just before leaving England, Wordsworth wrote to Cottle asking him to give up his interest in the volume.

On Friday, 14 September Coleridge, Chester and the Wordsworths took the overnight coach to Yarmouth, arriving at midday on the fifteenth. That night they slept aboard ship. At eleven o'clock the following morning the packet weighed anchor and set sail. Chester turned green, Dorothy retired in confusion to her cabin, and her queasy brother soon followed her below. Coleridge, who had never before been to sea, remained on deck, gazing at the receding shoreline.

---

* The poem may have been retitled to play down Coleridge's radical past; or perhaps to conceal the fact that it had already appeared in print.

9

SEPARATION

'Over what place does the Moon hang to your eye, my dearest Sara?' Coleridge enquired of his wife in a letter written two nights later. 'To me it hangs over the left bank of the Elbe; and a long trembling road of moonlight reaches from thence up the stern of our Vessel, and there it ends.'[1] The packet lay at anchor off Cuxhaven, in the mouth of the estuary. They had made an unusually speedy crossing, in only forty-eight hours. Early next morning the crew hauled anchor and sailed upriver. The party disembarked at Hamburg that same afternoon, Wednesday, 19 September 1798.*

They found Hamburg filthy, smelly, noisy and populated by avaricious rogues ready to cheat foreigners at every opportunity – though the locals were 'frantic with Joy' at the news of Nelson's crushing victory over the French Mediterranean fleet at the Battle of the Nile, which had left Bonaparte and his army stranded in Egypt. A celebratory dinner was held, commemorated by the firing of twenty-one guns, and when Coleridge entered the concert hall the band struck up 'Rule Britannia'.

An audience with Klopstock,† 'the venerable Father of German poetry', proved a disappointment, as Coleridge reported to Poole. 'There was no *comprehension* in the Forehead – no *weight* over the eyebrows – no expression of peculiarity, either moral or intellectual,

---

* The cost of the passage to Coleridge had been three guineas, plus as much again in fees and incidental costs, including provisions and porterage.
† Friedrich Gottlieb Klopstock (1724–1803), whose epic poem *The Messiah* was inspired by Milton's *Paradise Lost*.

in the eyes; – there was no *massiveness* in the general Countenance.' His upper jaw was toothless, his lower jaw all black teeth, his legs swollen. Worst of all, he wore a periwig and powdered his hair, '& Powder ever makes an old man's face look dirty. It is an honor to Poets & Great Men that you think of them as parts of Nature; and any thing of Trick & Fashion wounds you in them as much as when you see Yews clipped into miserable peacocks. – The Author of the Messiah should have worn his own Grey Hair. Powder and the Periwig were to the Eye what *Mr* Milton would be to the Ear.' Klopstock was known as 'the German Milton', but Coleridge indignantly repudiated the comparison: 'a very *German* Milton indeed!' He had read a little of Klopstock's verse, '& that little was *sad Stuff*!' Their conversation was conducted in French, Wordsworth interpreting Klopstock's words to Coleridge.[2]

Dorothy was distressed to see 'a surly-looking German driving a poor Jew forward with foul language, and making frequent use of a stick'. She noticed the 'cold unfeeling cruelty' in the countenance of the bystanders, and was shocked to discover that the law provided Jews with no protection against such insolence. 'The Jew had no right to *reign* in the city of Hamburgh,' a German told them in broken English. Coleridge later remarked on how 'the Jews are horribly, unnaturally oppressed & persecuted all throughout Germany'.[3]

Hamburg proved very expensive, and the Wordsworths in particular began to fret about costs as soon as they landed. They needed to move on, but were at first undecided where to go. There was not much point in settling in a university town until they had mastered the language sufficiently to be able to benefit from study in German. Within a fortnight the party had broken up. Coleridge and Chester found pleasant if highly priced* accommodation boarding with a Protestant pastor in the beautiful small town of Ratzeburg, only thirty miles north-east of Hamburg, at the head of a lake that drained down into the Baltic, while Wordsworth and his sister travelled south into lower Saxony in search of cheaper lodgings. 'I hear that the Two

---

* Two pounds and eight shillings for each of them a week, full board, excluding washing, tea and wine.

Noble Englishmen* have parted no sooner than they set foot on German earth,' Lamb wrote gleefully to Southey.[4]

Lamb implied that differences between the two men had caused them to separate. But there were practical reasons for them to have done as they did. Coleridge was planning to return to England after only three months – perhaps to fetch his family, perhaps not – so he did not want to venture too far. Transport within Germany was rumoured to be expensive – they found it hard to get reliable information on the subject – and poor roads made travelling both uncomfortable and slow (it took Coleridge and Chester almost as long to reach Ratzeburg as it had taken them to go from London to Yarmouth, a journey four times the distance). The Wordsworths, on the other hand, expected to stay in Germany two or three years, so it made sense for them to seek out a cheaper region of the country. While still in England they had been advised to try Saxony; 'some parts of that country are extremely beautiful and boarding is very cheap'.[5]

Coleridge's supporters welcomed this parting from Wordsworth, perhaps concerned that he was becoming subsumed. It was disturbing to hear him regularly proclaim his inferiority to his friend. 'So there is an end of our fear about amalgamation,' Poole wrote to Coleridge, on hearing that the Wordsworths had gone their own way. Whose fears, one wonders? Did Coleridge himself fear that he was in danger from proximity to Wordsworth? Josiah Wedgwood expressed to Poole his hope that the two poets would continue separated: 'I am persuaded that Coleridge will derive great benefit from being thrown into mixed society.'[6]

Poole urged Coleridge to 'attend wholly to those things which are better attained in Germany than elsewhere'. He discouraged him from attempting new poetry, or from wasting time on pieces for the *Morning Post*. He even warned him against being too much with Chester – though, as a relative nonentity, the latter represented far less of a distraction than the Wordsworths. 'Speak nothing but

* Probably a reference to the play *The Two Noble Kinsmen*, attributed jointly to Shakespeare and John Fletcher and written around 1613. The young noblemen referred to in the title profess their eternal friendship, but then quarrel ludicrously over a girl.

German. Live with Germans. Read in German. Think in German.'[7] And Coleridge seems to have done as Poole recommended. Over the winter he learned to read both high and low German, and to speak the former fluently, though he confessed that his pronunciation remained 'hideous'. As Wedgwood predicted, he gained by mixing with Germans. Living full board, he was able to converse at mealtimes with his host, a widower, increasing his vocabulary every day. Coleridge had brought with him several letters of introduction supplied by the Wedgwoods, and within five weeks of his arrival at Ratzeburg he could report to his wife that he had dined at 'all the Gentlemen's & Noblemen's houses' within the vicinity, as well as attending balls and dances, and skating on the lake.[8] 'Coleridge is in a very different world from what we stir in,' Dorothy informed her brother Christopher; 'he is all in high life, among Barons counts and countesses.' She noted that his expenses were more than theirs conjointly. 'It would have been impossible for us to have lived as he does; we should have been ruined.'[9]

But after the intimacy they had enjoyed before, living apart was bound to be difficult. Five months into their stay in Germany, Dorothy described the 'joy' she and her brother felt on receiving 'long desired' letters from Coleridge. On recognising his handwriting, 'I burst open the seals and could almost have kissed them in the presence of the post-master'. She and her brother 'devoured' Coleridge's letters, each relishing them 'for at least two hours'.[10] The separation was particularly hard for Coleridge. William and Dorothy were together, but Coleridge was deprived of both his family and his dearest friends. Though he had plenty of company (including, of course, Chester) he missed the Wordsworths acutely, as was clear from some English hexameters he wrote as an exercise 'when I was ill and wakeful' – probably in early December, after he had not seen them for more than two months. He addressed these to 'William, my teacher, my friend!'

> William, my head and my heart! dear Poet that feelest and thinkest!
> Dorothy, eager of soul, my most affectionate sister!
> Many a mile, O! many a wearisome mile are ye distant,
> Long, long, comfortless roads, with no one eye that doth know us.

These lines seem to have been written in an experimental, playful mood, so perhaps they should not be taken too literally as an expression of Coleridge's feelings. Nevertheless, when sending them to Wordsworth, he affirmed the truth of the sentiment of the concluding line, 'scarcely less true in company than in pain and solitude':

> William, my head and my heart! Dear William and dear Dorothea!
> You have all in each other; but I am lonely, and want you![11]

'William works hard,' Dorothy informed Coleridge, 'but not very much at the German.' Coleridge found this 'strange – I work at nothing else, from morning to night'.[12] The Wordsworths had come to rest in Goslar, a decaying medieval town at the foot of the Hartz Mountains, more than a hundred miles south of Hamburg, at the end of three days' weary journey. For reasons of economy they had chosen not to board; but eating their meals alone meant they were deprived of regular contact with German-speakers. Nor did they go out into society, as they were given to understand that a man and a woman who accepted invitations were expected to offer hospitality in return, and this they could not afford. They disliked the warm fug of the stove-heated rooms in which Germans received company, made worse by the fact that most of the local men smoked pipes, thickening the air so as almost to extinguish candles. In fact, as Wordsworth wryly confessed to Josiah Wedgwood, they mixed only with their landlady (a widow, 'respectable *in her way*', who nevertheless could not refrain from swindling her foreign guests), an émigré French priest, and a deaf neighbour missing many of his teeth – 'so that with bad German, bad English, bad French, bad hearing, and bad utterance you will imagine that we have had very pretty dialogues'.[13]

Coleridge told his wife that Wordsworth had been wrong to bring his sister: this prevented him from mixing in society, because 'it is next to impossible for any but married women or in the suit of married women to be introduced to any company in Germany. Sister is considered as only a name for Mistress.' It seemed to Coleridge (or so he wrote to Sara) that his friend had lost his inclination for male acquaintance – indeed, for any acquaintance, male or female, other than that of his sister.[14] Later he complained that 'dear Wordsworth' appeared to have 'hurtfully segregated & isolated his Being/Doubtless, his delights are more deep and sublime;/but he has likewise more hours, that prey on his flesh & blood.'[15]

Coleridge's uncharitable remark about the mistakenness of bringing Dorothy to Germany can perhaps be attributed to his unhappiness at being separated from the Wordsworths. His comment about how the name of 'sister' was considered code for mistress echoes the slur made by Dr Daniel Lysons, who had reported to the Duke of Portland in 1797 that Wordsworth had 'no wife with him, but only a woman who passes for his Sister'.

The Wordsworths' isolation was exacerbated by one of the coldest winters on record. The Elbe froze solid, so that communication with England was suspended for months. Brother and sister were confined to the house for most of the time, huddled around their black iron stove, venturing out for only an hour or so each day, wrapped in fur coats and hats to keep out the chill. There was little or no intellectual life in Goslar, and no good library. 'As I have had no books I have been obliged to write in self-defence,' Wordsworth wrote drily to Coleridge; 'I should have written five times as much as I have done but that I am prevented by an uneasiness at my stomach and side, with a dull pain about my heart.'[16] These seemed ominous signs in a man of only twenty-eight. Dorothy observed anxiously that 'William is very industrious: his mind is always active; indeed, too much so; he overwearies himself, and suffers from pain and weakness in the side.'[17] These were symptoms that she had noticed before – together with 'violent' or 'nervous' headaches – and would recur more and more frequently. They seem to have been associated with the strain of composition. 'I am absolutely consumed by thinking and feeling,' Wordsworth continued, suggesting that for him writing demanded physical effort, not just of the hand and mind, but of his whole body. To ease his strain Dorothy took down both poetry and prose from his dictation, and copied out lines of his verse to send to Coleridge. Often she would supplement a letter to Coleridge dictated by her brother with a message of her own.

*

In the same letter to Coleridge, dictated to Dorothy like so many others, Wordsworth included three passages of autobiographical blank verse, a first glimpse of the poem that would become known to posterity as *The Prelude*. This title was not used until after the poet's death, but it indicates how he conceived the poem, as a prelude to a greater work: *The Recluse*.* In its first form, as begun in the winter of 1798–99 and completed the following autumn, this work consisted of two books; later it would comprise five, then thirteen, and eventually fourteen. The poem was written in several bursts, years apart, and would be much revised thereafter. It is unlikely that Wordsworth envisaged a work on such a scale when he began to produce autobiographical fragments during that winter, and possible that he did not even think of it as a distinct work when he began. He was groping for a way forward with *The Recluse*; finding his path blocked, he began to explore in verse the origin and development of his powers, in the hope that this would reveal the route he should follow.

Many years later, Wordsworth would explain that he had undertaken 'a review of his own mind' in preparation for writing *The Recluse*, to 'examine how far Nature and Education had qualified him for such employment'. It was this process of self-analysis that so absolutely consumed him during the winter months in Goslar. As part of this preparation, he 'undertook to record, in verse, the origin and progress of his own powers, as far as he was acquainted with them'.

Lines of *The Recluse* written at Alfoxden in the spring had hinted that he might look inwards before tackling his main theme:

> . . . And if with this
> I mix more lowly matter; with the thing
> Contemplated describe the Mind and the man
> Contemplating; and who, and what he was –
> The transitory Being who beheld
> This vision; when and where and how he lived; –
> Be not this labour useless –

---

* Confusingly, Coleridge referred to it as a 'tail-piece' to *The Recluse*.

'Tintern Abbey', written just before he left for Germany, had taken Wordsworth into new territory, providing a means for him to express in simple yet magnificent lines the intense joy he felt in nature. Now his creative tide flowed strongly. In the bleak surroundings of Goslar, isolated from everyone but his sister, he delved deep into the riches of his memory. He retrieved incidents from his boyhood one after another, shaping them into passages of sublime verse. Three of these he now sent to Coleridge.

Whether Coleridge understood that these passages were fragments of a much larger work is unknown. It is clear that there was frequent correspondence between him and Wordsworth while they were in Germany, but most of this has not survived. Many years later, Coleridge referred to the thirteen books on the growth of an individual mind (*The Prelude*) as having been written to a plan 'partly suggested by me', yet what he went on to say suggests that he was referring to the plan for *The Recluse*.[18] He was certainly impressed by what he read that winter in Germany. A fragment of a letter he wrote to his friend refers to his pleasure at reading a passage of blank verse later incorporated into *The Prelude*. He picked out a couple of lines that 'I should have recognised any where; and had I met these lines running wild in the deserts of Arabia, I should have instantly screamed out "Wordsworth!" '[19]

In another passage written at this time, Wordsworth addressed Coleridge directly:

> Nor will it seem to thee, my friend, so prompt
> In sympathy, that I have lengthened out
> With fond and feeble tongue a tedious tale.
> Meanwhile my hope has been that I might fetch
> Reproaches from my former years, whose power
> May spur me on, in manhood now mature,
> To honourable toil. Yet should it be
> That this is but an impotent desire –
> That I by such inquiry am not taught
> To understand myself, nor thou to know
> With better knowledge how the heart was framed

Of him thou lovest – need I dread from thee
Harsh judgments if I am so loth to quit
Those recollected hours that have the charm
Of visionary things, and lovely forms
And sweet sensations that throw back our life
And make our infancy a visible scene
On which the sun is shining?[20]

It appears that Wordsworth was seeking Coleridge's endorsement for the direction he had taken. (Whether he sent this passage to Coleridge is not known.) Maybe he was anxious that Coleridge might think it a diversion from the main task of *The Recluse*. Wordsworth's unease was understandable, because he was attempting something previously untried. Such an emphasis on personal experience seemed to his contemporaries self-important. 'He sees nothing but himself and the universe,' wrote Hazlitt in his *Lectures on the English Poets*, describing Wordsworth's egotism as 'in some respects a madness'. In his letters Keats would criticise 'the wordsworthian or egotistical sublime'. Neither of these men had read *The Prelude*; had they done so, their criticism would surely have been even sharper. Such reactions help to explain Wordsworth's reluctance to publish the poem in his lifetime. Yet looking inward was an essential part of the Romantic revolution initiated by Wordsworth and Coleridge. It is significant that the term 'autobiography' would enter the English language in the first decade of the nineteenth century, and that Southey would be among the first to use it in print.

One of the autobiographical passages Dorothy copied out for Coleridge was a description of skating in the Lake District, based on a childhood memory of Wordsworth's. This was a response to a letter Coleridge had written from Ratzeburg, rhapsodising on the pleasures of skating. Dorothy admitted that they wished to 'decoy' him to the north of England, where he might enjoy skating with her brother: 'A race with William upon his native lakes would leave to the heart and the imagination something more Dear and valuable than the gay sight of Ladies and countesses whirling along the lake of Ratzeburg.' Was there a hint of jealousy in this remark?

Another passage Dorothy transcribed to send to Coleridge described a boyhood expedition to gather hazelnuts. 'I think I shall not tire you,' she wrote.

> It is like the rest, laid in the North of England, whither wherever we finally settle you must come to us at the latter end of next summer, and we will explore together every nook of that romantic country. You might walk through Wales and Yorkshire and join us in the county of Durham, and I would once more follow at your heels, and hear your dear voices again.[21]

The Wordsworths had already decided to return to England once the weather improved.

Dorothy also copied out two 'little Rhyme poems which I hope will amuse you'. These were early versions of 'She dwelt among the untrodden Ways' and 'Strange Fits of Passion I have known', two of the cycle of five known as the 'Lucy poems'. (In copying it out she described the latter as 'a favourite of mine – i.e. of me Dorothy'.) Soon afterwards Wordsworth sent Coleridge another, 'A Slumber did my Spirit seal'. These poems allude to the death or imagined death of 'Lucy', a beloved young woman whose identity has been the subject of much speculation. The theory has often been advanced that Dorothy was the model for Lucy, and there is certainly some evidence to support this identification. Wordsworth would use the name 'Lucy' in another poem not in this sequence, 'The Glow-worm', in which the narrator tenderly places a glow-worm for 'my Lucy' to see. When sending this poem to Coleridge in 1802, he explained that it was based on an incident that had taken place 'about seven years ago between Dorothy and me'.[22] In identifying Dorothy as the subject of these poems, it has even been suggested that the repeated harping on Lucy's death marked Wordsworth's repression of incestuous feeling towards his sister.[23] But other aspects of the Lucy figure point away from Dorothy. In creating characters a writer will mix elements from real individuals with others from his imagination, just as he may draw on real events without being limited by them. To infer

Wordsworth's thoughts and feelings from his poems is to deny his powers to create.

Nevertheless, it is reasonable to assume that in writing the 'Lucy' poems Wordsworth found inspiration from his life with his sister, his only companion in this period. Coleridge guessed that 'A Slumber did my Spirit seal' might refer to Dorothy. 'Whether it had any reality, I cannot say,' he wrote to Poole; 'most probably, in some gloomier moment he had fancied the moment in which his Sister might die.'[24]

Coleridge became increasingly anxious at having heard nothing from home. At last, on the final day of November 1798, when he had been away four months, he received a letter from his wife. It contained grim news. Sara apologised for not writing earlier, 'but I was at the time struggling under the most severe trial that I have ever had to undergo'. Little Berkeley had become infected with smallpox after a botched inoculation;* he had been close to death, and left disfigured with the characteristic pockmarks on his face. It had been a terrible ordeal for Sara. She had lost a great deal of weight, and much of her hair, with the result that she wore a wig ever after. 'What I felt is impossible to write – I had no husband to comfort me and share my grief – perhaps the boy would die, and he far away!'[25]

Coleridge was overcome, and cried fitfully all day. He wrote to commiserate with Sara, though characteristically the letter was all about his own feelings of distress, including swollen eyelids (perhaps brought on by so much weeping). Poole was determined to protect Coleridge from unnecessary anxiety, and made light of events at home. 'Mrs Col and the little ones are perfectly well,' he wrote breezily. 'Berkeley was, as you have heard, well peppered with the smallpox, but never in any danger.' He urged Coleridge not to come home 'till every object of your journey be attained'.[26]

---

* A very recent innovation: Jenner's first inoculation had been given only two years before, and his account of this and subsequent successful vaccinations had been published only months before Poole's sister-in-law initiated the inoculation of all the Nether Stowey children.

'My Wife, believe and know that I pant to be home & with you,' Coleridge assured her – but instead of returning as she obviously longed for him to do, he chose to extend his stay by another six months. Bolstered by Poole, he persuaded himself that this was his duty. Having already spent so much in coming to Germany, he could not leave before he had gathered materials for a work that would enable him to recoup his expenses. He had already decided what this should be: a life of Lessing,* '& interweaved with it a true state of German Literature, in it's rise and present state'. This would capitalise on the vogue for German literature in England (already on the decline, though Coleridge could not have been expected to know this). Like Coleridge himself, Lessing had been a polymath, with what Schlegel would later describe as a 'boldly combining mind'. Coleridge saw multiple similarities between himself and his projected subject. His interest had been captured by a 'very, very fine' portrait he had seen in Hamburg:

> His eyes were uncommonly like mine – if anything, rather larger & more prominent – But the lower part of his face & his nose – O what an exquisite expression of elegance and sensibility!

Though 'the effect of his Physiognomy' was marred by a toupee periwig.[27]

Coleridge was also collecting books and other materials for the great prose work of philosophical synthesis 'to which I hope to dedicate in silence the prime of my life'.[28] He aimed to achieve a philosophical resolution that would act as a 'friend', a guide to life. For all these reasons he would need to enrol at the University of Göttingen, and stay there at least until the summer term ended in May.

He had from the start written a journal of his activities and observations in Germany, sending this to Sara and to Poole alternately, so as to avoid time-wasting duplication. There was a good possibility that such a journal might in due course be published (as indeed it

---

* Gotthold Ephraim Lessing (1729–81), playwright and critic, an early champion of Shakespeare.

was, in *The Friend*).* It was assumed that the two recipients would share their letters from Coleridge. One disadvantage of this scheme was that his letters, particularly his letters to his wife, were more impersonal than one might expect.

Sara remained very worried about Berkeley, now eight months old, who had not fully recovered from his illness. On medical advice she took her two boys to Bristol for a change of air. Berkeley's illness had put her to considerable unexpected expense, and she could not afford to alienate Poole, who put pressure on her not to burden her husband with details that would upset him. Instead Poole took it upon himself to keep Coleridge informed of his child's health. 'Berkeley had a cough which prevailed amongst the children here' – but, as he assured Coleridge, 'the change of air has been of great service to him'. Poole felt that his brilliant young friend should be spared the responsibilities of a husband and a father. 'Let, my dear Col., nothing trouble you,' he urged.[29]

On 11 February 1799 Poole received a letter from a distraught Sara. 'Oh! My dear Mr Poole, I have lost my dear child!' Berkeley was dead. She had not yet written to her husband, she told Poole, 'and when I do – I will pass over all disagreeable subjects with the greatest care, for I well know their violent effect on him – but I account myself most unfortunate at being at a distance from him at this time, wanting his consolation as I do, and feeling my grief almost too much to support with fortitude'. Hartley too was feverish, though recovering. Southey undertook to arrange the baby's funeral, and he and Edith kindly offered Sara and Hartley a refuge at their house on the outskirts of Bristol, where they would soon be going, 'for this house at present is quite hateful to me' (Southey came over in a coach to collect them). She concluded by asking Poole to lend her money until her husband's return, as the amount he had left her was almost all spent.[30]

Poole persuaded Sara not to distract her husband from his studies by telling him of Berkeley's death. However well meaning, Poole's interventions would have a disastrous effect on Coleridge's marriage.

---

* In 1797 Cottle had published a volume of Southey's letters to Edith from Spain and Portugal.

Sara found herself without her husband's support at a moment of extreme distress. Ignorant of the tragedy at home, Coleridge prolonged his stay in Germany. On the day of Berkeley's death he was in Hanover, *en route* to Göttingen. While his wife was in mourning he sent her regular letters, often written in a tone that must have been painful to her. While she grieved for her lost child, he described high-spirited drinking bouts. It was only natural for Sara to resent his continuing absence, and to contrast Southey's uxoriousness with her own husband's neglect. Southey showed a manly care for his wife and sister-in-law, while Coleridge was spared his responsibilities like a pampered boy.

Meanwhile Coleridge struggled to balance his loyalty to Poole against his desire to be with Wordsworth. 'Of many friends, whom I love and esteem,' he assured Poole, 'my head & heart have ever chosen you as the Friend – as the one being, in whom is involved the full & whole meaning of that sacred Title.' Poole was 'my Friend, my best Friend, my Brother, my Beloved – the tears run down my face'. Coleridge protested that he could not write to Poole without tears: 'my spirit is more feminine than yours'. He could not endure to have an enjoyment in which Poole could not partake, he declared. 'My *whole Being* so yearns after you,' he wrote to Poole towards the end of his stay in Germany, 'that when I think of the moment of our meeting, I catch the fashion of German Joy, rush into your arms, and embrace you.'[31] His letters to his wife were not so passionate. But his dramatic expressions of affection for Poole should not be misinterpreted. He observed men kissing and embracing each other with distaste. After a riotous evening in Göttingen, at which bottles were smashed and drunken men embraced, he wrote to Sara that 'this Kissing is a most loathsome Business – & the English are known to have such an aversion to it, that it is never expected of them'.[32] If Coleridge's letters to Poole were in any sense an expression of physical desire, it was his response to an unconscious desire he may have sensed in his friend; for Coleridge it was almost second nature to present himself to others in the form that would please them most.

Coleridge's avowals of his determination to adhere to Poole became more vociferous as he felt himself pulled in a different direction. 'I am sure I need not say how you are incorporated into the better part of my being,' he told Wordsworth, 'how, whenever I spring forward into the future with noble affections, I always alight by your side.' In their correspondence during the winter of 1798–99 they seem to have discussed plans to settle 'in neighbourhood to each other' when they returned to England.[33] Where this should be remained unresolved. Though Wordsworth had left England with half a mind to return to the Quantocks,* in Germany his thoughts turned increasingly towards the Lakes. No doubt his inner journey into the country of his boyhood rekindled a desire to return there. If, as seems likely, he had not yet revealed to Coleridge the extent and the scope of the autobiographical poem on which he had been working, this made it difficult to explain his motives. 'Wordsworth is divided in his mind, unquietly divided, between the neighbourhood of Stowey & the N[orth]. of England,' Coleridge grumbled to Poole. 'He cannot think of settling at a distance from *me*, & I have told him that I *cannot* leave the vicinity of Stowey.' But Coleridge did not want to go back to the old cottage: 'it is not possible, I can be either comfortable or useful in so small a house'. He asked Poole to look out for somewhere else.[34]

'*I will not part from you, if you will not part from me,*' wrote Poole. 'I can truly say that your society is a principal ingredient of my happiness, a principal source of my improvement.'[35] Coleridge assured Poole that he felt the same: 'my Resolve is fixed, *not to leave you till you leave me!*' Nevertheless he felt drawn towards Wordsworth. The conflict came to a head when the Wordsworths visited Coleridge at Göttingen in the early spring. They had left Goslar almost two months earlier to 'saunter about' Germany, and were now on their way home. It was an emotional reunion. The three spent the day together, and towards evening Coleridge accompanied the two walkers five miles along their route. Wordsworth tried to persuade his friend to join them in the Lakes. 'W. was affected to tears at the thought of not

---

* Just before leaving Hamburg for Saxony, he asked Poole to 'keep your eye' on Alfoxden, in case it should become free again.

being near me,' Coleridge reported to Poole; 'it is painful for me too to think of not living near him; for he is a *good* and *kind* man, & the only one whom in *all* things I feel my Superior – & you will believe me, when I say, that I have few feelings more pleasurable than to find myself in intellectual Faculties an Inferior.' But he resisted; there was 'the expense of removing, & the impropriety of taking Mrs Coleridge to a place where she would have no acquaintance, two insurmountable objections'. Most of all, there was Poole himself. 'Finally, I told him plainly, that *you* had been the man in whom *first* and in whom alone, I had felt an *anchor!*' It was a contest of wills. 'I think it highly probable, that where I live, there he will live, unless he should find in the North any person or persons, who can feel & understand him, can reciprocate & react on him.'[36]

A month or so after Berkeley's death Poole relented, and wrote to tell Coleridge the melancholy news. Perhaps he feared that Coleridge was likely to hear of it soon one way or another. His letter made light of Sara's suffering: 'Don't conjure up any scenes of distress which never happened. Mrs Coleridge felt as a mother,' he assured his friend, '*but she never forgot herself.* She is now perfectly well and does not make herself miserable by recalling the engaging, though, remember, mere instinctive attractions of an infant a few months old.' Poole, a bachelor with little experience of children, digressed on the unreasonableness of affection towards babies: 'When the infant becomes a reasonable being, then let the affection be a thing of reason, not before.' Again he urged Coleridge not to come home 'till you have done your business'. In an act of unconscious cruelty, he sent the letter via Sara for her to read and forward.[37]

Coleridge read Poole's letter calmly, and afterwards walked out into the open fields, 'oppressed, not by my feelings, but by the riddles, which the Thought so easily proposes, and solves – never!' He could not truly say that he grieved: 'I am perplexed – I am sad – and a little thing, a very trifle would make me weep; but for the death of the Baby I have *not* wept!'[38]

He wrote to his wife by the same post. 'It is one of the discomforts of my absence, my dearest Love! that we feel the same calamities at different times.' He trusted that this sad event might 'in many and various ways be good for us – To have shared – nay, I should say – to have divided with any human Being any one deep Sensation of Joy or of Sorrow, sinks deep the foundations of a lasting love'. (Of course, this was just what they had not done.) He referred for the first time in their correspondence to difficulties within their marriage: 'When in Moments of fretfulness and Imbecility I am disposed to anger or reproach, it will, I trust, be always a restoring thought – "We have wept over the same little one – & with whom am I angry? – with her who so patiently and unweariedly sustained my poor and sickly Infant through his long Pains."' He concluded by saying that he hoped to be home 'at the end of 10 or 11 weeks', i.e. towards the end of June.[39]

Poor Sara had been counting on his return in May. She had already been forced to solicit a further ten guineas from Poole to tide her over. When Coleridge received a letter from her describing her misery and her longing for his return, he reacted tetchily: 'Surely it is unnecessary for me to say, how infinitely I languish to be in my native Country & with how many struggles I have remained even so long in Germany!' But it was impossible, he said, for him to collect what he had to collect in less than six weeks, even though he was reading and transcribing between eight and ten hours every day. If he was to return now, they would be embarrassed and in debt, but if he finished what he was doing they would be clear – 'not to add that so large a work with so great a variety of information from sources so scattered, & so little known even in Germany, will, of course, establish my character – for industry & erudition, certainly; & I would fain hope, for reflection & genius'. He hoped to be home in two months' time, late in June.[40]

Sara could not hide her disappointment, but declared herself 'fully satisfied with your reasons'. She was now once again living at the Nether Stowey cottage, 'this horrible place', with its 'hateful' associations. They must leave there when he came back, she continued. 'My dear dear Samuel, do not lose a moment of time in finishing your work – for I feel like a poor deserted thing.'[41]

Coleridge told Poole that he was homesick. He was depressed that he had not written any substantial poems in Germany, in stark contrast to Wordsworth. 'My poor Muse is quite gone – perhaps, she may return & meet me at Stowey.' The many nightingales around Göttingen had recalled to his mind his own poem on the subject, and then 'my *only* child' Hartley, who featured prominently in the poem. 'Dear Lamb! I hope, *he* won't be dead before I get home. – There are moments in which I have such a power of Life within me, such a conceit of it, I mean – that I lay the Blame of my Child's Death to my absence – *not intellectually*; but I have a strange sort of sensation, as if while I was present, none could die whom I intensely loved.'[42]

Despite such feelings, he still did not hurry home. Instead he found time for a week's walking tour in the Hartz Mountains with a group of other young Englishmen studying at the university, romping in apparent high spirits, like a carefree undergraduate. While they walked he recited 'Christabel', and it is possible that the reactions of his young friends persuaded him that he should continue with the poem. On his return to Göttingen he wrote to Josiah Wedgwood summarising what he felt he had achieved in Germany. Though the year was not yet five months old he had already spent more than two-thirds of his annuity, and he asked Wedgwood's permission to '*anticipate*' the following year's allowance.

On 24 June 1799 Coleridge and Chester left Göttingen. Even then they did not come directly home, but followed a circuitous route, returning first to the Hartz Mountains and then exploring the area to the north. They did not reach Cuxhaven until 18 July. The rest of the journey was straightforward enough. In London, Coleridge stopped to borrow a clean shirt from Richard Wordsworth. He probably visited Daniel Stuart, who had been disappointed not to receive any contributions to the *Morning Post* from him in Germany. Coleridge arrived in Nether Stowey towards the end of July. He had been away from home almost exactly a year.

The Wordsworths had reached England three months earlier. They were now without a home or any definite plan for the future. But they did have a temporary refuge. When they had decided to abandon the German experiment and to return to England as soon as it was warm enough to do so, they had arranged to stay indefinitely with Dorothy's friend Mary Hutchinson, who lived with her brothers and sisters in a substantial brick house at Sockburn-on-Tees in County Durham. The Hutchinsons, like the Wordsworths, had been orphans since childhood; Mary's brother Tom was farming at Sockburn, helped by his youngest brother George. An elder brother, John, a widower, was in business in nearby Stockton, and another brother was away at sea. Tom's three sisters, Mary, Sara and Joanna, all unmarried, kept house for him and his brothers. The Hutchinsons and the Wordsworths were related by marriage,* and Mary had been Dorothy's particular friend in Penrith, when both were living with relatives after the death of their parents. Dorothy had stayed some weeks at Sockburn in the spring of 1795, and almost two years later Mary had spent more than six months at Racedown, leaving the day before Coleridge's arrival.

Mary was the eldest sister, born in 1770, the same year as Wordsworth. Sara was five years younger, and Joanna five years younger still. Another sister, Margaret, had died in 1796, a tragedy which had affected all her siblings, strengthening in particular the already close bond between Mary and Sara. Back in 1787, during the summer when Dorothy was reunited with her brothers, she had introduced William to her friend Mary, and they were often in each other's company both that summer and the following year, when Wordsworth returned from Cambridge for the long vacation. It is likely that there was a brief romance between the two young people, then in their late teens. Mary was plain, with a squint in one eye, but she was tall and fair, with a gentle manner and a sweet temper, and she radiated a graceful womanliness that evidently attracted Wordsworth. Though they were not to see each other again for several years, it seems that some tender

---

* William Monkhouse, uncle to Mary Hutchinson and her siblings, and the Reverend William Cookson, uncle to Dorothy and her siblings, married two sisters, Ann and Dorothy Cooper. William Monkhouse and Ann Cooper were first cousins by birth. In 1812 Thomas Hutchinson would marry his first cousin Mary Monkhouse, William's niece.

feeling between them persisted, and was renewed during Mary's stay at Racedown. Many years later, Wordsworth wrote to Mary recalling her time there and imagining how, had things been only a little different, 'we should have seen so deeply into each others hearts, and been so fondly locked in each others arms, that we should have braved the worst and parted no more'.[43] What he meant by 'braved the worst' is uncertain, though it was probably a reference to his lack of prospects. Mary's wealthy uncle, whose support was important to the orphaned Hutchinsons, disapproved of the attachment for this reason. The other obstacle between them was of course Wordsworth's affair with Annette Vallon. Though his emotions for Annette had cooled, he felt a continuing obligation towards his former mistress and their child.

After landing at Yarmouth, William and Dorothy travelled straight to Sockburn, where they were to remain more than seven months. It was not yet certain where they would settle. There was some talk of taking a house nearby, while the possibility remained that they might return to West Somerset. 'We are yet quite undetermined where we shall reside,' Dorothy wrote to Poole on 4 July. 'If you hear of any place in your neighbourhood that will be likely to suit us we shall be much obliged to you if you will take the trouble of writing to us.'[44]

Once again, Wordsworth was troubled by money worries. His brother Richard wrote to say that he had received not 'a Farthing' from Montagu, while Montagu's friend Douglas had paid only £10 of the £100 he owed, and was now believed to be in the West Indies. A note Montagu had given Richard for £21.5s. had not been honoured when it fell due. Richard was determined to have nothing more to do with Montagu, and pressed on his younger brother 'the necessity of coming immediately to some conclusion' with him.[45] Meanwhile there was an urgent need to earn some money. During the last few months in Germany Wordsworth had revised both 'Peter Bell' and the Salisbury Plain poem, meaning to improve each of them to a publishable state. Now he set about trying to discover what had happened to the *Lyrical Ballads*. The volume had been published the previous autumn, only a fortnight or so after their departure from Yarmouth. From the different accounts he had heard, Wordsworth feared that there had been 'some sad mismanagement in the case'. It turned out that despite his rumoured financial difficulties Cottle had not given up his interest in the volume in favour of Joseph Johnson, as Wordsworth had wanted. Cottle's reason for not complying with Wordsworth's request was that he had already entered into an agreement to sell almost all his stock to Arch, another London bookseller, and indeed copies had been printed with Arch's name on the title page. (Cottle later claimed that the copies had been sold at a loss, but at least he had received something for them; if he had followed Wordsworth's instruction he might have received nothing at all.) In deciding to dispose of copies in this way Cottle may have been influenced by Southey, who seems to have read the poems while they were still in press and to have told Cottle that they would not sell.[46]

While still in Germany, Wordsworth may have received some inkling from Coleridge that the volume had not been well received. Sara had written to tell her husband that the *Lyrical Ballads* 'are not esteemed well here, but the Nightingale and the River Y [Wye]'. In her letters to Poole she had expressed herself more frankly. 'The Lyrical Ballads are laughed at and disliked by all with very few excepted,' she informed him.[47] These comments were written while Sara was living with Southey, whose verdict on the volume had been published in the *Critical Review*. 'The experiment, we think, has failed,' he wrote, though he praised several of the poems, particularly 'Tintern Abbey'. He reserved special scorn for the 'absurd, or unintelligible' 'Ancient Mariner': 'a Dutch attempt at German sublimity'. Southey's review maintained the fiction that the *Lyrical Ballads* was the work of a single, anonymous author, though he knew exactly who had written each poem. It is difficult to avoid the conclusion that his criticisms were motivated by a lingering resentment towards Coleridge.[48] Though Lamb's feelings about Coleridge were still raw, he took Southey to task: 'I am sorry you are so sparing of praise to the "Ancient Marinere"; – so far from calling it, as you do, with some wit, but more severity, "A Dutch Attempt", &c., I call it a right English attempt, and a successful one, to dethrone German sublimity.'[49]

Wordsworth was furious with Southey, not on Coleridge's behalf, but his own:

> He knew that I published these poems for money and money alone. He knew that money was of importance to me. If he could not conscientiously have spoken differently of the volume, he ought to have declined the task of reviewing it.

> The bulk of the poems he has described as destitute of merit. Am I recompensed for this by vague praises of my talents? I care little for the praise of any other professional critic, but as it may help me to pudding . . .[50]

Wordsworth's correspondence with Cottle makes it obvious that he regarded the *Lyrical Ballads* as his own work, to manage without reference to his co-author. Cottle never questioned that the copyright belonged entirely to Wordsworth.[51] It is perhaps indicative that Wordsworth expected to receive the entire thirty guineas agreed for the volume,* rather than sharing it with Coleridge, who therefore disposed of his most substantial poem, the crowning achievement of his poetical career (and three lesser poems), for no payment at all.

Very quickly Wordsworth formed the view that 'the Ancyent Mariner' had been injurious to the volume: 'I mean that the old words and the strangeness of it have deterred readers from going on'. Possibly that was true, but possibly too Wordsworth found it easier to accept criticism of his friend's poems than of his own. Dr Charles Burney's piece about the volume in the *Monthly Review* appeared soon after Wordsworth's return to England. The 'Ancient Mariner' was, in his opinion, 'the strangest story of cock and bull that we ever saw on paper', though he found in it 'poetical touches of an exquisite kind'. Coleridge's poem had 'more of the extravagance of a mad

---

* 'If you choose the volume of Poems, at the price mentioned, to be paid at the time specified, i.e. thirty guineas, to be paid sometime in the last fortnight of July, you may have them . . .'[52] Confusingly, a fragment of a letter from Dorothy refers to Cottle giving the same amount 'for William's share of the volume'.[53] It is conceivable that Cottle might have paid a separate sum to Coleridge, over and above the sum initially proposed. A letter from Margaret Spedding, a friend of Wordsworth's, to her brother mentions Wordsworth and Coleridge 'making forty pounds' from the volume.[54] However, the weight of evidence strongly suggests that Cottle paid thirty guineas and no more.

German poet,' declared the *Analytical Review*, 'than of the simplicity of our ancient ballad writers'. Wordsworth reacted to such criticism by planning to omit the 'Ancient Mariner' should the poems ever be reissued in a second edition.[55]

Sara insisted that Coleridge heal the breach with Southey, who had shown her such kindness after Berkeley's death. Within a day or two (possibly only an hour or two) of his arrival at Nether Stowey, Coleridge accordingly wrote to his former friend, who was on holiday with a sickly Edith not far off in Minehead. Sara and Hartley were due to join them there in a few days' time. Coleridge obviously found it hard to know what to write, and began stumblingly, but he was sensible enough to keep to generalisations in a short and touching letter. 'If we should meet at any time, let us not withhold from each other the outward expressions of daily Kindliness,' he entreated. 'We are few of us good enough to know our own Hearts – and as to the Hearts of others, let us struggle to hope that they are better than we think them/& resign the rest to our common maker.'

Southey could not be won over so easily, and replied with a letter of recrimination and self-justification. It was obvious that whatever he had heard from Lloyd had left scars. Coleridge drafted a long, detailed riposte, but then thought better of it, and instead wrote another short letter insisting that he had never accused Southey of anything but 'your deep & implacable enmity towards me', which he attributed solely to Lloyd's mischief-making. He cited Poole and Wordsworth as witnesses 'that I have ever thought & spoken of you with respect & affection'.[56] Poole supported his statement in a separate letter to Southey: 'Without entering into particulars, I will say generally that in the many conversations I have had with Coleridge concerning yourself, he has never discovered the least personal enmity against, but on the contrary the strongest affection for you; stifled only by the untoward circumstances of your separation.' Poole ascribed Lloyd's conduct to 'a diseased mind – be assured from me, who have seen his contradictory letters, that his evidence amounts to nothing'.[57] By now Southey had another reason to doubt Lloyd, who had 'behaved very ill' to a woman he admired and liked, Mary Hays.[58]* When Sara returned from Minehead with Edith, the two sisters were escorted by Southey. Coleridge dramatically embraced his old friend on the doorstep.

Southey was convinced that 'Lloyd reported as many unfavourable accounts of me to Coleridge – as he did of Coleridge to me – and manufactured conversations and speeches wholly out of his brain.' The visitors stayed at Nether Stowey about a fortnight, and the two former Pantisocrats were soon 'writing at the same table' once more.[59] One morning while shaving Southey composed the first few lines of a satirical ballad, 'The Devil's Thoughts', and showed these to Coleridge, who completed the poem before breakfast. This was political satire, a return to the 'Jacobin poetry' of the past, and was quickly published by Daniel Stuart in the *Morning Post*, where it was 'most *enthusiastically* admired'.[60] However, the poem was published anonymously, so that for many years the public was unaware that it had been written by Southey and Coleridge. It was attributed to Richard Porson, Regius Professor of Greek at Cambridge,† and even republished in 1830 with a memoir of Porson, illustrated with engravings based on drawings by Cruikshank.

The Southeys and the Coleridges made a trip together into Devon to visit Coleridge's family at Ottery St Mary, where George Coleridge had succeeded his father as headmaster of the local school. His brothers were good men, Coleridge told Poole, 'but alas! We have neither Tastes or Feelings in common.' He managed to hold his tongue when any controversial topics arose in conversation, however, and even drank the loyal toast of 'Church & King'.[61] Southey was amused by old Mrs Coleridge, who, seeing her youngest son arguing with his brothers, assumed that he must be in the wrong, even though she was too deaf to hear what they were saying. Afterwards Coleridge and

* Mary Hays (1760–1843), novelist and reformer. An admirer and biographer of Mary Wollstonecraft, she is credited with having introduced Wollstonecraft to Godwin. She had an unreciprocated passion for William Frend, and later carried on a sentimental correspondence with Charles Lloyd (fifteen years her junior), who mocked her cruelly and lampooned her in his novel *Edmund Oliver*.
† Richard Porson (1759–1808), distinguished classical scholar and famous eccentric.

FRIENDS

Southey made a five-day walking tour along the south Devon coast. The two poets laid plans for *Mahomet*, an epic poem in hexameters on a huge scale. They made a beginning while they were still together, and Southey continued after they parted, so that by the end of the year he had written more than a hundred lines. Coleridge promised to 'go on with the Mohammed', though, he said, 'something I must do for pecuniary emolument'. He was talking of writing a schoolbook, which he thought would be 'a lucrative Speculation'; he also had 'very serious Thoughts of trying to get a couple of Pupils'.[62] As the months passed it became increasingly clear to Southey that Coleridge would never produce more than the fourteen lines he had written at the start.

Coleridge had also promised to contribute to the popular *Annual Anthology*, which Southey edited in 1799 and 1800. Southey wanted 'Christabel' to open the anthology, and began to press Coleridge for the poem. But Coleridge was 'not in a poetical Mood'; it was still unfinished, and even if it were finished, it seemed to him an 'improper' opening poem; it ought to be last, not first. Perhaps influenced by Wordsworth's impression of the 'injurious' effect of the 'Ancient Mariner',* he argued that 'those who dislike it will deem it extravagant Ravings, & go on thro' the rest of the Collection with the feeling of Disgust – & it is not impossible that were it liked by any, it would still not harmonize with the *real-life* Poems that follow'. (Wordsworth would use a very similar argument to justify shunting the 'Ancient Mariner' towards the rear of the second edition of *Lyrical Ballads*.) In his next letter to Southey, Coleridge admitted to having 'scarce poetic Enthusiasm enough to finish Christabel'.[63]

While staying with Southey in lodgings at Exeter, Coleridge had received a letter from Wordsworth, who was again troubled by pain in his side. Coleridge was 'agitated' by the report of his friend's health, which he found 'alarming'. Possibly Wordsworth exaggerated his illness to lure Coleridge northwards. Coleridge had been trying to secure Alfoxden once more, in the hope that he might share it with

---

* He was with Wordsworth when he wrote this letter.

William and Dorothy, but Wordsworth made it clear that he had now firmly decided to settle in the north of England.[64]

Around this time, Coleridge wrote to Wordsworth that he was 'anxiously eager to have you steadily employed on "The Recluse"':

> My dear friend, I do entreat you go on with 'The Recluse'; and I wish you would write a poem, in blank verse, addressed to those, who, in consequence of the complete failure of the French Revolution, have thrown up all hopes of the ameliora- tion of mankind, and are sinking into an almost epicurean selfishness, disguising the same under the soft titles of dom- estic attachment and contempt for visionary *philosophes*. It would do great good, and might form a part of 'The Recluse', for in my present mood I am wholly against the publication of any small poems.[65]

Coleridge's stress on the utility of the poem is noticeable. He still hopes for 'the amelioration of mankind', but has come to believe that poetry will be the best means of achieving this, not politics.

It seems that Wordsworth must have replied explaining that he planned to dedicate the poem on the growth of his own mind to his friend, for a grateful Coleridge wrote to him again a few weeks later on the same subject:

> I long to see what you have been doing. O let it be the tail-piece of 'The Recluse'! for of nothing but 'The Recluse' can I hear patiently. That it is to be addressed to me makes me more desirous that it should not be a poem of itself. To be addressed, as a beloved man, by a thinker, at the close of such a poem as 'The Recluse', a poem *non unius populi*,* is the only event, I believe, capable of inciting in me an hour's vanity.[66]

Over the years that followed, Coleridge would continue to urge Wordsworth forward with *The Recluse*. The poem, this great ambitious project dwarfing all others, became a stick with which Coleridge chastised his friend. For Wordsworth, the subject was one of perpetual mortification. However high he soared, *The Recluse*

---

* Literally 'not of one people', i.e. a universal poem.

seemed out of reach. His other achievements seemed small by comparison with the ideal Coleridge kept constantly before him.

Coleridge's reference to the 'complete failure' of the French Revolution encapsulates the prevalent disillusionment felt by radicals. There was nothing happening in France to inspire idealists overseas. The Directory was pursuing increasingly illiberal policies at home, and expansionist policies abroad. Opposition to Pitt's government seemed pointless: there was no credible alternative to his policies; the Foxite Whigs had withdrawn from Parliament in despair. Coleridge was reading Spinoza, whose philosophy provided an anodyne for those wishing to retire from active engagement in politics in favour of a meditative quietism.[67] This drift of thought can be detected in Coleridge's letter urging Wordsworth to go forward with *The Recluse*. Since its publication in 1798, his poem 'The Recantation' had attracted much comment. It was taken to epitomise the retreat from radicalism, the change of sentiment of a generation initially sympathetic to the Revolution. While her husband was still in Germany, Sara had complained to Poole that 'it is very unpleasant to me to be often asked if Coleridge has changed his political sentiments – for I know not properly how to reply – pray furnish me'.[68] Southey suspected that Coleridge would be unhappy at the unwitting inclusion of 'The Recantation' in a new annual anthology.* Mary Hays asked Southey if he too had changed his principles. 'Had she known more of me I should have been hurt at the question.'[69]

In October, however, the political atmosphere was transformed by the sudden appearance of Napoleon in France, having abandoned his army in Egypt. Caesar had crossed the Rubicon; the collapse of the Directory seemed imminent, and peace possible. A measure of Coleridge's excitement can be gained from his letter to Southey on receiving the news: 'Buonaparte – ! Buonaparte! dear dear DEAR Buonaparte!'[70] Shortly after this letter was written, Coleridge left Nether Stowey for Bristol, supposedly *en route* to London to search

---

* *The Spirit of the Public Journals: Being an impartial selection of the most exquisite essays and jeux d'esprits, principally prose, that appear in the newspapers and other publications.*

for two travelling chests of books bought in Germany that had gone astray. (They appeared in Stowey two days after his departure.) There he met Humphry Davy,* the self-educated son of a Penzance carpenter, whom he immediately recognised as 'an extraordinary young man'. Within no time they were planning a philosophical epic in six books of blank verse, using the story of Moses to trace the progress of man from a primitive through a civilised to a degenerate state; like so many of Coleridge's schemes this came to nothing. In Bristol Coleridge saw Cottle, who was also about to leave for London, where, having finally decided to quit the publishing trade, he would sell all his remaining copyrights to Longman.† They decided first to make a journey north together to see Wordsworth, apparently on the spur of the moment. Who took the initiative in this decision is unclear. In his unreliable *Reminiscences*, Cottle presents the trip as if Coleridge was already set on going and pressed Cottle to accompany him.[72] Against this is a fragment of a letter from Wordsworth written seven weeks earlier, urging Cottle to pay a visit to the north of England and offering to accompany him on a tour of Cumberland and Westmoreland. Perhaps both men were contemplating a visit to Wordsworth when they met, and this discovery prompted them to go together. They left Bristol on 22 October, travelling by post-chaise, probably at Cottle's expense, and arrived at Sockburn about four days later.

---

* Humphry Davy (1778–1829), chemist and poet. In 1798 he was recruited by Dr Beddoes to join the Pneumatic Institution in Bristol, funded by the Wedgwoods. In 1801 he joined the new Royal Institution in London as Director of the Chemical Laboratory. He became a Fellow of the Royal Society at the age of only twenty-five; in 1812 he was knighted for his work, and in 1820 he became President of the Royal Society.

† Thomas N. Longman (1771–1842), publisher and bookseller, of Paternoster Row, London. He was the third successive Thomas Longman since the foundation of the firm in 1724, and had inherited the business from his father in 1792. A few years later he went into partnership with a Bristol bookseller, Cottle's near neighbour in Wine Street, Owen Rees. In 1798 Cottle had hoped to sell the first edition of *Lyrical Ballads* to Longman, as he had done Southey's *Joan of Arc*.

10

AMALGAMATION

Coleridge was relieved to find Wordsworth in good health. This was his first meeting with the Hutchinsons, who had of course heard much of the prized friend. After tea, Cottle asked Mary what she thought of Coleridge on first appearance. Her response is not recorded, but it seems to have been favourable. 'Few moments in life so interesting,' Coleridge noted in his pocket book, 'as those of an affectionate reception from those who have heard of you yet are strangers to your person.'[1]

The travellers set out on their tour the next afternoon, Wordsworth and Coleridge on foot and Cottle mounted on a mare. It was not an arrangement that made for easy conversation, and perhaps Cottle felt himself in the way. (Possibly he had never intended to accompany them any further than the nearest coach stop, and borrowed a horse from the Hutchinsons to take him there.) The party broke up after only a few days, on the old Roman road at Greta Bridge (near Barnard Castle); Cottle set off for London while the two poets took the mail coach over the Pennines to Temple Sowerby, a few miles short of Penrith. Cottle recorded afterwards that while he was in the north 'the subject of the "Lyrical Ballads" was mentioned but once, and that casually, and only to account for its failure!' Wordsworth ascribed its lack of success to the 'Ancient Mariner', which, he said, 'no one seemed to understand', and to the unfavourable reviews.[2]

At Temple Sowerby they were unexpectedly joined by Wordsworth's younger brother John, a sailor in the service of the East India Company, who had returned to England the previous month after a long voyage. He and William had not seen each other for some years, and he decided to take advantage of this chance meeting by joining the two walkers for the first part of their tour. Shy, gentle and warm-hearted, John was an easy companion. 'He interests me much,' Coleridge wrote to Dorothy. 'Your Br. John is one of you; a man who hath solitary usings of his own Intellect, deep in feeling, with a subtle Tact, a swift instinct of Truth & Beauty.'

The three walkers set out a day or two later. Now that he had attracted his friend north, Wordsworth was keen to show him as much as possible of the landscape he loved, then just beginning to be discovered by travellers. Over the next three weeks they would criss-cross the Lakes, exploring along the dales and over the passes, trekking across the fells, climbing the steep slopes, relishing the magnificent views from the peaks, and pausing to admire the many spectacular waterfalls. This being Wordsworth country, they were often able to stay the night under the roof of an acquaintance or relative. For the two Wordsworths this was a nostalgic journey into the land of their childhood; for Coleridge it was an expedition of discovery. It seems likely that William pointed out to his friend places of special significance for him, some of which Coleridge had already encountered in his autobiographical verse. In the process Wordsworth revealed to Coleridge the scale of the poem on the growth of his own mind, on which he had been working for more than a year, and which, it seemed, was almost complete in two books.

They began by walking south-west towards Haweswater, following the eastern shore. This was Coleridge's first sight of the Lakes, 'a world of scenery absolutely new to me'. No visitor can fail to be impressed by this landscape: under an ever-changing sky, brooding mountains tower over the dales, huge U-shaped valleys scraped out by glaciers millions of years before: a land made by giants, where humans appear puny and insignificant. Coleridge gazed awe-struck over a precipice, imagined a poor wretch dangling over a thundering waterfall, and shuddered at the thought of plummeting into a black lake where the steep sides of scree killed any hope of escape.

The mists hung so low over the mountains that they could not take the direct route across the fells and the Kirkstone Pass to Ambleside; instead they went by way of Longsleddale and then across the lower pass to Kentmere. After passing through Troutbeck they followed the road along Windermere to Bowness, and took the ferry across the lake. It was a cold crossing. On the other side of the lake they walked back up to Hawkshead, where both the Wordsworth brothers had been at school, and found 'great change among the people since we were last there'. Next morning they turned northwards again, across the head of Windermere and on up past Rydal to Grasmere. Here they rested for a few days. Coleridge was 'enchanted with Grasmere and Rydal', a satisfied Wordsworth reported to Dorothy. Perhaps seeing the place through his friend's eyes influenced Wordsworth, because after telling his sister again that 'C. was much struck with Grasmere & its neighbourhood', he talked of building a house by the lake; John had offered the money to buy the land. Another possibility was an empty, unfurnished cottage he had seen at Grasmere, 'which perhaps we may take'.

Coleridge was impressed above all by the grandeur of the surroundings – which he associated with the scale of Wordsworth's ambition. On a fine day, when 'Nature lived for us in all her grandest accidents', they climbed the slopes of Helvellyn as far as Grisedale Tarn, a small lake in a natural bowl high up the mountain. An ecstatic Coleridge described the walk to Dorothy: 'light and darkness coexisted in contiguous masses, & the earth and sky were but *one!*' From the edge of the bowl they peered down Grisedale to glimpse 'gloomy Ullswater' in the distance. There John left them, descending to Ullswater and continuing along the lakeside towards Penrith, while the two poets returned to Grasmere.

A few days later Wordsworth and Coleridge walked up to Keswick. Approaching Derwent Water towards evening, Coleridge exclaimed at its

> diversity of harmonious features, in the majesty of its beauties & in the Beauty of its majesty – O my God! & the Black Crags close under the snowy mountains, whose snows were pinkish with the setting sun & the reflections from the sandy

rich Clouds that floated over some & rested upon others! It was to me a vision of a fair Country.[3]

A letter from Daniel Stuart caught up with Coleridge in Keswick, offering him regular employment on the *Morning Post*. Coleridge immediately decided to accept. The pay would allow him to live with his family in London for the next four or five months, 'a thing I wish extremely on many & important accounts'.[4] One of these was the need to clear the arrears resulting from his stay in Germany, which had proved much more expensive than expected. Another was the opportunity to play a part in public affairs once more. On the very day that Coleridge received Stuart's offer, Napoleon seized power in a *coup d'état* that abolished the rule of the Directory and cleared the way for a new constitution, including his installation as First Consul, a suitably classical title.

From Keswick they walked west and towards Cockermouth, Wordsworth's childhood home. Afterwards they descended via Lorton and Crummock Water to Buttermere, turning west again to Ennerdale and circling back through Wasdale and up Borrowdale, and then along Derwent Water to Keswick once more, continuing along the Penrith road as far as Threlkeld. Next day they made their way east and then south, via Matterdale to Patterdale, at the foot of Ullswater, where they stayed the night. In the morning they walked back up the eastern side of Ullswater to Pooley Bridge, at the head of the lake, where they seem to have spent the night with Thomas Clarkson* and his wife Catherine. She wrote to her friend Priscilla Lloyd (sister of Charles Lloyd) about their visit. 'C. was in high Spirits & talk'd a great deal,' she reported. 'W. was more reserved but there was neither hauteur nor moroseness in his Reserve.' She thought Wordsworth 'rather handsome', with a 'fine commanding figure' and 'the manners of a gentleman'; and observed that he seemed very fond of Coleridge, 'laughing at all his Jokes & taking all opportunities of shewing him off'.[5]

---

* Thomas Clarkson (1760–1846), the celebrated abolitionist, who led the campaigns against slavery in 1787–94 and again from 1805 onwards. At St John's College, Cambridge, he had been a contemporary of his fellow abolitionist William Wilberforce and of Wordsworth's uncle William Cookson.

Somewhere around here the two men parted. Coleridge walked to Penrith and made for Sockburn, while Wordsworth remained in the Lakes, possibly returning to Grasmere to secure that cottage they had seen. Why Coleridge should have returned to Sockburn is unclear. Perhaps he already felt the first stirrings of the great passion of his life.

Sara Hutchinson was then twenty-four, short and fair, with reddish-brown hair that was often admired. She was not considered a beauty. After her death Coleridge's daughter, also called Sara, would describe her as 'dumpy', but Sara Coleridge could be forgiven for failing to acknowledge the attractiveness of the woman who had been the object of her father's obsessive love. Others described her looks as homely, and she tended towards plumpness – but she was lively and well-educated, with a particular love of poetry. Years later, when she was in her forties, John Keats – twenty years younger – would describe her as 'enchanting'. Fun and feminine, and possibly a little flirtatious, Sara Hutchinson was much as Sara Fricker had been five years before, when Coleridge had first seen her in Bristol in the heady days of Pantisocracy. Indeed, she was the same age now as Sara Fricker had been then. His Sara had changed, worn down by grief and disappointment. She had lost her lustrous hair. Here was another Sara, fresh, inquisitive and admiring. As he had been when he met Sara Fricker, Coleridge was elated, his mind full of sublime images and excited by his recent adventure. Maybe he was already dreaming of living in the north of England, close to Wordsworth. At Sockburn he found a houseful of young women eager to hear his stories and laugh at his jokes. For him this was delightful, like being with the Evans family again.

Coleridge stayed at Sockburn about four days. Fragments from his private notebooks suggest something of what may have happened while he was there. On 24 November, a Sunday, he stood around a fire, laughing and telling stories, exchanging puns and conundrums with John Hutchinson. One of his notebook entries describes the scene, and a passage written in Latin (presumably as a precaution against browsers, including his wife) suggests what Coleridge later believed to be the lasting significance of the moment: '. . . And pressed Sara's hand a long time behind her back, and then, then for the first time, love pricked me with its light arrow, poisoned alas! and hopeless.'[6]

This notebook entry may be misleading. It was made retrospectively, four years afterwards, by which time Coleridge had become infatuated with Sara Hutchinson. Time tricks the memory, forever reshaping the past to explain notions and feelings from the present. Coleridge probably did press Sara's hand as they stood in front of the fire, but this may not have seemed so significant then as it did later. For one thing, he seems to have been attracted to Mary as well as to Sara. But it was Sara who subsequently became the focus of his attention. She seems to have given him a lock of her hair, which months later he carried with him in his coat pocket.[7] Possibly an incident occurred similar to the one described in his later poem 'The Keepsake', which describes an early-morning assignation with a young woman in a 'woodbine bower' beside a 'smooth, scarcely-moving river-pool' – perhaps a pool on the Tees. She has left the bed she shares with her sleeping sister, and in the dawn light makes her way softly to meet the poet. The poem is suffused with sensual imagery. In the bower she weaves for him a silken keepsake, into which she has worked the flowers* she knows he loves,

> And, more belov'd than they, her auburn hair.

In the poem, the young woman modestly allows the poet to kiss 'my own warm tear of joy/From off her glowing cheek . . .' Later he refers to the 'entrancement of that maiden kiss'. This line is anticipated in a note he entered in his book while apparently still in Sockburn: 'The long Entrancement of a True-love's Kiss'. The same wording (with minute variations) appears in the retrospective note, where he added another date, Monday, 25 November, the day of his departure from Sockburn.[8] If Coleridge didn't kiss Sara, it seems that he was tempted to do so.

---

* Forget-me-nots – according to the *Oxford English Dictionary*, the poem marks the first known use of this term in print.

Wordsworth returned to Sockburn a day after Coleridge's departure. He had decided to take the small cottage he had seen at Grasmere at a rent of £8 a year, virtually the same price as Coleridge paid at Nether Stowey.* Three weeks later he and Dorothy left Sockburn on horseback, so early in the morning that it was still dark, escorted by George Hutchinson, who would take the horses home afterwards. They crossed the Tees by moonlight and rode past Richmond. Eight miles further on they parted from George, and continued up Wensley-dale on foot, pausing to admire a waterfall. That night they slept at Askrigg, after walking the last three miles in the darkness on half-frozen roads. The next morning a thin coat of snow lay on the ground. From Askrigg they continued across the fells to Sedbergh, leaving the road from time to time to admire caves and more waterfalls, and then descended to Kendal. This was an epic walk, more difficult in winter, particularly for Dorothy in her long skirts: an unusual feat, especially for a woman of good breeding. The next day, 20 December 1799, they bought some furniture in Kendal and then journeyed on to Grasmere by post-chaise, arriving in late afternoon. It was cold and frosty, stars standing out clear in the night sky. Ice was forming on the lake. At the cottage they found two letters from Coleridge waiting. They were greeted by a maidservant, Molly Fisher, who had made the beds. A fire smouldered in the parlour grate. This was the house that would become known as Dove Cottage,† their home for most of the next decade.

The next few days saw brother and sister busy painting the walls, making curtains, mending doors, and generally settling in. Dorothy papered one small upstairs room with old newspapers. She pro-nounced herself 'much pleased' with the house and its 'appurtenances', delighted especially by the old orchard behind, which sloped up steeply to a spot commanding a fine view over the roof of the cottage

---

* Eight guineas a year, according to Berta Lawrence;[9] £7 a year according to Mrs Henry Sandford.[10]

† But not while the Wordsworths were living there, when it was nameless and generally described by the name given to the group of cottages to which it belonged, Town End. The name Dove Cottage, used here for convenience, was given to the house almost a century after they had left, probably after its old name as an inn, the Dove and Olive.

across the lake, and past the church to Helm Cragg in the distance. (The front windows of the cottage offered an only slightly less impressive view.) In every direction were walks of seemingly perpetual variety. 'My dear friend,' Wordsworth wrote to Coleridge on Christmas Eve, after they had been in their new home four days, 'we talk of you perpetually, and for me I see you everywhere.'[11]

The cottage was small, being only six rooms, but 'quite large enough for us', and like Coleridge's equally small cottage it could accommodate a surprising number of guests. At the end of January their brother John arrived for a long visit, and a month later the three of them were joined by Mary Hutchinson, who stayed about a month. According to her sister Joanna, Mary reported on her return that she was 'very much delighted indeed with Grasmere, and the Wordsworth way of living'; she had never seen so complete a cottage in her life, nor one so very comfortable.[12] The Wordsworths' existing fondness for the Hutchinson sisters (particularly Mary and Sara) had been strengthened during their long stay at Sockburn, and after their departure the intimacy between the two families was maintained and even enhanced by regular exchange of letters. Though William was a reluctant letter-writer, Dorothy was an indefatigable correspondent; it has been estimated that when at home she wrote on average one letter every day. The majority of these were addressed to a small circle of intimate friends, of whom the principal figures were Coleridge and the Hutchinson sisters.[13]

Wordsworth would sometimes escape to the orchard to avoid an unwelcome visitor. Here he would pace to and fro, composing line after line of verse. Years later he would even consider dedicating an edition of his poems to the path through the orchard.[14] In front of the house he and Dorothy enclosed two or three yards of land to make a small garden, which in due course would supply them with runner beans, French beans, peas, kidney beans, spinach, potatoes, carrots, broccoli, onions, turnips and rhubarb, together with apples and pears from the orchard.[15] Against the whitewashed walls of the house they planted roses and honeysuckles, framing the views through the latticed windows. They kept a boat on the lake, where the two Wordsworth brothers often fished and brought back small pike for the table. 'We are daily more delighted with Grasmere, and its neighbourhood,' Dorothy wrote to her old friend Jane Marshall; her only complaints were that sound travelled easily through the small cottage and that it was rather too near the main road from Ambleside to Keswick.[16] There was a steady procession of itinerants passing, many of whom called at the cottage to beg: a little girl who had been sleeping in the open, turned out of home by her stepmother; a young woman from Manchester who had lost her husband and three children; a potter who could not get help from the parish because he still had the implements of his trade; a mutilated soldier; an old leech-gatherer bent almost double after an accident with a cart; and dozens of others. The Wordsworths provided hospitality to many such people and gave them food or small sums of money. A neighbour muttered sadly to Dorothy about the alteration in the times, and observed that soon there would be only two ranks of people, the very rich and the very poor, for small farmers were being forced to sell and land was being concentrated in fewer and fewer hands. Wordsworth was fascinated by stories of hardship and deprivation. Once these would have stirred him to revolutionary rhetoric, as when he and Beaupuy had encountered the 'hunger-driven girl' leading a heifer by a cord. Now, eight years on, he was still fighting against such injustice, but his tactics were different. Political change was not the solution; what was required was a renewal of old values, a rejection of the vast impersonal forces that drove men off the land and robbed them of their independence.

Once settled, Wordsworth at last returned to *The Recluse*. The autobiographical 'Poem to Coleridge' was complete – or so he thought, though he still harboured doubts about it. There was no excuse not to make a start, as Coleridge was constantly urging – 'I grieve that "The Recluse" sleeps.'[17] In the first few months of 1800, Wordsworth began his great philosophical work. The poem opened with his first glimpse of the vale of Grasmere, as a schoolboy one golden summer holiday, and posed an ambition for his former self:

... here
Must be his Home, this Valley be his World.

Grasmere is evoked as an earthly paradise, a haven from the 'vast
Metropolis' and 'crowded streets':

> Far from the living and dead wilderness
> Of the thronged World, Society is here
> A true community, a genuine frame
> Of many into one incorporate.

Here would gather a small group of loving friends: their brother John,
the Hutchinson sisters, and Coleridge:

> Our beautiful and quiet home, enriched
> Already with a Stranger whom we love
> Deeply, a Stranger of our Father's House,
> A never-resting Pilgrim of the Sea,
> Who finds at last an hour to his content
> Beneath our roof. And others whom we love
> Will seek us also, Sisters of our hearts,
> And One, like them, a Brother of our hearts,
> Philosopher and Poet, in whose sight
> These Mountains will rejoice with open joy.
> – Such is our wealth! O Vale of Peace, we are
> And must be, with God's will, a happy Band.

By early summer Wordsworth had finished 'Home at Grasmere', the
first of what would certainly be many books of *The Recluse*.

From Sockburn, Coleridge had gone directly to London, travelling by
coach through the night. He found lodgings at no. 21 Buckingham
Street, on the south side of The Strand, and around the beginning of
December wrote to Cottle asking if he knew whether Sara and Hartley
were in Bristol. He wanted to send her some cash for travelling
expenses, because, he announced grandly, 'we shall reside in London
for the next four months' – but he was unsure of her whereabouts.[18]
The cottage in Nether Stowey had been shut up (and at the end of
the year would be surrendered altogether). In fact Sara had been

staying with a friend of Poole's near Watchet. She had known nothing of Coleridge's journey north, assuming that he had been in London all this time. Thus neither wife nor husband knew where the other had been. Some days later Sara and Hartley arrived in London to join him, after a separation of more than six weeks.

Coleridge threw himself into London life with gusto. He quickly restored his friendship with Lamb. Perhaps Southey was instrumental in this reconciliation. Like Southey, Lamb became more wary of Lloyd, especially after learning how he had treated Mary Hays. As a result Lamb was less inclined to believe what Lloyd had told him about Coleridge. But neither did he place complete trust in what Coleridge said. In a letter to his friend Thomas Manning, Lamb remarked that as long as he had known Coleridge, he had known him to be 'in the daily & hourly habit of quizzing the world by lyes [lies], most unaccountable & most disinterested fictions'. (It is only fair to record that in the instance that prompted this observation, Coleridge's veracity was vindicated.)[19] Lamb remained on good terms with Lloyd, but he no longer sided with him against Coleridge. As in the past, Lamb lit up in the charge of Coleridge's electric company. 'The rogue has given me potions to make me love him,' he joked, echoing Falstaff.[20]*

Perhaps surprisingly, Coleridge also established a friendship with William Godwin, a widower since the death two years before of his wife, the pioneering feminist Mary Wollstonecraft. He called on Godwin soon after his arrival in London, taking with him Humphry Davy, who had come to town on a visit. Godwin was hugely impressed by this brilliant youth, but afterwards cried, 'What a pity that such a man should degrade his vast talents to Chemistry!' Coleridge saw a good deal of Godwin during these months in London,† engaging in lively discussions, often fuelled by alcohol. Godwin was then in retreat from the atheistic rationalism that had so provoked Coleridge, but

* 'I have forsworn his company hourly any time this two and twenty years, and yet I am bewitched with the rogue's company. If the rascal have not given medicines to make me love him, I'll be hanged.' *Henry IV, Part One*, II, ii.
† They saw each other at least thirty times, according to Godwin's manuscript diary. In February 1800, for example, they met on eleven separate occasions.

they still found plenty to argue about, and on one occasion a tipsy Coleridge talked so extravagantly that he felt obliged to write an apologetic letter to Godwin the next morning. On Christmas Day 1799 the Coleridge family dined with Godwin and his children,* whose silence Coleridge found oppressive. Nevertheless three-year-old Hartley selected two-year-old Mary Godwin (who would become Mary Shelley) as his future partner in life. For his part 'Mister Gobwin' (as Hartley called him) found the young Coleridge too boisterous. After Hartley had given the philosopher a rap on the shins with a ninepin, Godwin lectured Sara on the need for greater discipline.

The Christmas dinner was exceptional, in that Coleridge was accompanied by his family; in general he paid calls and dined out alone, whether he was in male or mixed company. Towards the end of his stay in London, when Sara had taken Hartley to the country, Coleridge stayed three nights at Godwin's house. Earlier Godwin had read the manuscript of his tragedy *Osorio*, afterwards offering his criticisms over tea. Godwin was intrigued enough by Coleridge's charismatic personality to contemplate writing a biography of the younger man. He kept some notes based on their conversations, recording in one of them that Coleridge 'always longed to know some man whom he might look up to, by that means to increase his sentiment of the importance of our common nature: every man knows himself to be little'.[21] Godwin considered Davy the most extraordinary human being he had ever met, but Coleridge disagreed, as he told Tom Wedgwood: 'I know one whom I feel to be the superior.'[22] This was of course Wordsworth.

Lamb teased Coleridge about the 'tribe of authoresses' who trailed in his wake. Coleridge certainly enjoyed the company of clever women, and in his fellow *Morning Post* contributor Mary Robinson he encountered a woman both clever and beautiful.† Mary, known as 'Perdita' Robinson after her most famous stage role, had been an actress and the young Prince of Wales's first mistress. She trod the

---

* His daughter Mary and her half-sister Fanny, the child of Mary Wollstonecraft's lover Gilbert Imlay, whom Godwin brought up as his own.
† Mary Robinson (1757?–1800), actress, novelist and poet.

narrow line between glamour and notoriety, skilfully manipulating her reputation, and after her stage career had ended, reinvented herself as a novelist and poet. A former lover of Fox's, she aligned herself with the radical Whigs; her 'very false notions of politics' drew criticism from the *Anti-Jacobin Review*. After her death she was described as 'the most interesting woman of her age'. Coleridge thought her 'a woman of undoubted Genius', and promoted her poetry. Her experiments in writing under the influence of opium echo his, and her 'Ode to S.T. Coleridge' quoted from 'Kubla Khan', which she had almost certainly heard him recite.[23]

Coleridge and Godwin dined one evening at the house of Horne Tooke,* the elderly radical and hero of the treason trials, in whose honour Coleridge had written verses after Tooke had succeeded in attracting nearly 3,000 votes in the 1796 election for the borough of Westminster. Also present was Tooke's close friend Sir Francis Burdett, the wealthy radical MP. On 7 February Godwin took tea at Coleridge's lodgings with Lamb, James Webbe Tobin,† John Frederick Pinney and Basil Montagu. The latter's politics had become much more conservative as he tried (and failed) to obtain a Fellowship at Cambridge. Coleridge speculated that Montagu's retreat from radicalism might be one reason why he was 'very cool to me'. Another was that Coleridge was pressing him to honour his financial obligations to Wordsworth.[24]

Daniel Stuart had agreed to pay all Coleridge's expenses in return for regular contributions. What Stuart wanted above all was thoughtful comment on the fast-changing political situation. Coleridge would in effect be a leader writer, setting the political tone of the *Morning Post*, which was on its way to becoming the biggest-selling newspaper in London. This was a powerful position, and one that he relished. But it made him visible again. A satirical poem, 'The New Morality', which had appeared the previous year in the short-lived but effective

* John Horne Tooke (1736–1812), radical parson, poet, philologist and eventually an MP, a veteran agitator who had been a supporter of John Wilkes in the 1760s.
† Eldest son of a Nevis planter in partnership with Azariah Pinney. He lived in London with his brother John, an attorney and aspiring playwright. A friend of Wordsworth and Tom Wedgwood, he visited Alfoxden in the late summer of 1797.

Anti-Jacobin; or Weekly Examiner and had been reprinted a month later alongside a superb cartoon by James Gillray, was now anthologised in a new publication, *The Beauties of the Anti-Jacobin*. The poem lampooned Coleridge as a Jacobin dupe, along with Southey and (curiously) Lloyd and Lamb. In the cartoon, books such as Mary Robinson's novel *Walsingham* and Wollstonecraft's *Wrongs of Women* cascaded from a 'Cornucopia of Ignorance'. Sorting through these were Coleridge and Southey, depicted with asses' heads, a reference to Coleridge's absurd poem 'To a Young Ass'. This was not enough in itself to upset Coleridge: the poem had appeared in print twice already, and was now out of date. Its feeble arrows failed to pierce his hide. The cartoon was quite amusing. What stung him was a biographical note newly added to the poem, which referred to his 'avowed deism' at Cambridge and his ludicrous enlistment in the army. Worst of all, the note alleged that he had quit his native country and become a 'citizen of the world', leaving 'his little ones fatherless' and 'his wife destitute'. It was not true, but there was enough truth in it to hurt. A bad conscience may have made Coleridge especially indignant. He contemplated (but did not pursue) a libel action, and was still complaining about the slur more than fifteen years later.

Cracks opened in the Coleridge marriage. He could not be unaware of how his wife had suffered during his absence in Germany, but his response was perversely resentful. In a letter to Southey he wrote enviously of Southey's happiness with Edith, while lamenting that he could never be completely happy with Sara, because their temperaments and interests were so different. These thoughts were expressed in Latin, presumably to hide them from Edith. He also added a Latin postscript to a letter to Josiah Wedgwood, grumbling that Sara appeared to be pregnant again. Wedgwood was no doubt surprised to be the recipient of such confidences from his protégé.[25]

Coleridge worked hard, often toiling through the night and not leaving his desk at the office of the *Morning Post* until dawn, by which time boys were already out on the streets selling newspapers containing articles he had written only hours before. His first piece for the paper under the terms of his new arrangement, on the new

French constitution, appeared on 7 December 1799. Over the next four months he supplied Stuart with an average of six columns of prose each week. Many of these were concerned with international affairs, with the war above all. Coleridge castigated the government for rejecting Napoleon's offer of peace negotiations. He also contributed poems and epigrams, and began to produce parliamentary reports. In early February 1800 he welcomed Fox's sensational return to the House of Commons after three years' absence. Probably his most original piece was a profile of Pitt, remarkable for its psychological insight. Indeed Coleridge seemed to envisage Pitt as an evil *alter ego*, a former child prodigy 'far beyond his fellows, both at school and at college', forced to perform in front of admiring adults. It was a characteristic of Coleridge's to draw on his own experience for insight into the lives of others.

The *Morning Post* advertised as a companion to the Pitt profile one of Bonaparte. Coleridge later claimed that a French official acting under instructions from Napoleon himself had enquired when this would appear. The great man was apparently expecting a eulogy, and his presumptuous eagerness was enough to make Coleridge pull the piece.[26] Some scepticism has been expressed about the veracity of this story.

Coleridge's attitude to his journalism was ambivalent. On the one hand, it was 'not unflattering to a man's Vanity to reflect that what he writes at 12 at night will before 12 hours is over have perhaps 5 or 6000 readers!' As he wittily remarked, few wine merchants could boast of creating more sensation. On the other hand, he was squandering his talents. He claimed to have 'Newspapered it' merely as a means of subsistence. 'My faculties appear to myself dwindling,' he moaned to Poole, 'and I do believe if I were to live in London another half year, I should be dried up wholly . . .' In a few weeks, he wrote to Josiah Wedgwood in early February, 'I shall have accomplished my purpose – & then adieu to London for ever!'[27] His plan was to write for the *Morning Post* in the afternoons, and to undertake freelance literary work in the mornings. The former would allow him to live, while the latter would enable him to clear his debts. He gathered up

Top left The Bristol lodgings shared by the Pantisocrats for most of the year 1795.
Top right Racedown Lodge in Dorset, occupied by Wordsworth and his sister Dorothy from 1795 to 1797.
Above left 'Our little hovel': home of the Coleridge family from the end of 1796 until the middle of 1799. The cottage was located on the edge of Nether Stowey, in the foothills of the Quantocks.
Above right Alfoxden Park, on the northern slopes of the Quantocks, rented for £24 per annum by William and Dorothy Wordsworth in the year 1797–98.

The first authenticated portrait of Wordsworth, showing the poet at the age of twenty-eight, painted during the time when he was living in the Quantocks and collaborating with Coleridge on *Lyrical Ballads*. It was commissioned by the publisher Joseph Cottle from a local artist, William Shuter. The bent arm with the hand lodged in the coat front, in the style later made famous by Napoleon, was said by Leigh Hunt to have been habitual with Wordsworth.

A more assured and perhaps more self-contained Wordsworth, aged thirty-six, then arguably at the height of his powers. This drawing by the fashionable artist Henry Edridge was one of two commissioned by Wordsworth's friend and benefactor Sir Charles Beaumont, and probably idealises his features.

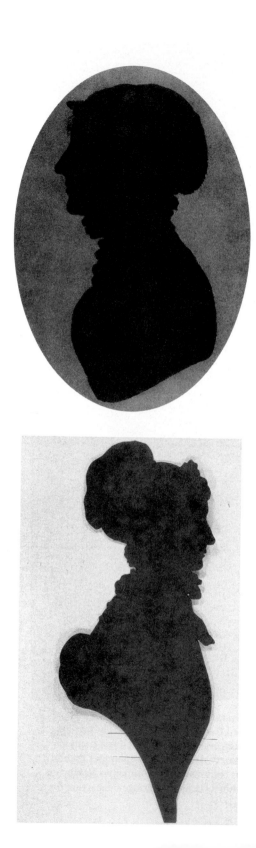

Silhouettes of Dorothy Wordsworth (*above left*), made in 1806, when she would have been in her mid-thirties, and of Sara Hutchinson (*above*) and her sister Mary Wordsworth (*left*), made in 1827, when both women were in their fifties.

Miniatures of Sara Coleridge (*left*), made in 1809 when she was in her late thirties, and of Annette Vallon (*below left*), made at an unknown date.

Below Hartley Coleridge, aged ten: the apple of his father's eye, and a favourite of the Wordsworths. Both poets envisaged Hartley as an ideal child, 'exquisitely wild'.

The Great Track over the top of the Quantocks, photographed in the 1930s.

'Alfoxton Park' by Miss Sweeting, from a book of views published in the 1830s. The house, which can be seen towards the right-hand edge of the picture, sits on the northern slopes of the Quantock Hills, facing out towards the sea.

Greta Hall in the 1880s.

'From the Window before me there is a great Camp of Mountains – Giants seem to have pitch'd their Tents there,' Coleridge enthused in one of several letters written on the evening of his first full day in his new home at Greta Hall, on the outskirts of Keswick. The house can be seen on raised ground towards the left of the picture.

'He is truly a man of *perpendicular Virtue – a down-right upright Republican!*' wrote Coleridge of his new friend Robert Southey early in 1795. This portrait (*above*) of Southey by James Sharples was probably painted later in the same year, by which time Southey's youthful idealism was coming under strain.

'. . . brow-hanging, shoe-contemplative, *strange* . . .' Coleridge's description of the young William Hazlitt, then in his early twenties, was written around the time of this self-portrait (*left*), while Hazlitt was trying to make a living as an artist.

Above left Thomas Poole, radical and benefactor, a steadfast friend to Coleridge: a stout, sensible, kind man with a rubicund complexion and a noticeable West Country burr.

Left Charles Lamb, Coleridge's friend from boyhood. Hazlitt (a painter) described his 'fine Titian head', his curly hair, and his startling eyes, each a different colour. Slightly built, with spindly legs, Lamb walked with a shambling gait, the legacy of childhood polio.

Above Joseph Cottle, the first publisher of Coleridge, Southey and (almost) Wordsworth.

Contemporary drawings by John Harden of Brathay Hall, not far from Grasmere, which perhaps give some sense of the poets' domestic life. The women in Wordsworth's household did much transcribing at the men's dictation.

Dove Cottage, photographed early in the twentieth century.

advances from publishers for a variety of projects, only one of which materialised: a translation of Schiller's *Wallenstein* trilogy, so new that the complete work had not yet appeared even in Schiller's native Germany, with the result that Coleridge worked from manuscripts. He soon wearied of 'this Translation Fag'. At the beginning of March, Sara took Hartley to stay with friends in the country,* while Coleridge moved in with Lamb at no. 36 Chapel Street, in Pentonville. He was concentrating on his translation of Schiller, which he found 'a *Bore* – *never, never, never* will I be so taken in again'.[28] He worked at home in his dressing gown, which Lamb said made him look like a conjuror. Lamb basked in the sunshine of his company, his doubts about Coleridge evaporating: 'I am living in a continuous feast,' he wrote to his friend Manning.[29]

'I have been in excessive Perplexity of mind lately on sundry subjects – and have besides over-worked myself,' Coleridge complained to Southey.[30] He was still struggling to finish his translation, an 'irksome and soul-wearying Labor'. He felt that he had made a 'very, very foolish bargain', he told Wedgwood, because he now had no hope of its success: 'I can say with truth, that I could have written a far better play myself in half the time.'[31] The translation proved a financial disaster for Longman – unbought copies were sold for waste paper. Coleridge later wrote that they became 'winding-sheets for pilchards' or remained 'extant only by the kind partiality of trunk-makers'.

Coleridge was determined not to stay in London beyond the beginning of April. Friends tried to change his mind: Godwin, for example, seemed to Lamb 'mortified' at the prospect of Coleridge's going away.[32] Stuart offered him a share in the *Morning Post* worth £2,000 to stay, but Coleridge was adamant. 'I told him, that I would not give up the Country, & the lazy reading of Old Folios for two Thousand Times two thousand Pound – in short, that beyond 250£ a year, I considered money as a real Evil – at which he stared; for such Ideas are not animals indigenous in the Longtitudes and Latitudes of a

---

* The Roskilly family: the Reverend Mr Roskilly, formerly curate at Nether Stowey, had been promoted to become rector of Kempsford in Gloucestershire.

Scotchman's Soul.'[33] But where in the country Coleridge would go was by no means decided. For a while he seemed more inclined to settle with the old friend rather than the new: with Southey, rather than Wordsworth. At the turn of the year he was certainly contemplating cohabiting with the Southeys: 'To be near you would be a strong motive with me, for my Wife's sake as well as for myself.' Initially he had tried to attract Southey to join him in London – 'You might have Lodgings in the same House with us' – and then talked about the two families sharing Alfoxden, which, he argued, 'would make two Houses sufficiently divided for unimpinging Independence'. Apparently the house was again empty, and available to let, though whether Mrs St Albyn would be more amenable to Coleridge and Southey as tenants than she had been to Wordsworth was unclear.

Coleridge's letters to Southey glowed with a renewed affection – but it was noticeable that when Southey felt a worrying pain in his heart, and an intermittent pulse, Coleridge did not rush to his side as he had done to Wordsworth's. After consulting doctors, Southey concluded that a warmer climate was the remedy for his disorder, and at first thought of Italy. He suggested that Coleridge might accompany him: 'now, if you could fall in with these schemes, we might plunder Italy as the French have done'.[34] Coleridge thought it not impossible 'that a number might be found to go with you'. As soon as he had finished in London, he told Southey,

> I fall to the Life of Lessing – till that is done, till I have given the Ws* some proof that I am *endeavouring* to do well for my fellow-creatures, I cannot stir. That being done – I would accompany you – & see no impossibility of forming a pleasant little Colony for a few years in Italy or the South of France. Peace will soon come.[35]

Coleridge was so taken with the idea of this colony that he invited his new friend Humphry Davy to join them. But that was before he learned that Sara was pregnant again, which rendered her unfit for a sea voyage and put the scheme for a colony on hold – but 'no day

---

* The Wedgwood brothers.

passes in which I do not as it were yearn after you'. A letter from Southey announced his impending departure for Lisbon. Coleridge promised that if he were to stay longer than a year on the Continent, *'I and mine will join you* – & if you return at that Time, you must join us. Where we shall be, God knows!'

He sent Southey a valedictory message:

> The time returns upon me, Southey! when we dreamt one Dream, & that a glorious one – when we eat [*sic*] together, & thought each other greater & better than all the World beside, and when we were bed fellows. Those days can never be forgotten, and till they are forgotten, we cannot, if we would, cease to love each other.[36]

Meanwhile Coleridge continued to correspond with Poole about moving back to west Somerset. When Poole suggested a house at Aisholt, three miles from Nether Stowey, Coleridge replied that the situation was 'delicious; all I could wish'. But, he lamented, Sara preferred to be in a town or else close to one. 'God knows where we can go; for that situation which suits my wife does not suit me; and what suits me does not suit my wife.' Later Poole suggested renting part of a farmhouse, an idea Coleridge seemed ready to accept, on condition that he had the use of the garden to grow vegetables – but the scheme was vetoed by Sara, who thought that sharing a kitchen would lead to continual squabbles. Poole feared that he was losing Coleridge, despite Coleridge's protestations of being 'ever, ever yours'. Among all his friends, declared Coleridge, he had always called and always felt Poole to be 'the Friend'. But his neglect had hurt Poole's feelings: 'I think you treated me with unmerited silence, and when you wrote you seemed to perform a duty, not a pleasure.' Poole told Sara of his dread that 'I was acquiring the *heart-withering* faculty of losing men's hearts though I retained their heads.'[37]

'How could you take such an absurd idea in your head, that my Affections have weakened towards you?' protested Coleridge. 'I write now merely to desire you to be on the look out for a House – I shall beyond all doubt settle at Stowey, if I can get a suitable House – that is – a House with a Garden, & large enough for me to have a Study out [of] the noise of Women and children – that is absolutely necessary for me.'

'*I have a huge Hankering for Alfoxden,*' he told Poole, tantalised by the memory of the idyllic year preceding his departure for Germany. 'I would to God, I could get Wordsworth to re-take Alfoxden – the Society of so great a Being is of priceless Value – but he will never quit the North of England – his habits are more assimilated with the Inhabitants there.' He complained that he was alone in fully appreciating Wordsworth's genius: 'no one, neither you, or the Wedgewoods [*sic*],* altho' you far more than any one else, ever entered into the feeling due to a man like Wordsworth – of whom I do not hesitate in saying, that since Milton no man has *manifested* himself equal to him'.[38]

Poole accused Coleridge of prostrating himself before Wordsworth, but the defendant pleaded guilty to the charge. 'Is it impossible that a greater poet than any since Milton may appear in our days? Have there any *great* poets appeared since him?'

> Future greatness! Is it not an awful thing, my dearest Poole? What if you had known Milton at the age of thirty, and believed all you now know of him? – What if you should meet in the letters of any then living man, expressions concerning the young Milton *totidem verbis* the same as mine of Wordsworth, would it not convey to you a most delicious sensation? Would it not be an assurance to you that your admiration of the *Paradise Lost* was no superstition, no shadow of flesh and bloodless abstraction, but that the *Man* was even so, that the greatness was incarnate and personal?

Coleridge's letter to Poole referred to 'other men's rash opinions concerning W'.[39] By other men he meant the Wedgwoods, who like Poole had strong misgivings about Coleridge's idolatry of Wordsworth. They had provided Coleridge with financial support in recognition of his own distinctive genius, not so that he could preach the

---

* Coleridge consistently mis-spelt his patrons' surname, both in letters to others and to the brothers themselves.

gospel of Wordsworth. The concern about 'amalgamation' was once more widely felt. As if to confirm the fears of his friends, Coleridge left London soon after writing to Poole – as Lamb put it, 'on a visit to his God, Wordsworth'.[40] He arrived at Dove Cottage around 6 April, and stayed almost a month. Some time during his stay he learned that a fine house was available to rent on the edge of Keswick, thirteen miles from Grasmere.

In mid-May the two Wordsworth brothers left Dove Cottage for a walking tour into Yorkshire, taking in some of the sights of the Yorkshire Dales, the landscape that had so impressed William and Dorothy the previous December. Their main object was to visit the Hutchinsons, now living at a farm called Gallow Hill, a few miles inland from Scarborough.

Dorothy began a new journal on the day her brothers left. It was written for her brother to read on his return, 'to give W[illia]m pleasure'. His departure was distressing to Dorothy. 'My heart was so full that I could hardly speak to W. when I gave him a farewell kiss,' she wrote. For the past five years they had been almost continuously together, sharing every thought and feeling. Much of that time had been spent in isolation, when each had no company but the other. Their love had intensified, and their shared sense of purpose gave an almost religious fervour to their happiness. They had been known to lie on the ground and imagine their bodies lying next to each other in their graves. The long-cherished dream of 'our little cottage' had become blissful reality. Now a shadow darkened the future: the possibility that her brother might marry threatened Dorothy's idyll. Her journal makes it obvious that she feared losing him. Though Mary Hutchinson had become her closest friend, a wife would surely displace a sister.

After they had parted she sat on a stone at the margin of the lake, crying. 'The lake looked to me, I knew not why, dull and melancholy, and the weltering on the shores seemed a heavy sound.' A few days later, she was disappointed to find no letters waiting for her at Ambleside. 'Grasmere was very solemn in the last glimpse of twilight; it calls home the heart to quietness. I had been very melancholy in my walk back. I had many of my saddest thoughts, and I could not keep the tears within me.' As the days passed and Dorothy remained alone, she recorded several such moods in her journal. 'The quietness and still seclusion of the valley affected me even to producing the deepest melancholy.' She had resolved not to 'quarrel with myself': not to succumb to resentment, jealousy or self-pity. Though she loved both brothers, her thoughts were entirely of William. After three weeks she was full of nervous expectation of his return. 'I lingered out of doors in the hope of hearing my Brother's tread.' She would not go far from home, for fear of missing his return. 'No William,' she noted one day; 'No William!' two days later. At last, at around eleven o'clock one night, she heard footsteps outside, and the sound of the gate opening. 'It was William!'

Wordsworth had left his brother at Greta Bridge and pushed on ahead, returning to Dorothy alone. He was sensitive to her anxiety, and wanted to reassure her as much as he was able. Later he stated that he had 'no thoughts of marrying' at this time. They stayed up talking until four o'clock in the morning, when the first signs of dawn were appearing and the birds had begun to sing.[41]

John returned the following evening. He would remain with William and Dorothy until the autumn, leaving Grasmere at the end of September to take command of a ship. In these months he came to share the vision of William's destiny, and to dedicate himself to its fulfilment. 'He encouraged me to persist in the plan of life which I had adopted,' Wordsworth wrote years later. John hoped to prosper by his voyages, and to share his wealth with his brother and sister. 'I will work for you,' he said to William before he left, 'and you shall attempt to do something for the world.'[42]

Coleridge intended to return from the Lakes to London (or so he told Stuart), but at Kendal he received letters 'which forced me Stowey-ward'.[43] Whose letters these were is unclear. Perhaps they were from his wife, who must have been anxious about where they were to live, now that she was approaching full term. Southey had always opposed taking Sara too far from her friends and family in Bristol – but Southey was now in Portugal. By 21 May Coleridge was in west Somerset, staying with Poole. He wrote to Dorothy, commissioning her to enquire about suitable lodgings around Grasmere, and in particular to enter into negotiations to rent Greta Hall, the Keswick house. This was large enough to accommodate two families, even though the owner had retained an apartment for his own use. Wordsworth seems to have encouraged his friend to take the house by holding out the prospect that he and Dorothy would join the Coleridge family there 'in about a year's time'.[44] In any case, they were not far away in Grasmere. 'If I cannot procure a suitable house at Stowey,' Coleridge wrote to Godwin, 'I return to Cumberland & settle at Keswick – in a house of such prospect, that if, according to you & Hume, impressions & ideas *constitute* our Being, I shall have a tendency to become a God – so sublime & beautiful will be the series of my visual existence.'[45]

Both Poole and the Wedgwoods had strong misgivings about Coleridge's proposed move north. All three men were concerned that he might become Wordsworth's satellite. In a letter to Josiah Wedgwood Coleridge attempted to justify such a move: he could not work in a small house, there was nothing suitable to be found near Stowey, Mrs Coleridge had scarcely any society there, Poole's relations had insulted her, the nearness to Bristol 'connected me too intimately with all the affairs of her family', Poole might be going abroad if peace came and his mother died (as seemed likely), and so on.[46] Tom Wedgwood was on the brink of setting off to the West Indies, in a desperate attempt to recover his lost health; many years later Coleridge wrote to Poole of 'T. Wedgewood's farewell Prophecy to me respecting W., which he made me write down, & which no human Eye ever saw – but mine'.[47] It is not hard to guess what that prophecy might have been. Coleridge continued to hunt for a house around Stowey, and even ventured as far as Porlock in his search, but his heart was elsewhere. The importance of living close to Wordsworth prevailed over all other considerations. In June the Coleridge family made the journey up to Grasmere. They stayed with the Wordsworths

until their new home was ready, and a month later moved into Greta
Hall.

'From the Window before me there is a great *Camp* of Mountains –
Giants seem to have pitch'd their Tents there,' Coleridge enthused to
Davy on the evening of his first full day in his new study, a splendid
room which commanded an uninterrupted view from Derwent Water
and Borrowdale on one side, across to Bassenthwaite on the other. A
wilderness of mountains formed the majestic backdrop. Towards the
end of the day, as the sun began to drop behind the peaks, great
shadows advanced across the lakes. 'I question, if there be a room in
England which commands a view of Mountains & Lakes & Woods &
Vales superior to that, in which I am now sitting,' he boasted to
Godwin. After writing to Davy, he climbed out onto the 'leads' of the
roof for an even better view of the sunset. Perched there he wrote at
least two further letters. 'My God!' he exclaimed, 'what a scene!' He
was encircled by 'the most fantastic mountains, that ever Earthquakes
made in sport; as fantastic, as if Nature had *laughed* herself into the
convulsion, in which they were made'.[48]

Greta Hall had originally been built as an observatory, a fine place
from which to contemplate the heavens. It stood isolated on high
ground above the River Greta, less than a mile downstream of Windy
Brow, William Calvert's farmhouse where the Wordsworths had stayed
in 1794, and about a quarter of a mile outside Keswick. The owner, a
successful carrier named William Jackson, had remodelled the old
observatory as a gentleman's residence, with spacious rooms, tall
windows and marble fireplaces. He occupied a set of separate rooms
at the back, letting the main rooms at the front to Coleridge for £42
per annum – perhaps not unreasonable for such a house, but something of an extravagance for a young writer with no regular income
and accumulating debts. The river ran almost in a semi-circle around
the back of the house, enclosing 'an *enormous* Garden' which sloped
down through shrubberies to 'a most delightful shaded walk' along
the river. Skiddaw loomed behind, while the Coleridges' bedroom at
the front offered a magnificent view of Helvellyn. 'My glass being

opposite to the Window, I seldom shave without cutting myself,' joked Coleridge.[49]

Dorothy thought their new home ideally situated for the Coleridges – '*she* likes to be near a Town, *he* in the country' – and Greta Hall combined both.[50] The relative position of the Wordsworths and the Coleridges was now inverted. In Somerset, the Wordsworths had inhabited a large furnished country mansion, while the Coleridges occupied an 'old hovel' they furnished themselves; in the Lakes, the Wordsworths lived in a small unfurnished cottage, while the Coleridges had taken the principal part of a substantial, well-furnished house with pretensions to grandeur. Coleridge signed a letter from his new residence 'S.T. Coleridge, Esq., Gentleman-poet and Philosopher in a mist'.

Of course there were walks in all directions, and Coleridge took full advantage of these. His notebooks filled with detailed and often lyrical descriptions of light, clouds, skies, lakes, streams, mountains and valleys. Standing one day at the very top of Skiddaw, he was joined by a lean, 'expressive-faced' man, who stood beside him a while, and then examined a piece of slate on which Coleridge had earlier scratched his own name among those of others who had done so before. '*Coleridge!*' the lean man exclaimed – 'I lay my life, that is the *Poet Coleridge.*'[51]

Coleridge's arrival in the Lakes opened the second, and longest, period of close proximity between the two poets. For the next three and a half years (except when one or the other was away) Coleridge and Wordsworth were constantly in contact with each other, as they had been in the Quantocks. Though the distance between Keswick and Grasmere was four times the distance between Nether Stowey and Alfoxden, and the journey between their two homes far more difficult, especially in poor weather as there were few places to shelter, they nevertheless contrived to spend much of their time in each other's company. In Coleridge's first six months in the Lakes, for example, he saw Wordsworth on eighty-one days, and for many of those they were together for most if not all of their waking hours, from rising in the morning until retiring to bed. In general, one man would come and stay a few days with the other, because the journey – about five hours' walk – made it impractical to come and go for shorter periods. Often at the end of such a stay the host would accompany his guest part of the way back. They passed much of their time outside, relishing the superb scenery, the ever-changing sky, and even the smallest manifestations of natural beauty: a flower, a butterfly, the leaves swirling in the breeze. Coleridge carried a magnifying glass, and would show his friend minute details of flowers or beetles. At night they often roamed out under the stars.

Dorothy usually accompanied them, though she was tactful enough to allow the poets time alone together when they needed it. She shared their observations and interests; her sensitivity to the splendour of the natural world delighted them both. The three of them understood each other, and relished the pleasure of being understood. For Coleridge, Dorothy's loving concern offset Wordsworth's more austere and distant manner. He was sometimes remote and self-contained; she was always warm and interested. If Wordsworth and Coleridge were brothers, she was sister to them both. All three felt easy in each other's company, to the extent that they resented others as intruders.

> We three dear friends
> In truth we groan
> Impatiently to be alone . . .

wrote Coleridge in a flippant *jeu d'esprit* when a worthy but unwelcome visitor made it impossible for them to relax as they usually did at Dove Cottage, and the steady rain prevented them from escaping together:

> . . . Well, he and I
> And she, whom we both call our own,
> Dear Rain! We want to be alone –
> We three, you see – & not one more
> We want to be alone so sore!
> We have so much to talk about,
> So many sad things to let out . . .

This close circle gradually widened to include the Hutchinson sisters, especially Mary and Sara, each of whom stayed at Grasmere for long spells. Though these five would never be assembled together during this period, they were often in a band of three or four, and regular, almost daily, letters between them reinforced their intimacy. Shared experiences bound them together. This group was an enlargement of 'The Concern': a team dedicated to the production of verse and the appreciation of Nature. They lived in each other's pockets, composing, transcribing, talking, eating, walking – a tiny community, a set, almost a family. Coleridge jokingly described them as a 'gang', with Wordsworth as its leader. Coleridge himself was central to this small community, as Dorothy implicitly acknowledged when she wrote their names in the shape of a heart, with his name in the middle. Sara Coleridge, on the other hand, was excluded. The character of the 'gang' was quasi-religious, a sect with a heartfelt common faith that excluded non-believers. They had places that were special to them: paths, groves, sites where they would habitually sit or pause to admire the view. They gave private labels to these places, often naming them after individuals in the group, associating them with memories of times spent together. Sara Hutchinson laid the first stone for a seat on White Moss Common, known thereafter as 'Sara's Seat', which would be completed by Coleridge, Wordsworth and Dorothy six months later. In particular, there was an upright rock with a smooth surface standing by the roadside, about halfway between Grasmere and Keswick, where they often paused and parted on their walks. They knew it first as 'Sara's Rock', because her initials had been inscribed in the face of the stone; afterwards Coleridge cut his own initials above Sara's with a pocket-knife and Dorothy's below; when Dorothy discovered this, she kissed each letter in turn. Later Wordsworth added his initials and those of Mary Hutchinson, and 'Sara's Rock' became known to them as 'The Rock of Names'. John Wordsworth left Grasmere within three months of Coleridge's arrival. Though from this time forward he was away at sea most of the time, he was much in their thoughts, and for this reason he was admitted as a sixth, largely honorary member of their circle. His initials too were carved into the rock.

*

Wordsworth had decided to publish a second edition of *Lyrical Ballads*. This was something of a *volte-face*. Though he had talked about the possibility of a second edition after his return from Germany in the spring of 1799, he had taken no further action. The slow sale and poor reviews were dispiriting. 'My aversion from publication increases every day,' he had told Cottle that summer, 'so much so, that no motives whatever, nothing but pecuniary necessity, will, I think, ever prevail upon me to commit myself to the press again.'[52] Towards the end of that year Wordsworth had written to Coleridge in London telling him not to bother to contradict the story that 'the L.B. are entirely yours. Such a rumour is the best thing that can befall them.'[53] This attitude may seem curious, until one considers that Wordsworth was still virtually unknown to the public. Though his poetical powers were fully developed, and indeed Coleridge was lauding him as the greatest poet since Milton, it remained true that Wordsworth had published only two immature works under his own name, seven years before. Coleridge, on the other hand, had published two editions of his collected poems, plus three further poems in quarto. Moreover he was a prominent polemicist.

Since the turn of the year, however, Wordsworth's attitude to the *Lyrical Ballads* had undergone another revolution. One reason may have been that he now had control of the copyright. When Cottle had sold all his copyrights to Longman, they had been valued as one lot. Subsequently Cottle discovered that the copyright in *Lyrical Ballads* had been 'reckoned *as nothing*'. He asked whether in that case he might reclaim the copyright on behalf of the author, and Longman generously agreed. Cottle was thus able to present the copyright to Wordsworth, in the form of a receipt for thirty guineas, which he gave to Coleridge for onward transmission to his friend.[54] Coleridge's enthusiastic championing of Wordsworth's work was crucial to its republication.[55] Indeed, it was probably Coleridge who prompted Wordsworth to reconsider the possibility of a second edition, when he arrived at Grasmere in early April 1800, perhaps bearing Cottle's receipt. The first indication that Wordsworth had changed his mind came in a letter Coleridge wrote from Grasmere during his stay.[56] It seems to have been decided then to reissue *Lyrical Ballads* in two volumes, the first of these to be essentially the same as the original edition, and the second to consist of new poems.

Another reason for reviving the possibility of a second edition was that sales, though slow, had trickled on, helped by reviews that continued to appear eighteen months after publication. By the early summer of 1800 the initial impression of five hundred copies was exhausted. On Wordsworth's behalf Coleridge persuaded Longman that a new, enlarged edition was required, this time in two volumes. Thus Longman, bamboozled by Coleridge's eloquence, found himself offering £80 for a work whose value he had previously reckoned as nil.

Though the second edition of *Lyrical Ballads* was conceived as a joint volume, it was understood that the proceeds should go to Wordsworth alone, as had been the case for the first edition. After the publication of the second edition, Wordsworth would assume a debt of £30 advanced by Longman to Coleridge, but more as a favour to his friend than in recognition of his contribution.[57] Coleridge repaid this loan within three months.

Coleridge also arranged for the second edition to be printed in Bristol by the firm of Biggs & Cottle, a partnership between Nathaniel Biggs and Joseph Cottle's younger brother Robert. When he travelled down to Bristol from Grasmere at the beginning of May, Coleridge carried with him several new poems of Wordsworth's for the second volume. Someone on the spot was needed to supervise the printing, especially checking proofs and revises, which would require close liaison with the printer, and Coleridge secured Humphry Davy's agreement to undertake this burdensome task, though Davy and Wordsworth had yet to meet or even to correspond.

When Coleridge returned to Grasmere in June 1800, accompanied by Sara and Hartley, he was suffering from a heavy cold, which soon worsened, forcing him to take to his bed for several days. He wrote afterwards that he was more unwell than at any time since leaving school. His eyelids swelled painfully, making it difficult for him to read even four weeks later. Meanwhile several obligations demanded his attention. He had agreed to prepare an account of his German tour for Longman; he had accepted an advance from another publisher, possibly for a 'bookseller's compilation'; and he had yet to begin the life of Lessing, long promised to the Wedgwoods and ostensibly the reason why he had not returned to England immediately on receiving news of the death of his son. Lurking in the background were the great philosophical works to which he had pledged himself. Moreover, though he had resisted Stuart's blandishments to join the permanent staff of the *Morning Post*, he had promised a regular supply of contributions, both essays and poems, and Stuart was already pressing him hard.

Instead of tackling any of these, however, he plunged wholeheartedly into the task of preparing the second edition of *Lyrical Ballads*. This required meticulous work, transcribing Wordsworth's new poems, and writing out careful instructions to the printer. Wordsworth's habit of revising already-published poems, often making minute changes, added considerably to the labour, which continued through the summer into the autumn. Very little of it was done by the poet himself, however; the work was shared between his sister and Coleridge, who chided his friend as 'a lazy fellow' in a letter to Davy. 'I bemire myself by making promises for him,' he continued.[58]

Coleridge persuaded Wordsworth to write a preface elaborating the principles underlying the poems. This was a manifesto for a new type of poetry, with very few personifications of abstract ideas and 'little of what is usually called poetic diction'; he would speak in 'the real language of men'. Such poetry was both more 'genuine' and more 'manly'. Thus Wordsworth met the most usual criticism of his poems – that they were 'low' – head-on. With remarkable boldness he claimed a moral place for poetry, in opposition to the 'multitude of causes' now acting to 'blunt the discriminating powers of the mind', of which the most obvious was the 'increasing accumulation of men in cities'. He was arguing that poetry could and should play a central role in the culture, as a means of countering the alienating effects of urbanisation and industrialisation. This was a confident assertion of the importance of poetry, a key assumption behind the idea of *The*

Recluse. It was reiterated in the letters Wordsworth would send accompanying presentation copies of the poems, particularly the letter to Fox, still the most prominent progressive politician. Wordsworth declared that each of the poems in this volume 'has a worthy *purpose*'. He defended his decision to choose 'low and rustic life' for the setting of his poems:

> . . . because in that situation the essential passions of the heart find a better soil in which they can attain their maturity, are less under restraint, and speak a plainer and more emphatic language; because in that situation our elementary feelings exist in a state of greater simplicity and consequently may be more accurately contemplated and more forcibly communicated; because the manners of rural life germinate from those elementary feelings; and from the necessary character of rural occupations are more easily comprehended; and are more durable; and lastly, because in that situation the passions of men are incorporated with the beautiful and permanent forms of nature. The language, too, of these men is adopted (purified indeed from what appear to be its real defects, from all lasting and rational causes of dislike or disgust) because such men hourly communicate with the best objects from which the best part of language is originally derived; and because, from their rank in society and the sameness and narrow circle of their intercourse, being less under the influence of social vanity they convey their feelings and notions in simple and unelaborated expressions. Accordingly such a language arising out of repeated experience and regular feelings is a more permanent and a far more philosophical language than that which is frequently substituted for it by Poets, who think that they are conferring honour upon themselves and their art in proportion as they separate themselves from the sympathies of men, and indulge in arbitrary and capricious habits of expression in order to furnish food for fickle tastes and fickle appetites of their own creation.

As Wordsworth remarked in his letter to Fox, two of the longer poems in the collection, 'The Brothers' and 'Michael', 'were written with a view to shew that men who do not wear fine cloaths can feel deeply'.[59]

The preface to the second edition of *Lyrical Ballads* is the best-known of all Wordsworth's prose writings. Some of its phrases – 'the real language of men', 'Poetry is the spontaneous overflow of powerful feelings', 'emotion recollected in tranquillity' – have become familiar. Ironically, in years to come Wordsworth would disown the preface, maintaining that he 'never cared a straw about theory', and that he had written it solely to oblige Coleridge.[60] But this is surely very far from how he felt at the time. Though the ideas he expressed were not necessarily original, the style of the preface was very personal, in places almost autobiographical. And while in old age Wordsworth's poems had become part of the canon, when he wrote the preface they were widely derided, and he was extremely sensitive as a result. He felt that they needed defending.

Coleridge later claimed that the preface was 'half a child of my own Brain', that it had first been intended that he should write it, and that Wordsworth had drawn on his notes.[61] Some doubt has been expressed about the degree of Wordsworth's debt to Coleridge, but it is surely true, as Coleridge also maintained, that the ideas in it had arisen from their conversations about poetry, which had been so frequent that neither of them could say who started any particular thought.[62] In the preface Wordsworth referred to the help he had received from a friend, and affirmed, 'our opinions on the subject of poetry do almost entirely coincide'. And in a letter to Daniel Stuart written around the end of September, Coleridge had stated, 'the Preface contains our joint opinions on Poetry'.[63]

On his return from Germany the previous year Wordsworth had talked about omitting the 'Ancient Mariner' altogether from subsequent editions, in the belief that it had been an 'injury' to the volume. He had convinced himself that its 'old words' and the 'strangeness' of the poem had 'deterred readers from going on'. It seems that he now discussed this problem with Coleridge, who readily offered to 'suppress' the poem. On further consideration Wordsworth allowed it to remain, though now displaced from its opening position.

In the second edition, the 'Ancient Mariner' became the penultimate poem in the first volume, placed just before 'Tintern Abbey'.

In response to the criticisms of the 'Ancient Mariner' that had so troubled Wordsworth, Coleridge revised the poem extensively. He made more than seventy changes, some of them substantial: in one place, for example, he omitted five successive stanzas, and elsewhere supplied completely new stanzas. Most of the revision entailed pruning or removing altogether the archaic language in which the original poem had been written – thus 'eldritch' became 'ghastly', and so on. The spelling too was modernised. The very title of the poem changed from 'The Rime of the Ancyent Marinere' to 'The Ancient Mariner: A Poet's Reverie'. The result was a different type of work from the one Coleridge had originally envisaged.

Coleridge also supplied a new poem for the first volume in place of one Wordsworth had decided to omit. The Godwinian radicalism that had inspired 'The Convict' now embarrassed Wordsworth, and he felt that the continued inclusion of such an overtly political poem was damaging to the rest. As a substitute Coleridge modified a poem he had already published in the *Morning Post* under the title 'Introduction to the Tale of the Dark Ladie', and gave it a new title, 'Love'. This had probably been written on his return to Sockburn after the walking tour with Wordsworth, and seems to have drawn on his passionate feelings for Sara Hutchinson. Wordsworth commented sourly, 'there was too much of the sensual in it'.[64] Now often overlooked, in Coleridge's lifetime this was one of the most popular of his poems.

All the work for the first volume had been done by the time the Coleridges moved into Greta Hall in July 1800. In the following few weeks there was much coming and going between Keswick and Grasmere. Within a week Coleridge was back at Dove Cottage, settling the contents of the second volume. He brought with him the recently published *Annual Anthology*, which contained fifteen of his poems (including 'This Lime-Tree Bower My Prison') and a further twelve poetical epigrams. Possibly he hoped that one or more of these might be included in the new *Lyrical Ballads* – if so, he was to be disappointed. Wordsworth had already supplied many new poems (including the 'Lucy' poems) for the second volume, and over the coming months would compose several more. It was agreed that Coleridge would contribute a few under the classification 'Poems on the Naming of Places', and that the volume should conclude with the as yet incomplete 'Christabel'. Nevertheless, and despite what had been said before, it was decided that the second edition would appear solely under Wordsworth's name. On 13 August Wordsworth wrote to the printer that 'the Title Page must stand thus: Lyrical Ballads/with other poems./ By W. Wordsworth' – followed by a Latin epigraph and the description '2nd Edition'. Far from encouraging the story that the work was 'entirely yours', as Wordsworth had urged Coleridge only months before, he was now advertising to the world that it was 'entirely mine'.

It is not known what discussions, if any, took place on this subject. Later Coleridge claimed that he had agreed to the work being published under Wordsworth's name, even insisted upon it, in recognition of the fact that all but five of the eventual sixty-five poems were Wordsworth's.* But by the time he made this claim it was a *fait accompli*, which he was obliged to explain somehow, to himself if not to others. The rationale for the decision to publish under Wordsworth's name was much less obvious when it was made; then it seemed likely that Coleridge's contribution would be much more significant. His poems occupied more than one-third of the first volume. And it remained true that the longest poem in either edition was Coleridge's 'Ancient Mariner', which indeed had inspired the volume in the first place. The *Lyrical Ballads* had originated in an attempt at joint composition, and when this failed, had continued as a form of poetic dialogue, which Coleridge, apparently with Wordsworth's assent, had insisted was '*one work*': one which should therefore be published anonymously, as if by a single poet. Insensibly, perhaps, this principle had been lost, and Coleridge's contribution sidelined.

* According to Earl Leslie Griggs, editor of Coleridge's letters, Wordsworth's instruction to the printer about the wording of the title page has a postscript in Coleridge's hand, implying that the latter was consulted about and agreed to the work's being published under Wordsworth's name. But the editors of the Wordsworth letters believe that the postscript may be in Wordsworth's hand.[65]

Wordsworth's decision to publish the second edition under his own name alone represented the final abandonment of the ideals in which the volume had been born.

There was a late flurry about the title when it was discovered that a volume of Mary Robinson's verse entitled *Lyrical Tales* was due to be published later in the year. She intended this as a tribute to *Lyrical Ballads*, and for this reason had fixed on the same publisher and the same printer, even requesting that her book should be printed in the same typeface. Wordsworth's reaction was to fear that a work with such a similar title from the famous Mrs Robinson might overshadow his own.[66] He informed the printer of his wish to alter the title to 'Poems/in two Volumes/By W. Wordsworth' as a result, though he left it up to Longman, who preferred not to make the change. The eventual title of the second edition was *Lyrical Ballads, with Other Poems.*[67]*

While Wordsworth seems to have consulted his friend on most if not all of these decisions, he does not appear to have considered Coleridge's interests. Indeed, obtaining Coleridge's consent to the changes only served to accentuate his subjugation. His meekness in complying with Wordsworth's wishes was remarkable. He seemed ready to agree to any demand, no matter what the cost to himself. This was no longer a friendship of equals. In a letter urging Godwin to visit the Lakes, Coleridge offered the prospect of meeting Wordsworth, 'the latch of whose Shoe I am unworthy to unloose'.[68] This was an allusion to the words of John the Baptist:

> He it is, who coming after me is preferred before me,
> Whose shoe's latchet I am not worthy to unloose.†

Coleridge was content to be prophet to the new Messiah.

Coleridge's letter to Godwin referred to the imminent arrival of Charles Lloyd in the Lakes. Now married, and with a new baby,

---

* It had been originally intended that the title of the second edition should be *Lyrical Ballads, and Pastorals.*
† I John 1:26.

Lloyd had taken a house at Old Brathay near Ambleside, only four miles from Grasmere. Though Coleridge pretended to be indifferent to Lloyd's presence, it seems to have caused him considerable anxiety. Lloyd had already poisoned two of his most valuable friendships. Dorothy confided to her friend Jane Marshall that she and her brother were 'by no means glad' that the Lloyds were to be their neighbours, because 'Charles Lloyd is a man who is perpetually forming new friendships, quarrelling with his old ones, and upon the whole a dangerous acquaintance.'[69] They could hardly ignore him, however, because their brother Christopher had become engaged to his sister Priscilla. She was due to come and spend the winter with the Lloyds, after first staying with her friend Mrs Clarkson at Ullswater.

On 23 September Lloyd called at Dove Cottage while Coleridge was there. It is not known what took place, but in a note about Lloyd and the Wordsworths many years later Coleridge remembered 'the fear of *his* coming in & receiving an unpleasant agitation occasioned such Looks & Hurry & Flurry & anxiety that I should be gone from Grasmere, as gave me many a heart-ache'.[70]

Over the months that followed the Wordsworths saw a lot of the Lloyds, and Charles Lloyd called frequently at Dove Cottage. 'We have not much society but the Wordsworths,' Lloyd wrote to a Cambridge friend after he had been in the Lakes almost five months. 'Miss Wordsworth I much like, but her brother is not a man after my own heart.'[71] At some point Coleridge clashed with Dorothy on the subject of Lloyd, calling him a 'rascal' – at which Dorothy 'fired up', and defended him with 'great warmth'.

On 30 September Lloyd dined alone with the Wordsworths, and they walked home with him after dinner. That same evening Dorothy finished writing out the preface to the new edition of *Lyrical Ballads*, and two accompanying notes. Apparently without consulting Coleridge, Wordsworth added an apologetic footnote to the 'Ancient Mariner' acknowledging the many criticisms of the poem, which 'had indeed great defects'. He elaborated these defects before listing what he considered to be the merits of the poem. He claimed credit for its continued presence in the volume, 'as the Author was himself very desirous that it should be suppressed'.

One might think that Wordsworth would have been kinder to have discarded the poem, rather than to have retained it on such terms. To mention Coleridge's willingness to suppress it only deepened his humiliation. Wordsworth's disregard of his friend's feelings contrasted sharply with his own sensitivity. The other note he wrote at the same time warmly defended his own poem 'The Thorn' against the criticisms it had received.

Was it possible that Wordsworth had been influenced by Lloyd? The latter had a record of making trouble for Coleridge, even with his close friends; he had an insinuating manner, and was skilled at wounding without appearing to be hostile. Moreover, he was well connected. It would have been easy for him to represent opinion in London, Cambridge and elsewhere as contemptuous of the 'Ancient Mariner'. The negative reviews of the first edition of *Lyrical Ballads* had predisposed Wordsworth to think of the 'Ancient Mariner' as a drag on the collection. Perhaps, encouraged by Lloyd, he persuaded himself that retaining the poem was favour enough, and that some qualification was needed if it were not to jeopardise the rest. Wordsworth did not much care for Lloyd, whose very presence reminded him of the emotional instability he dreaded and deplored. No doubt he was exasperated with Coleridge for the delay in finishing 'Christabel'. Ambition blinded him to the predicament of his friend, who had helped him in so many ways to reach the commanding point where he now stood. Coleridge's prostration made it easy for Wordsworth to walk all over him.

Before publication, Wordsworth asked Longman to let Lamb have a copy of the new edition of *Lyrical Ballads*. He wrote to Lamb, apparently eager for his comments. Lamb acknowledged both gift and letter in a thoughtful response of the type he had often sent to Coleridge in the past, uninhibitedly dispensing both praise and criticism. Wordsworth's poem 'The Old Cumberland Beggar' he thought too didactic; 'an intelligent reader finds a sort of insult in being told, I will teach you how to think upon this subject'. In his view, he told Wordsworth, there was 'an unwritten compact between Author and reader; I will tell you a story, and I suppose you will understand it'.

> I am sorry that Coleridge has christened his Ancient Marinere 'a poet's Reverie' – it is as bad as Bottom the weaver's declaration that he is not a lion but only the scenical representation of a Lion. What new idea is gained by this title, but one subversive of all credit, which the tale should force upon us, of its truth? For me, I was never so affected with any human Tale. After first reading it, I was totally possessed with it for many days . . .

Lamb countered the criticisms of the poem in Wordsworth's note. 'You will excuse my remarks,' he continued, 'because I am hurt and vexed that you should think it necessary, with a prose apology, to open the eyes of dead men that cannot see.' Lamb's reproaches were consistent with his defence of the poem against Southey's criticisms two years earlier. He summed up his opinion of the second volume by saying that no poem in it had struck him so forcibly as the 'Ancient Mariner', 'The Mad Mother' and 'Tintern Abbey' in the first. He also regretted the preface, which he thought had a *'diminishing'* effect on the poems that followed and should have been published separately.[72]

Wordsworth's reply has not survived, but Lamb summarised it in a letter to his confidant Thomas Manning: 'I had better be cautious henceforward what opinion I give of the Lyrical Ballads. All the North of England are in turmoil. Cumberland and Westmoreland* have already declared a state of war,' he began. He referred to Wordsworth's self-professed 'almost insurmountable aversion from Letter-writing'. After he had sent his opinions to Wordsworth,

> The Post did not sleep a moment. I received almost instantaneously a long letter of four sweating pages from my Reluctant Letter-Writer, the purport of which was, that he was sorry his 2d vol. had not given me more pleasure (Devil a hint did I give that it had *not pleased me*), and was 'compelled

---

* i.e. Coleridge and Wordsworth. Keswick was in Cumberland, Grasmere in Westmoreland.

to wish that my range of sensibility was more extended . . .' –
With a deal of Stuff about a certain Union of Tenderness and
Imagination . . .

Wordsworth had copied out several passages which he considered
that Lamb had missed, underlining some to emphasise his points.
Nor was this all:

> Coleridge, who had not written to me some months before,
> starts up from his bed of sickness, to reprove me for my
> hardy presumption: four long pages, equally sweaty and more
> tedious, came from him; assuring me that, when the works
> of a man of true genius, such as W. undoubtedly was, do not
> please me at first sight, I should suspect the fault to lie 'in
> me and not in them', etc. etc. etc. etc. etc. What am I to do
> with such people?[73]

While Wordsworth had been writing his preface, Coleridge was struggling to complete 'Christabel'. This had been intended as his most
significant new contribution to the second edition of *Lyrical Ballads*.
By mid-September the first part of the poem had already been set up
in type. Unfortunately composition of the second part took longer
than hoped,* and Wordsworth began to chafe at the delay. In his first
draft of the preface he had anticipated its completion, explaining that
'a friend' had contributed 'the long and beautiful† Poem of Christabel,
without which I should not yet have ventured to present a second
volume to the public'. Coleridge's continuing failure to produce
'Christabel' therefore threatened the *raison d'être* for the second volume. 'The delay in Copy has been owing in part to me, as the writer
of Christabel,' Coleridge confessed when the poem was still apparently
unfinished. 'Every line has been produced by me with labour-
pangs,' he lamented. In a burst of misery, he announced that 'I abandon Poetry altogether – I leave the higher and deeper kinds to

* On the evening of 31 August Coleridge had walked over to Grasmere to read the
Wordsworths 'a part of *Christabel*' – presumably what he had by then written of the
second part, since they were already familiar with the first. His route took him over
the top of Helvellyn in the gathering darkness, and he arrived at eleven o'clock, while
Dorothy was walking in the garden by moonlight.
† The words 'long and beautiful' have been struck out in manuscript.

Wordsworth, the delightful, popular & simply dignified to Southey; & reserve for myself the honourable attempt to make others feel and understand their writings, as they deserve to be felt & understood.'[74]

Coleridge was feeling the strain. Even while he was grappling with 'Christabel', Stuart was pressing him for contributions. In late September he began to supply Stuart with essays. Though he was now again very short of money, he felt unable to seek help from the Wedgwoods after ignoring their warnings about moving to the north, and was therefore reduced to borrowing from Godwin.[75]

There were plenty of reasons why he should have found it so difficult to finish 'Christabel'. Indeed, both Lamb and Wordsworth were subsequently to conclude that the whole attempt was misguided; the poem was complete as already written.* Moreover, to proceed with the poem led Coleridge into forbidden territory. Its first part had ended in Christabel's apparent seduction, but his mind sheered away from such a disturbing thought. The sexual theme was both fascinating and revolting to him. He was tormented by hideous nightmares arising from guilty memories of brothel creeping in his undergraduate years. The first part of 'Christabel' had evoked such illicit pleasures, reaching a climax in the moment when Geraldine lets drop her robes, leaving her body uncovered. This is the moment of horror that would later cause Shelley to run from the room screaming. Coleridge could not describe the naked Geraldine; he had reached the threshold, but he could not go in.[76]

His inhibition would intensify as he became besotted with Sara Hutchinson. The need for self-control increased as the temptation grew. In November, Sara Hutchinson arrived to spend the winter in the Lakes. Coleridge accompanied Wordsworth towards Penrith to meet her. They escorted her to Greta Hall, where she and Wordsworth stayed a few days before going on to Grasmere. A week later Coleridge joined them at Grasmere. That night he awoke screaming, after a nightmare of being attacked by a woman who tried to pull out his right eye. Wordsworth called out on hearing his friend's screams, but

* See page 229.

did not come to comfort him, a dereliction that Coleridge thought cruel.[77]

An entry in Coleridge's notebook, which he dated 30 October, described his predicament:

> He knew not what to do – something, he felt, must be done – he rose, drew his writing-desk suddenly before him – sate down, took the pen – & found that he knew not what to do.[78]

Afterwards he attempted to rationalise his writer's block. 'The deep unutterable Disgust, which I had suffered in the translation of that accursed Wallenstein, seemed to have stricken me with barrenness – for I tried & tried, & nothing would come of it.'[79] He took many a walk up the mountains in an attempt to find inspiration; but none came. Eventually (or so he said) his faculties returned to him after drinking too much one night. Conditions at home were far from ideal: in mid-September Sara gave birth to a son, whom they called Derwent; the baby emitted a noise like a creaking door, while his little body was convulsed by fits. He was not expected to live. Poor Sara was distraught at the prospect of losing another child. Fortunately, Derwent recovered quickly, and was soon being described as 'a fat pretty child, healthy and hungry'.[80]

By late September Coleridge had written a second part of 'Christabel' as long as the first, but the poem was no more complete than it had been before; if anything, less so. The effort had exhausted him, and his inability to conclude the poem left him demoralised. Of course he was anxious not to fail Wordsworth, and the knowledge that Lloyd was often at Grasmere heightened his anxiety. It seems that, in despair of finishing the poem in the near future, Coleridge clung to the hope that it might be published as a fragment: this is one interpretation of a letter he wrote to Daniel Stuart at the end of September.[81] Somehow he convinced himself that Wordsworth was again dangerously ill, and needed him – though Dorothy's journals for this period show no indication of this; on the contrary, her brother was taking long walks as usual. On 3 October Coleridge worked through the night writing essays for the *Morning Post*, and the next

day walked over to Grasmere, arriving very wet while the Wordsworths were still at dinner. They sat up until midnight talking, and
Coleridge recited to his friends what he had written. 'Exceedingly
delighted with the second part of "Christabel"', Dorothy noted in her
journal. The next morning Coleridge read the poem to them again;
'we had increasing pleasure'. Wordsworth *was* now ill, and took to
bed after working hard on an addition to the preface. Coleridge and
Dorothy walked to Ambleside to post a letter, returning after dark.
Coleridge had intended to leave the next day, but it was wet out of
doors and he remained. Had it not rained that day, much might have
been different, because after tea Wordsworth announced a change of
plan: 'determined not to print "Christabel" with the L.B.'.[82] Dorothy's
journal records this decision, but does not explain it. Coleridge left
Grasmere the next morning, carrying with him a letter from Wordsworth to the printer cancelling all references to his 'long and beautiful'
poem.

Coleridge defended the decision to omit 'Christabel' in letters to
friends. To Davy, he claimed that the poem 'was running up to
1300 lines' (twice the length of any surviving manuscript*), and that
Wordsworth thought it 'indelicate to print two Volumes with *his
name* in which so much of another man's was included'. This was
the very reverse of the argument that Wordsworth had used in the
preface to justify presenting a second volume to the public. And in
fact the two parts of 'Christabel' together were only a little longer
than the 'Ancient Mariner'. It is scarcely credible that the final length
of the poem could have been envisaged as any shorter when the
original decision had been made to include it in the second edition
of *Lyrical Ballads*. Another excuse Coleridge gave to Davy was that
'the poem was in direct opposition to the very purpose for which the
Lyrical Ballads were published – viz – an experiment to see how far
those passions, which alone give any value to extraordinary Incidents,
were capable of interesting, in & for themselves, in the incidents of

* In a letter to Poole written around the same time, Coleridge reported that 'Christabel'
had 'swelled into a poem of 1400 lines'.

common Life'.[83] This was a reasonable point, but one that should have been obvious from the moment when the second edition was first discussed, and of course the criticism was equally true of the 'Ancient Mariner'. In a letter to Longman apologising for the delay in providing copy for the second volume, Wordsworth fell back on differences of style to explain 'Christabel's' omission: 'A Poem of Mr Coleridge's was to have concluded the Volumes; but upon mature deliberation I found that the Style of this Poem was so discordant from my own that it could not be printed along with my poems with any propriety.'[84] But the style of the poem had been known for more than two years. Moreover, Wordsworth's argument seemed to contradict what he had written in the preface, where he had acknowledged 'the assistance of a Friend' in providing five poems, 'for the sake of variety'. Somewhat lamely, he argued that these poems had 'the same tendency as my own; and that, though there would be found a difference, there would be found no discordance in the colours of our style'. In fact, the difference between the two styles was obvious to even the most casual reader. Wordsworth utilised the same reasoning to explain the exclusion of 'Christabel' as he had used to justify the inclusion of the 'Ancient Mariner'.

To soften the blow of the rejection, Wordsworth seems to have suggested publishing 'Christabel' separately, in tandem with his own poem 'The Pedlar' (a segment extracted from 'The Ruined Cottage'). But the two poems had nothing in common; 'Christabel' was no more concordant with 'The Pedlar' than it was with Wordsworth's poems in the *Lyrical Ballads*.

In a letter to Josiah Wedgwood, Coleridge reported that the poem had grown 'so long, & in Wordsworth's opinion so impressive, that he rejected it from his volume as disproportionate both in size & merit, & as discordant in it's character'.[85] The fact that the two poets used the same term – 'discordant' – to explain the poem's omission suggests that they had agreed this formula between them.

None of the justifications used by either poet stands up to scrutiny. Neither appears to have advanced the obvious argument, namely that the poem was incomplete. It ended abruptly, suggesting that the second part was itself incomplete. Long afterwards Coleridge would append some lines about Hartley as 'The Conclusion to Part II', though these seemed to have little if any relation to the rest of the poem.* It is not obvious why 'Christabel' was rejected, only that it was. Possibly Wordsworth was alarmed about how it might be received. The 'Ancient Mariner' had damaged the first edition of *Lyrical Ballads* (or so he believed); another 'strange' poem might sink the second.

The quality of the poem does not seem to have come into the reckoning – unless one accepts Coleridge's unconvincing explanation that Wordsworth found it too impressive to print alongside his own poems. Perhaps it was simply not to his taste – though Dorothy's testimony that she and her brother had been 'exceedingly delighted with the second part of "Christabel"' seems to indicate otherwise. Increasingly, Wordsworth was concentrating on incidents of everyday life, eliminating from his poems all that was unusual or outlandish. The supernatural had no place in his work. Perhaps he thought that 'Christabel' was a piece of ephemeral Gothic, destined not to last. In fact nothing could be further from the truth: the poem, circulating in manuscript, had an influence almost impossible to overestimate, and through the work of a second generation of Romantic poets it would kindle the Victorian fascination with the medieval. One could describe it without exaggeration as one of the seeds of nineteenth-century culture; and it remains one of the most popular poems written in English. This would be of little benefit to the author, however. 'Christabel' would not be published for another fifteen years, by which time, as Coleridge himself recognised,[86] it appeared far less original than it would have done had it been published soon after it was written.†

Wordsworth might not have admitted it to himself, either then or later, but subconscious resentment of Coleridge may have played a

---

* For reasons that appear mysterious, the first of theses line alludes to his own contribution to Wordsworth's 'We are Seven'.
† Walter Scott's hugely successful 'The Lay of the Last Minstrel' (1805) was an imitation (perhaps unconscious, perhaps not) of 'Christabel', echoing the content, style and metre of Coleridge's poem and including at least one phrase taken directly from it, written after his friend John Stoddart had recited it to him in the autumn of 1802.

part in the decision to reject 'Christabel'. His friend regularly reminded him about the need to make progress with *The Recluse*; this was more important than anything else. Wordsworth thought so too, which made Coleridge's persistence a form of torment. Coleridge's adulation made it impossible for Wordsworth to disappoint him. However much he twisted and turned, Wordsworth could not escape from *The Recluse*. Yet he could not write it either. Frustration bred a suppressed antagonism, which erupted in his cruel dismissal of his friend's work. How dare Coleridge urge him to write *The Recluse* when he could not even finish 'Christabel'?

In a letter to Poole, Coleridge complained that the effort to finish the poem 'threw my business terribly back – & now I am sweating for it'. He was receiving 'dunning letters', i.e. demands for payment from creditors. He poured out his frustration to Stuart: 'I do nothing, but almost instantly it's defects & sillinesses come upon my mind, and haunt me, till I am completely disgusted with my performance, & wish myself a Tanner, or a Printer, or any thing but an Author.' Having explained to Stuart his failure to produce more essays, he enclosed some verse: 'I shall fill up these Blanks with a few Poems.'[87] He could not bring himself to claim the poems as his own, though they were printed under his name. In fact Wordsworth had written them. At the very moment when Coleridge ought to have asserted himself, circumstances forced him to go cap in hand to Wordsworth, for scraps from his pocket book.

One of the poems published under Coleridge's name in the *Morning Post* at this time, 'The Mad Monk', could have been written by either man, and is included in the standard editions of both's work. It resembles Wordsworth's past and future work in several ways, but whether it was written by him, or written by Coleridge in imitation of his style, or some combination of the two, is impossible to determine. Coleridge's skill was such that he could well have succeeded in an imitation even at a time when he was unable to find the inspiration to write anything wholly original.

On 15 October Wordsworth walked over to Keswick to see how much progress Coleridge had made in writing other poems for the

Lyrical Ballads. Two days later he was back. An entry in Dorothy's journal summarised his findings: 'Coleridge had done nothing for the L.B. Working hard for Stuart.' He had done nothing, and would do nothing more. There would be no Coleridge poems in the second volume of *Lyrical Ballads*. Meanwhile Wordsworth was writing a new poem to fill the vacant place at the end of the second volume. 'Michael' was the very antithesis of 'Christabel', a pastoral poem evoking the sturdy qualities of the sheep farmers among whom he was now living. It was not finished until 9 December, and the next day the Wordsworths walked over to Keswick with Sara Hutchinson. They remained at Greta Hall four days, while Coleridge discussed with Wordsworth plans to publicise the new edition. He proposed to send a set of volumes to various 'persons of eminence': two MPs, Fox and the anti-slavery campaigner William Wilberforce; the fashionable Duchess of Devonshire; the actress (and royal mistress) Mrs Jordan; Mrs Barbauld; and Sir James Bland Burges, government servant and man of letters. Coleridge drafted these letters and wrote out several of them himself. 'I am especially pleased that I have contributed nothing to the second volume,' he wrote to Longman, 'as I can now exert myself loudly and everywhere in their favor without suspicion of vanity or self-interest. I have written Letters to all my acquaintance whose voices I think likely to have any Influence. In all this I am guided, if I know my own heart, wholly & exclusively by my almost unbounded admiration of the poems.'[88]

Wordsworth apologists have claimed that Coleridge accepted the rejection of 'Christabel' 'cheerfully', and quote his own self-justificatory letters afterwards in support of this argument. They cite too Dorothy's comment on Coleridge's next visit to Dove Cottage; 'we were very merry'.* But Dorothy, though very fond of Coleridge, was blind to the possibility that her brother might be at fault. And Coleridge tried to put a brave face on his disappointment. In reality

---

* After supper Coleridge again read 'Christabel' to the Wordsworths and to their guest John Stoddart, who in due course was to recite the poem to Scott.

he had suffered a mortal blow; his spirit was broken; he would never be the same man again. 'I have too much trifled with my reputation,' he reflected sadly to Poole.[89] A week before Christmas, he wrote to Thelwall for the first time in years, listing his current literary pursuits, which no longer included poetry. 'I have altogether abandoned it,' he told Thelwall, 'being convinced that I never had the essentials of poetic Genius, & that I mistook a strong desire for original power.'[90] He compared himself to an ostrich: 'I cannot fly, yet I have wings that give me the feeling of flight.' He pictured himself as a 'bird of the earth', running along the plain, looking up and seeing birds that could really fly.[91] The contrast with Wordsworth was painfully evident. 'He is a great, a true Poet,' he affirmed to Francis Wrangham; 'I am only a kind of a Metaphysician.' In the same breath he informed Wrangham that Wordsworth had just sent off the last sheet of copy for 'his' *Lyrical Ballads*.[92]

Coleridge concealed his distress from the Wordsworths, and perhaps they remained unaware of its true cause. His mind would no longer be wholly open to them. The wound continued to fester. As the years passed, entries critical of Wordsworth began to appear in Coleridge's notebooks. Though the friendship remained warm a long time, it could never recover the same closeness – when each man gave and received in complete confidence, when each shared the same vision, and neither felt anything to fear from the other. Wordsworth had eclipsed his friend, and afterwards Coleridge would always be in his shadow.

Two months after the appearance of *Lyrical Ballads*, after a prolonged illness in which he had increasingly resorted to laudanum to combat pain, Coleridge wrote to Godwin lamenting that 'my imagination (or rather the Somewhat that had been imaginative) lies, like a Cold Snuff on the circular Rim of a Brass Candle-stick, without even a stink of Tallow to remind you that it was once cloathed and mitred with Flame'. He asked Godwin if he had seen the new *Lyrical Ballads*, and singled out three of the poems Wordsworth had written for the second volume: 'I should judge of a man's heart, and intellect precisely according to the degree & intensity of the admiration, with which he read those poems.' He referred to Godwin's plan to write his biography:

> If I die, and the Booksellers will give you any thing for my Life, be sure to say – 'Wordsworth descended on him, like the γνῶθι σεαυτόν* from Heaven; by shewing to him what true Poetry was, he made him know, that he himself was no Poet.'[93]

Coleridge's confidence was in ruins. As he told Godwin, 'the Poet is dead in me'. He was twenty-eight years old.

---

* 'Know Thyself', the advice inscribed on the Temple of Apollo at Delphi.

PART III

Acquaintances

'My Friend (O me! what a word to give permanence
to the mistake of a Life!)'[1]

11

SUBORDINATION

At about six o'clock in the evening of 19 April 1801, a Sunday, William and Dorothy arrived at Greta Hall, after walking up from Grasmere. Both felt anxious about their friend. Only the previous day they had received an alarming account of Coleridge's condition; he had begun to talk of dying.[1] Dorothy reported on their visit to Mary Hutchinson: 'We both trembled, and till we entered the door I hardly durst speak.' They found Coleridge sitting in the parlour, looking 'dreadfully pale and weak'. Dorothy described him as 'very, very unwell – ill all over', so weak that he changed colour whenever he exerted himself in any way.[2]

For more than five months the Wordsworths had been concerned about Coleridge's health. He had been ill on and off since the middle of November, confined to bed much of the time, staging recoveries only to relapse, suffering such a succession of distressing symptoms that he seemed like a man accursed: inflamed eyes, headaches, nausea, constipation, diarrhoea, swollen knees, arthritic hands, aches in his hips and calves, excruciating back pain, rheumatic fever, itches, boils, even a swollen testicle. He wrote his friends pitiful bulletins detailing his symptoms; indeed, for the rest of his life he would scarcely ever write a letter without an account of his health, regardless of the recipient. His letters now were filled with gloomy predictions that he was 'going down into the Grave'. In a period of respite he explored Easedale, above Grasmere, and there discovered a hollow place in the rock shaped like a coffin, exactly his own length; he lay down in it and slept, a sycamore bush shielding the sun from his eyes.[3] 'It grieves me to think that he should be throwing himself away,' John Wordsworth wrote in reply to a letter from Dorothy.[4]

At Christmas the whole Coleridge family had come to Grasmere for three weeks' visit. Coleridge had walked from Keswick, arriving soaked to the skin, and so ill that he was confined to bed for the remainder of his stay. Early in the New Year he had been carried back to Keswick by chaise,* and had crept into his bed at Greta Hall. He was sleepless and irritable; the pain in his back was acute enough to cause him to cry out at any sudden movement. The local surgeon-apothecary diagnosed 'a species of irregular gout', and prescribed leeches, blisters, bark† and large quantities of Kendal Black Drop, a solution of opium in vegetable acids or spirits, at least twice as powerful as the more usual laudanum.[5] Coleridge supplemented this with brandy. The result was to blur the distinction between day and night, between wakefulness and sleep. He remained in his room dreaming, his obligations to publishers unmet while his debts accumulated. A sick husband and a baby made a lot of work for Sara Coleridge, and her namesake Sara Hutchinson came over from Grasmere for a few weeks to help. Meanwhile Coleridge produced nothing except a series of long, half-brilliant, half-mad philosophical letters to his patron, from which he desisted only at Wordsworth's 'fervent entreaty'. He claimed to have 'completely extricated the notions of Time, and Space', and to be about to 'solve the process of Life & Consciousness'. The 'intensity of thought' made him 'nervous and feverish'. He was annoyed at the lack of response from Josiah Wedgwood, who later confessed to putting aside his letters unread.[6]

'I do think he will never be quite well till he has tried a warm climate,' mused Dorothy.[7] Coleridge had begun to cast around for somewhere suitable. He proposed to Southey – still in Portugal, where he had gone for the sake of *his* health – that both families should relocate to the Pinney estate on the Caribbean island of Nevis; 'Words-

---

* A light open carriage for one or two people.
† The bark of various species of the South American cinchona tree, ground into a powder, taken as a medicine; its active ingredient is quinine.

worth would certainly go, if I went.' (He did not seem troubled by the prospect of living among slaves.) He even revived the idea of settling in the valley of the Susquehanna, if Wordsworth would come too. 'Another Winter in England would *do for me,*' he forecast, hinting that Poole should advance him the money for a trip to the Azores, above and beyond the £37 he already owed.[8] Early in July Wordsworth wrote to Poole on Coleridge's account, asking him to lend their mutual friend the necessary funds. For once, Poole was disinclined to help. He had been hurt to discover that Coleridge no longer wrote to him with as much pleasure as before.* And he was stung by Coleridge's railing against the hard-heartedness of the rich, 'wallowing in the wantonness of wealth'. A man could not be a moral being without having felt the pressure of hardships, Coleridge had informed Poole. Such remarks seemed pointed at Poole himself, especially unfair at a time when Poole was particularly active in organising relief for the local poor. The war had pushed up the price of bread to unprecedented levels, and there had been food riots in the West Country; Poole had met a delegation from the hungry protesters. Surrounded by so much suffering, he was irritated by Coleridge's constant complaints of poverty. After all, Coleridge received an annuity of £150; those whom Poole was trying to help were forced to survive on much less.[9]

Poole replied not to Wordsworth, but to Coleridge. To hear of the state of Coleridge's health grieved him more than he could express. Tom Wedgwood was planning to winter in Sicily; might not Coleridge accompany him? Alluding to Wordsworth's proposal, Poole referred to the 'many claims' on him. He offered a loan of £20, pointing out that Coleridge already owed him not £37, but £52.

In an earlier letter, Poole had expressed scepticism about whether 'your disease be really *bodily,* and not the consequence of an irritated mind'. It seemed to him impossible to imagine that Coleridge could not be well, if only his mind were 'freely at ease'. It was 'a curious

---

* Poole happened to be with the Wedgwoods when a letter arrived from Coleridge, which was read aloud to the assembled company.

thing' for a man under thirty to predict his imminent death.* If Coleridge's mind could purge itself of its tendency to alternate between restlessness and torpor, 'it would make you great and happy'.[10]

Poole's letter seemed to hint at the underlying cause of his friend's ailments: it was the medicine itself that was poisoning him. Ever since his teens Coleridge had resorted to laudanum when he felt ill or anxious. Not only did it alleviate the symptoms, it also induced pleasurable sensations, liberating his mind to float free, evoking images of sensual delight. Over time, his body had built up a high degree of tolerance towards the drug, so that to achieve the same palliative effect required him to consume ever-increasing amounts. Now came a sudden collapse in his health, chaos in his digestive system, increased sensitivity to pain in every part of his body (which Coleridge diagnosed as 'flying' or 'irregular' gout), anxiety bordering on panic, and extreme despondency – all classic signs of opium addiction. Without opium, he suffered all manner of agony; when it was given, he felt immediate relief. Yet the more opium he took, the more he needed.

The effect of opium-taking on the body was then little understood. Most doctors regarded opium as a general-purpose analgesic, much as aspirin is regarded today. Moreover, it was a tranquilliser, calming the nerves and aiding rest. The danger of addiction went unrecognised. Many sensible people saw no harm in opium. The evangelical reformer William Wilberforce, for example, took opium daily for the last forty-five years of his life.[11] Coleridge's respectable brother George had experienced the pleasurable effects of opium. Laudanum was routinely given to babies; Dorothy took it to alleviate toothache.

One curious aspect of Coleridge's addiction was that his symptoms could disappear as quickly as they had arrived, leaving him in apparent robust good health, and supporting the illusion that laudanum was efficacious in curing him. Eventually he would come to appreciate

---

* Though not then so curious as it might seem today. Among Coleridge's contemporaries, Robert Lovell and Margaret Hutchinson had died in 1796; Joseph Hucks and Amos Cottle (Joseph's older brother, a poet) died in 1800; and Robert Allen died in 1805.

that the opposite was true: that most, if not all, of 'the direful sufferings, I so complained of, were the mere effects of Opium, which I
even to that hour imagined a sort of Guardian Genius to me!'[12] In later
years, when the pernicious effect of the drug had become apparent to
him, Coleridge traced his dependence back to this period, when he
was 'seduced into the ACCURSED Habit ignorantly'. He recollected
that he had tried opium as a remedy for swollen knees after reading
in a medical journal of the cure of a similar case. In truth, he had
been an occasional user of opium for at least a decade, but it was not
until the winter of 1800–01 that he became enslaved to the drug.[13] It
seems likely that mental distress tipped him over the edge. Opium
had become a crutch on which he leant at times of agitation or
anxiety. The financial pressures upon him, his deteriorating relations
with his wife, his difficulties in completing 'Christabel', his concern
not to disappoint Wordsworth, and his misery when his poem was
rejected – all these drove him to seek solace in opium. The crisis of
confidence he suffered that winter turned him into an addict. The
effect was disastrous, not just to his health, but to his personality.
Dependence on the drug exacerbated all the most deplorable aspects
of his character: self-pity, evasiveness, secrecy, duplicity, indifference,
passivity, apathy, paralysis, self-loathing and shame. Some of these
traits were already present, but the addiction made them much worse.

After a delay of almost six weeks, Coleridge responded to Poole,
shrugging off his advice. To have accompanied Tom Wedgwood
abroad was the very last thing he could have submitted to, he protested. 'Two invalids – & two men so utterly unlike each other in
opinions, habits, acquirements, & feeling!' (He had offered to accompany Wedgwood abroad the previous November, and would do so
again.) 'It is impossible that you should feel with regard to pecuniary
affairs as Wordsworth or as I feel,' he declared loftily. It was the same
'parade of superior feeling' of which Kitty Wedgwood had complained. 'Let us for the future abstain from all pecuniary matters,'
Coleridge urged. Within weeks, however, he was again soliciting
money from Poole.[14]

*

In the middle of July, Coleridge travelled across the Pennines, ostensibly because he wanted to study the manuscripts of the medieval philosopher-cleric John Duns Scotus in the library of Durham Cathedral; in reality because he could not keep away from Sara Hutchinson, who had left the Lakes around the end of March. He based himself at nearby Bishop Middleham, where she was staying with her brother George. After a fortnight or so he rode with Sara to Tom Hutchinson's farm at Gallow Hill, near Scarborough, where he soothed his swollen knee by bathing in the sea, remaining there ten days before returning with her to Bishop Middleham. To Coleridge, Sara was an ideal companion, a soulmate, 'my comforter', his 'Best-beloved! who lovest me the Best!' In his mind she was a symbol of purity and innocence, his 'good angel', a woman at once desirable and untouchable. He was afire with a longing that grew ever more fervent as it remained unconsummated. What she felt about him is unclear. Perhaps she was flattered by his attention at first, though later it became oppressive. Certainly she sympathised with him in his difficulties with his wife. Many years later she would warn her cousin Thomas Monkhouse to be wary of marrying: 'I have seen such misery in the marriage life as would *appal* you if you had seen it. Such millstones about the necks of worthy men!'[15]

Coleridge's passion for Sara Hutchinson drew him still closer to the 'family of love' centred at Grasmere. For Coleridge, this new 'family' was an echo of the old one. Once again, he and a fellow-poet, a 'brother', were linked to two sisters, this time Hutchinsons instead of Frickers. But their situations were not the same. While Wordsworth was unencumbered, Coleridge was not. Blocking his path to Sara Hutchinson was another Sara, his wife. His resentment of her increased accordingly.

Dorothy was contemptuous of Sara Coleridge, whom she thought shallow and trivial, 'the lightest weakest silliest woman!'[16] She referred disparagingly to her breastfeeding, and her preoccupation with the children. 'She is indeed a bad nurse for C,' she wrote to Mary Hutchinson, though 'an excellent nurse to her sucking children'. In Dorothy's view, Coleridge and his wife were 'ill matched', and both to be pitied.

'She would have made a very good wife to many another man, but for Coleridge!! Her radical fault is want of sensibility, and what can such a woman be to Coleridge?'[17] The Hutchinson sisters took their cue from Dorothy. Mary described Coleridge's wife as 'a stuffed turkey' and Sara called her 'a silly prating thing'.

Dorothy was unlikely to have thus criticised Sara had she not heard similar criticism from Coleridge himself. In his notebook he complained that his wife was 'the willing Slave of the Ears & Eyes of others'; moreover, she was 'uncommonly *cold* in her feelings of animal Love'.[18] Relations between husband and wife deteriorated during Coleridge's long months of illness. It is not hard to imagine the substance of their frequent quarrels. Sara must have been exasperated by his opium habit. It drove her frantic to see her husband inactive month after month, while their indebtedness increased and creditors became importunate. There was something unmanly about a husband who could not provide for his wife and children. She remonstrated with him; and she was irritated further to find herself depicted to his friends as a shrewish, nagging wife. She resented the Wordsworths' influence on her husband, which distracted him from productive activities and which so manifestly excluded her. She was not as welcoming to them as he would wish. Dorothy complained that they did not stay long at Greta Hall, because 'we are never comfortable there after the first 2 or 3 days'. Whenever he felt well enough, Coleridge escaped to Grasmere, apparently frittering away more precious time.

Early in May Coleridge travelled by post-chaise to Grasmere, taking Hartley with him. There he felt well enough to undertake a six-mile walk before suffering a relapse and returning a week later to Keswick. Hartley remained behind, attending the local school during his stay, which lasted five or six weeks. Coleridge's elder son (and later Derwent too) would be a frequent visitor to Grasmere in the years that followed, often without the presence of either parent. Hartley was a favourite with the Wordsworths; more than that, he represented an ideal of childhood, 'exquisitely wild'. Wordsworth wrote a poem about him, 'To H.C., Six Years Old', and he would be the subject of a stanza of Wordsworth's 'Immortality' ode, just as he had been portrayed in Coleridge's 'Frost at Midnight'. In time, Hartley would inspire the conclusion to the second part of 'Christabel'.

Coleridge was back at home in time to receive the Southeys, newly returned from Portugal, who arrived at Greta Hall (accompanied by Southey's mother) for an indefinite stay in response to his repeated invitations. 'I am willing to believe,' Coleridge had written to Southey earlier in the year, 'that the blessed Dreams, we dreamt some 6 years ago, may be auguries of something really noble which we may yet perform together.' Southey had seemed excited about the prospect. 'Time & absence make strange work with our affections; but mine are ever returning to rest upon you. I have other & dear friends, but none with whom the whole of my being is intimate – with whom every thought & feeling can amalgamate.' For his part, Coleridge had been equally enthusiastic – 'oh! how I have dreamt about you', he exclaimed, 'how I yearned toward you...'[19]

After such a build-up, the reality was disappointing. 'I feel your absence more than I enjoy your society,' Coleridge admitted to Southey after he had gone; 'that I do not enjoy your society so much, as I anticipated that I should do, is wholly or almost wholly owing to the nature of my domestic feelings, & the fear, or the consciousness, that you did not or could not sympathize.'[20] On their arrival in early September the Southeys experienced the tension in the Coleridge household. They were inclined to side with Sara, who naturally confided in her sister, while Coleridge was at first inhibited from complaining about his wife to his brother-in-law. Southey always felt protective towards Sara; there was a story in the family that he had originally courted her before switching his attentions to Edith. After his stay at Greta Hall was over he commented that 'in no instance was Mrs Coleridge ever to blame'. Coleridge's complaints that she irritated him, and made him so ill that he could do nothing, were merely a 'wretched excuse for idleness'; he was venting his vexation on his wife. The disciplined Southey was shocked to find that Coleridge did not open letters. He regretted his old friend's 'constant sacrifice to present impulse which marks his character and blasts the brightest talents that I have ever witnessed'.[21]

In October Southey made a brief trip to Ireland, leaving his wife and his mother behind at Greta Hall. Coleridge sent a letter after him, in which he assured Southey of his continuing affection and esteem, apologised for his gloominess, and unburdened his heart about his wife: 'alas! we are not suited to each other'. Coded references in the letter hinted at a new love. He began to talk openly of separating from Sara, 'foolish gossiping' that Southey very much deplored.[22]

An informal separation would have made little difference to Sara in practice; in recent years her husband had been away from home much of the time anyway. Such long absences were not unusual at the time, nor were they a cause for comment. So long as Coleridge continued to provide for the family as best he could, and so long as there was no open break to expose her to unkind gossip, she remained comparatively content. Jealousy was a luxury she could little afford. A public separation was another matter altogether. And divorce – which could then be granted only on grounds of cruelty or adultery – was a disaster. A woman's reputation was her most precious asset. A divorced woman was assumed to be adulterous, and branded a whore; she could not be received in respectable company. Moreover, the law gave a divorced woman no rights over her children; they could easily be taken away. And for Coleridge too, divorce was not an option. It ran contrary to all his most fundamental principles. A deeply religious man, he believed in the sanctity of the marriage vows. He could not abandon these without abandoning part of himself. And he would have been forced to eat his words; he had often campaigned against the tendency of Godwin and his supporters towards 'vice'. 'Carefully have I *thought thro*' the subject of marriage,' he wrote to Southey, '& deeply am I convinced of it's indissolubleness.'

When the Wordsworths urged Coleridge to separate from his wife, they were far from encouraging him to take up with Sara Hutchinson. She too had a reputation to protect. His passion for her was acceptable, indeed welcome in so far as it bound him closer to them. But his love must remain chaste; she was inviolable.

337

The more Coleridge longed for Sara Hutchinson, the more insistent he was on the need for restraint. Though he might separate from his wife, he would never be free of her, free for his beloved. He struggled to shape his illicit yearnings into an acceptable form, frequently describing Sara as a 'sister'. Part of his frustration was that he was unable to give public expression to his love. He began to refer to her in his notebooks as 'Asra', to distinguish her from the other Sara. Asra was an anagram, of course, but it was also a shortened form of Asahara, the Moorish maid of his imagination, a composite of all that he found most desirable in a woman, echoed perhaps in the seductive 'Abyssinian maid' of 'Kubla Khan'.[23] In long opium reveries he dreamed of happiness with 'Asra', his fantasy version of the real Sara. Though he could never have Sara, in his imagination Asra was his.

In his notebook he sketched what seems to have been a plan for a poem:

> A lively picture of a man, disappointed in marriage, & endeav-
> ouring to make a compensation to himself by virtuous &
> tender & brotherly friendship with an amiable Woman – the
> obstacles – the jealousies – the impossibility of it. – Best
> advice that he should as much as possible withdraw himself
> from pursuits of morals &c – & devote himself to abstract
> sciences –[24]

Southey returned from Ireland towards the end of October and took his family south to London. Desperate for money and unhappy at home, Coleridge decided that he too should winter in town, working for the *Morning Post* once more. It was an interesting time to be back in the thick of things. Pitt's government had fallen earlier in the year, and Addington's new administration reflected the public's war weariness. Already preliminaries of a peace had been signed between Britain and France. Letters were beginning get through again. Soon it would be possible to go back and forth between the two countries, and to roam freely across Europe.

*

Coleridge had seen little or nothing of the Wordsworths since early July, as they had gone to Scotland for a month* around the time that he had returned from Gallow Hill. He longed to be alone with them – 'so many sad things to let out'. Soon after their return he had spent a night at Dove Cottage, but the rain and the presence of another visitor (perhaps Southey) made uninhibited talk impossible. Dorothy's journal records two more visits from him in October. On 4 November, less than a week before Coleridge's departure for London, her otherwise invariable daily record is interrupted for almost five days, as a page has been torn from her journal at this point. It seems possible that the missing entries described conversations of a personal nature that someone thought better destroyed. Perhaps it was only now that Coleridge confided to his dearest friends the full extent of his feelings for Asra.

The night before he left, the Wordsworths came to stay at Keswick – Sara and the children were away, which was a relief. 'We enjoyed ourselves in the study and were *at home*,' Dorothy wrote in her journal. Walking back to Grasmere the next day, she found that 'every sight and every sound reminded me of him'. She had been upset by their conversation the previous evening. 'I was melancholy, and could not talk, but at last I eased my heart by weeping.' Her brother dismissed her tears as 'nervous blubbering', but she insisted that it was not so: 'O! how many, many reasons have I to be anxious for him.'[25] Dorothy's journals for the months that followed are full of loving thoughts of Coleridge. She wrote to him regularly, and was often made uneasy by his replies, detailing as they did his poor health, his unhappiness, and his ever-changing plans. Towards the end of January 1802, when she and her brother received a 'heart-rending letter' from Coleridge, Wordsworth talked of going to London to see him.[26]

In town, Daniel Stuart rented a first-floor set of rooms for Coleridge above his tailor's in King Street, Covent Garden. 'My practice was to call on him in the middle of the day,' Stuart later recalled, 'talk over the news, and project a leading paragraph for the next morning.'

---

* To attend Basil Montagu's wedding (his second).

He soon found, however, that Coleridge 'never could write a thing that was immediately required of him'. One evening he called on Coleridge around six o'clock to find him 'stretched out on the sofa groaning with pain'. He had written not a word. Back in his office, Stuart wrote the piece himself, and then returned, begging Coleridge to read it over, correct it and 'decorate it a little with some of his graceful touches'. But Coleridge proved incapable even of this. 'I am a Starling self-incaged,' he explained to Godwin, '& always in the moult, my whole Note is, Tomorrow, & tomorrow, & tomorrow.'[27]

A notebook entry written around this time provides a powerful image of his mental state:

> Mind, shipwrecked by storms of doubt, now mastless, rudderless, shattered, – pulling in the dead swell of a dark & windless sea.[28]

Mary Hutchinson had arrived in the Lakes around the beginning of November 1801, just as Coleridge was leaving,* and stayed at Dove Cottage until the end of the year. She and Wordsworth had plenty of opportunity to be alone together during these winter weeks; the understanding between them deepened. Six weeks after Mary had left, Wordsworth, dressed 'in his blue spencer,† and a pair of *new* pantaloons, fresh from London', rode to Penrith, a two-day journey, just to spend a couple of hours with Mary. Nine days later Coleridge announced to his wife that a wedding would take place 'soon after my return' from London (which he had indicated was imminent).[29] Why this did not happen can only be surmised. If Wordsworth were to marry – and perhaps he hesitated – he needed first to resolve matters with Annette Vallon, and to make arrangements for the support of his daughter Caroline. It is possible that she put pressure on him to do so. Before Christmas a letter 'from France' had arrived – presumably from Annette, or from someone writing on her behalf. Wordsworth wrote to Annette in January, and maybe he hoped that he would soon be able to go to France to make a settlement with her.

---

* She too was at Greta Hall the night before his departure.
† A short, close-fitting jacket.

But the peace talks dragged on slowly. On 8 February, Dorothy's journal records that a letter from Coleridge 'somewhat damped us; it spoke with less confidence about France'.*

If Wordsworth still hesitated, that would have been understandable. Marrying Mary would mean more than severing the connection with his half-forgotten mistress. It would mean distancing himself from his sister, or at least an end to the exclusive intimacy they had enjoyed for so long. This had been a possibility for the past year or more, but the decision had become no easier.

By comparison with the harvest of the previous autumn, the year 1801 had been a fallow one for Wordsworth. He spent much of it revising poems he had already written. This upset his stomach – 'he is always very ill when he tries to alter an old poem', observed Dorothy, 'but new composition does not hurt him so much'.[30] Early in the year he seems to have tinkered with his autobiographical poem, but then laid it aside. In March John Wordsworth had referred to his brother 'going on with the recluse', but this may indicate no more than an intention to do so.[31] At the end of the year Wordsworth returned briefly to the autobiographical poem, before putting it aside once again. Over the next two months he revised the preface for the third edition of the Lyrical Ballads; and recast 'The Pedlar'. He worked with furious intensity; one day his mood was so compelling that even though he wished to break off composition, he found himself unable to do so, and made himself ill.[32]

Something happened around the end of February that changed Wordsworth's course. In the margin of Dorothy's journal entry for the last day of the month is written 'Disaster Pedlar'; perhaps a manuscript was destroyed by mistake,† or perhaps he hit a wall. Three days later she records, 'I was so unlucky as to propose to rewrite The Pedlar.' It sounds as though Dorothy, usually so tactful, had struck a nerve, and earned a rebuke – but in any case Wordsworth 'got to

---

* The Treaty of Amiens between Britain and France was eventually signed on 27 March 1802.
† The Wordsworths had a habit of burning earlier drafts once a new one had been completed.

work, and was worn to death'. The next morning he set out for Keswick on horseback, leaving Dorothy alone for several days. She was obviously in an unusual state, because her journal slipped momentarily into the present tense:

> Wm has a nice bright day ... Now for my walk. I *will* be busy. I *will* look well, and be well when he comes back to me. O the darling! Here is one of his bitten apples. I can hardly find in my heart to throw it into the fire ... I walked round the two Lakes ... Sate down where we always sit. I was full of thoughts about my darling.

Four days later, on 7 March, Wordsworth reappeared, seemingly a changed man. While away he had written two new stanzas of 'Ruth' for the third edition of *Lyrical Ballads*; now his powers returned in full flood, and one fine poem after another flowed from him. On 14 March, for example, he finished a poem in bed before rising, and wrote another at the breakfast table. 'He ate not a morsel, nor put on his stockings, but sate with his shirt neck unbuttoned, and his waistcoat open while he did it.'[33]

Most of the poems he wrote now were short and simple. Later he would say that these had been 'chiefly composed to refresh my mind during the progress of a work of length and labour, in which I have been for some time engaged; and to furnish me with employment when I had not resolution to apply myself to that work'.[34] The apologetic tone was perhaps intended to appease Coleridge, who disapproved of 'small poems' as a distraction from more substantial employment. Yet among the poems Wordsworth started in the spring of 1802 was one of his greatest works, the 'Immortality' ode, as well as several lesser but still significant poems evoking his childhood. For Wordsworth, this was a moment of anticipation: he looked forward eagerly to marriage with Mary, but he also looked back to his youth, through the door that Dorothy still held open for him. He composed tender celebrations of the love he felt for his sister, and of the life they had made together, over which the shadows were already lengthening.

*

After an angry exchange of letters with his wife in the New Year, Coleridge's health and spirits recovered. By February he was positively skittish. 'I am quite a man of *fashion* – so many titled acquaintances – & handsome carriages stopping at my door – & fine *Cards* . . .' He teased his wife with accounts of flirting with aristocratic ladies. He was again toying with the idea of going abroad later in the year. 'What do you say to a two years' Residence at Montpelier – under blue skies & in a rainless air?' he asked her. He explained that the Wordsworths would join them in the south of France after William and Mary were married, and maybe Southey too, with whom he had been dining.[35]*

At the end of February Coleridge left London and headed north for Gallow Hill. He told his wife that he was going there so as to be able to escort Sara Hutchinson to Grasmere for her sister's wedding, but this seems to have been no more than a cover story. Dorothy wrote that she and her brother had been 'perplexed about Sara's coming' when they heard about it, presumably from Sara Coleridge – especially since by then Mary Hutchinson had been gone from Grasmere two months. Perhaps Coleridge simply felt that he had to see Asra somehow. What happened at Gallow Hill is obscure. Coleridge was there eleven days. A notebook entry for the day before he left reads '& wept aloud' – though these words are in inverted commas, suggesting that he may be quoting somebody else.† It continues, 'you made me feel uncomfortable' – but though it is reasonable to assume that 'you' and 'me' stand for Coleridge himself and Sara, it is not obvious which is which. Coleridge continued to Keswick, contemplating subjects for poems:

> Poem on this night on Helvellin/William & Dorothy & Mary/ – Sara & I

> Poem on the length of our acquaintance/all the hours that I have been thinking of her &c.[37]

---

* Southey may have allowed Coleridge to think him willing for them to go abroad together, but he confided to another friend that he did not wish to do so – 'our habits are not enough alike'.[36]
† The phrase occurs several times in the King James Bible; also in Homer and in Schiller's *Don Carlos* (1787).

A few days after his return to Greta Hall, Coleridge made his way over to Grasmere for a couple of nights. No record survives of what was said, but there was obviously much for these three to discuss. After he had gone Dorothy and William 'talked a good deal about C. and other interesting things'. Dorothy seems to have stiffened her brother's resolution to see Annette, and offered to accompany him to France. First he should go to Bishop Middleham, to set matters straight with Mary, to decide when they might marry, and perhaps to discuss the settlement he would make with Annette. It was an act of self-abnegation for Dorothy to urge her brother to commit himself in this way. She had been living with him for almost seven years, and for most of that time they had been alone together. She knew that once he was married she could never again have him to herself. The prospect of his marriage threatened the home she and her brother had made together: the cottage was not large enough for a substantial family, unlike Gallow Hill, where Mary had suggested that they might live with Tom and Sara. Mary did not want to be parted from them, and William did not want to be parted from Dorothy, who made a vow that they should not leave 'this country' for Gallow Hill.[38]

A week later the Wordsworths walked over to Greta Hall, where they based themselves for another week, with much coming and going. On 3 April Wordsworth and Coleridge climbed Skiddaw together. At some point during this stay, perhaps on the mountain itself, Wordsworth recited some lines that he had been writing only the morning before leaving Grasmere, the opening stanzas of his ode 'Intimations of Immortality from Recollections of early Childhood'. This returns to the themes of 'Tintern Abbey'; it is a poem about the irrevocable loss of inspiration:

> There was a time when meadow, grove, and stream,
> The earth, and every common sight,
> To me did seem
> Apparelled in celestial light,
> The glory and the freshness of a dream.
> It is not now as it hath been of yore; –

> Turn wheresoe'er I may,
> By night or day,
> The things which I have seen I now can see no more.

And the attempt to salvage something from this loss:

> Though nothing can bring back the hour
> Of splendour in the grass, of glory in the flower;
> We will grieve not, rather find
> Strength in what remains behind;

As Coleridge recognised, this was to be one of Wordsworth's finest poems, a sublime expression of his genius, embracing an evocative lyricism within a strong rhythmic structure. The poem laments the lost glories – but it nevertheless radiates a mood of triumphant joy. The first stanza is both verbally and metrically reminiscent of lines in 'The Mad Monk'.[39] Was this Wordsworth's acknowledgement of his debt to Coleridge? Or was it a demonstration of his independence? It is very difficult to know who is following whom in this dialogue, but it is clear that a conversation is taking place.

The resurgence of Wordsworth's creativity had come from within, but over the coming months it would be sustained through a poetic exchange with Coleridge, a reprise of the creative closeness the two men had achieved in the Quantocks five years before. Once again, one poet would develop a theme that would then be taken up by the other, before being handed back again. At the heart of these poems is the struggle against those forces that drain the poet of energy: the blunting experiences of adulthood, domestic unhappiness and distractions, material concerns. On the one hand, feelings of loss and desolation: on the other, revival and consolation.

On the night of 3 April, the two talked until dawn. Seemingly Wordsworth was still hesitant about committing himself to Mary, because Coleridge afterwards recorded that he had been 'urging him to conclude on marrying'.[40] The conversation must have been agonising for Coleridge. He was urging Wordsworth to unite himself with the woman he loved and to discard the woman he no longer loved – both of which Coleridge longed to do but would not allow himself.

The following evening Coleridge worked late into the night on a 'verse letter' addressed to Sara Hutchinson, into which he poured all his misery and frustration (whether this was ever sent to her is unknown). The 'Letter to —' opens in Coleridge's familiar conversational style, but the second stanza plunges into an expression of the deepest unhappiness; and from that point on the poem veers between howls of pain, lamentations, pleas for sympathy, and rapturous affirmations of love. The 'Letter to —' follows the plan he had sketched out in his notebook: 'a lively picture of a man, disappointed in marriage . . .' He confessed to sometimes feeling so miserable that he even regretted the births of his 'little Angel children'. It seems a poignant irony that the Coleridges' fourth child was conceived even as he was working on this poem.

A large number of allusions to the 'Immortality' ode make it explicit that the 'Letter to —' is (amongst other things) a response to Wordsworth's poem. The ode had lamented the fading of the 'celestial light' that had surrounded Wordsworth as a child:

> Whither is fled the visionary gleam?
> Where is it now, the glory and the dream?

As yet, it seemed, Wordsworth had no answer to these questions, for he would not complete the poem for another couple of years. Coleridge had no doubt why his own light had dimmed:

> E'er* I was wedded, tho' my path was rough,
> The joy within me dallied with distress.
> And all misfortunes were but as the Stuff
> Whence Fancy made me Dreams of Happiness:
> For Hope grew round me, like the climbing Vine,
> And Leaves, and Fruitage, not my own, seemed mine!
> But now ill-tidings bow me down to Earth –
> Nor care I, that they rob me of my Mirth;
> But O! each visitation

* Presumably a mistranscription for 'Ere'.

Suspends, what Nature gave me at my birth,
My shaping Spirit of Imagination!
I speak not now of those habitual Ills,
That wear out Life, when two unequal Minds
Meet in one House, & two discordant Wills . . .

His solution to his domestic unhappiness was to bury himself in his books:

For not to think of what I needs must feel,
But to be still and patient, all I can;
And haply abstruse Research to steal
From my own nature all the Natural Man;
This was my sole Resource, my wisest Plan!
And that, which suits a part, infects the whole,
And now is almost grown the temper of my Soul!

And yet the poem seems to hold out the possibility of revival, through the figure of Sara Hutchinson – 'Sister and Friend of my devoutest Choice!' – and concludes on a note of rejoicing. These last stanzas are full of conjugal references; Coleridge seems to be imagining the two of them united in some kind of marriage sanctified by nature.

Wordsworth rode across the Pennines on a borrowed horse to see Mary. She may still have been hoping that they might live at Gallow Hill after they were married, but Dorothy was determined to stay at Grasmere, and Wordsworth would not leave her. His heart was divided between the two women. As he rode back from Bishop Middleham a week later his mind was full of his sister, and he composed 'The Glow-worm', a poem redolent of his love for her, recalling a tender incident that had occurred when they were first living together at Racedown. He had been riding home one stormy night when he spotted a glow-worm, something that he knew 'my love' had never seen; so he dismounted, picked it up and brought it back, placing it in the garden for her to see. 'O Joy it was for her, and joy for me!'

While William was away, Dorothy had been staying with her friends the Clarksons on the banks of Ullswater. She was walking by the lake when the Clarksons' maid came to tell her that her brother had arrived. She screamed, and began to run back to the house – before collecting herself, and walking the rest of the way.

Two days later the two of them began a two-day journey back to Grasmere, over the Kirkstone Pass. As they walked along Ullswater; the wind was so furious that it 'seized their breath'. It blew across the lake, whipping up the waves to make a sound like the sea. They noticed a long belt of daffodils, some blown over, the rest tossing and reeling and dancing 'as if they verily laughed with the wind'.[41] This was the occasion that inspired Wordsworth's poem 'I wandered lonely as a cloud', written two years later.

The Wordsworths arrived back at the cottage at midnight, to find a letter from Coleridge waiting for them. Wordsworth replied immediately, enclosing a copy of 'The Glow-Worm' and another poem he had written while walking home that very afternoon.

Coleridge came over to Grasmere soon after their return. The day after he arrived, William and Dorothy 'sauntered a little in the garden'; Coleridge joined them, and 'repeated the verses he wrote to Sara'. Dorothy recorded that she was 'affected with them' and 'in miserable spirits' afterwards.[42]

In the twelve weeks that remained before the Wordsworths left for France, Coleridge was often at Grasmere. At a rough count, he spent about one-third of the late spring and early summer in the company of one or both Wordsworths. On 22 May, for example, a very hot morning, the Wordsworths met him at Sara's Rock (the 'Rock of Names'); they sat a long time under the wall of a sheep-fold and 'had some interesting melancholy talk about his private affairs'. It seems that Coleridge was again contemplating 'a very aweful Step' – separating from his wife.[43] Later in the day they returned to Grasmere. There the three of them sat in the orchard for a while until Dorothy left the two friends alone and went indoors to prepare a supper of mutton chops and potatoes.

Dorothy was especially sympathetic to Coleridge at this time. While he was struggling to come to terms with the unhappiness in his marriage, she was resigning herself to a future as a spinster aunt. At the end of May one of her teeth broke – an irreparable change, diminishing the already small likelihood that she might ever attract a husband. She expected the rest of her teeth to follow. 'They will soon be gone,' she wrote in her journal. 'Let that pass, I shall be beloved – I want no more.'[44]

Moreover, Dorothy acted as a go-between. She wrote out William's poems to send to Coleridge. It was to Dorothy that Coleridge sent his poems, though of course they were for Wordsworth to read. They were communicating though her, and she seems to have been an essential bridge between them.

By now it had been settled that William and Mary would live with Dorothy in the Lakes after they were married. Coleridge tried to attract them to Keswick, to share Greta Hall; there was plenty of room for two families. Sara Coleridge apparently made no objection. But Dorothy did; and the scheme was scotched. Even after this decision Coleridge did not give up altogether, and continued to search for houses in and around Keswick to accommodate his friends.

Early in May Wordsworth had worked furiously on a poem, known at first as 'The Leech Gatherer' and later published under the title 'Resolution and Independence'.* Based on a man he and Dorothy had met on the road not far from their cottage, the leech gatherer of the poem perseveres with his humble work despite many hardships. This poem was a continuation of the dialogue between the two poets, responding in particular to Coleridge's 'Letter to —'. The poem's narrator, who has been feeling dejected, encounters this feeble but dignified old man and afterwards laughs himself 'to scorn to find/In that decrepit man so firm a mind'. The moral of the poem is the need for self-reliance and stoicism in the face of adversity – a message to Coleridge not to succumb to the unhappiness that threatened to overwhelm him, but instead to take command of his own destiny:

---

* More than a dozen years later, Coleridge would write in his *Biographia Literaria* that 'this fine poem is especially characteristic of the author. There is scarce a defect or excellence in his writings of which it would not present a specimen.'

But how can He expect that others should
Build for him, sow for him, and at his call
Love him, who for himself will take no heed at all?

Wordsworth drew a comparison that Coleridge himself had once made:

I thought of Chatterton, the marvellous Boy,
The sleepless Soul that perished in his pride;
Of Him who walked in glory and in joy
Following his plough, along the mountain-side:*
By our own spirits are we deified:
We Poets in our youth begin in gladness;
But thereof come in the end despondency and madness.

On the same day that he finished this poem Wordsworth began
another, in the style of James Thomson's 'The Castle of Indolence'.†
As if to balance the stern message of 'Resolution and Independence',
this poem evoked the delight of Coleridge's company:

A noticeable Man with large grey eyes,
And a pale face that seemed undoubtedly
As if a blooming face it ought to be;
Heavy his low-hung lip did oft appear,
Deprest by weight of musing Phantasy;
Profound his forehead was, though not severe;
Yet some did think that he had little business here:

Sweet heaven forefend! his was a lawful right;
Noisy he was, and gamesome as a boy;
His limbs would toss about him with delight
Like branches when strong winds the trees annoy.
Nor lacked his calmer hours device or toy
To banish listlessness and irksome care;
He would have taught you how you might employ
Yourself; and many did to him repair, –
And certes not in vain; he had inventions rare.

* Robert Burns.
† James Thomson (1700–48), poet and tragedist (and probable author of 'Rule Britannia').
'The Castle of Indolence' appeared in 1748, a few weeks before his death. Wordsworth
admired his depictions of nature.

Expedients, too, of simplest sort he tried:
Long blades of grass, plucked round him as he lay,
Made, to his ear attentively applied,
A pipe on which the wind would deftly play;
Glasses he had, that little things display,
The beetle panoplied in gems and gold,
A mailed angel on a battle-day;
The mysteries that cups of flowers enfold,
And all the gorgeous sights which fairies do behold.

He would entice that other Man to hear
His music, and to view his imagery:
And, sooth, these two were each to the other dear:
No livelier love in such a place could be:
There did they dwell – from earthly labour free,
As happy spirits as were ever seen . . .

Considering the emotional context, it is perhaps unsurprising that Wordsworth and his sister reacted tetchily when they received a letter from the Hutchinson sisters criticising the first draft of 'The Leech Gatherer'. Dorothy wrote in schoolmistressy style to Sara:

> When you happen to be displeased with what you suppose to be the tendency or moral of any poem which William writes, ask yourself whether you have hit upon the real tendency and true moral, and above all never think that he writes for no reason but merely because a thing happened – and when you feel any poem of his to be tedious, ask yourself in what spirit it was written . . .[45]

Dorothy fiercely defended her brother's work against all criticism. One instance, which seemed insignificant at the time, would come to rankle with Coleridge in the future. Charles Lloyd was again responsible for the trouble, albeit this time by apparently praising Coleridge. Someone reported Lloyd as having publicly expressed the opinion that Coleridge was 'a greater poet, & possessed of more genius by nature', than Wordsworth. 'Instantly', as Coleridge recalled more than eight years afterwards, Dorothy pronounced Lloyd 'a VILLAIN'.[46] For the next few years the Wordsworths avoided the Lloyds whenever possible. 'We are determined to cut them entirely,' Dorothy wrote to Sara Hutchinson.[47]

Coleridge himself had made 'a sort of reconciliation' with Lloyd, though they never became close again. He stayed a night under Lloyd's roof during an epic solitary walking tour of the Lakes he undertook in August, described in a series of rapturous letters to Sara Hutchinson. Throughout the summer he reworked his 'Letter to —', condensing it into the ode he called 'Dejection', removing the more obvious references to his personal unhappiness. In a series of changes, the poem was transformed from a private (and unpublishable) letter to Asra (4 April), through manuscript laments addressed first apparently to Poole (7 May) and then to Wordsworth (19 July), into a work published in the *Morning Post* (4 October), addressed to 'Edmund', unidentified but obviously a pseudonym for Wordsworth. In the process Coleridge revised the beginning of one of his stanzas so that it now alluded to the opening of Wordsworth's 'Immortality' ode:

> There was a time when, though my path was rough . . .

In one sense, of course, the poem in all its forms was addressed to Coleridge's poetical twin. It continued the exchange with Wordsworth, responding to his 'Resolution and Independence', a relationship that Coleridge would make explicit by juxtaposing the two poems in a letter the following year.[48]

The revisions made 'Dejection' even more explicitly a lament for his fading powers. Coleridge felt very keenly that his light was going out. 'All my poetic Genius, if I really possessed any *Genius*, & it was not a mere general *aptitude* of Talent, & quickness in . . . Imitation is gone,' he lamented to Southey.[49] For Coleridge, happiness was essential to creativity; illness was a manifestation of misery. Many years later, in trying to elaborate this process in his *Confessions of Inquiring Spirit* (1828), he seems to have coined the term 'psychosomatic'.[50]

In September the *Morning Post* published his 'Hymn before Sunrise, in the Vale of Chamouny', which, as he later acknowledged, derived in part from the work of the German poet Friederike Brun.* It was perhaps not a very serious plagiarism; but it was ominous that both the poem itself and the introductory note he added to the published version should falsely suggest first-hand experience. He was not being truthful to the public, and he was not being true to himself. Chamonix was a place that Wordsworth had seen, but Coleridge had not. He had lost his independent vision; he was beginning to see the world though Wordsworth's eyes.

William and Dorothy passed the month of August in Calais, where Annette brought Caroline, now nine years old, to meet her father for the first time. They bathed in the sea, and walked by the shore in the evening. Some kind of accommodation was reached for Caroline's financial support, and it seems to have been agreed too that Annette might continue to call herself 'Madame Williams' for the sake of appearances. For Wordsworth this visit to France was not just personal; he was returning to the country he had left with such reluctance almost a decade earlier. Then his heart had been given to the Revolution; now he felt only repugnance. When a passer-by greeted him as 'citizen' he reflected on the emptiness of the term. In returning to France he was closing a chapter in his life, renouncing a cause no less than a woman.

The Treaty of Amiens had reopened the doors of Europe to British visitors, who now flocked to France in large numbers, eager to see the changes that had taken place since the Revolution thirteen years before. There was a sense that the peace might not last, so those who were interested and could afford to do so decided to go while they had the opportunity. While Wordsworth and his sister were in Calais, Tom Poole was in Paris, where he called on Paine. There is an unverified story that he attended a *levée* and was presented to the First Consul. Fox too was in Paris, and perhaps like Poole attended one of

---

* Friederike Brun (1765–1835), pioneer woman poet and travel writer, a *protégée* of Klopstock among others. Following a severe illness she became completely deaf. She passed some time in spas in Switzerland and Italy in an attempt to recover her health. Her poem in the manner of Klopstock, 'Chamouny at Sunrise', was published in 1791.

Napoleon's *levées*. He allowed himself to be presented to the First Consul, and a week later dined with him in private: actions which Coleridge condemned in a pair of open letters 'To Mr Fox' in the *Morning Post*. Coleridge's position completed a *volte-face*: he now supported the administration's increasingly belligerent attitude to France, and deplored the policies of appeasement pursued by the Foxite Whigs.

William and Dorothy returned via London, where they were able to spend a few days with their brother John, whose ship had just arrived back from China. In these few weeks in the capital Wordsworth composed a number of splendid sonnets evoking his deep love of his native country, including 'Westminster Bridge', 'Great men have been among us' and 'Milton! thou shouldst be living at this hour'. In writing about men like Milton, Sidney, Marvell, Vane and Harrington, Wordsworth was reclaiming these seventeenth-century republican heroes for their native land. They had been appropriated by the Revolution; Wordsworth was taking them back. Milton is mentioned in at least four of these sonnets, which seems significant, given that Coleridge was constantly comparing Wordsworth to Milton. The poem addressed directly to Milton invokes the poet's help in moral renewal: 'England hath need of thee'. In conjuring the spirit of Milton, Wordsworth is setting out a programme for himself.

The Wordsworths left London on 22 September and made straight for Gallow Hill. There, early in the morning of 4 October 1802, William and Mary Hutchinson were married. This was a difficult time for Dorothy. As the wedding approached, her behaviour became increasingly emotional. Wordsworth was sensitive to her distress, and did what he could to reassure his sister of her continuing importance in his life. At his insistence she spent the night before the ceremony with Mary's wedding ring on her finger. She did not attend the wedding itself, but threw herself on his bed, 'neither hearing or seeing anything' until the couple returned, when she ran downstairs to greet 'my beloved William and fell upon his bosom'.

Coleridge too was disturbed by the change. The night before the wedding he dreamed of Wordsworth and his bride, of Dorothy 'altered in every feature' but still Dorothy, and of being pursued by 'a frightful pale woman, who, I thought, wanted to kiss me, & had the property of giving a shameful Disease by breathing in the face . . .'[51] He chose Wordsworth's wedding day (the seventh anniversary of his own) to publish 'Dejection: An Ode', emphasising the contrast between his friend's happiness and his own misery. A week later he published an anonymous epigram, 'Spots in the Sun', which teasingly referred to Wordsworth's French mistress, mentioning Annette by name. It is hard to interpret this act as anything other than suppressed antagonism breaking through the surface of their friendship.

Coleridge's birthday was always an occasion when he took stock of his life. On the eve of his thirtieth he wrote gloomily to Tom Wedgwood. When they had last seen each other, the previous winter, 'I could scarcely keep from communicating to you the tale of my domestic distresses'. Now he kept nothing back. Since his return to Keswick in the spring, he said, 'scarce a day passed without a such a scene of discord between me and Mrs Coleridge, as quite incapacitated me for any worthy extension of my faculties by degrading me in my own estimation'.

> If any woman wanted an exact & copious Recipe, 'How to make a Husband completely miserable', I could furnish her with one . . . Ill tempered Speeches sent after me when I went out of the House, ill-tempered speeches on my return, my friends received with freezing looks, the least opposition or contradiction occasioning screams of passion . . . all this added to the utter negation of all, which a Husband expects from a Wife – especially, living in retirement – & the consciousness, that I was myself growing a worse man /O dear sir! No one can tell what I have suffered.[52]

Coleridge longed to escape: from his marriage, from his ill-health, from the psychological trap in which he found himself. Increasingly his mind dwelt on the thought of going abroad. If he could come back 'healed & renovated from all infirm Habits', and somehow unencumbered – then perhaps the beloved woman could be his. He had tried to persuade both Wordsworth and Southey to accompany him to some warm, dry place, but neither man would budge. There remained Tom Wedgwood, now more seriously ill than ever. Travelling with a rich man had its advantages. Notwithstanding what he had written about its being the very last thing he could have submitted to, Coleridge decided his duty required him to attend his patron; he offered to come whenever Wedgwood needed a companion, and on 3 November 1802 he received a summons. He left Keswick early the next morning, not knowing how long he would be away or where he might be headed after making a rendezvous with Wedgwood in Bristol. His wife was apparently reconciled to his going away to an unknown destination for an indefinite period. She made no objection to being abandoned once again when she was near full term; but she seems to have been furious when she discovered that Coleridge had spent a day with Sara Hutchinson in Penrith after he was unable to obtain a place on the early-morning mail coach to London. The letter she then wrote to him has been lost, but its tenor can be surmised from his responses. He wrote that he would have been inclined to dismiss her 'Feelings concerning Penrith' as 'a little tiny Fretfulness', but for a sentence 'of a very, very different cast', which 'immediately disordered my Heart, and Bowels'. He sent his wife a long analysis of the differences between them, pointing out in particular how much she was influenced by the opinions of others. He insisted on his right to 'move, live, & love, in perfect Freedom, limited only by my own purity & self-respect'. He demanded that she 'should to a certain degree love, & act kindly to, those whom I deem worthy of my Love', i.e. Sara Hutchinson and the Wordsworths. When his wife wrote to him in placatory mood, Coleridge was 'overpowered':

> I have a faith, a heavenly Faith, that our future Days will be
> Days of Peace, & affectionate Happiness.[53]

In his next letter he suggested to his wife that while she was lying in, Sara Hutchinson should come to help. This suggestion does not seem to have been taken up.[54]

Coleridge told his wife that 'the more you sympathize with me in my kind manners & kind feelings towards those of Grasmere, the more I shall be likely to sympathize with you in your opinions respecting their faults & imperfections. I am no Idolater at present; & I solemnly assure you, that if I prefer many parts of *their* characters, opinions, feelings, & habits to the same parts of your's, I do likewise prefer much, very much of your character to their's – Of course, I speak *chiefly* of Dorothy & William . . .'[55]

Contrary to expectations, Wedgwood proved 'a delightful & instructive Companion', as Coleridge outlined to his wife: 'He possesses the *finest*, the *subtlest* mind & taste, I have yet met with.'[56] It was still uncertain whether they would be going abroad, and meanwhile the two men toured south Wales by chaise before heading back to the Lakes – calling at Grasmere on the morning of Christmas Eve, where the Wordsworths informed Coleridge that he had a daughter, born the previous day. The two travellers hurried on to Keswick. It was an echo of Coleridge's arrival with Charles Lloyd the day after Hartley's birth – though to be fair to Coleridge, both children were born prematurely. The 'little Coleridgiella' was named Sara (without an 'h', Coleridge's preferred spelling).

In less than a month Coleridge and Tom Wedgwood were off again. The plan now was to stay a month or two at Josiah Wedgwood's house near Blandford, in Dorset, and then head for Paris, from which they would travel overland into Italy and Sicily, remaining abroad at least a year. But during the next few weeks there was much hesitation. Wedgwood became apprehensive that Coleridge's ill-health might incapacitate *him*. Looming over their discussions was the threat of renewed war. Towards the end of March 1803 Wedgwood departed for France, taking another travelling companion in Coleridge's place. He was forced to return hurriedly when war was declared on 17 May.

Left behind in London, Coleridge took out an expensive life insurance policy* to provide a sum of £1000 for his wife in the event of his death, and made a will, naming Poole and Wordsworth as trustees. Almost incidentally he arranged with Longman for a third edition of his poems, entrusting Lamb with the responsibility for supervising the book through the press. Although he had for the past

---

* The initial premium was £31, £27 in subsequent years.

five years contemplated a second volume of new poems to accompany the reissued first volume, he seems to have been too depressed to carry this through.[57] Southey was distressed by the collapse in Coleridge's confidence. It perplexed him that Coleridge seemed incapable of applying himself. He remembered Coleridge in his glorious, unclouded youth, and he was pained to see his friend brought so low. 'All other men whom I have ever known are mere children to him,' he remarked sadly to his friend William Taylor, 'and yet all is palsied by a total want of moral strength. He will leave nothing behind him to justify the opinion of his friends to the world; yet many of his scattered poems are such, that a man of feeling will see that the author was capable of executing the greatest works.'

In letters to Southey, Godwin and others, Coleridge poured out a stream of ambitious schemes for new works, often in multiple volumes. 'You spawn plans like a herring,' commented Southey. 'Coleridge and I have often talked of making a great work upon English literature,' Southey confided in Taylor; 'but Coleridge only talks, and, poor fellow! He will not do that long, I fear.'

> By God, it provokes me when I see a set of puppies yelping at him, upon whom he, a great, good-natured mastiff, if he came up to them, would just lift a leg and pass on. It vexes & grieves me to the heart that when he is gone, as go he will, nobody will believe what a mind goes with him – how infinitely and ten-thousand-thousand-fold the mightiest of his generation![58]

Early in April Coleridge returned to Keswick, bringing with him the 'flu, picked up from an old man in the coach, to which the whole family (except Hartley) succumbed in turn. Coleridge was confined to the house for six weeks or so, first with 'flu and then with what he described as 'rheumatic fever'; he seems to have felt some resentment that Wordsworth never came to visit him during this period.[59] He may have been irked to receive a letter from Wordsworth asking him 'in a very particular manner' to set out his thoughts in detail 'on a poetic subject' – probably *The Recluse*.[60]

Wordsworth was distracted by both business and personal matters. Viscount Lowther,* who had succeeded Lord Lonsdale in 1802, had indicated his intention to honour his predecessor's longstanding debts, and had begun to settle the claim of the Wordsworth family for monies owing to their late father; between them the five Wordsworth children would receive £8,500. Wordsworth and his sister reinvested some of the capital they received in the voyage of their brother John's ship, the *Earl of Abergavenny*, which sailed on 7 May 1803. On 18 June the Wordsworths' first child was born, a boy who was named John after both his uncle and his grandfather. Coleridge was one of his godparents, together with Dorothy and her brother Richard.

'If God grant me only tolerable health this summer,' Coleridge wrote to Poole, 'I pledge myself to all who love me, that by next Christmas the last three years of my Life shall no longer appear a Blank.'[61] In letters to Godwin he claimed to be 'ready to go to Press' with a philosophical work, an '*Instrument* of practical Reasoning', and asked Godwin's help in finding a suitable publisher. Nothing more was heard of this work in Coleridge's lifetime.

William Hazlitt, who was trying to make a living as an artist, was a surprise visitor to Keswick during the summer of 1803. Both Wordsworth and Coleridge commissioned him to paint their portraits – 'very much in the manner of Titian's', according to the latter.† Another visitor was the wealthy baronet Sir George Beaumont, himself an amateur artist of considerable skill, who rented Jackson's half of Greta Hall in July and August. Beaumont, who owned a London house in Grosvenor Square as well as estates in Essex and Leicestershire, had objected strongly to Coleridge's political opinions when they had first met in town, but his initial dislike quickly turned to admiration now that he found the radical firebrand had 'utterly renounced' his former views. His wife Margaret was a woman of sensibility; quoting from his own *Osorio*, Coleridge described her cynically to Wordsworth as

* Formerly Sir William Lowther, Viscount Lowther took the title on the death of his cousin Lord Lonsdale, who died without issue.
† Wordsworth paid Hazlitt three guineas. How much Coleridge paid is unknown.

. . . A deep Enthusiast, sensitive,
Trembles & cannot keep the Tears in her eye –
Such ones do love the marvellous too well
Not to believe it. You may wind her up
With *any* Music! –

Coleridge informed his friend that 'Sir G & Lady B.' were 'half-mad to see you'. Lady Beaumont had been so impressed on reading Wordsworth's poetry that had he entered the room immediately afterwards, she told Coleridge, she believed she would have fallen at his feet. She and her husband admired Hazlitt's portrait of Wordsworth – though Southey, who saw the picture later in the year, thought it made him look 'as if he had been a month in the condemned hole, dieted upon bread and water, and debarred the use of soap, water, razer and combs'.[62]* But the picture gave the Beaumonts an idea of Wordsworth as 'a profound strong-minded Philosopher, not as a Poet' – to which Coleridge responded that Wordsworth's poetry *was* his philosophy, 'under the action of strong winds of Feeling – a sea rolling high'.[63] A few days later Wordsworth came to Keswick, and the Beaumonts were able to meet him in the flesh. 'It is most pleasing to see the pure affection which subsists between the two bards, free from all bias of jealousy or weakness,' Sir George reported in a letter to a friend; 'they correct the errors of each other with manly freedom, & to their mutual advantage.' Wordsworth talked to Beaumont about the long autobiographical poem on which he was at work. This 'will probably take up years in the completion, for his health will not permit him to work upon it at all times, he says it prevents his sleeping & he is obliged to quit all thoughts of it for months together'.[64] Sir George was so convinced of the importance of bringing 'these two genius's' together that he purchased a farmstead at the foot of Skiddaw, not two miles from Greta Hall, and presented it to Wordsworth as a gift. The property, valued at £100, included two small fields and farm buildings

---

* 'The best of this good joke is,' wrote Southey, 'that the Wordsworths are proud of the picture . . . how the devil the painter had contrived to make a likeness of so well-looking a man so ridiculously ugly poozles everybody.'

which might be converted into a house for the Wordsworths. Beaumont's purpose, as he explained to Wordsworth subsequently, was for Wordsworth and Coleridge to be 'able to communicate more frequently' to each other the 'sensations' they received from 'the beauties of Nature'. This 'would be a means of contributing to the pleasure and improvement of the world, by stimulating you both to poetical executions'.[65]

Beaumont's generous offer was communicated through Coleridge, and may have been engineered by him as a means of attracting Wordsworth to the neighbourhood. It was a mark of Wordsworth's perplexity that it took him eight weeks to respond. After apologising at length for not replying earlier, he stated that 'few things would give me greater pleasure than to realise the plan which you had in view for me of building a house there'. But the chances were very much against it, partly because he could not afford to do so, 'and still more from the improbability of Mr C's remaining in the Country'.[66]

In mid-August Coleridge set out in a jaunting-car* with Wordsworth and his sister on a tour of Scotland. Mary was of course busy with a new baby (as was Sara), but it is by no means certain that she would have been invited even if she had been unencumbered. The tour was not a success. The arrangement of the vehicle made conversation difficult. Coleridge had been very ill before they left and was too weak to share the driving, so Wordsworth did it all. Nor did Coleridge join the Wordsworths on their after-dinner strolls. He was beginning to recognise the nature of the habit into which he had fallen, and he tried to reduce his intake of opium, with the result that he suffered distressing withdrawal symptoms, including 'hysterical attacks', seizures so convulsive that he feared a paralytic stroke. Worst of all were the nightmares, so horrifying that he dreaded sleep:

> But yester-night I prayed aloud
> In anguish and in agony,

---

* An open horse-drawn cart; the driver sat in a 'dicky box' at the front, while passengers sat in hanging seats facing out to either side.

Up-starting from the fiendish crowd
Of shapes and thoughts that tortured me:
A lurid light, a trampling throng,
Sense of intolerable wrong,
And whom I scorn'd, those only strong!
Thirst of revenge, the powerless will
Still baffled, and yet burning still!
Desire with loathing strangely mixed
On wild or hateful objects fixed.
Fantastic passions! Madd'ning brawl!
And shame and terror over all!
Deeds to be hid which were not hid,
Which all confused I could not know
Whether I suffered, or I did:
For all seemed guilt, remorse or woe,
My own or others still the same
Life-stifling fear, soul-stifling shame!

More than ever he was pining for Sara Hutchinson. 'O Asra,'* he confided to his notebook, 'wherever I am, & am impressed, my heart ak[ch]es for you.'[67] Many years later Wordsworth recalled that 'poor Coleridge was at that time in bad spirits, and somewhat too much in love with his own dejection';[68] while Coleridge found Wordsworth silent and withdrawn, as he often was in company. After a fortnight they decided to part. Later hints suggest tension between the two men: 'I soon found that I was a burthen on them,' Coleridge wrote on his return.[69]

The Wordsworths left Coleridge at Loch Lomond and continued up the west coast as far as Glencoe, afterwards working their way across country to Blair Atholl, and then descending via Edinburgh and the Borders to Carlisle, arriving back at Grasmere on 25 September. Towards the end of their journey they had called on Walter Scott, and spent a few days with him in the Borders. At Jedburgh Scott had recited part of his as yet incomplete poem 'The Lay of the Last Minstrel'. Both Wordsworths were struck with the resemblance between this and

---

* Someone has largely blotted out the words 'O Asra' in the notebook.

Coleridge's 'Christabel', and knowing that Scott had been much impressed by the latter poem when he heard it from their mutual friend John Stoddart, feared that it might be an 'unconscious imitation'. Subsequently, when 'The Lay of the Last Minstrel' was published with great success in 1805, Wordsworth 'blamed himself exceedingly' for not having mentioned the resemblance to Scott on hearing his recital. Dorothy did not think the matter of much importance, Coleridge's poem being 'so very superior to the other'; but Wordsworth and his wife believed that the prior publication of 'The Lay of the Last Minstrel' would 'tarnish the freshness' of 'Christabel' when it eventually appeared, 'and considerably injure the first effect of it'. Scott eventually admitted his debt to Coleridge.[70]

Meanwhile Coleridge continued on foot, walking more than thirty miles a day, 'in the hopes of forcing the disease into my extremities' by sheer physical exertion.[71] In this way he covered 263 miles in a mere eight days. Even when he burnt his shoes trying to dry them by the fire, he was not deterred, but carried on barefoot. At Perth he found a letter waiting for him from an anguished Southey, whose only child, his infant daughter Margaret, had died; the distraught parents were heading for Greta Hall, bringing a third Fricker sister, Mary Lovell, now dependent on them. (Though they came there as a temporary refuge, they were to stay the remainder of their lives.) Coleridge cut short his tour and caught the mail coach back to Keswick, arriving exhausted and dishevelled. This was natural enough after such an epic journey, but Southey was shocked to see the physical deterioration in him.

There was no cure for Coleridge's sickness; he was trapped, consumed by a passion he could not articulate. 'Month after month, year after year, the deepest Feeling of my Heart hid & wrapped up in the depth & darkness . . .' He seemed to recognise that his lost creativity was in some manner linked to his hopeless yearning for Sara Hutchinson, whom he had not seen since the beginning of the year. In the privacy of his notebooks he brooded on his forbidden love. 'I *long* for you, till Longing turns to Grief – & I close up again, despondent, sick at heart.'[72]

Conscience battled with desire; hideous thoughts crept out from the dark places of his mind; he made frantic efforts to thrust them back. Opium dulled his brain, but only for a while. In the daylight he could keep the fiends at bay by distracting activity, but in the dark he was defenceless. Each night he fought a losing battle against sleep. Then he was haunted by nightmares so terrifying that he would wake screaming, sweat streaming from him, his body locked in a convulsion. His cries were loud enough to bring the whole household running to his bedside.

'I now see very little of Wordsworth,' Coleridge complained to Poole after his return from Scotland, explaining that his health prevented him from going over to Grasmere as often as he used to, while Wordsworth's 'indolence' kept him at home. 'Indeed, were I an irritable man, and an unthinking one,' he continued, 'I should probably have considered myself as having been very unkindly used by him in this respect.' Not for the first time, Coleridge expressed concern about Wordsworth's 'Self-involution', and his tendency to hypochondria. In fact, Wordsworth had been in Keswick with Coleridge only a few days before Coleridge voiced these complaints, and only a week later Coleridge would go to Grasmere to see him. Coleridge's grumbling about Wordsworth's neglect may have been a carryover from tensions during the Scottish tour. Or he may have been exaggerating for Poole's benefit, knowing Poole's fears about his subservience to Wordsworth.

The sight of his friend surrounded by female admirers (Dorothy, Mary, and sometimes Sara Hutchinson too) irritated Coleridge, who deplored his 'living wholly among *Devotees* – having every the minutest Thing,* almost his very Eating & Drinking, done for him by his Sister, or Wife – & I trembled, lest a Film should rise, and thicken on his moral Eye'. He, by contrast, was now surrounded by the three Fricker sisters, who viewed him rather more critically.

Coleridge believed that writing 'small poems' had been harmful to his friend, even making him ill:

---

* Possibly this is a mistranscription, and should read 'even the minutest Thing'.

I rejoice therefore with a deep & true Joy, that he has at length yielded to my urgent & repeated – almost unremitting – requests and remonstrances – & will go on with the Recluse exclusively. – A Great Work, in which he will sail; on an open Ocean, & a steady wind; unfretted by short tacks, reefing & hawling & disentangling the ropes –[73]

Since war with France had resumed in May, the threat of invasion had returned, now more serious than ever before. Bonaparte had been able to concentrate his attention on plans for a strike in which he hoped to eliminate his most persistent enemy. A vast 'Army of England' was assembled on the Channel coast, and by the end of 1803 a flotilla of more than 2,000 transports was ready to carry them across the Straits of Dover. The French were expected to make their move at any moment. The British responded by constructing a system of fortified coastal defence, while raising volunteer regiments to support the army. Meanwhile the navy remained on constant alert. A succession of naval victories had made the British supremely confident of their fighting prowess. 'I do not say that the French will not come,' Earl St Vincent, the First Lord of the Admiralty, declared in Parliament, 'I say only they will not come by sea.'* But the danger remained that the enemy might slip across the Channel if the navy relaxed its guard, or was somehow lured or driven off station.

Soon after his return from Scotland, Wordsworth had gone to Ambleside to offer his services in response to the government's appeal for volunteer companies to defend their country. The expected French invasion brought out the differences between the two men: while Coleridge recoiled from the anticipated bloodshed, Wordsworth sprang forward in solidarity at this moment of national danger. Ten years before he had sat alone, in sullen silence, as vicars called their flocks to pray for English victories; now he joined in the general upsurge of feeling, penning a succession of patriotic sonnets.

Coleridge's response to the national emergency was to write a very long letter to the Beaumonts, recanting the radicalism of his

---

* This was a jocular reference to the French experiments with hot-air balloons.

youth: 'My *opinions* were the drivel of a Babe . . .' He told them that
he had been 'extremely affected' by the execution of the young (he
was twenty-four) Irish patriot Robert Emmet, whose ridiculous but
romantic uprising had collapsed for want of French support.* He
recalled how he had felt at 'poor Emmet's age', full of anger against
injustice and plans for a better world; to the Beaumonts he confessed
the 'unwise & unchristian feelings' he had felt towards 'all persons of
your rank in Society'. It was typical of Coleridge that his imagination
should lead him to identify with Emmet:

> Like him, I was very young, very enthusiastic, distinguished
> by Talents & acquirements & a sort of turbid Eloquence; like
> him, I was a zealous Partisan of Christianity, a Despiser &
> Abhorrer of French Philosophy & French Morals; like him, I
> would have given my body to be burnt inch by inch, rather
> than that a French Army should have insulted my native
> Shores/& alas! alas! like him, I was unconsciously yet actively
> aiding & abetting the plans, that I abhorred . . .

Had Emmet been spared, 'we *might* have had in him a sublimely
great man, we assuredly should have had in him a good man, & heart
& soul an *Englishman!*'[74]

Coleridge, Southey and Wordsworth were already associated in the
public mind, even before Southey arrived in the Lakes. In a hostile
notice of Southey's epic poem *Thalaba* in the first number of the new
Edinburgh Review, Francis Jeffrey† had attacked the 'followers of
simplicity' for their 'perverted taste', and suggested that there was
something subversive in their rejection of the established principles
of poetry. He quoted from Wordsworth's revised preface to the third
edition of *Lyrical Ballads*, which he described as 'a kind of manifesto'.
Wordsworth had no doubt that this review of *Thalaba* was throughout
a disguised 'attack upon me' – though he pretended not to have read

---

* Southey too had been affected by Emmet's death, and wrote a poem on the occasion.
† Francis Jeffrey (1772–1850), journalist, lawyer and Whig politician. A persistent scourge
of the 'Lake poets', he was described by Wordsworth as 'a blockhead' who 'knew nothing
about the Business'. In later years he and Wordsworth came to be on friendly terms.

it in full.[75] Jeffrey had described him as one of the 'chief champions and apostles' of this new 'sect'. In a letter to Poole, Coleridge acknowledged that Wordsworth was now called, rightly or wrongly, the 'Head & founder of a *Sect* in Poetry'.[76] It is remarkable that Wordsworth, for so long unknown by comparison with Coleridge and Southey, was being seen as spokesman for the three of them. As early as 1801 he had been described as 'the senior professor' of this 'new school'.[77] Paradoxically, he had risen to prominence by being so regularly and violently attacked. And though Wordsworth for many years continued to be reviled by the reviewers, he was revered by a small but increasing number of admirers, many of them young men inspired by the ethical principles they detected at the heart of his poetry. *Lyrical Ballads* sold steadily: the third edition of 1802 would be followed by a fourth in 1805.

Bracketing the three poets together in this way 'originates entirely in our not hating or envying each other', Coleridge had explained to the Beaumonts back in the summer; 'it is so unusual, that three professed poets, in every respect unlike each other, should nevertheless take pleasure in each other's welfare – & reputation'.[78] If this had ever truly been so, it was about to change. In the autumn Coleridge was disturbed to feel envious at a report that Wordsworth had written an 'excellent' new poem. He mused at length on the subject in his notebooks, disguising himself as 'A' and Wordsworth as 'B':

> A. thought himself unkindly used by B. – he had exerted himself for B. with what warmth! honoring, praising B. beyond himself. – &c &c – B. selfish . . . quite backward to poor A. . . . A. had been long, long idle owing perhaps in part to his Idolatry of B.

Coleridge's note mentioned 'the *up*, askance, pig look, in the Boat' – perhaps a reference to an incident on the Scottish tour. He used this long note to purge his distressing feelings of envy, and it seems that he may have made a brief visit to Grasmere in the next day or two in an attempt to relieve his mind.[79] A few days afterwards, however, a 'most unpleasant Dispute' left Coleridge hurt and bewildered. He was sitting for another Hazlitt portrait, commissioned by Beaumont. One afternoon he became upset when Hazlitt and Wordsworth joined in speaking irreverently 'of the Divine Wisdom'. Hazlitt was an angry young man, easily roused to feelings of rage – 'but *thou*, dearest Wordsworth . . . O dearest William!'[80]

Coleridge was becoming increasingly desperate about his failure to produce anything of worth. His poetic gifts seemed to have deserted him. He referred to himself half-jokingly as 'the ci devant Poet in rus & now Metaphysician'.[81] He spent day after day in his study, paralysed by fear and self-loathing. His wife satirically contrasted his 'indolence' with Southey's assiduousness. On the eve of his thirty-first birthday, Coleridge lacerated himself for his lack of achievement:

> O me! my very heart dies! – This *year* has been one painful Dream/I have done nothing! – O for God's sake, let me whip & spur, so that Christmas may not pass without some thing having been done . . .[82]

He decided he must go abroad. Southey's arrival meant that Sara and the children could be left safely in his care for a couple of years or so. In mid-December 1803 Coleridge left Greta Hall, intending to spend Christmas with the Wordsworths before journeying on to London, and then for a foreign destination still unsettled. (Resumption of the war had narrowed the choice.) But once at Grasmere he again became very ill, and took to bed, where he was nursed by Dorothy and Mary 'with Sister's and Mother's Love'. Then he recovered, and made ready to depart. Wordsworth stood security for a much-needed loan of £100 (which Coleridge would eventually repay, unlike many of the loans he received). Early in the New Year the two friends made their way up to 'the highest & outermost of Grasmere';* there, looking down on the vale so precious to them both, Wordsworth read Coleridge the second book of 'his divine

---

* Possibly at Hause Riggs, the last point on the path up to Grisedale Tarn (and Helvellyn beyond) from which Grasmere can be seen.

Self-biography', the poem that would eventually become known as *The Prelude*.[83] This was a sacred moment between the two men. Coleridge was leaving, perhaps never to return; Wordsworth was about to resume the task Coleridge had set him. A phrase towards the end, 'This melancholy waste of hopes o'erthrown', was a reference to Coleridge's request to Wordsworth to write a poem addressed to those disappointed by the failure of the French Revolution. The second book of the 'Poem for Coleridge' ends with a passage addressed to him directly:

> . . . Thou, my Friend! wast reared
> In the great city, 'mid far other scenes,
> But we by different roads at length have gained
> The self-same bourne. And from this cause to thee
> I speak, unapprehensive of contempt,
> The insinuated scoff of coward tongues,
> And all that silent language which so oft
> In conversation betwixt man and man
> Blots from the human countenance all trace
> Of beauty and of love. For thou hast sought
> The truth in solitude, and thou art one
> The most intense of Nature's worshippers,
> In many things my brother, chiefly here
> In this my deep devotion. Fare thee well:
> Health and the quiet of a healthful mind
> Attend thee, seeking oft the haunts of men –
> And yet more often living with thyself,
> And for thyself – so haply shall thy days
> Be many, and a blessing to mankind.

Coleridge was profoundly moved. He recognised the sublime power of the poem. He now had no doubt that Wordsworth would come to be seen by posterity as 'the first & greatest philosophical Poet':

> I feel myself a better Poet, in knowing how to honour *him*, than in all my own poetic Compositions, all I have done or hope to do – and I prophesy immortality to his Recluse, as the first & finest philosophical Poem . . .[84]

He pressed his friend to continue the great work, and promised to provide him with a detailed plan of its structure. At Coleridge's request Dorothy and Mary copied out all Wordsworth's unpublished verse – some eight thousand lines – so that he could take this abroad with him and provide his considered criticisms.

Wordsworth's 'Ode to Duty', composed around this time and perhaps sent south to Coleridge before he left the country,[85] could be read as a pledge to his friend:

> And oft, when in my heart was heard
> Thy timely mandate, I deferred
> The task, in smoother walks to stray;
> But thee I now would serve more strictly, if I may.

On 14 January 1804 Coleridge set out from Grasmere, walking the nineteen miles to Kendal in only four and a half hours. Wordsworth accompanied him almost as far as Troutbeck. The next day Coleridge reflected at length on his friend. Wordsworth, he decided, was 'a happy man':

> . . . not from natural Temperament – for therein lies his main obstacle – not by enjoyment of the good things of this world – for even to this Day from the first Dawn of his Manhood he has purchased Independence and Leisure for great & good pursuits by austere frugality and daily Self-denial – nor yet by an accidental confluence of amiable and happy-making Friends and Relatives, for every one near to his heart has been placed there by Choice and after Knowledge and Delib-eration – but he is a happy man, because he is a Philosopher – because he knows the intrinsic value of the Different objects of human Pursuit, and regulates his Wishes in Subordination to that Knowledge – because he feels, and with a *practical* Faith . . . that we can do but one thing well, & that therefore we must make a choice – he has made that choice from his early youth, has pursued & is pursuing it . . .[86]

Though the relationship between the two poets was now reversed, with Wordsworth unquestionably the dominant personality, still he remained dependent on Coleridge's guidance and good opinion. In particular he seemed unable to proceed with *The Recluse* without instructions from Coleridge, and immediately began to press him to provide the detailed notes he had promised: 'I cannot say how much importance I attach to this,' he wrote anxiously to Coleridge, who at that moment was still in England, waiting to embark for the Mediterranean (on the advice of the geographer George Bellas Greenhough, Coleridge had decided to go to Malta, and from there to Sicily). Wordsworth referred to the possibility that Coleridge might die before he had provided the notes: 'I should reproach myself for ever in writing the work if I had neglected to procure this help.'[87] On the same day that he wrote to Coleridge, Wordsworth outlined his plans to the seventeen-year-old Thomas De Quincey,* who had written to him care of his publishers expressing admiration for *Lyrical Ballads*:

> I am now writing a Poem on my own earlier life ... This Poem will not be published these many years, and never during my lifetime, till I have finished a larger and more important work to which it is tributary. Of this larger work I have written one Book and several scattered fragments: it is a moral and Philosophical poem ... To this work I mean to devote the Prime of my life and the chief force of my mind. I have also arranged the plan of a narrative poem.† And if I live to finish these three principal works I shall be content.[88]

Three weeks later the Wordsworths again wrote to Coleridge, by now in lodgings at Portsmouth waiting to sail. Because of the war, ships were travelling in convoy, with the inevitable concomitant delays. 'Our hearts are full of you,' wrote Dorothy. 'Farewell, my beloved Coleridge, dear friend, Farewell!' Coleridge had been smitten by especially violent diarrhoea, and had told at least one of his friends

---

* Thomas De Quincey (1785–1859), son of a Manchester linen merchant, a tiny, delicate man. He began to take opium while an undergraduate at Worcester College, Oxford. A passionate admirer of Wordsworth from boyhood, he was later alienated from his former idol. Once he had exhausted his inheritance he made a precarious living from journalism. His most famous book, *Confessions of an English Opium Eater*, was published in 1822. Like Coleridge, he was fascinated by dreams, and he planned a study of the subject which remained unfinished at his death.
† i.e. *The Excursion*.

that he had been suffering from cholera. 'My dearest Coleridge,' wrote Wordsworth, 'Your last letter but one informing us of your late attack was the severest shock to me, I think, I have ever received':

> I cannot help saying that I would gladly have given 3 fourths of my possessions for your letter on The Recluse at that time. I cannot say what a load it would be to me, should I survive you and you die without this memorial left behind. Do for heaven's sake, put this out of the reach of accident immediately . . . Heaven bless you for ever and ever. No words can express what I feel at this moment.[89]

Humphry Davy sent a farewell letter to Coleridge in which he attempted to articulate how much their friendship had meant to him. He urged Coleridge not to waste his marvellous talents:

> You must not live much longer without giving to *all men* the *proof of power*, which those who know you feel in admiration. Perhaps at a distance from the applauding and censuring murmurs of the world, you will be best able to execute those great works which are justly expected from you; you are to be the historian of the Philosophy of feeling – Do not in any way dissipate your noble nature/Do not give up your birth-right.

'Alas!' replied Coleridge, 'there *is* a something, an essential something wanting in me.' (This was by no means the only occasion when he said something to this effect.*) 'I seem to myself to distinguish power from strength & to have only the power.'[91]

'Coleridge is gone for Malta, and his departure affects me more than I let be seen,' Southey confided to his friend Mary Barker. The two poets had spent a happy few months together in the Lakes, taking long walks whenever Coleridge's health allowed. 'Coleridge and I are the best companions possible,' Southey reflected, 'in almost all moods of mind, for all kinds of wisdom, and all kinds of nonsense . . .' There

---

* e.g. He expressed to Southey the fear that he had '*power* not *strength*', that he was 'an involuntary Impostor', that he had 'no real Genius, no real Depth'.[90]

was still a bond between them: 'we were two ships that left port in company'.

Like Poole, Southey felt that Coleridge's malaise was psychological.

> Ill he is, certainly and sorely ill; yet I believe if his mind
> was as well regulated as mine, the body would be quite as
> manageable. I am perpetually pained and mortified by think-
> ing of what he ought to be . . .'[92]

While still in London, Coleridge had received a 'heart-wringing Letter' from Sara Hutchinson, 'that put Despair into my Heart'. Perhaps he had tried to see her before leaving England. What she wrote is unknown, though it seems reasonable to infer from his reaction that she discouraged any thought of her ever being able to return his feelings, in the hope that these might fade in time. As if to deny this possibility, his immediate response was to sketch an outline for an 'Ode on a Suicide for Love, whose punishment after his Death consisted in the continuance of the same appetiteless heart-Gnawing Passion which he could not reveal'. This was part of a projected sequence of poems he called 'The Soother of Absence'.[93]

His yearning for her did not diminish while he was away. 'Why are you not here?' he cried out in misery. When he was talking about some quite unconnected subject, such as government, or war, or chemistry, a memory of her would come into his mind, of walking with her along a ridge, high above Crummock Water, or sitting on a rock beside a waterfall – 'when they laughed at us for two lovers'. His dreams were always connected with her in some way or another. He fantasised about returning to her and solemnising 'the long marriage of our Souls'. He doodled her name in his notebook. 'O yes, Sara!' he wrote there, 'I did feel how being with you I should be so very much a better man . . .'[94]

Coleridge's feeling for Sara Hutchinson was intertwined with his feelings for the three Wordsworths. He often bracketed their five names together in his notebooks, or framed pages by writing the initials of members of the Grasmere circle in each corner. He coined a Greek word to link them, 'Ενοπεντας' (henopentas), meaning five in one, an echo of Wordsworth's line 'many into one incorporate'.

His ship the *Speedwell* reached Malta in May. Coleridge quickly found temporary employment as acting Secretary to the Governor, Sir Alexander Ball. Exigencies of war meant that communication with England was slow and irregular, with many letters failing to arrive; Coleridge had been on the island almost three months before he received his first letter from home, and that was unintelligible because of allusions to others which he had not seen. In August he crossed to Sicily, where he stayed more than two months and climbed Mount Etna. While there he began a flirtation with a young Sicilian woman, the *prima donna* Cecilia Bertozzi. It seems that he found her very attractive: only 'the heavenly vision' of Sara's face, 'the Guardian Angel of my innocence and Peace of mind', strengthened him to resist the allure of the 'too fascinating siren, against whose witcheries Ulysses's wax would have proved but a Half-protection . . .'[95] Perhaps a short-lived surrender to the siren of Syracuse might have released him from a more permanent enslavement.

Coleridge continued working for Sir Alexander Ball for more than a year, until a replacement arrived in September 1805. Then he returned to Sicily before crossing to the Italian mainland. His powers remained dormant. Indeed, he wrote no poetry of any substance while abroad. In his notebooks he castigated himself for achieving so little, and for failing to see things through. He feared that he must seem '*little*' beside Wordsworth, and lamented 'my want of so much that must be lovely in the Heart of Woman, Strength, Manliness, & Manly Beauty . . . O! SARA!' His notebooks reveal hints of jealousy, even as he wrote of 'venerated William' or 'dear and honoured W. Wordsworth'. He confessed to 'sickly thoughts' about Sara and Wordsworth married after Mary's death.[96]

At a reception in the Governor's Palace in Valetta, Coleridge was stunned to hear the news of John Wordsworth's death in a shipwreck.* In his mind he had already given up Sara Hutchinson to John, 'by an

* His ship, the *Earl of Abergavenny*, was wrecked off Portland on 5 February 1805 with the loss of about three hundred passengers and crew.

effort of agonising Virtue' – though it seems that no one beside himself had any notion of those two as lovers. 'O dear friends! Death has come amongst us!' he grieved to the Wordsworths, who knew that the news would distress him and hoped that it might bring him home. Coleridge feared that he might next hear of Sara's death, or William's. He imagined how his friends were feeling: 'They are expecting me – did they not even so expect him!' His notebook professed that he would 'very, very gladly' have died in John's place.[97]

During a becalmed sea journey he noted that the ship had made no progress despite five days' toil. 'Alas! alas! what have I been doing on the Great Voyage of Life since my Return from Germany but fretting upon the front of the Wind . . . !' On his birthday he was as usual plunged into a pit of misery: 'O Thought of Agony! O Thought of Despair! drive me not to utter Madness!' He found passing relief by dosing himself nightly with opium, though conscious that the practice was a form of '*usury* against myself'. Despair led him several times to thoughts of suicide. He contemplated hurling himself into the crater of Mount Etna, wondering whether he might somehow achieve a mystical union with Wordsworth: 'O that my Spirit purged by Death of its Weaknesses, which are alas! my *identity* might flow into *thine*, & live and act in thee, & be Thou.'[98]

Encouraged by Coleridge's response to his reading above Grasmere, Wordsworth surged forward with his autobiographical poem. He had decided to expand the original two books into five; possibly he had discussed this with Coleridge while the latter was still at Grasmere. In the ten weeks following Coleridge's departure he wrote another 1,500 lines, as well as 'a few small poems'. He walked every day, generally marching back and forth along a route of perhaps a quarter or half a mile, composing as he went. 'While he is so engaged he seldom knows how the time slips away,' wrote Dorothy, 'or hardly whether it is rain or fair.' In wet weather he took an umbrella.[99] Some time in early March he finished the poem in five books, and he may have sent it in that form to Coleridge with the remainder of his unpublished poetry. But it was already clear to him that a further stage of expansion was needed. The five books had followed the course of his inner life until his years at Cambridge; but he now realised that he needed to go on, to explore his response to the French Revolution and his infatuation with Godwinism. He immediately started to plan a much longer poem, in thirteen books.

Coleridge was never far from the surface of his mind: so much so that in recalling his reunion with Dorothy in 1787, when both had been in their teens, he could scarcely believe that his friend had not been with them:

> O friend, we had not seen thee at that time,
> And yet a power is on me, and a strong
> Confusion, and I seem to plant thee there.
> Far art thou wandered now in search of health,
> And milder breezes – melancholy lot –
> But thou art with us, with us in the past,
> The present, with us in the times to come.
> There is no grief, no sorrow, no despair,
> No languor, no dejection, no dismay,
> No absence scarcely can there be, for those
> Who love as we do. Speed thee well!* divide
> Thy pleasure with us; thy returning strength,
> Receive it daily as a joy of ours;
> Share with us thy fresh spirits, whether gift
> Of gales Etesian† or of loving thoughts.

On Christmas Day 1804 Wordsworth outlined 'the plan of my poetical labours' to Sir George Beaumont. He was 'at present chiefly engaged' on the poem 'on my earlier life or the growth of my own mind'; when this was finished, 'I purpose to fall with all my might' on *The Recluse*, 'which is the chief object upon which my thoughts have been fixed these many years'. By May 1805 he was reaching the end of his autobiographical poem. 'It will not be less than 9,000 lines,' he informed Beaumont: 'an alarming length! and a thing unprecedented in Literary history that a man should talk so much about himself.' It

---

* A pun on the name of Coleridge's ship, the brig *Speedwell*.
† Mediterranean winds. Perhaps also a play on Coleridge's initials ('esteesee').

was not conceit, he explained, that had made him write at such length, but humility; when he had begun the poem he had felt unsure of his own powers and unprepared to tackle a more arduous subject. To write about the development of his own mind was a way into a more ambitious work. 'This work may be considered as a sort of portico to the Recluse, part of the same building, which I hope to be able erelong to begin with, in earnest; and if I am permitted to bring it to a conclusion, and to write, further, a narrative Poem of the Epic Kind, I shall consider the *task* of my life as over.'[100]

In tracing the history of his own mind Wordsworth looked back to his feelings about the Revolution, both during his stay in France and immediately afterwards. In keeping faith with his mission, it was essential not to falsify the past, or to replace the perspective of the young revolutionary with the very different view he had formed subsequently. Equally, it was important to show how his sentiments had afterwards changed. The crowning of Napoleon as Emperor of France on 2 December 1804 symbolised the final 'catastrophe' of the Revolution, '... when we see the dog/Returning to his vomit ...', the French once more embracing monarchy. The disillusionment that Coleridge had spoken of was complete. The keen young Republican had cheered as the French King was deposed; now the disappointed older man groaned as a French Emperor was proclaimed. The ceremony was especially grotesque: Pope Pius VII was summoned from Rome to crown the tyrant, but at the crucial moment Bonaparte rose from his throne, seized the crown and placed it on his own head himself.

In the penultimate book of his long poem, Wordsworth described how he freed himself of 'this degradation', the prostitution of his soul to a political cause, and thereby restored his imaginative powers:

> ... I had felt
> Too forcibly, too early in my life,
> Visitings of imaginative power
> For this to last: I shook the habit off
> Entirely and for ever, and again

In Nature's presence stood, as I stand now,
A sensitive, and a *creative* soul.

The loss of their brother in the wreck of the *Abergavenny* hit William and Dorothy very hard. 'God keep the rest of us together!' Wordsworth exclaimed to Richard, from whom he had heard the tragic news; 'the set is now broken.'[101] John's death stiffened Wordsworth's resolve to persist with *The Recluse*. In his eyes, the two of them had made a compact: John had gone out into the world so that William could pursue his calling. In fulfilling his part of the bond between them, John had sacrificed his life. *The Recluse* became more than an ambition; it became a sacred duty.[102]

In this moment of extreme distress Coleridge was much in their minds. Wordsworth knew that he would be severely affected by the news: 'I tremble for the moment when he is to hear of my brother's death,' he wrote to Sir George Beaumont; 'it will distress him to the heart, and his poor body cannot bear sorrow.'[103] Dorothy was afraid for Coleridge, as he had known she would be. 'O my dear Lady Beaumont!' she wailed, 'I shall be thankful when he is off the sea, and once again upon English ground. Since he parted from us so much hope has been cut out of my heart that whatever I look at I feel the difference.'[104]

Towards the end of March the Wordsworths received a letter from Coleridge, dated 19 January, lamenting that his notes for *The Recluse* were lost. He had despatched them, together with a series of letters to Daniel Stuart, in the safekeeping of a soldier returning to England, who had unfortunately died of the plague at Gibraltar, and whose papers had been destroyed for fear of infection. A few months later a further batch of Coleridge's letters was thrown overboard to prevent them falling into the hands of the enemy, in the misapprehension that they were official papers, when the convoy carrying them was attacked by French frigates. Coleridge had unwittingly contributed to this mishap by presenting his package to the captain 'with great pomp of Seriousness', as if in his capacity as acting Secretary to the Governor. He wrote to Wordsworth in apparent dismay: 'My Ideas respecting your Recluse were burnt as a Plague-garment, and all my long letters to you and Sir George Beaumont sunk to the bottom of the Sea!'[105]

Without Coleridge's guidance Wordsworth was at a loss. 'He is very anxious to get forward with The Recluse, and is reading for the nourishment of his mind, preparatory to beginning,' Dorothy wrote to Lady Beaumont towards the end of 1805, 'but I do not think he will be able to do much more till we have heard of Coleridge.'[106] In the meantime Wordsworth composed the 'Character of the Happy Warrior', a poem that drew on memories of his sailor brother to commemorate the death of Nelson, whose annihilating victory over the French at Trafalgar in October that year had eliminated the threat of French invasion.[107] But while Britannia ruled the waves, the French were dominant on land: Napoleon inflicted a succession of crushing defeats on Britain's European allies, and the French army pushed down into Italy. Coleridge was almost cut off by the French advance, escaping only by passing himself off as a neutral, with the help of a sympathetic American sea-captain.

The Wordsworths continued to be anxious about Coleridge, and looked forward impatiently to his return. The importance of his company prevailed over all other considerations. In 1805 they were even ready to sacrifice their beloved home to be with him. They did not expect him to come back to the north because of the damp climate, and they had made up their minds to leave the Lakes to join him: 'we shall go wherever he goes'. Indeed, Dorothy did not want him to spend another winter in Keswick because of the risk to his health, and asked for the Beaumonts' help in dissuading him from doing so. To posterity, Wordsworth has become so much associated with Grasmere that it is startling to find him willing to abandon the Lake District altogether. Nevertheless, this is what he had decided. Moreover, he expected this move to be permanent; a letter from Dorothy in August 1805 mentions the possibility of another tour of Scotland 'before we finally quit the North of England'.[108] By now the Wordsworths had two children,* with another due. The cottage had

* John, born in 1803, and Dorothy, born the following year. Another son, Thomas, was born in June 1806.

become much too small for them, and they were looking around for a larger house – but they would not take anything except on a temporary basis, to keep themselves free to move wherever Coleridge wanted to settle on his return. By 1806 Wordsworth was thinking of building a house near Grasmere, but as Dorothy explained to Lady Beaumont, all their schemes were 'so far connected with Coleridge that we cannot *decide* upon anything till we hear from him or see him'.[109]

12

ESTRANGEMENT

Coleridge stayed away more than two years, travelling in Italy after leaving Malta. Originally the Wordsworths had hoped that he might return for the summer of 1805; by the end of the year they were 'in daily expectation' of his arrival.[1] Wordsworth was nervous about how Coleridge might react to his much-enlarged autobiographical poem, and asked Beaumont not to mention this should he see Coleridge first. In the spring of 1806 Wordsworth spent more than a month in London, hoping to intercept his friend there. Still there was no sign of Coleridge. Wordsworth returned to Grasmere, where he composed more than a thousand lines of *The Recluse* – though it seems likely that these were a continuation of work already begun, rather than a start on the main body of the *magnum opus*.[2] He could not tackle the latter without Coleridge's help: 'Should Coleridge return, so that I might have some conversation with him upon the subject, I should go on swimmingly.'[3]

At last, in the middle of August 1806, they received 'the blessed news' that Coleridge was back, his ship in quarantine, anchored off Portsmouth. They had heard nothing *from* him for more than a year, though they had received occasional reports *of* him from other travellers. Wordsworth had been 'vexed' and 'grieved' to hear from one of these that Coleridge had lost '*all* his papers', including the collection of Wordsworth's poems that had been copied out for him to take abroad.[4]

In anticipation of the imminent arrival of 'dearest Coleridge', Wordsworth immediately cancelled a planned trip to the Borders to see Walter Scott. But once landed, a dishevelled and penniless Coleridge made his way to London, and seemed in no hurry to return to the Lakes. He wrote to Southey, rather than to his wife, 'because I can write more tranquilly', to inform the household that he had arrived safely. 'I will come as soon as I can come,' he said, but it was not obvious why he could not come at once.[5] As he explained in a letter to Wordsworth, he so much recoiled from the thought of once more 'domesticating' with his wife that he dared not go home. In reply, Wordsworth urged the absolute necessity that 'Mrs Coleridge should be furnished with some reason for your not coming down as her present uncertainty and suspense is intolerable.'[6]

Time passed. After a month had gone by, Coleridge did at last write to his wife, at Mary Lamb's insistence. But this letter was just the first of a series of excuses for his non-appearance. It would be more than two months after his landing in England before he began the journey north. Wordsworth felt frustrated; he had been willing to go to London again to meet Coleridge, but had not done so for fear of missing him on the road. Coleridge's arrival was expected imminently, and repeatedly postponed. Moreover, the Wordsworths had been offered the use of a large farmhouse on Sir George Beaumont's estate at Coleorton, near Ashby de la Zouch in Leicestershire, where they planned to spend the winter; but they delayed their departure in the hope of his arrival. At last, despairing of him, they set out towards the end of October. At Kendal they were joined by Sara Hutchinson, who told them that Coleridge was not far off. He had been hoping to intercept her in Penrith, but arrived little more than half an hour after she had left for her rendezvous with the Wordsworths. Coleridge pursued Sara south to Kendal, though earlier, when the Wordsworths had suggested meeting there, he had replied that he could not come just to see them briefly, and then to part. They went in a group to greet him at his inn. 'Never never did I feel such a shock as at first sight of him,' Dorothy confessed afterwards; 'he is utterly changed.' Coleridge was still only in his mid-thirties, but already he looked middle-aged. His face and body were bloated almost beyond recognition – and worse, he seemed a different man, distant and unfamiliar, his once restless, impatient eyes now still and remote. Far from curing him and restoring his health, his period of exile abroad had increased his reliance on opium and alcohol. Dorothy noted in dismay that the 'divine expression of his countenance' had all but disappeared.[7] Occasionally the ingratiating smile of one too long dependent on the favours of others would cross his features.

After Dorothy and Mary had left for Coleorton with the children, Wordsworth and Sara stayed with Coleridge another day discussing what was to be done. There was no possibility, Coleridge told them, of his returning to live at Greta Hall, where the Southeys were now permanently ensconced with his wife: the thought of resuming marital relations filled him with horror. No doubt Wordsworth steeled him to face the inevitable confrontation when he reached home. Dorothy hoped that he might have 'strength of mind to abide by his resolution of separating from Mrs C'.[8] Within a matter of weeks Coleridge reported that he and his wife had agreed to part 'absolutely and finally', though apparently she tried everything she could think of to make him stay, and eventually consented to a separation only on condition that it should not be made public.[9] Southey thought the proposed separation 'a good thing':

> ... his habits are so murderous of all domestic comfort that I am only surprised Mrs C. is not rejoiced at being rid of him. He besots himself with opium, or with spirits, till his eyes look like a Turks who is half reduced to idiotcy by the practice – he calls up the servants at all hours of the night to prepare food for him – he does in short all things except at the proper time – does nothing which he ought to do, and every thing which he ought not.[10]

Dorothy was confident that, removed from conflict with his wife, and living quietly with them, Coleridge would recover his health. They would not serve him brandy, she explained to Lady Beaumont; 'if he is not inclined to manage himself, *we* can manage him, and he will take no harm, while he has not the temptations which variety of company leads him into of taking stimulants to keep him in spirits while he is talking'. But she also confided to her intimate friend Catherine Clarkson that her brother had 'suffered much' since Coleridge's return.[11] In his long isolation, Coleridge had withdrawn from human intimacy, sharing thoughts with his notebook rather than with those around him. Though he could still switch on the charm, he exuded the air of a man wronged. Self-pity and resentment lurked in the dark corners of his heart. Wordsworth's 'A Complaint', written around this time, was suggested by 'a change in the manner of a friend'; there was little doubt which friend was meant.[12]

> There is a change – and I am poor;
> Your love hath been, nor long ago,
> A fountain at my fond heart's door,
> Whose only business was to flow;
> And flow it did; not taking heed
> Of its own bounty, or my need.
>
> What happy moments did I count!
> Blest was I then all bliss above!
> Now, for that consecrated fount
> Of murmuring, sparkling, living love,
> What have I? Shall I dare to tell?
> A comfortless and hidden well.
>
> A well of love – it may be deep –
> I trust it is, – and never dry:
> What matter? If the waters sleep
> In silence and obscurity.
> – Such change, and at the very door
> Of my fond heart, hath made me poor.

Wordsworth too had changed. He was now a married man, the father of three children, responsible for providing for a family of six, including his sister – seven, if Sara Hutchinson was also included. He was no longer free to set out on spontaneous expeditions, or to stay up late into the night talking. The household had other, more domestic priorities; it was no longer devoted solely to the production of poems.

Coleridge followed the Wordsworths to Coleorton in mid-December, taking Hartley with him. Sara Hutchinson was of course there too. 'Your name sake takes upon her all the duties of his Mother & darling Friend,' he wrote unfeelingly to his wife, 'with all the Mother's love & fondness'.[13] Dorothy was delighted that he was back with them. 'I think I was never more happy in my life than when we had him an hour by the fireside,' she told Lady Beaumont; his looks were 'much more like his own old self'.[14] But the impression was short-lived; he soon relapsed into low spirits. The apparent recovery in his health did not last, either; he began to suffer seizures, which precipitated vomiting. It was assumed that from now on he would be living with the Wordsworths, but there would be no space for him when they returned to the already crowded Dove Cottage. Coleridge hoped that the Southeys might vacate Greta Hall, taking Sara Coleridge with them wherever they went, so that he might move back in there with the Wordsworths; while Southey hoped that the Wordsworths would settle with Coleridge in the West Country, so that the Southeys might have Greta Hall to themselves. The Wordsworths were uneasy about the possibility of displacing Sara from her home, especially when it emerged that the separation from his wife was neither so final nor so absolute as Coleridge had given them to believe. They quickly discovered not to put too much reliance on his word; dissimulation had become a habit with him, so that he hardly knew where the truth lay. He left letters unopened that he suspected might contain unwelcome news; nor could he summon the moral courage to write several painful letters of duty. Prudence as well as humanity dictated that he should write to his patron Josiah Wedgwood, whose brother Tom had died while Coleridge was in Malta. Coleridge had not written to the Wedgwoods while he was abroad, nor did he write now in response to Josiah's appeal for material for a life of his late brother. Wedgwood was indignant at Coleridge's neglect: 'even a total stranger' would not have refused such information if he possessed it. 'I cannot continue to esteem him,' Wedgwood fumed to Poole.[15]

Coleridge fretted that his annuity might be withdrawn, but even so he did not write to Wedgwood.

His love for Asra burned as bright as ever. He could not accept that his feelings were not reciprocated. In his journal he addressed her as 'Elpizomene', the hoped-for one. 'I know, you love me! – My reason knows it, my heart feels it . . .'[16] But almost as soon as they were together, Coleridge's pent-up jealousy erupted. One Saturday morning, less than a week after his arrival in Coleorton, he had a nightmare vision, real or imagined, apparently of Wordsworth and Sara in bed together, her 'most beautiful breast uncovered'. Three ensuing pages of his notebook that presumably described this discovery have been cut out, but a scrawled later entry reveals his continuing torment, even nine months afterwards:

> O agony! O the vision of that Saturday Morning – of the Bed/ – O cruel! is he not beloved, adored by two – & two such Beings – /and must I not be beloved *near* him except as a Satellite? – But O mercy, mercy! is he not better, greater, more manly, & altogether more attractive to any [?but] the purest Woman?[17]

Perhaps Coleridge knew that the incident was no more than a horrid fantasy, the product of an overwrought imagination, the diseased dream of a mind made wretched by unfulfilled longing and smouldering jealousy. Otherwise it is hard to explain his behaviour only a few days afterwards. Early in the New Year, the household at Coleorton assembled after supper to hear Wordsworth begin reading the 'Poem to Coleridge', now at last complete in thirteen books. The recitation continued over several successive evenings. Throughout were references to the 'honoured' and 'beloved' friend to whom the work was addressed, indeed offered as a present. Wordsworth highlighted the importance of Coleridge's faith in his work:

> When thou dost to that summer turn thy thoughts,
> And hast before thee all which then we were,
> To thee, in memory of that happiness,
> It will be known – by thee at least, my friend,

Felt – that the history of a poet's mind
Is labour not unworthy of regard:
To thee the work shall justify itself.

The subsequent passage movingly depicted the poem as a form of consolation for the sorrows both men had endured:

The last and later portions of this gift
Which I for thee design have been prepared
In times which have from those wherein we first
Together wandered in wild poesy
Differed thus far, that they have been, my friend,
Times of much sorrow, of a private grief,*
Keen and enduring, which the frame of mind,
That in this meditative history
Have been described, more deeply makes me feel,
Yet likewise hath enabled me to bear
More firmly; and a comfort now, a hope,
One of the dearest which life can give,
Is mine: that thou art near, and wilt be soon
Restored to us in renovated health –
When, after the first mingling of our tears
'Mong other consolations, we may find
Some pleasure from this offering of my love.

And in conclusion Wordsworth envisaged how he and Coleridge would work together, 'joint-labourers' in the work of man's redemption, 'surely yet to come'. This was a reference to their anticipated future collaboration on *The Recluse*, and to their glorious shared ambition for the poem.

Prophets of Nature, we to them will speak
A lasting inspiration, sanctified
By reason and by truth; what we have loved,
Others will love, and we will teach them how;
Instruct them how the mind of man becomes
A thousand times more beautiful than the earth
On which he dwells . . .[18]

* i.e. the death of John Wordsworth.

The evening that Wordsworth concluded his recital, Coleridge retired to his room and stayed up most of the night composing lines in which he attempted to express his response – seemingly the only poem he would write that troubled year, and arguably his last poem of any substance. 'To William Wordsworth' opens with an interpretation of the poem he has just heard, dwelling a while on his own failures, and sense of awe at the greatness of his friend's achievement. Lastly he describes the scene just closed:

> And when – O Friend! My comforter and guide!
> Strong in thyself, and powerful to give strength!
> Thy long sustained Song finally closed,
> And thy deep voice had ceased – yet thou thyself
> Wert still before my eyes, and round us both
> That happy vision of beloved faces –
> Scarce conscious, and yet conscious of its close
> I sat, my being blended in one thought
> (Thought was it? Or aspiration? Or resolve?)
> Absorbed, yet hanging still upon the sound –
> And when I rose, I found myself in prayer.

'If any thing good is to be done for him, it must be done by me,' Wordsworth had told Sir George Beaumont on Coleridge's arrival back in England.[19] The Wordsworths had convinced themselves that Coleridge needed to be with them, for the sake of his health and his sanity. Southey believed that the contrary was true. After confirming to a friend in London the truth of the rumour that Coleridge was separating from his wife, he held the Wordsworths responsible:

> It is from his idolatry of that family that this has begun –
> they have always humoured him in all his follies, listened to
> his complaints of his wife, and when he has complained of
> his itch, helped him to scratch, instead of covering him with
> brimstone ointment, and shutting him up by himself.

Southey was cynical about their motives. 'Wordsworth and his sister,' he continued, 'are of all human beings whom I have ever known the most intensely selfish.'

The one thing to which W. would sacrifice all others is his own reputation, concerning which his anxiety is perfectly childish – like a woman of her own beauty: and so he can get Coleridge to talk his own writings over with him, and critise [*sic*] them, and (without amending them) teach him how to do it – to be in fact the very rain and air and sunshine of his intellect, he thinks C. is very well employed and this arrangement a very good one.[20]

In April Coleridge accompanied Wordsworth and his wife down to London, taking Sara Hutchinson and Hartley with them. He had been expected to leave Coleorton before this, but as Wordsworth told Walter Scott, 'he is of a procrastinating habit'.[21] Coleridge planned to rendezvous with his wife in Bristol before continuing together to Ottery St Mary, where his brother George had invited them, in the hope that Coleridge might join him as a fellow schoolmaster. Coleridge seems to have clutched at this as a lifeline which might save him from drowning in debt. He made much of the sacrifice it would be to separate himself from Wordsworth and his family; yet later he gave as one reason for accepting his brother's offer the fact that he had been 'very unhappy at Coleorton from causes, I cannot mention'.[22] Maybe the proposed move to Ottery was an attempt to assert his independence of his friend – though he accepted a loan of £50 from Wordsworth before he left. Coleridge's notebooks suggest conflict between the two men over his attentions to Sara Hutchinson. His wife may have hoped that a new start would induce him to relent in his decision to separate from her; she certainly behaved as if nothing had changed between them. At the very least, being received by the family would lessen the shame resulting from their separation. Perhaps at Wordsworth's prompting, Coleridge wrote to George from Coleorton to explain 'the true state of my domestic affairs' in advance of his arrival.[23]

Wordsworth went to town to supervise the publication of a new collection of his verse, *Poems in Two Volumes*. In due course this was greeted with extraordinary scorn by the reviewers, who gave it a roasting hot enough to melt the confidence of most poets.* 'If the printing of trash such as this be not felt as an insult on the public taste,' sneered Francis Jeffrey in the *Edinburgh Review*, 'we are afraid that it cannot be insulted.' It was precisely to shield him from the heat of such sustained and potentially fatal criticism that Coleridge's encouragement, confidence and good opinion had always been so important to Wordsworth. Outwardly, he managed a cool response. He reassured the Beaumonts that he was not disheartened by such 'petty stings', and quoted to them Coleridge's maxim that 'every great and original writer, in proportion as he is great and original, must himself create the taste by which he is to be relished'.[24]

Inwardly, however, bitterness flowed through Wordsworth's veins, poisoning his heart. He felt ill-used. He was tempted into answering critics when it would have been wiser to have kept silent; and he became increasingly disdainful of those who failed to appreciate his work. In company, he exhibited a combination of resentment and conceit; people were often astonished, or even offended, when he proclaimed the superiority of his own works.[25] Many years later, in a superb essay, Hazlitt described how disappointment had left Wordsworth 'morbid':

> We are convinced, if he had been early a popular poet, he would have borne his honours meekly, and would have been a person of great *bonhommie* and frankness of disposition. But the sense of injustice and of undeserved ridicule sours the temper and narrows the views. To have produced works of genius, and to find them neglected or treated with scorn, is one of the heaviest trials of human patience. We exaggerate our own merits when they are denied by others, and are apt to grudge and cavil at every particle of praise bestowed on those to whom we feel a conscious superiority. In mere self-defence we turn against the world, when it turns against us; brood over the undeserved slights we receive; and thus the genial current of the soul is stopped, or vents itself in effusions

* e.g. 'a silly book ... puerile' (*Critical Review*); 'namby-pamby ... tedious, affected' (*Edinburgh Review*); 'miserable trash' (*The Satirist*); 'ridiculous' (*The Cabinet, or Monthly Report of Polite Literature*); 'puerile ... feeble' (*British Critic*); 'drivelling nonsense ... insufferable' (*Poetical Register*).

of petulance and self-conceit. Mr. Wordsworth has thought too much of contemporary critics and criticism; and less than he ought of the award of posterity, and of the opinion, we do not say of private friends, but of those who were made so by their admiration of his genius. He did not court popularity by a conformity to established models, and he ought not to have been surprised that his originality was not understood as a matter of course. He has *gnawed too much on the bridle*; and has often thrown out crusts to the critics, in mere defiance or as a point of honour when he was challenged, which otherwise his own good sense would have withheld.[26]

Later than he had promised, Coleridge made for Bristol, where he found his wife, who had been waiting for him there two months, staying with one of her unmarried sisters. He lingered another month in Bristol before they set out for Poole's house at Nether Stowey, *en route*, as he supposed, to Ottery. At Poole's he read a letter from his brother George, written two months before, in reply to his letter from Coleorton. The letter had been waiting for him in Bristol, but he had left it unopened until now. An agitated George explained that it was impossible for Coleridge and his family to be received at Ottery. In due course Sara Coleridge received a more formal letter from George's wife to the same effect. Coleridge was furious; his future was in disarray. He had no work, no income, and no home. And now he was burdened with his wife and children.

The family spent the summer of 1807 as guests of Poole in Nether Stowey, while Coleridge pondered his next move. The young Thomas De Quincey, visiting the area in the hope of gaining an introduction to Coleridge, whose work he admired almost as much as that of his idol Wordsworth, spent two or three days in Nether Stowey, waiting for Coleridge to return from what was supposed to be a day trip to Bridgwater. While De Quincey was there, Lord Egmont, one of Coleridge's local admirers, called on Poole with a present of snuff for Coleridge, and the three men fell into conversation. Egmont argued that Coleridge should undertake 'some great monumental work, that might furnish a sufficient arena for the display of his various and rare accomplishments; for his multiform erudition on the one hand, for his splendid power of theorizing and combining large and remote notices of facts on the other'. He suggested a history of Christianity. 'But, at any rate, let him do something,' urged Lord Egmont, 'for at present he talks very much like an angel, and he does nothing at all.'

From the sort of laugh which Lord Egmont gave at his own simplicity in having expected Coleridge to be at home when he had said he would be there, De Quincey gathered that procrastination had become 'a marking feature in Coleridge's daily life':

> Nobody who knew him ever thought of depending on any appointment he might make: spite of his uniformly honourable intentions, nobody attached any weight to his assurances *in re futura*: those who asked him to dinner or any other party, as matter of course, sent a carriage for him, and went personally or by proxy to fetch him; and, as to letters, unless the address were in some female hand that commanded his affectionate esteem, he tossed them all into one *deadletter bureau*, and rarely, I believe, opened them at all.

De Quincey decided to seek out Coleridge in Bridgwater. There, on a lovely summer evening, he found the poet standing in a gateway, in a deep reverie:

> In height he might seem to be about five feet eight; (he was, in reality, about an inch and a half taller, but his figure was of an order which drowns the height;) his person was broad and full, and tended even to corpulence; his complexion was fair, though not what painters technically style fair, because it was associated with black hair; his eyes were large and soft in their expression; and it was from their peculiar appearance of haze or dreaminess, which mixed with their light, that I recognised my object.

Coleridge started when De Quincey announced his name, and seemed at a loss, repeating rapidly 'a number of words which had no relation to either of us'; but he recovered himself, and received the young man graciously. De Quincey noticed how passers-by greeted Coleridge with smiles of recognition, and several asked after his health; and a later stroll about town together confirmed his impression of the deep affection and esteem for the visiting poet in which the whole town seemed to share.

Coleridge led De Quincey into a dining room, and rang the bell for refreshment. For about three hours he continued to talk, seldom giving the young man an opportunity to contribute to the conversation. At one point a lady entered, whom his host introduced in a frigid tone as 'Mrs Coleridge', before she quickly retired. It was immediately obvious to De Quincey that this was not a very happy marriage. Never had he 'beheld so profound an expression of cheerless despondency' as he saw on the face of his host. At dinner that evening, with a large party of people present, Coleridge was evidently finding it an effort to talk, and seemed to De Quincey to be struggling with gloomy thoughts. He interpreted the restless activity of Coleridge's mind in chasing abstract truths, and in burying himself in the dark places of human speculation, as an attempt to escape from his own personal wretchedness.

At about ten o'clock in the evening De Quincey took his leave of Coleridge. Excited by all that he had seen and heard, he felt that he could not sleep, so decided to walk the forty-odd miles back to Bristol. After the sultry heat of the day, the summer night felt refreshingly cool; hardly a sound disturbed the stillness, 'and all things conspired to throw back my thoughts on the extraordinary person whom I had quitted'. After Coleridge's death De Quincey would describe his as 'the largest and most spacious intellect, the subtlest and most comprehensive, that has yet existed among men'. Yet even at their first meeting he perceived the 'sad spectacle of powers so majestic already besieged by decay'. Coleridge had obviously intimated that he was in financial difficulty, because once in Bristol De Quincey sought out Joseph Cottle and enquired how he could discreetly contrive 'a particular service' to Mr Coleridge, 'which might have the effect of liberating his mind from anxiety for a year or two, and thus rendering his great powers disposable to their natural uses'. Cottle dissuaded De Quincey from offering a gift of £500, one-fifth of his entire inheritance, suggesting the lesser sum of £300 instead. In due course Coleridge accepted this as a loan, which he hoped to be able to pay back in two years' time. (In fact it would never be repaid.) The gift was made anonymously, to save Coleridge from embarrassment; but the identity of the donor was probably clear to him. Coleridge seems to have used some of the money to repay Wordsworth for the loan of £100 made as he was on the brink of setting out for Malta in 1804. In an extract from a letter to Cottle, now lost, which presumably concerned repayment of this loan, Coleridge referred to Wordsworth as one whom 'I love and honour as far beyond myself, as both morally and intellectually he is above me'.[27] But he never wrote to the Wordsworths, and they believed that their letters to him remained unopened.

In the autumn Coleridge received an invitation from Humphry Davy to come to London and give a course of lectures on the principles of poetry at the Royal Institution. The proposal had first been put to him the previous year, on his return from Malta, when Wordsworth had persuaded him to decline. Now he decided to accept. He and his family returned to Bristol. From there De Quincey undertook to escort Mrs Coleridge and her three children back to the Lakes by post-chaise, leaving Coleridge free to go directly to London.

This provided De Quincey with an opportunity to meet a man he respected even more than Coleridge, 'that man whom, of all the men from the beginning of time, I most fervently desired to see'. De Quincey had been in correspondence with Wordsworth for four years or so, but had yet to meet him. Though he had been in the Lakes the previous year, and had gazed down reverently at Wordsworth's cottage from the hills above, he had not dared to descend and introduce himself. Now, after a journey from Bristol of about a fortnight, the post-chaise was straining up the hill towards Grasmere. De Quincey and the two boys alighted and walked ahead; Hartley sprinted forward as they neared the familiar cottage. Trembling, De Quincey turned in at the gate and walked rapidly towards the door. He heard a step,

> and, like a flash of lightning, I saw the figure emerge of a
> tallish man, who held out his hand, and saluted me with the

most cordial manner, and the warmest expression of friendly welcome that it is possible to imagine.

Just then, however, the chaise pulled up outside, and Wordsworth advanced past the stunned De Quincey to greet Mrs Coleridge.

Still in Bristol, Coleridge fell violently ill while dining at the St James's Square house of his friend John Morgan, and remained there a month or so while he recuperated. He had known Morgan, a contemporary of Lamb's at Christ's Hospital, since 1795, the year when he was living in College Street with Southey and George Burnett. Morgan, a lawyer from a Unitarian background, had since married, and his wife Mary and her sister Charlotte Brent cared for Coleridge, once again in his favourite situation, nursed and pampered by a household of women. Coleridge acknowledged a resemblance between the Brent sisters and the Hutchinson sisters in a letter to Dorothy, and later in the year he would publish under a transparent pseudonym a poem, 'To Two Sisters', drawing the same comparison, an action resented – albeit for different reasons – both in Keswick and in Grasmere. Coleridge recovered enough to travel to London in November, but his lectures were postponed by an illness of Davy's, and he returned to Bristol. In the next few years he would frequently return to stay with the Morgan family, and while he was away he would send the two sisters affectionate letters that trod a fine line between flirtatiousness and familiarity – a line which he sometimes crossed. In at least one of these, he appeared to suggest that were he still healthy and young, and had he not 'cut the throat of my Happiness' by marrying, he would be paying court to Charlotte. In this, as in other letters on the subject, he would increasingly blame Southey for having cajoled him into marriage with a woman fundamentally unsuited to him.[28]

Later in the year, in an act of almost unbelievably poor taste, Coleridge would ask for a seal to be made bearing the legend 'Che sarà sarà' (this motto was not then as familiar as it has recently become). 'O that S. were S.,' he sighed in his notebook.[29]

In the New Year of 1808 Coleridge again travelled back to London and settled in some noisy rooms in The Strand above the busy office of the *Courier*, an evening paper owned but not edited by Daniel Stuart.* De Quincey visited him there, and left a vivid portrait of Coleridge, still in his nightclothes in the early afternoon, bellowing down three or four flights of stairs to his attendant, an old woman called Mrs Brainbridge. Here, stupefied with opium, he was often unable to rise from his bed to give the lectures at the appointed hour of two o'clock. De Quincey described the reaction of fashionable ladies arriving outside the Royal Institution in Albemarle Street in their carriages, only to find a lecture cancelled because 'Mr Coleridge had been taken ill' – 'expressions of concern, repeated too often, began to rouse disgust'.

Even when Coleridge was available to lecture, the result was disappointing.

> His appearance was generally that of a person struggling with pain and overmastering illness. His lips were baked with feverish heat, and often black in colour; and in spite of the water, which he continued drinking through the whole course of the lecture, he often seemed to labour under an almost paralytic inability to raise the upper jaw from the lower.

He generally chose to speak extempore, with unfortunate results. Long, embarrassing silences were interrupted by digressions onto subjects that seemed barely relevant, if relevant at all. Much of the lectures consisted of readings, apparently chosen haphazardly and read in a monotone. On one occasion he began his talk by announcing that he had prepared and written down quotations from various different authors to illustrate the points he wished to make, and interleaved these in his pocketbook, which had been stolen as he was entering the building. Henry Crabb Robinson,† who attended one of the later lectures in the series, commented that the speaker 'kept his

---

* In 1803 Stuart had sold the *Morning Post* to supporters of the Prince of Wales.

† Henry Crabb Robinson (1775–1867), solicitor, barrister and friend of Wordsworth, Coleridge, Lamb, Hazlitt and Carlyle. His extensive diaries are a useful source for the period.

audience on the rack of pleasure and offence two whole hours and ten minutes'.[30]

After one of the lectures Coleridge found himself confronted by a woman who introduced herself as Mrs Todd. He was confused that this stranger seemed to know him and to expect recognition in return. Then it flashed on him that this was Mary Evans, whom he had once loved 'almost to madness'. He had not seen her for fourteen years. A brief, embarrassed conversation followed. Afterwards Coleridge received an apologetic letter from her, explaining that she had acted on impulse. At her invitation he called on the Todds at home, where he witnessed, in exaggerated form, 'a counterpart of the very worst parts of my own Fate': an unhappy and deteriorating marriage. Within a few years Mary's husband would have lost all his money, the family home was broken up, and their son placed in the care of a maternal uncle.[31]

Illness forced the postponement of the lecture series, and confined Coleridge to his rooms. He informed Southey gloomily that he had not many months to live. Late in February, Wordsworth came to London for a visit that lasted a little more than a month. He and Dorothy had been alarmed by reports of Coleridge's illness, and by two long and melancholy letters from Coleridge himself. Wordsworth hoped to persuade Coleridge to join them in the north as soon as he was at liberty to do so. In a few months' time they would be moving into a larger house on the edge of Grasmere.

In London, Wordsworth was irritated not to be able to gain admittance to Coleridge's rooms until four o'clock in the afternoon. When he did at last see Coleridge, he found him not as ill as he had feared. His powers of recovery were astonishing; as Dorothy commented: 'how Coleridge does rise up, as it were, almost from the dead!'[32] Indeed he soon recovered sufficiently to dine out. Wordsworth reported to Walter Scott afterwards that they had dined in a large party as guests of the publisher Thomas Longman: 'upon the whole it was but a dull business, saving that we had some good haranguing, talk I cannot call it, from Coleridge'.[33]

Wordsworth was not alone in making such a distinction. At another dinner around this time, Coleridge completely dominated the conversation, though again it was a large party. 'For nearly two hours he spoke with unhesitating and uninterrupted fluency.' It was 'an intellectual exhibition altogether matchless'. His auditors appeared 'rapt in wonder and delight'. To at least one of those present, the bibliographer and librarian Thomas Dibdin, it seemed as if 'a second JOHNSON' had visited the earth to make wise the sons of men, and he regretted that he had not the powers of 'a second BOSWELL, to record the wisdom and eloquence which had that evening flown from the orator's lips'. All the same, the speaker would not allow give and take. 'His generosity was illimitable, for he would receive nothing in return.'[34] Madame de Staël later commented that while very great in monologue, Coleridge had no idea of dialogue.

Wordsworth's other motive for coming to town was to make arrangements for the publication of a new long poem, 'The White Doe of Rylstone'. But he seemed in two minds about this; he offered the poem to Longman, but was unwilling to allow him to inspect the manuscript. 'I do not chuse to send it to be thumbed by his criticasters,' he wrote to Dorothy. He still smarted from the mugging he had received from the critics over the publication of *Poems in Two Volumes*. 'I do not think it likely I shall publish it at all – indeed, I am so thoroughly disgusted with the wretched and stupid Public, that though my wish to *write* for the sake of the People is unabated yet my loathing at the thought of publication is almost insupportable.' He had virtually decided not to proceed when he received a letter of remonstrance from Dorothy arguing the importance of earning some money from the poem to fund their increasing expenses. 'Do, dearest William!' she wrote: 'do pluck up your Courage – overcome your disgust to publishing.'[35] At this Wordsworth, who was on the brink of leaving London, seems to have left the matter in Coleridge's hands.

Coleridge negotiated with Longman's partner Rees a fee of £100 – only a little less than the hundred guineas Wordsworth had demanded. He made some small modifications, apparently along lines he and Wordsworth had discussed, and offered to see the poem through the press. In early May he received a letter from Dorothy stating her anxiety that the poem should be published 'as soon as possible'. He was therefore mortified to hear from Longman that Wordsworth had withdrawn it, claiming that Coleridge had 'proceeded without authority'. Coleridge wrote Wordsworth a dignified and reasoned letter of complaint.[36] Wordsworth's response, if there was one, has not survived. But he could hardly have taken offence at such a mild rebuke. A week or two later, however, Wordsworth received a letter of a very different character. Perhaps inflamed by drink, Coleridge delivered a series of wild and angry accusations, unleashing the resentments that he had restrained for so long.[37] The bitterest of these concerned Sara Hutchinson. He accused the Wordsworths of cruelty in attempting to persuade her that she was the cause of his unhappiness, and suggested that her letters to him had been written under their supervision. He was *'convulsed'* with fury to hear that she had visited Charles Lloyd, and all his paranoia about Lloyd poured out, like pus leaking from a wound.

Wordsworth wrote a firm letter of reply – though there is some doubt as to whether it was ever sent. In the surviving draft, he stated that there was more than one sentence in Coleridge's letter 'which I blushed to read'; most of the accusations against him were 'utterly unworthy of notice, coming as they needs must have done from a man in a lamentably insane state of mind'. Those charges he deemed proper to notice were mostly petty misunderstandings dating back years, and easily answered: 'Let me sweep away some of the rubbish of which I hoped never to have heard more.' As for Coleridge's indignation at Sara's having stayed with the Lloyds, 'it may be proper to remind you that you yourself five or six years ago when surely you had not reason to think very highly of Mr Lloyd, volunteered a visit to his House and stayed with him all night'. Wordsworth hotly denied the 'unmanly and ungentlemanly' charge that Sara's letters had been written under his supervision: 'she is 34 years of age and what have I to do with overlooking her letters!'

I come now to the keystone of our offences viz. our cruelty, a hope in infusing into Sara's mind the notion that your attachment to her has been the curse of all your happiness. So far from our having done this the very reverse is the truth. They* did not pretend to deny (for my part I have meddled little with the affair) that your passion was a source to you of much misery; but they always told her that it was a gross error to appropriate this to herself . . .[38]

Whether or not Wordsworth's letter was sent, the friendship survived this eruption, and at the beginning of September a noticeably stouter Coleridge arrived in the Lakes as if nothing had happened. So began by far his longest stay with the Wordsworths, still in Grasmere but now living in a large, ugly house called Allan Bank. Sara Hutchinson was now living with them permanently, so there were five adults in the house, Coleridge, the married couple and the two unmarried sisters. There were also three children, with another due imminently.†

By 'a very painful Effort of moral Courage' Coleridge had successfully cut down his use of opium, and with renewed energy set about a new project, a periodical called *The Friend*. Unlike *The Watchman*, this would not sully itself with the ephemera of current events or party politics, but would concentrate on fundamental principles of philosophy, morality and law. He solicited his friends to collect subscriptions, and several of them put up money to fund the initial costs. Wordsworth was privately sceptical about Coleridge's ability to carry on the publication for any length of time: 'He neither will nor can execute any thing of important benefit either to himself his family or mankind,' he wrote in confidence to Poole around the end of May 1809, just before the appearance of the first number. 'Neither his talents nor his genius mighty as they are nor his vast information will avail him anything: they are all frustrated by a derangement in his intellectual and moral constitution.'[39] It was a sad conclusion for

* i.e. Dorothy and Mary Wordsworth.
† Catharine, born less than a week after Coleridge's arrival. On the day of her birth, he and Wordsworth had gone over to Keswick for a brief visit; Wordsworth never liked to be at home when his wife was in labour.

one who ten years earlier had been dazzled by Coleridge's energy and eloquence.

Coleridge rashly insisted on publishing *The Friend* himself, convinced that a publisher would cheat him of the profits, though in fact it always ran at a considerable loss.* There were many practical difficulties as a result, and Coleridge was unused to business; he confessed to finding the writing of essays 'quite delightful by comparison with the troubles of *setting up shop*'.[41] The arrangements he made were so impractical as to be perverse: he walked over the passes in all weathers to deliver the copy by hand to the printer in Penrith. Nevertheless, he somehow managed to sustain *The Friend* for twenty-eight numbers over a period of nine months. Wordsworth confessed that Coleridge had applied himself more steadily than he (or anyone else) had expected. Coleridge wrote most of it himself, though Wordsworth helped with contributions. Much of the copy was dictated to Sara Hutchinson; indeed, one advantage for Coleridge of the scheme was that it brought them together, the two of them often working into the small hours of the morning. As De Quincey, who had taken over the tenancy of Dove Cottage, remarked, 'he lived chiefly by candle-light'. The emotional pressure on Sara Hutchinson was intense: Coleridge was as demanding as the most jealous lover. He grumbled when she seemed restless in his company, and he remained suspicious of her attachment to Wordsworth. He brooded on 'that dreadful Saturday morning' in Coleorton when he thought he had seen the two of them in bed together. He took offence at 'the astonishing Effect of an unbecoming Cap' on Sara's appearance – 'it is not, cannot be, other than morally culpable'. In his happier moods he dreamed of the children they would have together: 'O wife that art! O wife thou wilt be!' When the Wordsworths complained about his obsessive attentions to Sara, he protested that his love for her was pure, and therefore innocent. He resented the fact that they seemed incapable of distinguishing between love and lust.[42]

Even Coleridge's admirers were forced to admit that *The Friend*

---

* Coleridge later estimated that he had lost £200 from *The Friend*.[40]

was often 'very obscure'. Not only was the subject-matter uncompromisingly difficult, the presentation was a further deterrent to the general reader, with multiple digressions reminiscent of the worst of his lectures. In defiance of journalistic principles, Coleridge ended one number in mid-sentence, completing it in the next. Despite being told that *The Friend* was '*unreadable*', he remained oblivious to advice or criticism. He asked Southey to submit a lively letter 'in a humorous manner' on the periodical's faults, for publication alongside a self-mocking reply, but when Southey did so, he failed to publish it.[43] Southey was also irritated when in the second number Coleridge used a footnote to deny the charges of deserting his wife and country made against him ten years earlier in *The Beauties of the Anti-Jacobin*. This was folly, since the charges against Coleridge and his friends had long been forgotten by all except perhaps those immediately concerned, and resurrecting them now could only do him damage. Still worse than folly, in Southey's opinion, was to deny what was patently true: 'if he was not a Jacobine, in the common acceptation of the name, I wonder who the Devil was. I am sure I was, am still, and ever more shall be . . .'[44]

After the first dozen numbers Coleridge yielded to pressure to lighten the content of *The Friend*, but the effect of this new policy was far from satisfactory. The new material was much more miscellaneous, and the result was incoherent. It became harder and harder to know what *The Friend* was for. The few loyal subscribers began to drift away.

'So deeply do I now enjoy your presence,' an ecstatic Coleridge wrote in his notebook early in 1810, 'so totally possess you in myself, myself in you . . .'[45] Eventually the strain of working long hours alongside her besotted admirer became too much for Sara Hutchinson, and in March she left Grasmere to go and live with her brother.* *The Friend* promptly ceased publication. For some weeks Coleridge spoke

---

* Tom Hutchinson was now farming at Hindwell, in the Welsh border country near Kington. Some of Coleridge's notebook entries seem to suggest that Sara departed without his knowledge. Afterwards he felt that the Wordsworths had connived with her to deceive him.

of persisting, but nothing happened. Dorothy was by no means certain that it would have continued even if Sara had stayed to help him:
'He was tired, and she had at last no power to drive him on.' Dorothy
denied that his love for Sara had stopped him in his work: 'do not
believe it: his love for her is no more than a fanciful dream – otherwise
he would prove it by a desire to make her happy. No! He likes to have
her about him as his own, as one devoted to him, but when she stood
in the way of other gratifications it was all over.' Dorothy seems to
be hinting that Sara had presented Coleridge with an ultimatum –
probably a demand that he leave off opium and perhaps drink too –
with which he had failed to comply.

By now the Wordsworths were despairing of Coleridge. 'We have
no hope of him,' Dorothy wrote sadly to Catherine Clarkson,

> none that he will ever do anything more than he has already
> done. If he were not under our Roof, he would be just as
> much the slave of stimulants as ever; and his whole time and
> thoughts, (except when he is reading and he reads a good
> deal), are employed in deceiving himself, and seeking to
> deceive others. He will tell me that he has been writing, that
> he *has* written half a Friend; when I *know* that he has not
> written a single line ... He lies in bed, always till after 12
> o'clock, sometimes much later; and never walks out – Even
> the finest spring day does not tempt him to seek the fresh
> air; and this beautiful valley seems a blank to him. He never
> leaves his own parlour except at dinner and tea, and some-
> times supper, and then he always seems impatient to get back
> to his solitude – he goes the moment his food is swallowed.
> Sometimes he does not speak a word ...[46]

This was not the same man with whom they had rambled joyously
in the Quantocks.

Coleridge's presence does not seem to have inspired Wordsworth to
progress with *The Recluse*, as he had once trusted it would. Before
his friend's return to the Lakes Wordsworth had composed three
fragments for the great work, the most substantial, 'The Tuft of

Primroses', broken off in mid-line. Indeed, the period of Coleridge's stay at Allan Bank was a barren one for Wordsworth, much of it taken up with writing a pamphlet attacking the recently concluded Convention of Cintra, the terms of which were felt to be unnecessarily generous to the French.* Whether this was a profitable use of Wordsworth's time may be doubted. He fussed and fretted over the publication, at one moment belligerent, the next cautious, harassing the printer with changes in proof, so that by the time the pamphlet appeared the controversy had cooled. Wordsworth's poems written while Coleridge was living at Allan Bank were unremarkable. It was not until Coleridge was on the brink of leaving that Wordsworth resumed *The Recluse*, and then he began working on the part of least interest to Coleridge, the narrative later published as *The Excursion*. Indeed, it is not obvious that Coleridge took any interest in it at all.

With *The Friend* defunct, Coleridge was now at a loose end, and Sara Hutchinson was no longer there to keep him at Grasmere. She did not write to him; he bemoaned 'her *cruel neglect* and *contemptuous silence* ever *since!*' He returned to Greta Hall to take up residence again with his wife and children, and with the Southeys. According to Dorothy, he did 'nothing but read'. Southey said much the same: Coleridge had been 'reading very hard and to no purpose – for nothing comes of it, except an accumulation of knowledge equal to that of any man living and a body of sound philosophy superior to what any man either of this or of any former age has possessed – all of which will perish with him'. Southey felt compassion for his old friend: 'what a mind is here overthrown!'[47]† In August Sara Coleridge wrote to Poole that 'S.T.C. has been here the last four or five months, and I am sorry to add that in all that time he has not *appeared* to be

---

* Following the victory of the British forces under Sir Arthur Wellesley (later Duke of Wellington) sent to relieve Lisbon at the Battle of Vimiero in August 1808, an armistice was agreed. The French army in the Iberian Peninsula under General Junot was allowed to return to France with all its arms and equipment, which provoked indignation in England.

† 'O! what a noble mind is here o'erthrown': *Hamlet*, III, i. Mary Evans had utilised the same quotation in her 1794 letter attempting to persuade Coleridge to abandon Pantisocracy.

employed in composition, although he has repeatedly assured me he was. The last No. of the "Friend" lies on his Desk, the sight of which fills my heart with grief, and my Eyes with tears; but I am obliged to conceal my trouble as much as possible, as the slightest expression of regret never fails to excite resentment.'[48]

Coleridge's notebook was now 'My only Confidant, my only faithful Friend'.

> What I lately began to do out of prudence, I now do with pleasure, as an act of affection & the sacred shame of a fond affection – lock it up carefully, and never write in it but when alone![49]

In September Basil Montagu arrived at Grasmere for a stay of more than three weeks, accompanied by his third wife, his second wife like his first having died in childbirth. On a visit to Keswick, the Montagus seem to have listened sympathetically to Coleridge's account of his struggle with opium addiction. Coleridge had formed a plan to go to Edinburgh, and there place himself under the care 'of some medical man', in the hope of effecting a cure. Montagu suggested that Coleridge might like to consult his own physician in London, and offered him a bed at his house in Soho.* Coleridge was welcome to share Montagu's carriage when he and his wife returned to London. Sara Coleridge endorsed this proposal, and Coleridge 'acquiesced'. He had been thinking about going to London anyway.

His decision placed Wordsworth in a dilemma. First he tried to convince Montagu that Coleridge would not be comfortable in his house. When Montagu failed to take the hint, Wordsworth felt obliged to warn him, in confidence, about Coleridge's unsociable habits. The terms he used afterwards became a matter of dispute, but Wordsworth never denied that the conversation had taken place.

Coleridge knew nothing of this until a couple of days after their arrival in London. According to a later account by De Quincey, a quarrel arose when Montagu tried to prevent Coleridge from opening

---

* No. 55 Frith Street. Kathleen Coburn, the editor of Coleridge's notebooks, thinks this may have been an apartment owned by the Montagus rather than their home.[50]

a bottle of wine in honour of his guest, a sea captain he had known in Malta. (Montagu was a teetotaller, and was later to write a pamphlet condemning the practice of drinking at mealtimes.) In the ensuing argument, Montagu blurted out what he said Wordsworth had told him: that Coleridge was 'a rotten drunkard', who was 'rotting out his entrails by intemperance'; that he was '*in the habit* of running into debt at little Pot-houses for Gin'; and that for years past he had been 'an absolute nuisance in the family'. Coleridge was devastated, particularly when Montagu alleged that he had been 'authorised' or 'commissioned' to say that Wordsworth had 'no hope of me!'

Montagu's disclosures took Coleridge completely by surprise. He was shocked by the sudden revelation of how the Wordsworths saw him, and he was mortified that Wordsworth should have exposed his weaknesses to others.* As was usual with him, it took some time before he felt the full impact of the blow. In the days that followed he brooded over what he had learned, becoming more and more unhappy as the words echoed in his mind. Fragments from his note-books give a sense of his misery: 'a compressing and strangling Anguish, made up of Love, and Resentment, and Sorrow—'.

Coleridge left Montagu's house immediately for Hudson's Hotel, in nearby Covent Garden.† He felt as if he were whirling about in a vortex. Trying to make sense of his confusion, he drew up a 'Confessio Fidei', listing everything in which he believed. This was followed by a long passage of self-analysis, headed 'Ego-ana'. All the old grievances swelled to the surface, even the quarrel with Lloyd and what he saw as the Wordsworths' failure to side with him. For more than a decade he had subjugated himself to Wordsworth, even (so he told himself) at the expense of losing Sara Hutchinson's respect. He had set aside his own writing, containing his envy and frustration only at the price of his health. He had devoted himself to Wordsworth's interest, at the price of alienating his benefactors and being dismissed as a deluded

* In retrospect, it may seem surprising that Montagu appears to have said nothing about Coleridge's opium-taking, but the context of the quarrel is sufficient to explain the emphasis on drunkenness.
† No. 43 King Street.

fanatic by many otherwise disposed to think highly of him. He had championed Wordsworth's reputation, though in return Wordsworth had shown only a languid, or very desultory interest in his own. So long as Coleridge had been Wordsworth's sole admirer, he had been loved in return. Now there were others to fill his place. The friend for whom he had sacrificed so much had abandoned him, or so it seemed. His love had been spurned.[51] Months afterwards, he burst in on Mary Lamb, crying 'Wordsworth, Wordsworth has given me up.'

After a few days at the hotel Coleridge moved in with the Morgans, now living in Hammersmith,* where he would remain more than a year. He was further upset to hear that John Morgan had been warned to be 'on his guard' against Coleridge. Morgan 'told me that I had enemies at work against my character'. Coleridge does not seem to have shared his unhappiness with his friends; on the contrary, he seemed 'very cheerful' when the Lambs saw him a fortnight later. In due course he was further mortified to find that Montagu's physician, Anthony Carlisle, had violated his confidence; his struggle with addiction was now the subject of common gossip.

Montagu wrote to Wordsworth, confessing that he had repeated what Wordsworth had told him to Coleridge, who had been very angry. Wordsworth was annoyed, but contented himself with telling Montagu that he had done unwisely. He received no letters from Coleridge, but such silences were not uncommon. They had heard from other sources that Coleridge was well and in good spirits – indeed, that he was powdering his hair:† evidence, Dorothy concluded with a sniff of disapproval, that he was not seriously affected. It was not until some months had passed that the Wordsworths received a letter from Mary Lamb in which she referred to 'a coolness' between Coleridge and Wordsworth. Dorothy wrote back immediately to say that there was no coolness on her brother's part. Mary Lamb begged Wordsworth to come to London immediately, eliciting a 'cold answer' from Wordsworth that Lamb judged inadvisable to show his

---

* No. 7 Portland Place (now known as Addison Bridge Place).
† Coleridge later explained that he had been advised to powder his hair 'to prevent my taking Cold after my Hair had been thinned'.[52]

friend. Then fragmentary details reached the Wordsworths of a letter Coleridge had sent to his wife, in which he wrote as one who had been 'cruelly injured'; he appeared to suggest that Wordsworth's unjust conduct had driven him to the brink of madness. Dorothy's reaction was to be indignant at the slur on her brother.

Wordsworth was disinclined to write to Coleridge. He felt confident of his own rectitude; Dorothy expressed their joint view that 'having deserved no blame we are easy on that score'. If Coleridge asked for an explanation, then Wordsworth was ready to give one; but Dorothy thought it 'more likely that his fancies will die away of themselves'.[53] Wordsworth did not seem to feel that he had done Coleridge a wrong, or that he owed him an apology. Indeed, as more reports reached Grasmere of Coleridge's hurt feelings, Wordsworth increasingly resented the implication that he was responsible. When Southey returned from London in the summer and repeated what Coleridge had told him, Wordsworth denied that Montagu had ever 'said those words' and hypothesised that Coleridge 'had invented them'.* He persuaded himself that Coleridge had concocted the story as a pretext to break with him. Dorothy referred angrily to 'the delusions of his own self-deceiving heart'.[54] Meanwhile Coleridge had been waiting in vain for an explanation. It was not for him, as the injured party, to make the first approach; the mere thought of Wordsworth made his insides feel fluttered and disordered. 'So deep and so rankling is the wound, which Wordsworth has wantonly and without the slightest provocation inflicted in return for a 15 years' most enthusiastic, self-despising & alas! self-injuring Friendship,' Coleridge complained to Daniel Stuart after six months, 'that I cannot return to Grasmere or it's vicinity.'[55] He felt betrayed, both by the Wordsworths and by Sara Hutchinson, who had returned from her brother's to live with them once more. When word reached him that the Wordsworths dismissed his misery as 'pretence' and were openly questioning his veracity, he was bitterly resentful. He came to believe that Wordsworth had spoken as he did to Montagu in the knowledge that his words would be

* The evidence of Coleridge's notebooks tends to support his version of the conversation with Montagu.

repeated to him. Thus both men felt aggrieved, and both believed the other had meant to put an end to their friendship.

Months passed, with no contact between them. In February 1812 Coleridge arrived back in the Lakes for a six-week visit to his family. His chaise took him through Grasmere, which he had never before been known to pass without calling on the Wordsworths; but he drove past their door without stopping, ignoring the speechless astonishment of his sons whom he had collected from school in Ambleside beforehand. Derwent 'fixed his eyes full of tears upon his father, who turned his head away to conceal his own emotions'. Later, when Sara Coleridge explained to Hartley that 'Mr W. had a little vexed his father by something he had said to Mr Montagu,' Hartley 'turned as white as lime'.[56]

Friends tried to arrange a meeting so that they might be reconciled, but neither man would make the first move. Wordsworth did not expect Coleridge to be able to leave Keswick without seeing him. Coleridge admitted that his reason pulled one way, while his heart pulled in the opposite direction. He was offended to hear from his wife that Wordsworth 'treats the affair as a trifle'.[57] She received numerous messages and letters from Dorothy urging Coleridge not to leave the Lakes without seeing them, 'but he would not go to *them* and *they* did not come to him'.[58]

In April Coleridge returned to London, where he again took up residence with the Morgans, now living in Soho.* Later that same month Wordsworth set off for London himself, determined to confront Coleridge. He came in a spirit of cold resentment rather than of reconciliation. Arriving at the Beaumonts' house in Grosvenor Square, he was angered to find that Coleridge had told his side of the story to them 'with plentiful abuse of me'. Wordsworth thought this 'scandalous conduct on his part, and most ungrateful' – so much so that he was tempted to 'put an end to all intercourse with him for ever'. The MP Richard Sharp showed him a letter in which Coleridge had referred to Wordsworth (though not by name) as 'my bitterest

* At no. 71 Berners Street.

Calumniator'. Wordsworth was livid: 'this conduct is insufferable and I am determined to put an end to it'.[59] But it was not obvious how this should be achieved. A further complication was that Coleridge required 'the most perfect tranquillity of mind', being about to begin a new course of lectures.

Lamb reluctantly agreed to become involved as intermediary. Wordsworth proposed that Coleridge should submit himself to cross-examination before Montagu and himself, in the presence of a neutral referee; he suggested Josiah Wedgwood for this role. 'Woe is me, that a friendship of 15 years should come to this!' lamented Coleridge to Lamb, 'and such a friendship . . .'[60] He had no objection to meeting Wordsworth, either alone or in company, but he was not prepared to submit himself to examination, or to meet Wordsworth and Montagu together in circumstances that might end in one accusing the other of lying, which could lead to a duel. He pointed out that he had never declined to explain himself, but he expected an explanation from Wordsworth, and felt that he had a right to one. The temperature was rising; both men demanded satisfaction. At this point Lamb withdrew from his role as mediator, feeling that it was impossible to heal the breach. Coleridge appealed directly to Wordsworth, but Wordsworth refused to open his letter.

Eventually, through the intercession of the lawyer Henry Crabb Robinson, it was agreed that both men should exchange letters setting out their positions, in a manner that would enable them to meet without awkwardness. This was done, and the two resumed contact. They met on several occasions in the week that followed, and one morning they walked up to Hampstead together. 'I never ceased to have faith in you, to love & revere you,' Coleridge wrote to his old friend.[61] Wordsworth felt that he had 'settled the business' with Coleridge. But though the wound was closed, the hurt remained.

Coleridge informed Poole that 'a Reconciliation has taken place – but the *Feeling*, which I had previous to that moment, when the 3/4ths Calumny burst like a Thunder-storm from a blue Sky on my Soul – after 15 years of such religious, almost superstitious, Idolatry and Self-sacrifice – O no! no! that I fear, never can return. All outward actions, all inward Wishes, all Thoughts & Admirations, will be the same – *are* the same – but – aye there remains an immedicable *But*.'[62]

Sara Coleridge believed that 'there will never more be *that* between them which was in days of yore':

> but it has taught C. one useful lesson; that even his dearest & most indulgent friends, even those very persons who have been the great means of his self-indulgence, when he comes to live wholly with them, are as clear-sighted to his failings, & much less delicate in speaking of them, than his Wife, who being the Mother of his children, even if she had not the slightest regard for himself, would naturally feel a reluctance to the exposing of his faults.[63]

Wordsworth's four-year-old daughter Catharine died at the beginning of June, while he was still in London. (It was this tragedy that prompted his sonnet 'Surprised by Joy'.) Six months later the Wordsworths suffered a second bereavement, the death of their son Thomas, then aged six, the 'darling of the family'. Coleridge had been particularly fond of Thomas, and he was invited to join the grieving family up in Grasmere. Dorothy thought that nothing would do her brother so much good as Coleridge's company and conversation.[64] Coleridge's initial reply was warm but evasive. He commiserated with his friend, and gave thanks that they were no longer estranged at such a moment. On being pressed, he claimed to be so busy with rehearsals for his play *Remorse* (a rewritten version of *Osorio*), due to be put on at the Drury Lane Theatre early in the New Year, that he did not know when he would be able to get away. When the Wordsworths heard that he had left London for Margate, they realised sadly that they could never again hope to see him in Grasmere.

Wordsworth's *The Excursion*, a long poem in nine books, with the subtitle *Being a Portion of The Recluse*, was published in the summer of 1814. It was an ambitious work, and in a preface to the poem Wordsworth set out his still more ambitious plans for *The Recluse* as a whole. He referred to the already completed 'review of his own mind':

That Work, addressed to a dear Friend, most distinguished for his knowledge and genius, and to whom the Author's Intellect is deeply indebted, has been long finished; and the result of the investigation which gave rise to it was a determination to compose a philosophical poem, containing views of Man, Nature, and Society; and to be entitled, 'The Recluse'; as having for its principal subject the sensations and opinions of a poet living in retirement. – The preparatory poem is biographical, and conducts the history of the Author's mind to the point when he was emboldened to hope that his faculties were sufficiently matured for entering upon the arduous labour which he had proposed to himself; and the two Works have the same kind of relation to each other, if he may so express himself, as the ante-chapel has to the body of a Gothic church. Continuing this allusion, he may be permitted to add, that his minor Pieces, which have been long before the Public, when they shall be properly arranged, will be found by the attentive Reader to have such connection with the main Work as may give them claim to be likened to the little cells, oratories, and sepulchral recesses, ordinarily included in those edifices.

And as 'a kind of Prospectus' of the design and scope of *The Recluse*, Wordsworth offered the concluding hundred or so lines of his 'Home at Grasmere'.

Hazlitt's review, which ran over three parts in the *Examiner*, was perceptive and appreciative, though its criticisms irritated Wordsworth and his sister. But Francis Jeffrey's malicious piece in the *Edinburgh Review* left him almost incoherent with rage. The opening sentence set the tone: 'This will never do.' Jeffrey proceeded to ridicule the whole enterprise. The following year, when Wordsworth at last issued 'The White Doe of Rylstone', Jeffrey had another swipe: 'This, we think, has the merit of being the very worst poem we ever saw imprinted in a quarto volume.'

From Coleridge, however, the Wordsworths heard nothing, though he had been singled out in the preface and there had been much speculation that he might write a review. At the end of the year

Wordsworth voiced his doubt that Coleridge had read more than three lines of the poem. At last, almost nine months after the poem's publication, Coleridge broke his silence in the most oblique way possible, by a passing remark in a letter to Lady Beaumont, in which he asked for the return of a manuscript that he had lent her,* the poem addressed to Wordsworth ('To William Wordsworth') after hearing him recite 'the Work on the Growth of his own spirit' (*The Prelude*). Coleridge praised *The Excursion*, but yet – 'the fault may be in my own mind' – he did not think it equal to the latter:

> I have sometimes fancied, that having by the conjoint oper-
> ation of his own experiences, feelings and reason *himself*
> convinced *himself* of Truths, which the generality of persons
> have either taken for granted from their Infancy, or at least
> adopted in early life, he has attached all their own depth and
> weight to doctrines and words, which come almost as Truisms
> or Common-place to others.[65]

Coming from this source, from the man who so long ago had pro-posed the scheme of a great philosophical poem to Wordsworth, this comment was especially damaging. Coleridge knew that Lady Beaumont was likely to share the contents of his letter with Words-worth, which indeed she did. Wordsworth suppressed his hurt feelings sufficiently to write a dignified letter to Coleridge: 'I have rather been perplexed than enlightened by your *comparative* censure.' He asked his old friend for more specific criticisms: 'Pray point out to me the most striking instances where I have failed.'

Wordsworth's letter was addressed to 'My dear Coleridge' and signed, 'believe me my dear Coleridge in spite of your silence/Most affectionately yours/W. Wordsworth'. Nevertheless, he begged Cole-ridge to 'relinquish the intention of publishing the Poem addressed to me after hearing *mine* to you'. He believed that the commendation would be 'injurious to us both, and my work when it appears, would labour under a great disadvantage in consequence of such a precur-sorship of Praise'.

---

* She never returned the poem; Wordsworth may have asked her not to do so.

In a long reply Coleridge explained that *The Excursion*, though excellent in many ways, had disappointed the expectations aroused by *The Prelude*. He had hoped for *The Recluse*, and now, at last, he set out in detail what he felt that poem should contain, the notes that Wordsworth had begged him to supply before leaving for Malta.[66]*

It was too late. Wordsworth was now in his late forties, and if ever there was a moment when he might have written *The Recluse*, it was past. Though he would make another sustained attempt at it, this too would be unsuccessful. He would never complete the visionary work which he had so long believed would be his masterpiece (though more than twenty years later his wife was still hoping that he might return to it), and the rest of his life would be lived under the shadow of this disappointment. His talent shrivelled, and though he produced many more poems, few of them were of the quality he once exhibited in abundance. *The Prelude* – his greatest achievement – would remain unpublished in his lifetime.

Many years after, when he was nearly seventy, Wordsworth alluded to his failure to write *The Recluse* in a conversation with a visitor. Talking of the poet Thomas Gray, he remarked that Gray 'had undertaken something beyond his powers to accomplish. And that is my case.'

Coleridge had not intended to douse his friend's fire. But he sensed that the fire was going out nonetheless. In his notebooks there is a recurrent stress on the imperative need of the creative imagination for freedom – from prosperity, from respectability, from domesticity. In 1812 Wordsworth had written to Lord Lonsdale soliciting his aid in obtaining some lucrative office, and the following year Lonsdale helped him to obtain a post as Distributor of Stamps for Westmoreland and the Penrith District of Cumberland. It was not quite a sinecure; there was some real work involved, but Wordsworth was free to hire an assistant to do most of this and keep whatever profit remained. Gradually he achieved the financial security he craved, and

* See Appendix, page 427.

in the process, respectability gained on him. He was made a magistrate. His political views became steadily more reactionary, so that he even opposed the very modest reforms for the extension of the franchise and the elimination of the more blatant abuses proposed in the Bill that finally passed through Parliament in 1832. Southey too was in retreat from his radical youth, especially after he was appointed Poet Laureate in 1813. In two long articles in the Tory *Quarterly Review* he denounced the agitation for reform. He was therefore deeply embarrassed when his 1794 revolutionary epic *Wat Tyler* was announced for publication; he tried to prevent this, arguing that it was being published without his authorisation, but the Lord Chancellor refused an injunction on the grounds that seditious works could not claim protection under the copyright laws. To the delight of Southey's critics, his poem became a bestseller. It derived from a manuscript Southey had left with the radical printer Ridgeway when he had visited him in prison at the time of the treason trials more than twenty years earlier. Thomas Love Peacock's satirical novel *Melincourt* (1817) was a sharp response to Southey's *Quarterly Review* articles; its central set-piece describes an election in the rotten borough of One-Vote: Wordsworth and Southey are mockingly portrayed as 'Mr Paperstamp' and 'Mr Feathernest'. In his notebooks Coleridge (himself depicted by Peacock as 'Mr Mystic') deplored the 'apostacy' of men of genius.[67]

Years earlier Coleridge had expressed the fear that living among adoring female devotees might damage Wordsworth: that a film might arise and thicken his moral eye. In 1818 Coleridge copied out a passage from Jean Paul's *Geist** that argued the deadly effect of marriage on the poetic imagination. Mary Barker, a clever woman with whom Southey often flirted, joked that both Wordsworth and Southey each had three wives: as well as their own spouses, Wordsworth had his sister and his wife's sister, and Southey had his wife's two sisters living

* Jean Paul Richter (1763–1825), known colloquially as Jean Paul, grotesque and humorous novelist, essayist and reviewer, shaped many of the Romantic poets' preoccupations with nature, religion and psychology, including dreamlike states. He introduced the concept of the *Doppelgänger*. His *Geist* was published in 1801.

with him. It was not simply jealousy that made Coleridge fear the 'she-petticoats around WW'.[68]

For more than fifteen years Coleridge's unfinished 'Christabel' had circulated widely in manuscript and had been greatly admired, so much so that some were able to recite it by heart. Though several attempts had been made to persuade him to publish the poem, he had always refused, in the hope of one day being able to complete it. But early in 1815, and desperate for money, he decided not to wait any longer, and sought the help of Lord Byron in publishing his poems. It was something of a climbdown for Coleridge to look for assistance from the younger Byron, whose *English Bards and Scots Reviewers* (1809) had lampooned 'ballad monger Southey', 'simple Wordsworth' and 'gentle Coleridge . . . to turgid ode and tumid stanza dear'. But Coleridge was in no position to harbour grudges. He had only recently emerged penniless from another crisis in his health, in which attempts to withdraw from opium use had brought him to the verge of complete collapse. He had been in the habit of swallowing as much as a pint of laudanum a day, at a ruinous cost of £5 a week.[69]

Byron introduced Coleridge to his publisher John Murray, who agreed to publish a volume consisting of 'Christabel' and two shorter poems inspired by opium, 'Kubla Khan' and 'The Pains of Sleep'. It was a desperate measure to present the public with a still unfinished poem after keeping it back for so long. In his preface Coleridge acknowledged that the poem's originality would have been much more apparent had he published it when the second part was completed in 1800. Since then, 'my poetic powers have been, till very lately, in suspended animation'. He hoped to complete the three parts yet to come 'in the course of the present year'.

Like 'Christabel', 'Kubla Khan' too was incomplete. 'Oh! When will he ever give his friends anything but pain?' sighed Sara Coleridge, who was almost certainly echoing Southey in judging it 'unwise' of her husband to have published his fragments; 'we were all sadly vexed when we read the advertizement of these things.'[70] The revelations about opium-taking may have embarrassed her.

Coleridge knew that publishing these poems uncompleted was likely to attract criticism. 'Forth steps Mr Coleridge, like a giant refreshed from sleep,' read an unsigned notice in the *Edinburgh Review*;* it had been almost twenty years since Coleridge had last produced a volume of new poems. But the patient public would be disappointed; the awakened colossus had produced 'one of the most notable pieces of impertinence of which the press has lately been guilty'.[71]

Introducing 'Kubla Khan', Coleridge made a virtue of necessity. He was publishing it, he said, as a fragment, 'at the request of a poet of great and deserved celebrity,† and as far as the author's own opinions are concerned, rather as a psychological curiosity, than on the ground of any supposed *poetic* merits'. He continued with the tale of the opium-inspired vision, and the interruption by the person from Porlock. The poem 'had been originally, as it were, given to him' in the opium dream; and then lost. As he had done for 'Christabel', Coleridge announced his intention of finishing the poem from the 'still surviving recollections in his mind'. The text itself referred to such a wish:

> Could I revive within me
> Her symphony and song . . .

Whether or not there was any truth in this story, introducing it here was a brilliant framing device. The public was fascinated by the idea that poetry could be written without effort, under the influence of drugs; and the concept of the lost poem was infinitely tantalising. By setting 'Kubla Khan' within this context, Coleridge not only found a way to intrigue the public in his poems, but also legitimised his failure to finish them.

In 1815 Wordsworth published an edition of his collected poems, with a new preface outlining his poetical principles, a development of the preface to the second edition of *Lyrical Ballads*. Coleridge, who was

---

* This review has been ascribed to Thomas Moore.
† i.e. Byron.

planning a collected edition of his own poems, was thrown off course. For more than a dozen years he had suspected that 'some where or other there is a radical Difference in our theoretical opinions respecting Poetry'.[72] Wordsworth's preface to the second edition of *Lyrical Ballads* had started these suspicions. Though 'half a child of my own brain', that preface had been nurtured by Wordsworth into something rather different from Coleridge's original conception. Now Coleridge decided to set out his own ideas about poetry in response to Wordsworth. He worked furiously, dictating his thoughts to his devoted friend Morgan. He was motivated in part by the sense that Wordsworth had appropriated his ideas without understanding them fully, and perhaps too by a sense of resentment that he was associated in the public mind with Wordsworth and Southey, and repeatedly attacked as such.

At first Coleridge thought a preface to his poems sufficient for his purpose. But soon he began to think of two volumes, one prose volume outlining his thoughts on poetry and criticism, and a separate volume of poems. He instructed the printer that his words should be set in the same font and in the same size as Wordsworth's. His critique of Wordsworth was a central theme. On the one hand he sought to subvert the critical theory put forward by Wordsworth, and to reclaim for himself some of his central concepts publicised by Wordsworth – in particular, the distinction between 'fancy' and imagination'; on the other he hailed Wordsworth as a great poet. He traced the poetic revolution initiated by himself and Wordsworth in *Lyrical Ballads*, and demonstrated that Wordsworth was the commanding poetic genius of the age, despite the inadequacy of his 'critical remarks'. One of Coleridge's motives was to correct the harm done to Wordsworth and his contemporaries by unprincipled and ignorant reviewers, and to establish a new standard of authoritative and impartial literary judgement founded on philosophical principles.[73]

The manuscript that Coleridge produced was a complex, often obscure work combining autobiography, philosophy and criticism – a history of his own mind, a prose counterpoint to *The Prelude*. The seed of this tangled tree was planted back in 1803, during Coleridge's heroic tramp across Scotland. 'Seem to have made up my mind to write my metaphysical works, as *my Life*, & *in* my Life – intermixed with all the other events/or history of the mind & fortunes of S.T. Coleridge.'[74] It was appropriate that he should use this semi-autobiographical form to express ideas so personally important to him. One interpretation of the book is as a middle-aged man's critique of his younger self. Indeed, it was a form of apologia, as Hazlitt was swift to point out when the book was eventually published. Coleridge decided to call it *Biographia Literaria*, with the subtitle *Biographical Sketches of My Literary Life and Opinions* – a deliberate echo of *The Life and Opinions of Tristram Shandy*, and perhaps an allusion to the complex structure of both works, with multiple digressions, and footnotes so long that they threatened to overwhelm the body of the text. He was conscious of this tendency in his writing: years before he had compared his thoughts to 'Surinam Toads – as they crawl on, little Toads vegetate out from back & side, grow quickly, & draw off attention from the mother toad'. He envied Southey's ability to say one thing at a time 'in short and close sentences'.[75]

Meanwhile Coleridge had assembled his poems into a volume which he called *Sibylline Leaves*, 'in allusion to the fragmentary and widely scattered state in which they have been long suffered to remain'.[76] The title refers to the enigmatic prophecies of the Sibyl, written in verse on leaves which she discarded to be dispersed by the wind, making them disordered and difficult to interpret. The Sibyl was said to have gathered these leaves together and bound them into nine volumes, which she offered for sale to the Roman King Tarquin. When he rejected her price as outrageously high, she burned three of the books, offering the remaining six at the same high price. Again he refused, and she burned three more volumes, offering the last three at the original price, which Tarquin wisely accepted.[77] Coleridge's use of this myth for the title of his collected poems was characteristically perverse.

For *Sibylline Leaves* Coleridge made substantial revisions to the 'Ancient Mariner', adding and deleting whole stanzas, and making numerous alterations elsewhere, transforming the nature of the poem into a more subtle, less judgemental tale. Though he was to make further changes in years to come, this is the essence of the version best known to subsequent generations. He also added a marginal gloss, as if written by a devout scholar of an earlier age trying to make sense of the poem in terms of orthodox religion. This device accentuated the sense of the poem as a timeless and mysterious parable, and distanced it from Coleridge himself as the author.

Two years earlier, after Wordsworth had begged him not to publish 'the poem addressed to me after hearing *mine* to you', Coleridge had assured Wordsworth that he had never thought of doing so without first consulting his old friend. Now, however, he included in *Sibylline Leaves* a revised version of the poem, entitled 'To a Gentleman: Composed on the Night after his Recitation of a Poem on the Growth of an Individual Mind'. This omitted some of the more personal passages from the original private tribute, particularly those referring to Coleridge's own unhappiness. But though Wordsworth was no longer mentioned by name, the identity of the 'Gentleman' was obvious – not least because a new line in the revised version of the poem* alluded to the concluding line of Wordsworth's 'Immortality' ode.

Though Coleridge had written *Biographia Literaria* at tremendous speed, so that it was in the hands of the printers by September 1815, it traced a tortuous route to publication and was not to appear in print until almost two years later. By this time Coleridge had left Morgan's house and was living in retreat in Highgate (where he would spend the rest of his life) with his doctor, James Gillman. He was anxious how Wordsworth might react to the book. But his old friend never wrote a line to him on the subject. Nor did he comment on the belated publication of 'Christabel' and 'Kubla Khan'. Wordsworth pretended to friends that he had only skimmed parts of *Biographia Literaria*, though later it became obvious that he had read the whole book – without pleasure. 'The praise is extravagant and the censure inconsiderate.'[78] Coleridge had pressed him to write a preface to *Lyrical Ballads*, and then nearly two decades later attacked him for

* 'Thoughts all too deep for words!'

doing so. Once Wordsworth had valued Coleridge's criticism of his work above all things – but not in public, not after the work itself had been written and published.

Towards the end of the year 1817, the Wordsworths came to London with Sara Hutchinson. One evening they dined in a small party which included Coleridge and his son Hartley. This seems to have been the first meeting between the two poets since the resolution of their quarrel five years before, and the first time Coleridge had seen Sara in almost eight years, since she had left Grasmere exhausted by her work on *The Friend*. After dinner they were joined by Lamb and his sister. Henry Crabb Robinson, who was also present, recorded the conversation, which he felt was 'not altogether as it ought to have been'. When Coleridge spoke, Wordsworth answered by dry, unfeeling contradiction. 'The manner of Coleridge to Wordsworth was most respectful, but Wordsworth towards Coleridge was cold and scornful.' After a while Coleridge accused Wordsworth of putting an unkind question, but Wordsworth made no apology. 'I was for the first time in my life not pleased with Wordsworth,' Crabb Robinson recorded in his diary; 'Coleridge appeared to advantage in his presence.' Coming away with the Lambs afterwards, he found that they felt the same.

A few days later Crabb Robinson called at Lamb's house after dinner and found a large party collected round the two poets. Coleridge, who was 'philosophising in his rambling way', had the larger body of listeners, while for most of the time Wordsworth was engaged in a *tête-à-tête*. At one point Crabb Robinson overheard Wordsworth reciting his own verse, while Coleridge too began to recite from memory: not his own poetry, but Wordsworth's.[79]

The young Keats (who revered Wordsworth and saw him several times during his stay in London) was sorry to find that his idol 'has left a bad impression where-ever he visited in town by his egotism, vanity, and bigotry'.[80] On one occasion when Keats called on Wordsworth he had been irritated to be kept waiting a long time, and then somewhat disgusted to find his host dressed in a stiff collar, and in a great hurry as he was due to dine with one of the commissioners of stamps.

Sara Coleridge reported to Poole on what she had heard of the meeting between Wordsworth and Coleridge (presumably from Hartley). Coleridge had been 'much agitated' at seeing the Wordsworths, 'but was very agreeable on the whole'. She had learned that her husband was now 'quite grey haired'.[81]

Over the next ten years the two old friends saw each other only a handful of times, when Wordsworth made one of his periodic visits to London. Both were now famous, revered as pioneers and reviled as defectors by a younger generation of Romantic poets. Their quarrel, and the reconciliation, were common knowledge. Anecdotes began to pile up. One described a salon where Wordsworth sat stiffly at one end of the room, surrounded by male admirers, while Coleridge lounged at the other, his audience mainly of women.

In 1820 Wordsworth published a book of sonnets, united by the theme of a single river. It was a variant of the idea Coleridge had proposed twenty years earlier, as Wordsworth conceded in an aggressively defensive postscript, saying that if he had been 'trespassing' or 'encroaching' on Coleridge's ground, he had done so 'insensibly'. Later in that year Coleridge was embarrassed by the unauthorised publication in *Blackwood's Magazine* of a private letter he had written critical of 'Atticus', clearly a pseudonym for Wordsworth.

Wordsworth's manner had become stern and withdrawn. The years of strain showed in his pinched, lined features and his pained, weary expression. His now sparse hair revealed a vast domed forehead. Visitors found him a formidable, brooding man, his form rigid as if from effort, or suffering.

Coleridge's hair was white, his body shrunk; his eyes, once so animated, appeared lost in an expressionless face. He now seemed an old bachelor, more like a distant uncle than a husband or father. In January 1823 his wife and their beautiful, clever daughter Sara (now twenty) visited Highgate for almost a month; he had not seen either of them for more than ten years. In April William and Mary came to

London with Sara Hutchinson, and dined in a party which included Coleridge, Lamb, Samuel Rogers and Thomas Moore: five poets around one table. Coleridge dominated the conversation, as he usually did. The following day Sara and the Wordsworths joined Coleridge and others for a musical evening, which Coleridge enjoyed greatly. Wordsworth pronounced himself 'perfectly delighted and satisfied', but sat alone, with his face covered, and was generally assumed to be asleep. Holidaying at Ramsgate later that year, Sara Hutchinson was surprised by a visit from Coleridge, who inveigled himself into her party, alarming her into leaving the resort suddenly.[82]

In the eyes of the public, Coleridge was seen as a sage, who (in the young Carlyle's words) had withdrawn 'from the inanity of Life's battle'. His table talk was taken down by admirers and published. The great philosophical prose work, like the great philosophical poem, remained unwritten. Coleridge seemed calm, almost resigned. Indeed he was spoken of nostalgically, as if he were already dead.[83]

In the summer of 1828 the two poets toured Belgium, Germany and the Netherlands, together with Wordsworth's daughter Dorothy, known in the family as Dora to avoid confusion with her aunt, and jokingly called Rotha (after the river that runs through Grasmere Vale) by Coleridge, who thought of himself as her godfather, though there seems to have been some doubt about this. Wordsworth and his daughter had decided to undertake the tour on the spur of the moment, during a visit to London, and they invited Coleridge to join them. In Brussels they met the novelist Thomas Colley Grattan, who afterwards accompanied them some of the way. He described Coleridge as 'of a full and lazy appearance, but not actually stout'. His expression was 'placid and benevolent', his grey eyes 'full of intelligent softness'. He dressed in black, with black silk stockings and breeches buttoned and tied at the knees, so that he resembled a dissenting parson, or even an itinerant preacher. Wordsworth was 'a perfect antithesis to Coleridge – tall, wiry, harsh in features, coarse in figure, inelegant in looks'. His manner was 'unrefined and unprepossessing'. He was 'roughly dressed' in a long brown *surtout*, striped duck

trousers, fustian gaiters and thick shoes; he looked more like a mountain farmer than a poet.

'We get on delightfully,' Dora reported to her friend and future
husband Edward Quillinan, though she added that Coleridge had
been overpowered by the heat during the first part of their journey
and for two days had been very ill. Coleridge became irritable when
Wordsworth appeared to be directing the arrangements without con-
sultation. In German code he reflected in his notebooks on Wordsworth's egoism, his meanness, and his tedious monologues:

> Never does he turn round, or ponder, whether one has
> [already] understood him, but each word is followed by three,
> four, five syn- or homonyms, in a tiring sequence of eddies,
> and in this manner for three, four hours . . . I was repelled by
> the infinite number of dissonances which his way of thinking,
> feeling and arguing created with my own – the worst being
> his great worries over money and trifling money matters.
> Recently, all the shortcomings, which marked him in his
> early manly years, have increased considerably; the grand
> flourishings of his philosophic and poetic genius, have with-
> ered and dried.[84]

Coleridge objected to Wordsworth's 'continuous, never-intermitting,
deep murmuring', which he interpreted as a ruse to prevent auditors
from escaping.

In December 1830 Wordsworth and his wife passed through London,
and on Christmas Day they dined with Coleridge, in a party that
included his daughter Sara and her husband and cousin Henry Nelson
Coleridge. This was the last recorded meeting between the two old
friends, and Coleridge recorded it as 'a happy Christmas Day
throughout'.[85]

In the late spring of 1834 Sara Hutchinson again came to London,
and this time she visited Coleridge in Highgate. He was in great pain,
and it was obvious to her that he was dying: 'Greatly was I shocked
at the changed appearance of my dear old Friend.' She came to see
him twice more during her stay. A couple of months later, when she
was back in the Lakes, she had word that 'poor dear Coleridge is

gone!' He had died on 25 July, aged sixty-one; for more than half his life he had been predicting his imminent death. The end had been calm and happy, so she had been told; 'the disease was at his heart'.[86]

Wordsworth showed no emotion on receiving the long-expected news. He reflected sadly that though they had seen little of each other for the past twenty years,

> his mind has been habitually present with me, with an accompanying feeling that he was still in the flesh. That frail tie is broken and I, and most of those who are nearest and dearest to me must prepare and endeavour to follow him.[87]

In a brief burst of the old affection, like a sudden ray of sunshine on a cloudy day, he described his old friend as 'the most *wonderful* man that he had ever known'.[88]

In Coleridge's 'Christabel' there is a prophetic passage of lament for a lost friendship:

> Alas! They had been friends in youth;
> But whispering tongues can poison truth;
> And constancy lives in realms above;
> And life is thorny; and youth is vain;
> And to be wroth with one we love
> Doth work like madness in the brain.
> And thus it chanced, as I divine,
> With Roland and Sir Leoline.
> Each spake words of high disdain
> And insult to his heart's best brother:
> They parted – ne'er to meet again!
> But never either found another
> To free the hollow heart from paining –
> They stood aloof, the scars remaining,
> Like cliffs which had been rent asunder;
> A dreary sea now flows between;
> But neither heat, nor frost, nor thunder,
> Shall wholly do away, I ween,
> The marks of that which once had been.

APPENDIX

Coleridge's Plan for *The Recluse*

(Extracted from Coleridge's letter to Wordsworth,
30 May 1815)

In order therefore to explain the *disappointment* I must recall to your mind what my *expectations* were: and as these again were founded on the supposition, that (in whatever order it might be published) the Poem of the growth of your own mind was as the ground-plat[form] and the Roots, out of which the Recluse was to have sprung up as the Tree . . .

. . . THE RECLUSE I had (from what I had at different times gathered from your conversation on the Plan) anticipated as commencing with you set down and settled in an abiding Home, and that with the Description of that Home you were to begin a *Philosophical Poem*, the result and fruits of a Spirit so fram'd and so disciplin'd, as had been told in the former. Whatever in Lucretius* is Poetry is not philosophical, whatever is philosophical is not Poetry: and in the very Pride of confident Hope I looked forward to the Recluse, as the *first* and *only* true Phil. Poem in existence. Of course, I expected the Colours, Music, imaginative Life, and Passion of *Poetry*; but the matter and arrangement of *Philosophy* – not doubting from the advantages of the Subject that the Totality of a System was not only capable of being harmonized with, but even calculated to aid, the unity (Beginning, Middle, and End) of a *Poem*. Thus, whatever the Length of the Work might be, still it was a *determinate* Length: of the subjects announced each would have it's own appointed place, and excluding repetitions each would relieve & rise in interest above the other –. I supposed you first to have meditated the faculties of Man in the abstract, in their correspondence with his Sphere of action,

* A reference to Lucretius' philosophical poem *De Rerum Natura*.

and first, in the Feeling, Touch, and Taste, then in the Eye, & last in the Ear, to have laid a solid & immoveable foundation for the Edifice by removing the sandy Sophisms of Locke, and the Mechanic Dogmatists, and demonstrating that the Senses were living growths and developments of the Mind & Spirit in a much juster as well as higher sense, than the mind can be said to be formed by the Senses –. Next, I understood that you would take the Human Race in the concrete, have exploded the absurd notion of Pope's Essay on Man, Darwin,* and all the countless Believers – even (strange to say) among Xtians† of Man's having pro-gressed from an Ouran Ooutang state‡ – so contrary to all History, to all Religion, nay, to all Possibility – to have affirmed a Fall in some sense, as a fact, the possibility of which cannot be understood from the Nature of the Will, but the reality of which is attested by Experience & Con-science – Fallen men contemplated in the different ages of the World, & in the different states – Savage – Barbarous – Civilized – the lonely Cot, or Borderer's Wigwam – the Village – the Manufacturing Town – Sea-port – City – Universities – and not disguising the sore evils, under which the whole Creation groans, to point out however a manifest Scheme of Redemption from this Slavery, of Reconciliation from this Enmity with Nature – what are the Obstacles, the *Antichrist* that must be & already is – and to conclude by a grand didactic swell on the necessary identity of a true Philosophy with true Religion, agreeing in the results and differing only as the analytic and synthetic process, as discursive from intuitive, the former chiefly useful as perfecting the latter – in short, the necessity of a general revolution in the modes of developing & disciplin-ing the human mind by the substitution of Life, and Intelligence (con-sidered in it's different powers from the Plant up to that state in which the differences of Degree becomes a new kind (man, self-consciousness) but yet not by essential opposition) for the philosophy of mechanism which in every thing that is most worthy of the human Intellect strikes *Death*, and cheats itself by mistaking clear Images for distant conceptions, and which idly demands Conceptions where Intuitions alone are possible or adequate to the majesty of Truth. – In short, Facts elevated into Theory – Theory into Laws – & Laws into living & intelligent Powers –

* Erasmus Darwin (1731–1802), author of *The Botanic Garden.*
† Christians.
‡ Lord Monboddo (1714–99) had put forward the hypothesis that mankind was descen-ded from orang-utans.

true Idealism necessarily perfecting itself in Realism, & Realism refining itself into Idealism. –

Such or something like this was the Plan, I had supposed that you were engaged on . . .[1]

ACKNOWLEDGEMENTS
NOTES
INDEX

ACKNOWLEDGEMENTS

It was my old friend Sean Magee who suggested that I should write about the friendship between Wordsworth and Coleridge. In the equivalent place in one of his books, Professor Peter Hennessy refers to its genesis in 'the extraordinarily fertile mind of the incomparable Sean Magee', and I should like to make a similar acknowledgement. 'Eclipse is first, and the rest nowhere.'

Anyone who writes about either Wordsworth or Coleridge owes a great debt to the many fine scholars, too numerous to list here, who have edited their poems and letters, and in the case of Coleridge, his notebooks. I have also found invaluable Mark L. Reed's two-volume chronology of Wordsworth.

I should like to thank Oxford University Press for permission to quote from the letters of both men, and Routledge & Kegan Paul for permission to quote from the Coleridge notebooks.

In writing this book I have tried to form my own conclusions from primary sources. But it would be churlish not to acknowledge my special debt to the excellent biographies of Wordsworth by Mary Moorman and Stephen Gill, and of Coleridge by Richard Holmes and Rosemary Ashton; as well as to two stimulating books which concentrate on particular periods, Nicholas Roe's study of Wordsworth and Coleridge in the radical 1790s, and John Worthen's account of the 'gang' in 1802. Bibliographical details of these works are given in the list of abbreviations that precedes the notes.

I am particularly grateful to those friends who kindly agreed to read and comment on my book in draft: Paul Cheshire, David Fairer, Sean French, Felicity James, Sean Magee, George Misiewicz, Keith Perry and Duncan Wu. My wife Robyn read the book several times and as always provided many helpful criticisms. I am grateful too to Pamela Clemit who read passages from my book and corrected more than one careless error; to Hugh Griffith for his translations from the Latin; and to Pepsy

Dening for translating Annette Vallon's letters and reading and commenting on various drafts. I have benefited much from the advice I have received, but I have not always taken it, and responsibility for the flaws and errors in this book is mine alone.

I must thank Derrick Woolf for allowing me to look round Coleridge's cottage at Nether Stowey when it was not open to the public; Elspeth Scothern for showing me Alfoxton Park Hotel; the staff of Wordsworth's house in Cockermouth for keeping it open for me until the last possible moment on the last day of the season; and Jeronime Palmer and Scott Ligertwood for showing me Greta Hall, now a highly-recommended guest house.

The London Library has been customarily helpful and efficient in finding and supplying books; I am grateful to its staff, and also to the former Librarian, Alan Bell, who very generously allowed me to buy his set of the Wordsworth letters at what I now realise to have been a ridiculously low price.

I should particularly like to thank Doug and Claudie Hawes for their hospitality in Paris and in the Dordogne; and Lucy Trench and Robert Collingwood for several times lending me their cottage on the Welsh border when I needed to get away.

I am grateful to my editors for their belief in the book and for their many valuable comments on the typescript: Mike Fishwick and then Richard Johnson in England, and Paul Slovak in America. I must also thank Robert Lacey for his tactful copy-editing, and Douglas Matthews for preparing the index with his usual skill. Finally I wish to thank my agent Andrew Wylie for his encouragement and support throughout.

ADAM SISMAN
Bath, May 2006

NOTES

ABBREVIATIONS

Bondage	*Samuel Taylor Coleridge: The Bondage of Opium* by Molly Lefebure (London, 1974)
CL	Charles Lamb
Cottle	*Reminiscences of Samuel Taylor Coleridge and Robert Southey* by Joseph Cottle (London, 1847)
De Quincey	*Recollections of the Lakes and the Lake Poets* by Thomas De Quincey, ed. David Wright (Harmondsworth, 1970)
DW	Dorothy Wordsworth
DWJ	*Journals of Dorothy Wordsworth*, ed. Ernest de Selincourt (London, 1941) 2 vols
Essays	*Essays on His Times*, ed. David V. Erdman (Princeton, 1978) (*Collected Works of Samuel Taylor Coleridge*, 3) 3 vols
FW	Francis Wrangham
Gang	*The Gang: Coleridge, the Hutchinsons and Wordsworth in 1802* by John Worthern (New Haven & London, 2001)
GB	Sir George Beaumont
GC	George Coleridge
GCB	Grosvenor Charles Bedford
Gill	*William Wordsworth: A Life* by Stephen Gill (Oxford, 1989)
HCR	*Henry Crabb Robinson on Books and their Writers*, ed. Edith J. Morley (London, 1938) 3 vols
Holmes	*Coleridge: Early Visions & Later Reflections* by Richard Holmes (London, 1989 & 1998) 2 vols
HWB	Horace Walpole Bedford
JC	Joseph Cottle
JP	Jane Pollard (later Mrs John Marshall)
JPE	John Prior Estlin
JT	John Thelwall
JW	Josiah Wedgwood

LCML	*Letters of Charles and Mary Anne Lamb*, ed. Edwin W. Marrs, Jr (Ithaca & London, 1975–) 3 vols to date
Lectures	*Lectures 1795 on Politics and Religion*, ed. Lewis Patton and Peter Mann ((Princeton, 1971) (*Collected Works of Samuel Taylor Coleridge*, 1)
Love	*The Bondage of Love: A Life of Mrs Samuel Taylor Coleridge* by Molly Lefebure (London, 1986)
LSTC	*Collected Letters of Samuel Taylor Coleridge*, ed. E.L. Griggs (Oxford, 1956–71) 6 vols
LWDW	*Letters of William and Dorothy Wordsworth*, ed. E. de Selincourt, 2nd edition revised by Chester L. Shaver, Mary Moorman and Alan G. Hill (Oxford, 1967–93) 8 vols
MB	Margaret, Lady Beaumont
Memoirs	*Memoirs of William Wordsworth*, ed. Christopher Wordsworth (1851)
MH	Mary Hutchinson
Minnow	*Minnow among Tritons: Mrs S.T. Coleridge's Letters to Thomas Poole, 1799–1834*, ed. Stephen Potter (London, 1934)
Moorman	*William Wordsworth: A Biography* by Mary Moorman (Oxford, 1957 & 1965) 2 vols
Mrs RS	Edith Southey
Mrs STC	Sara Coleridge
NBSTC	*The Notebooks of Samuel Taylor Coleridge*, ed. Kathleen Coburn (New York & London, 1957–2002) 5 double vols
NLRS	*New Letters of Robert Southey*, ed. Kenneth Curry (New York & London, 1965) 2 vols
Poetry	*Poetical Works*, ed. J.C.C. Mays (Princeton, 2001) (*Collected Works of Samuel Taylor Coleridge*, 16) 3 vols
Poole	*Thomas Poole and His Friends* by Elizabeth Sandford (London, 1888) 2 vols
Prelude	*The Prelude, or The Growth of a Poet's Mind by William Wordsworth* (text of 1805 unless otherwise specified), ed. Ernest de Selincourt (Oxford, 1933)
Radicals	*Wordsworth and Coleridge: The Radical Years* by Nicholas Roe (Oxford, 1988)
RS	Robert Southey
RW	Richard Wordsworth
STC	Samuel Taylor Coleridge
Storey	*Robert Southey: A Life* by Mark Storey (Oxford, 1997)
Table Talk	*Table Talk and Omniana* by Samuel Taylor Coleridge (Oxford, 1917)

TP   Thomas Poole

Watchman   *The Watchman* ed. Lewis Patton (Princeton, 1970) (*Collected Works of Samuel Taylor Coleridge*, 2)

WCEY   *Wordsworth: The Chronology of the Early Years, 1770–1799* by Mark L. Reed (Cambridge, Massachusetts, 1967)

WCMY   *Wordsworth: The Chronology of the Middle Years, 1800–1815* by Mark L. Reed (Cambridge, Massachusetts, 1975)

WM   William Mathews

WProse   *The Prose Works of William Wordsworth*, ed. W.J.B. Owen & Jane Worthington Smyser (Oxford, 1974) 3 vols

WPW   *The Poetical Works of William Wordsworth*, ed. E. de Selincourt & Helen Darbyshire (Oxford, 1940–49) 5 vols

WW   William Wordsworth

INTRODUCTION

1 Mary Wordsworth to Mrs STC, 7 November 1845, *LWDW*, 7, 719
2 Quoted in Kathleen Coburn: *In Search of Coleridge* (London, 1977), 82
3 *Gang*, 6

PROLOGUE

1 RS to Caroline Bowles, 13 February 1829; Edward Dowden (ed.): *The Correspondence of Robert Southey with Caroline Bowles* (Dublin, 1881), 52
2 H.T. Dickinson: *British Radicals and the French Revolution, 1789–1815* (Oxford, 1985), 7; Gregory Claeys (ed.): *Political Writings of the 1790s* (London, 1995), 3, 21–2

PART I: STRANGERS

1 *Prelude*, X, 693–4

1 : REVOLUTION

1 WW to WM, 6 & 17 September 1790; *LWDW*, 1, 36
2 *Prelude*, VI, 352–4
3 *Prelude*, VI, 408–13
4 WW to DW, 6 & 16 September 1790; *LWDW*, 1, 36
5 *Prelude*, VI, 694–6
6 Robin Jarvis, 'Landscape and Locomotion: Coleridge the Walker', in the *Coleridge Bulletin*, New Series 13, Spring 1999, 39–40; Rebecca Solnit: *Wanderlust: A History of Walking* (London, 2001)
7 *Prelude*, VI, 681–6
8 *Prelude*, IX, 18–19
9 *Prelude*, VII, 524–43; & 1850 *Prelude*, VII, 512–43
10 *Radicals*, 24–37
11 DW & WW to JP 26 June 1791; *LWDW*, 1, 51
12 WW to WM, 23 November 1791 & 19 May 1792; *LWDW*, 1, 62 & 76
13 *Prelude*, III, 79–118 & VI, 55–76
14 *Prelude*, III, 75–120
15 DW & WW to JP, 7 December & 26 June 1791; *LWDW*, 1, 66 & 52

16 *Prelude*, IX, 63–80
17 *Prelude*, X, 191–201 & 659–65
18 WW to WM, 19 May 1792; *LWDW*, 1, 77
19 *Prelude*, IX, 164–8
20 Moorman, 1, 190
21 WW to RW, 19 December 1791, *LWDW*, 1, 70
22 *Prelude*, IX, 218–21
23 *Prelude*, IX, 230–6
24 '. . . every word/They uttered was a dart . . .' *Prelude*, IX, 261–2
25 WW to WM, 19 May 1792; *LWDW*, 1, 77–8
26 *Prelude*, IX, 288–93
27 *Prelude*, IX, 124–5
28 *Prelude*, X, 689–702
29 Radicals, 49ff
30 Quoted in ibid., 68
31 *Prelude*, X, 728–35
32 *Prelude*, IX, 415–24
33 *Prelude*, IX, 316–17 & 512–24
34 Quoted in Simon Schama: *Citizens* (London, 1989), 640
35 *Prelude*, X, 222–3
36 *Prelude*, X, 102–3 & 131–6
37 Radicals, 82
38 WW to RW, 19 December 1791; *LWDW*, 1, 71
39 De Quincey, 175
40 *Prelude*, X, 194–201
41 *Citizens*, op. cit., 649
42 WW to RW, 3 September 1792; *LWDW*, 1, 81
43 *Prelude*, X, 190–1

2 : REACTION

1 Quoted in Radicals, 100
2 WW to WM, 23 May 1794; *LWDW*, 1, 120
3 *Prelude*, X, 275–8
4 *Prelude*, X, 249–58
5 *WProse*, 1, 31–49
6 Blair Worden: *Roundhead Reputations: The English Civil Wars and the Passions of Posterity* (London, 2001), 207
7 Radicals, 16
8 *Gentleman's Magazine*, ii (December 1834), 606
9 STC to Mary Evans, 7 February 1793; *LSTC*, 1, 51
10 Radicals, 101–8
11 STC to GC, 24 January 1792; *LSTC*, 1, 20
12 STC to GC, 11 November 1792; *LSTC*, 1, 42
13 Holmes, 1, 39
14 STC to TP, 9 October 1797; *LSTC*, 1, 347 & 347–8
15 STC to TP, 16 October 1797; *LSTC*, 1, 354
16 Alethea Hayter: *Opium and the Romantic Imagination* (London, 1968), 34
17 STC to Mrs Evans, 13 February 1792; *LSTC*, 1, 21
18 Henry Gunning: *Reminiscences of the University, Town, and County of Cambridge* (Cambridge, 1854), 1, 274
19 *Gentleman's Magazine*, ii (December 1834), 606
20 STC to GC, 23 February 1794; *LSTC*, 1, 67
21 STC to GC, 13 January & 5 August 1793; *LSTC*, 1, 46 & 59
22 STC to GC, 23 February 1794; *LSTC*, 1, 68
23 Emile Legouis: *William Wordsworth and Annette Vallon* (London & Toronto, 1922), 124–33
24 DW to JP, 16 June 1793; *LWDW*, 1, 95
25 Introductory note to *Guilt and Sorrow*; *WPW*, 1, 94–5
26 Gill, 74. In quoting Professor Gill, I do not mean to suggest that he has succumbed to this temptation.
27 WW to John Kenyon, summer 1838; *LWDW*, 6, 616
28 *Prelude*, XII, 318–26
29 Quoted from a letter of WW's now

lost in DW to JP, 10 & 12 July 1793; *LWDW*, 1, 102

30 DW to JP, July 1787; *LWDW*, 1, 2–3

31 WW to DW, 6 & 16 September 1790; *LWDW*, 1, 35

32 DW to JP, 26 June 1791, 16 February and 10 & 12 July 1793; *LWDW*, 1, 51, 87 & 98

33 DW to JP, 16 June 1793; *LWDW*, 1, 95

34 DW to JP, 10 & 12 July 1793; *LWDW*, 1, 98

35 Ibid., 103

36 DW to JP, 30 April 1790; *LWDW*, 1, 28

37 DW to JP, 16 June 1793 & 16 February 1793; *LWDW*, 1, 93 & 88

38 Moorman, 1, 212–13

39 For a contrary view, see Kenneth Johnston's *The Hidden Wordsworth: Poet, Lover, Rebel, Spy* (New York & London, 1998), 358–400

40 DW to Mrs Christopher Crackanthorpe, 21 April 1794; *LWDW*, 1, 116–17

41 DW to unknown correspondent, April 1794; *LWDW*, 1, 113

3 : IDEALISM

1 RS to GCB, [?] 22 November 1793; cited Storey, 52. Storey's reference does not tally. Also cited in Radicals, 166

2 RS to HWB, 12 December 1793; *NLRS*, 1, 40

3 RS to GCB, June 1794; *NLRS*, 1, 57 & 58; ibid, 29 October 1793; quoted in Storey, 37

4 RS to GCB, February & 29 October 1793; *NLRS*, 1, 19 & quoted in Storey, 37

5 RS to HWB, 12 December 1793 & to GCB, 1 June 1794; *NLRS*, 1, 39 & 54

6 WW to WM, 17 February 1794; *LWDW*, 1, 112

7 WW to WM, 23 May 1794; *LWDW*, 1, 120

8 WW to Anne Taylor, 9 April 1801; DW to JP, 16 February 1793; *LWDW*, 1, 327–8 & 89

9 Jonathan Wordsworth: *The Music of Humanity* (London, 1968), 184–5

10 WW to WM, 8 June & 23 May 1794; *LWDW*, 1, 123–4 & 120

11 RW to WW, 23 May 1794; DW to RW, 28 May 1794; *LWDW*, 1, 120–1

12 WW to WM, 8 June 1794; *LWDW*, 1, 123–4

13 William St Clair: *The Godwins and the Shelleys* (London, 1989), 85

14 STC to GC, 8 February 1794; *LSTC*, 1, 63–4

15 STC to RS, 6 July 1794; *LSTC*, 1, 83

16 STC to George Dyer, February 1795; *LSTC*, 1, 152–3; Holmes, 1, 63

17 RS to GCB, 12 June 1794; *NLRS*, 1, 58

18 Ibid., 56

19 RS to GCB, 20 July, & to HWB, 1 August & 12 November 1794; *NLRS*, 1, 61, 65–6 & 87

20 RS to GCB; *NLRS*, 1, 14

21 STC to RS, 6 July 1794; *LSTC*, 1, 83–5

22 STC to RS, 13 July 1794; *LSTC*, 1, 85–90

23 Ibid., 87–8

24 RS: *Letters from England* (1807, reissued and edited by Jack Simmons, London, 1951), 479

25 Tom Mayberry: *Coleridge and Wordsworth: The Crucible of Friendship* (Stroud, 1992, revised edition 2000), 41

26 Cottle, 6

27 RS to GCB, 21 August 1794; *NLRS*, 1, 68–9

28 *Poole*, 68–9

29 Quoted in Radicals, 209

30 *Prelude*, X, 335 & 373–80

31 *Prelude*, X, 411–12 & 416

32 *Prelude*, X, 177–88

33 *Prelude*, X, 429–39

34 WW to WM, 8 June 1794; *LWDW*, 1, 128

35 *Prelude*, X, 306–12

36 *Prelude*, X, 361–5

37 *Prelude*, X, 466–9

38 *Prelude*, X, 577–85

39 *Poole*, 72. Mrs Sandford, writing in the 1880s and influenced by Southey's later reputation, casts some doubt on this story, but it fits with comments made in his more recently discovered letters of the time.

40 RS to HWB, 22 August 1794; *NLRS*, 1, 73

41 STC to Charles Heath, 29 August 1794; *LSTC*, 1, 97

42 RS to HWB, 22 August 1794; *NLRS*, 1, 71 & 74

43 WW to William Calvert, 1 October 1794; *LWDW*, 1, 130

44 WW to GB, 23 February 1805, *LWDW*, 1, 546

45 RW to WW, 13 October 1794; *LWDW*, 1, 132n

4 : SEDITION

1 STC to RS, 1 September 1794; *LSTC*, 1, 98

2 STC to RS, 11 & 19 September 1794; *LSTC*, 1, 101 & 106

3 STC to RS, 1 September 1794; *LSTC*, 1, 99

4 STC to RS, 21 October and 3 November 1794; *LSTC*, 1, 114 & 122–3

5 RS to HWB, 22 August 1794; *NLRS*, 1, 72

6 STC to RS, 18 September 1794; *LSTC*, 1, 103

7 STC to FW, 26 September 1794; *LSTC*, 1, 107

8 STC to RS, 9 December 1794; *LSTC*, 1, 132

9 Quoted in STC to RS, 13 November 1795; *LSTC*, 1, 164

10 STC to Edith Fricker, 17 September 1794; *LSTC*, 1, 102

11 STC to RS, 21 & 23 October 1794; *LSTC*, 1, 112–18 & 120

12 STC to RS, 17 December 1794; *LSTC*, 1, 143

13 STC to FW, 24 October 1794; *LSTC*, 1, 121

14 STC to Mary Evans, early November 1794; *LSTC*, 1, 129–31

15 STC to GC, 6 November 1794; *LSTC*, I, 125–6

16 *Poole*, 68–9

17 RS to Thomas Southey, 6 November 1794; *NLRS*, 1, 86

18 STC to RS, 29 December 1794; *LSTC*, 1, 147

19 STC to RS, 17 December 1794; *LSTC*, 1, 138–9

20 STC to RS, 21 October 1794; *LSTC*, 1, 115

21 STC to RS, 13 July 1794; *LSTC*, 1, 86

22 STC to RS, 29 December 1794; *LSTC*, 1, 145

23 STC to RS, 9 & 29 December 1794; *LSTC*, 1, 132 & 146

24 STC to RS and RS to Sarah Fricker, 2 & 9 January 1795; *LSTC*, 1, 148 & 148n

25 WW to WM, 7 November 1794; *LWDW*, 1, 135

26 *Prelude*, X, 645–56

27 WW to WM, 24 December 1794 & 7 January 1795; *LWDW*, 1, 137 & 139

28 WW to WM, 7 November 1794; *LWDW*, 1, 136

29 WW to FW, 20 November 1795; *LWDW*, 1, 159

30 STC to George Dyer, late February 1795, *LSTC*, 1, 152

31 RS to Thomas Southey, 21 March 1795; *NLRS*, 1, 93: RS to GCB, 8 February 1795; C.C. Southey (ed.): *Life and Correspondence of Robert Southey* (London, 1849–50), 1, 231

32 Cottle, 11–12

33 STC to George Dyer, 10 March 1795; *LSTC*, 1, 155

34 Introduction to *Lectures*, xxxv–xxxvi; STC to RS, 13 November 1795; *LSTC*, 1, 172

35 Introduction to *Lectures*, liii–lxxx

36 *The Observer* (Bristol, 1794); quoted in Seamus Perry (ed.): *S.T. Coleridge: Interviews and Reflections* (Basingstoke, 2000), 39

37 RS to HWB, 11 December 1793; *NLRS*, 1, 37

38 Robert Woof: 'Wordsworth and Coleridge: Some Early Matters' in Jonathan Wordsworth (ed.): *Bicentenary Wordsworth Studies* (1970), 83–7

39 Note to 'Lines Written at Shurton Bars', in *Poems on Various Subjects* (1796)

40 See Paul Magnuson: 'The "Conversation" Poems' in Lucy Newlyn (ed.): *The Cambridge Companion to Coleridge* (2002), 32–44

41 RS to GCB, October 1795; *NLRS*, 1, 101

42 STC to RS, 13 November 1794; *LSTC*, 1, 163–73

43 DW to JP, 2 & 3 September 1795; *LWDW*, 1, 149

44 Ibid., 150

45 Ibid.

46 Holmes, 1, 176, drawing on research by William St Clair

47 WW to WM, 20 & 24 October 1795; *LWDW*, 1, 153–4

48 Kathryn Cave (ed.): *Diary of Joseph Farington* (New Haven & London, 1982), 10, 3628

49 Mary Wordsworth to Mrs STC, 7 November 1845, *LWDW*, 7, 719

50 See Tim May, 'The Pantisocrats in College Street', *Notes and Queries*, December 2005, 456–60, on the location of these lodgings

51 WW to FW, 20 November 1795; *LWDW*, 1, 158

52 'Wordsworth and Coleridge: Some Early Matters', op. cit., 83ff

53 *Memoirs*, 2, 443

54 *Poole*, 78–9

55 DW to JP, 16 February 1793; *LWDW*, 1, 89

56 Christopher Wordsworth: *Social Life at the English Universities* (1874), 589–90

57 *Prelude*, VI, 292–6, 305–9 & 316 –26

PART II: FRIENDS

1 *NBSTC*, 13

5 : CONTACT

1 DW to JP, 19 March 1797 & 7 March 1796; *LWDW*, 1, 180–1 & 166

2 WW to WM, 20 & 24 October 1795; *LWDW*, 1, 154

3 DW to ?, 1799; *LWDW*, 1, 281

4 WW to FW, 20 November 1795; *LWDW*, 1, 159

5 WW to WM, 20 & 24 October 1795 and DW to JP, 30 November 1796; *LWDW*, 1, 154 & 162

6 WW to JC, January 1796; *LWDW*, 1, 163

7 *Star*, 17 & 20 November 1795; *Lectures*, Appendix B1, 361

8 *Watchman*, xxxii–xxxiii

9 Cottle, 75–6

10 G.L. Tuckett to Robert Allen, [?] February 1796; *LSTC*, 1, 192n

11 STC to John Edwards, 29 January, and to Josiah Wade, 18 January 1796; *LSTC*, 1, 179 & 176

12 STC to John Edwards, 29 January 1796; *LSTC*, 1, 179–80

13 STC to Josiah Wade, c.10 February 1796; *LSTC*, 1, 184–5

14 STC to JC, 22 February 1796; *LSTC*, 1, 185–6

15 STC to JC, October 1795; *LSTC*, 1, 162

16 STC to JC, early March & c.12 March 1796; *LSTC*, 1, 187 & 189

17 STC to Josiah Wade, c.14 March 1796; *LSTC*, 1, 190

18 STC to John Edwards, 12 March 1796; *LSTC*, 1, 188

19 STC to John Edwards, 20 March 1796; *LSTC*, 1, 191

20 Ibid., 192

21 STC to JC, late March 1796; *LSTC*, 1, 193–4

22 Mark Storey sees 'good reason to believe that Southey was the author of the piece' (Storey, 95). But this seems unlikely, since Southey did not return from Portugal until after *The Watchman* folded.

23 STC to TP, 30 March 1796; *LSTC*, 1, 195

24 STC to JT, late April 1796; *LSTC*, 1, 205

25 STC to RS, 11 December 1794; *LSTC*, 1, 137

26 STC to TP, 5 May 1796; *LSTC*, 1, 207

27 STC to JPE, 4 July 1796; *LSTC*, 1, 224

28 Quoted in STC to TP, 30 March 1796; *LSTC*, 1, 195

29 CL to STC, 8–10 June & 1 December 1796; *LCML*, 1, 17 & 65–9. Marrs prints 'top' rather than 'loss' (as Lucas, an earlier editor of Lamb's letters, has it), but Lucas's transcription makes more sense to me.

30 CL to STC, 27 May & 8–10 June 1796; *LCML*, 1, 4 & 19

31 CL to STC, 10 December 1796; *LCML*, 1, 78

32 CL to STC, 28 January 1798; *LCML*, 1, 127

33 CL to STC, 30–31 May 1796; *LCML*, 1, 10

34 CL to STC, 8 November 1796; *LCML*, 1, 60

35 STC to JT, late April 1796; *LSTC*, 1, 204–5

36 *Poetry*, 1, 264–5

37 Duncan Wu, 'Coleridge, Thelwall, and the Politics of Poetry', in *The Coleridge Bulletin* (New Series), 4 (Autumn 1994), 23–44

38 STC to JT, 13 May 1796; *LSTC*, 1, 215–16

39 Ibid., 213–14 & 215

40 STC to JT, 13 November, 17 December & 13 May 1796; *LSTC*, 1, 253, 277 & 216

41 *NBSTC*, 6783

42 STC to JT, 13 & 19 November 1796; *LSTC*, 1, 254 & 259–60

43 STC to Benjamin Flower, 11 November 1796; *LSTC*, 1, 268

44 *Prelude*, X, 791–4

45 STC to TP, 5 May 1796; *LSTC*, 1, 208

46 WW to FW and DW to JP, 7 March 1796; *LWDW*, 1, 168 & 166

47 Azariah Pinney to WW, 25 March 1796; Beregen Evans & Hester Pinney: 'Racedown and the Wordsworths', *Review of English Studies* (January 1932), VIII, no. 29, 13

48 Azariah Pinney to James Tobin, 12 April 1796; ibid., 12

49 STC to JT, 13 May 1796; *LSTC*, 1, 215–16

50 Though a fragment of a letter published in James Gillman's *Life of Samuel Taylor Coleridge* (reprinted in *LWDW*, 1, 156) appears to suggest a subsequent visit by Wordsworth to Bristol to see Southey and Coleridge, Robert Woof ('Wordsworth and Coleridge: Some Early Matters', op. cit.) has shown that this is almost certainly garbled.

51 STC to JPE & TP, 4 July 1796; *LSTC*, 1, 222 & 226–7

52 CL to STC, 17 October 1796; *LCML*, 1, 51

53 STC to Benjamin Flower, 27 December 1796; *LSTC*, 1, 247

54 CL to STC, 28 October 1796; *LCML*, 1, 57

55 STC to RS, 27 December 1796;
   LSTC, 1, 290–1
56 Cottle, 106–7
57 STC to JT, 31 December 1796; *LSTC*,
   1, 294

6 : RETREAT

1 STC to TP, 4 July, 22 August,
   24 September, 1 & 7 November
   1796; *LSTC*, 1, 226, 230, 235, 241 &
   251; TP to STC, 8 August 1796;
   Poole, 92–3
2 E.V. Lucas: *Charles Lamb and the
   Lloyds* (London, 1898), 20
3 STC to Charles Lloyd, Senior,
   15 October 1796; *LSTC*, 1, 240
4 STC to JT, 17 December 1796; *LSTC*,
   1, 277
5 STC to George Dyer, 10 March
   1796; *LSTC*, 1, 154
6 STC to TP, 5 & 7 November 1796;
   LSTC, 1, 248 & 251
7 STC to TP, 12 & 13 December 1796;
   LSTC, 1, 269–276
8 WW to WM, 21 March 1796, & to
   FW, 25 February 1797; *LWDW*, 1, 169
   & 178
9 *Prelude*, XI, 74–8
10 WW to WM, 21 March 1796;
   LWDW, 1, 169
11 DW to JP, 19 March 1797; *LWDW*, 1,
   181
12 *Prelude*, X, 760–70
13 *Prelude*, X, 807–9 & 815–30
14 *Prelude*, X, 872–8
15 Gill, 108–9
16 *Prelude*, X, 888–900
17 *Prelude*, XI, 3–7
18 WW to WM, 21 March 1796;
   LWDW, 1, 170
19 *The Borderers*, III, 1493–6
20 WW to William Rowan Hamilton,
   25 June 1832; *LWDW*, 5, 535–6
21 *Prelude*, X, 908–21
22 *WPW*, 4, 463

23 'The Sparrow's Nest', *WPW*, 1, 227
24 'Tintern Abbey', *WPW*, 2, 262
25 'The Sparrow's Nest', *WPW*, 1, 227
26 *Prelude*, X, 905 & 906–7
27 Jonathan Wordsworth, M.H.
   Abrams, and Stephen Gill: *The
   Prelude 1799, 1805, 1850* (New York
   & London, 1979), 408 n9
28 STC to JT, 17 December 1796; *LSTC*,
   1, 282
29 DW to JP, 16 October 1792; *LWDW*,
   1, 83
30 STC to TP, 6 February 1797; *LSTC*,
   1, 303
31 STC to JPE, January 1797; *LSTC*, 1,
   301
32 STC to JT, 6 February 1797; *LSTC*,
   1, 308 & 305
33 CL to STC, 7–10 January 1797;
   LCML, 1, 87 & 90
34 STC to JT, 6 February 1797; *LSTC*,
   1, 308
35 STC to Benjamin Flower,
   2 November & 11 December, to JT,
   13 November & 31 December 1796,
   and to JC, early April 1797; *LSTC*, 1,
   247, 253, 267–8, 293 & 320
36 STC to JC, 10 March 1797; *LSTC*, 1,
   312
37 STC to JC, 6 January 1797; *LSTC*, 1,
   297
38 CL to STC, 7–10 January &
   5–6 February 1797; *LCML*, 1, 87–8
   & 97; *NBSTC*, 1, 161
39 STC to JC, 10 March 1797; *LSTC*, 1,
   313
40 STC to William Lisle Bowles,
   16 March 1797; *LSTC*, 1, 318
41 STC to JC, 15 March 1797; *LSTC*, 1,
   315
42 STC to JC, early April 1797; *LSTC*,
   1, 319–20
43 STC to JC, 8 June 1797; *LSTC*, 1, 325
44 WW to WM, 21 March 1796;
   LWDW, 1, 169
45 STC to JT, 31 December 1796; *LSTC*,
   1, 294

46 STC to JC, early April 1797; *LSTC*, 1, 320–1

47 STC to JC, 10 May 1797; *LSTC*, 1, 324

48 STC to JPE, 10 June 1797; *LSTC*, 1, 327

7 : COMMUNION

1 DW to MH, June 1797; *LWDW*, 1, 188–9

2 STC to JPE, 10 June 1797, *LSTC*, 1, 326

3 STC to JC, 8 June 1797; *LSTC*, 1, 325

4 STC to JPE, 18 May 1798, *LSTC*, 1, 410

5 Ibid.

6 STC to MB, 3 April 1815; *LSTC*, 4, 564

7 Extract from a letter from Richard Reynell; *Illustrated London News*, 22 April 1893, 500

8 STC to JC, 8 June & c.3 July 1797; *LSTC*, 1, 325 & 330–1

9 De Quincey, 132–3, 52–3

10 STC to JC, c.3 June 1797; *LSTC*, 1, 330

11 DW to MH, 4 July 1797; *LWDW*, 1, 189

12 *WPW*, 4, 411–12

13 Cottle, 150–1

14 Extract from a letter from Richard Reynell; *Illustrated London News*, 22 April 1893, 500

15 Moorman, 1, 354–5

16 DW to MH, 5 March 1798; *LWDW*, 1, 199

17 CL to STC, 19 or 26 July 1797; *LCML*, 1, 118

18 DW to MH, 14 August 1797; *LWDW*, 1, 190

19 STC to RS, 17 July 1797; *LSTC*, 1, 334 & 336

20 *Prelude* (1850), XIV, 420 & 397–9

21 STC to Godwin, 19 November 1801; *LSTC*, 2, 775

22 STC to the editor of the *Quarterly Review*, ? April 1828; *LSTC*, 6, 733 & 733n

23 CL to STC, 19 or 26 July 1797; *LCML*, 1, 118

24 *Poole*, 117

25 STC to Josiah Wade, 1 August 1797; *LSTC*, 1, 339

26 *Table Talk*, 122

27 James Dykes Campbell: *Samuel Taylor Coleridge: A Narrative of the Events of his Life* (2nd edn, 1896), 73

28 STC to TP, July 1797; *LSTC*, 1, 338

29 *Poole*, 131

30 Nicolas Roe: 'Coleridge and John Thelwall' in Richard Grevil & Molly Lefebure (eds): *The Coleridge Connection* (London, 1990), 74

31 STC to JT, 19 August 1797; *LSTC*, 1, 341

32 Mrs Andrew Crosse: *Red Letter Days of My Life* (1892), 1, 105.

33 STC to JT, 21 August 1797; *LSTC*, 1, 343–4

34 'Coleridge and John Thelwall', op. cit., 76

35 STC to JT, 14 October 1797; *LSTC*, 1, 349

36 CL to WW, 26 April 1816; *LCML*, 3, 215

37 STC to William Lisle Bowles, 16 October 1797; *LSTC*, 1, 355–6

38 Charles Lloyd to RS, ?15 September 1797; *LSTC*, 1, 345n–6n

39 Jenny Uglow: *The Lunar Men* (London, 2002), 462–3

40 Moorman, 1, 332–6

41 Cottle, 182–5. It is unclear when this visit took place, but late September/early October is certainly one possible time.

42 *WPW*, 1, 361–2

43 STC to JC, c.20 November 1797; *LSTC*, 1, 357

44 Ibid., 357–8

45 CL to STC, 15 April 1797; *LCML*, 1, 109

46 Charles Lloyd to Robert Lloyd, 1811;

quoted in *Charles Lamb and the Lloyds*, op. cit., 247–8

47 CL to STC, 28 January 1798; *LCML*, 1, 126

48 CL to STC, c.20 September 1797; *LCML*, 1, 123

49 *NBSTC*, 4006

50 RS to Charles Danvers, 5 September 1797; *NLRS*, 1, 144

51 STC to RS, 7 December 1797; *LSTC*, 1, 358–9

52 STC to JC, c.20 November 1797; *LSTC*, 1, 357

53 STC to JT, 14 October 1797; *LSTC*, 1, 352; RS to John May, 6 October 1797; *NLRS*, 1, 152

54 STC to JC, 2 December 1797; *LSTC*, 1, 358

55 DW to Mrs William Rawson, 13 June & 3 July 1798; *LWDW*, 1, 223

56 DW to MH (?), 20 November 1797, and Edward Ferguson & Elizabeth Threlkeld to Samuel Ferguson, 13 & 14 February 1798; *LWDW*, 1, 194 and 197n

57 STC to JPE, 30 December 1797; *LSTC*, 1, 361

58 STC to JT, 14 October 1797; *LSTC*, 1, 349

59 STC to JW, 5 January 1798; *LSTC*, 1, 364–7

8 : COLLABORATION

1 STC to TP, 17 & 27 January 1798; *LSTC*, 1, 374–5 & 381

2 WW to James Webbe Tobin, 6 March 1798; *LWDW*, 1, 211

3 JT to Dr Peter Crompton, 3 March 1798; quoted in Nicholas Roe, 'Coleridge and John Thelwall: Medical Science, Politics, and Poetry', *Coleridge Bulletin*, New Series No 3, Spring 1994

4 STC to GC, 10 March 1798; *LSTC*, 1, 394–8

5 Clement Carylon: *Early Years and Late Reflections* (1843–58); quoted in *S.T. Coleridge: Interviews and Reflections*, op. cit., 80; see also STC to William Sotheby, 10 September 1802, *LSTC*, 2, 866

6 DW to MH, 5 March 1798; *LWDW*, 1, 200

7 STC to WW, 30 May 1815; *LSTC*, 4, 574

8 See Duncan Wu: *Wordsworth: An Inner Life* (Oxford, 2002), especially 109–17

9 STC to Mrs STC, 3 October 1798; *LSTC*, 1, 421

10 Kenneth R. Johnston: *Wordsworth and The Recluse* (New Haven & London, 1984), 5–6

11 STC to JPE, 18 May 1798; *LSTC*, 1, 410

12 STC to JC, 7 March 1798; *LSTC*, 1, 391

13 *Table Talk*, 188

14 STC to JC, 7 March 1798; *LSTC*, 1, 391

15 WW to James Losh, 11 March 1798; *LWDW*, 1, 214

16 STC to JC, [April 1798]; *LSTC*, 1, 403. The original of this letter is lost, and the text is taken from JC's *Early Recollections; chiefly relating to the late Samuel Taylor Coleridge* (1837). Griggs, the editor of Coleridge's letters, has tentatively dated it early April 1798, on the basis of internal evidence in other paragraphs. One of these refers to 'our plan' of visiting Germany, which seems inconsistent with Coleridge's urgency to find another house for Wordsworth near Stowey, as expressed in the paragraph quoted. Cottle had the deplorable habit of stitching together passages from different letters to suit his narrative, and it therefore seems to me likely that this paragraph was taken from an earlier letter.

17 DW to MH, 5 March 1798; *LWDW*, 1, 199–200

18 WW to James Webbe Tobin, 6 March 1798; *LWDW*, 1, 211

19 WW to James Losh, 11 March 1798; *LWDW*, 1, 213–14

20 DW to Mrs William Rawson, 13 June & 3 July 1798; *LWDW*, 1, 221–2

21 STC to JC, c.13 March & early April 1798; *LSTC*, 1, 399–400 & 402–3

22 STC to GC, 14 May 1798; *LSTC*, 1, 409

23 Kathleen Jones: *A Passionate Sisterhood: the Sisters, Wives and Daughters of the Lake Poets* (London, 1998), 3–5

24 De Quincey, 51–5

25 STC to WW, 23 January 1798; *LSTC*, 1, 378–9

26 Conversation with Wordsworth in 1830, quoted in Moorman, 1, 489–90; see also *Poetry*, 1, 479

27 James Gillman: *The Life of Samuel Taylor Coleridge* (1838), 302–3; see also the introduction to 'Christabel' in *Poetry*, 1, 477–81

28 *Poetry*, 1, 483n

29 *WPW*, 2, 527

30 WW to JC, 12 April & 6 May 1798; *LWDW*, 1, 215 & 218

31 DW to MH, 20 November 1797; *LWDW*, 1, 194

32 Cottle, 174–8. JC describes two visits to the Quantocks in the spring of 1798, but this is hard to reconcile with the surviving correspondence. It is possible, indeed likely, that this visit coincided with that of Hazlitt, though neither man mentions the other in his account.

33 WW to JC, 28 August 1798; *LWDW*, 1, 227

34 *WPW*, 2, 527

35 STC to JC, 28 May 1798; *LSTC*, 1, 411–12

36 WW to James Webbe Tobin, 6 March 1798; *LWDW*, 1, 211

37 *LSTC*, 1, 400n

38 STC to JC, 7, c.13 & c.17 March 1798; *LSTC*, 1, 390, 399 & 400–1

39 Gurion Taussig: *Coleridge and the Idea of Friendship* (Newark & London, 2002), 239

40 RS to JC, 19 January 1798; *NLRS*, 1, 158

41 WW to JC, 9 May 1798; *LWDW*, 1, 218

42 *STCNB*, 4006

43 STC to TP, 14 May, & to JPE, 18 May 1798; *LSTC*, 1, 408 & 410

44 STC to JPE, 14 May 1798; *LSTC*, 1, 407

45 STC to TP, 19 May 1799; *LSTC*, 1, 516

46 STC to TP, 14 & 20 May 1798; *LSTC*, 1, 408 & 411

47 CL to WW, 26 April 1816; *LCML*, 3, 215

48 *Watchman*, 102–3 & *Morning Post*, 9 January 1798; 1, 111–12. For a while I thought proudly that I was the first to notice this, but I soon realised that I had been anticipated by Felicity James; see her 'Coleridge and the Fears of Friendship, 1798'; *Coleridge Bulletin*, New Series, no. 24, Winter 2004

49 CL to STC, 23 May–6 June 1798; *LCML*, 1, 128–9

50 CL to STC, 10 January 1820; E.V. Lucas (ed.): *Letters of Charles and Mary Lamb* (London, 1935), 2, 267–8

51 For an exposition of the ideas underlying this argument, see Duncan Wu, 'The Road to Nether Stowey'; *Coleridge Bulletin*, New Series No 23, Spring 2004

52 Emile Legouis, 'Some Remarks on the Composition of the Lyrical Ballads of 1798', in *Wordsworth & Coleridge: Studies in Honour of*

George MacLean Harper (New York, 1962), 5

53 STC to TP, 3 August 1798; *LSTC*, 1, 414

54 STC to Mrs STC, 3 October 1798; *LSTC*, 1, 420

9 : SEPARATION

1 STC to Mrs STC, 18 September 1798; *LSTC*, 1, 415–16

2 STC to TP, 20 November 1798; *LSTC*, 1, 441–5

3 *DWJ*, 30 September 1798; STC to Mrs STC, 10 March 1799; *LSTC*, 1, 473

4 CL to RS, 28 November 1798; *LCML*, 1, 152

5 DW to Mrs William Rawson, 13 June & 3 July 1798; *LWDW*, 1, 221

6 TP to STC, 8 October 1798; *Poole*, 150; JW to TP, 1 February 1799; *LSTC*, 1, 419n

7 TP to STC, 8 October 1798; *Poole*, 150

8 STC to Mrs STC, 8 November 1798; *LSTC*, 1, 439

9 DW to Christopher Wordsworth, 3 February 1799; *LWDW*, 1, 245

10 DW & WW to STC, 27 February 1799; *LWDW*, 1, 250–4

11 STC to WW & DW, December 1798; *LSTC*, 1, 451–2

12 STC to TP, 20 November 1798; *LSTC*, 1, 445

13 WW to JW, 5 February 1799; *LWDW*, 1, 249

14 STC to Mrs STC, 14 January 1799; *LSTC*, 1, 459–60

15 STC to TP, 6 May 1799; *LSTC*, 1, 491

16 DW & WW to STC, 14 or 21 December 1798; *LWDW*, 1, 236

17 DW to ?, c.3 February 1799; *LWDW*, 1, 247

18 *Table Talk*, 188–9

19 STC to WW, 10 December 1798; *LSTC*, 1, 452–3

20 *Two-Part Prelude* (1799), 1, 447–64; *The Prelude 1799, 1805, 1850*, op. cit., 13

21 DW & WW to STC, 14 or 21 December 1798; *LWDW*, 1, 238–9

22 WW & DW to STC, 16 April 1802; *LWDW*, 1, 348

23 F.W. Bateson: *Wordsworth: A Reinterpretation* (London, 1954)

24 STC to TP, 6 April 1799; *LSTC*, 1, 479

25 Mrs STC to STC, 1 November 1798; *Love*, 105

26 STC to Mrs STC, 2 December 1798; *LSTC*, 1, 449; TP to STC, 22 November 1798; *Poole*, 151

27 STC to Mrs STC, 8 November, & STC to TP, 20 November 1798; *LSTC*, 1, 437 & 443

28 STC to JW, 21 May 1799; *LSTC*, 1, 519

29 TP to STC, 24 January 1799; *Poole*, 153

30 Mrs STC to TP, 11 February 1799; *Minnow*, 1–2

31 STC to TP, 15 & 28 September & 26 October 1798, & 6 May 1799; *LSTC*, 1, 415, 420, 430, 435 & 490

32 STC to Mrs STC, 10 March 1799; *LSTC*, 1, 476

33 STC to WW, [December 1798]; *LSTC*, 1, 453

34 STC to TP, 4 January 1799; *LSTC*, 1, 455

35 TP to STC, 24 January 1799; *Poole*, 153

36 STC to TP, 6 May 1799; *LSTC*, 1, 490–1

37 TP to STC, 15 March 1799; *Poole*, 156–8

38 STC to TP, 6 April 1799; *LSTC*, 1, 478–9

39 STC to Mrs STC, 8 April 1799; *LSTC*, 1, 481–3

40 STC to Mrs STC, 23 April 1799;
LSTC, 1, 484

41 Mrs STC to STC, 15 May 1799; *Love*,
118

42 STC to TP, 6 May 1799; *LSTC*, 1,
493, 490

43 WW to MH, 11 August 1810;
LWDW, 8, 29

44 DW to TP, 4 July 1799; *LWDW*, 1,
266

45 RW to WW, 15 May 1799; *LWDW*, 1,
Appendix IV, 673

46 D.F. Foxon: 'The Printing of *Lyrical
Ballads*, 1798', *The Library*, vol. 9
no. 4 (1954)

47 Mrs STC to STC, 25 March 1799;
LSTC, 1, 489n; Mrs STC to TP,
March & 2 April 1799; *Minnow*, 4 &
5

48 RS to C.W. Williams Wynn;
17 December 1798; *NLRS*, 1, 176–7

49 CL to RS, 8 November 1798; *LCML*,
1, 142

50 WW to JC, [summer?] 1799;
LWDW, 1, 267–7

51 Cottle, 259–60

52 STC to Cottle, early April 1798;
LSTC, 1, 402

53 DW to ?, 13 September 1798;
LWDW, 1, 227

54 Margaret Spedding to her brother,
22 November 1799; quoted in Gill,
163n. I have not seen this letter.

55 WW to JC, 2 & 24 June 1799;
LWDW, 1, 263 & 264

56 STC to RS, 29 July & 8 August 1799;
LSTC, 1, 523–5

57 TP to RS, 8 August 1799; *LSTC*, 1,
524n

58 RS to Mrs RS, 15 May 1799; *NLRS*,
1, 187–8

59 RS to Thomas Southey,
6 September, & to Charles Danvers,
20 August 1799; *NLRS*, 1, 199 &
199n

60 STC to RS, 19 December 1799;
LSTC, 1, 550

61 STC to TP, 16 September 1799;
LSTC, 1, 528

62 STC to RS, 25 & 30 September 1799;
LSTC, 1, 531 & 535–6

63 STC to RS, 15 October,
30 September, 10 November &
19 December 1799; *LSTC*, 1, 540,
535, 545 & 549

64 STC to TP, 10 September 1799;
LSTC, 1, 526–7

65 STC to WW, c.10 September 1799;
LSTC, 1, 527

66 STC to WW, 12 October 1799;
LSTC, 1, 538

67 *Essays*, 1, lxxxiv & lxxxivn

68 Mrs STC to TP, 2 April 1799;
Minnow, 5

69 RS to Mrs RS, 16 May 1799; *NLRS*,
1, 191

70 STC to RS, 15 October 1799; *LSTC*,
1, 539

71 Molly Lefebure: 'Humphry Davy:
Philosophic Alchemist'; in *The
Coleridge Connection: Essays for
Thomas McFarland*, op. cit., 102–3

72 Cottle, 259

10 : AMALGAMATION

1 *NBSTC*, 493, 1587

2 Cottle, 259

3 WW & STC to DW, c.10 November
1799; *LSTC*, 1, 542–5

4 STC to RS, 10 November 1799;
LSTC, 1, 545

5 Catherine Clarkson to Priscilla
Lloyd, 12 January 1800; quoted in
WCEY, 280–1

6 *NBSTC*, 1575

7 *NBSTC*, 718, which reads as follows:
'Mr Coleridge/A little of Sara's Hair
in this Pocket'. Kathleen Coburn,
editor of *NBSTC*, links this note
with Coleridge's poem 'The
Keepsake'. John Worthern (*Gang*,
94) challenges this interpretation of

Coleridge's note, suggesting that it records something said to him, perhaps by a servant in Somerset, and therefore cannot refer to Sara Hutchinson, since no servant would have known Sara Hutchinson's name or been able to identify her hair; but neither would a servant have been likely to have referred to Sara Coleridge by her first name, certainly not without prefixing it with the title 'Mrs'.

8 *NBSTC*, 578 & 1575

9 *Wordsworth and Coleridge in the West Country* (Newton Abbot, 1970), 84

10 *Poole*, Appendix A, 315

11 This sentence was in a draft and omitted from the letter actually sent to Coleridge; see WW to STC, 24 & 27 December 1799 & Appendix V; *LWDW*, 1, 273 & 679

12 Joanna Hutchinson to John M—, c.26 April 1800; quoted in *WCMY*, 61

13 *Gang*, 65–8

14 *Gang*, 48

15 *Gang*, 3

16 DW to JP, 10 & 12 September 1800; *LWDW*, 1, 295

17 STC to WW, February 1800; *LSTC*, 1, 575

18 STC to JC, c.1 December 1799; *LSTC*, 1, 547

19 CL to Thomas Manning, 8 February, Manning to CL, 9 March 1800; *LCML*, 1, 183 & 184

20 CL to STC, probably 16 or 17 April 1800; *LCML*, 1, 198

21 Holmes, 1, 258

22 STC to Thomas Wedgwood, 2 January 1800; *LSTC*, 1, 559

23 Paula Byrne: *Perdita: The Life of Mary Robinson* (London, 2004), esp. 286–8

24 STC to JW, 4 February 1800; *LSTC*, 1, 567

25 STC to RS, 12 February, & to JW, 4 February 1800; *LSTC*, 1, 571 & 569

26 *Essays*, 1, 226n–228n

27 STC to JW, 4 February, & to TP, 31 March 1800; *LSTC*, 1, 568–9 & 585

28 STC to Samuel Purkis, 27 March 1800; *LSTC*, 1, 583

29 CL to Thomas Manning, 17 March 1800; *LCML*, 1, 189

30 STC to RS, 10 April 1800; *LSTC*, 1, 585

31 STC to JW, 21 April 1800; *LSTC*, 1, 587

32 CL to STC, 16 or 17 April 1800; *LCML*, 1, 200

33 STC to TP, 21 March 1800; *LSTC*, 1, 582

34 STC to RS, 19 December 1799 & 12 February 1800; *LSTC*, 1, 547–50 & 571; RS to STC, 23 December 1799; *NLRS*, 1, 209

35 STC to RS, 19 & 24 December 1799; *LSTC*, 1, 547–50 & 552–3

36 STC to RS, 25 January & 10 April 1800; *LSTC*, 1, 562–3 & 585–6

37 STC to TP, January & 21 March 1800, *LSTC*, 1, 562 & 582; TP to STC, 1 January 1800; *Poole*, 167–71

38 STC to TP, 14 & 25 February, 21 & 31 March 1800; *LSTC*, 1, 575 & 582

39 STC to TP, 31 March 1800; *LSTC*, 1, 584

40 CL to Thomas Manning, 5 April 1800; *LCML*, 1, 191

41 WW to James Losh, 16 March 1805; *LWDW*, 1, 563

42 *DWJ*, 14 May–8 June 1800

43 STC to Daniel Stuart, 15 July 1800; *LSTC*, 1, 603

44 STC to TP & to JW, both 24 July 1800; *LSTC*, 1, 608 & 610

45 STC to William Godwin, 21 May 1800; *LSTC*, 1, 588

46 STC to JW, 24 July 1800; *LSTC*, 1, 609–10

47 STC to TP, 13 February 1813; *LSTC*, 3, 438

48 STC to Humphry Davy, James Webbe Tobin & Samuel Purkis, all 25 July; & to William Godwin, 8 September 1800; *LSTC*, 1, 611, 613, 614–15 & 620

49 STC to FW, 19 December 1800; *LSTC*, 1, 658

50 DW to JP, 10 & 12 September 1800; *LWDW*, 1, 298

51 STC to TP, 14 August 1800; *LSTC*, 1, 618–19

52 WW to JC, 27 July 1799; *LWDW*, 1, 267

53 WW to STC, 24 & 27 December 1799; *LWDW*, 1, 281

54 Cottle, 259–60

55 James Butler and Karen Green: Introduction to the Cornell Wordsworth edition of *Lyrical Ballads* (Ithaca, 1992), 24

56 STC to RS, 10 April 1800; *LSTC*, 1, 585

57 WW to Messrs Longman & Rees, 27 March, & to RW, 23 June 1801; *LWDW*, 1, 321 & 336

58 STC to Humphry Davy, 25 July 1800; *LSTC*, 1, 611

59 WW to Charles James Fox, 14 January 1800; *LWDW*, 1, 315

60 *WProse*, 1, 167

61 STC to William Sotheby, 13 July 1802; *LSTC*, 2, 811

62 STC to RS, 29 July & to William Sotheby, 13 July 1802; *LSTC*, 2, 830 & 811

63 STC to Daniel Stuart, c.30 September 1800; *LSTC*, 1, 627

64 *Poetry*, 605

65 WW to Biggs & Cottle, c.13 August 1800; *LSTC*, 1, 617 & *LWDW*, 1, 293

66 *Perdita: The Life of Mary Robinson*, op. cit., 383–4

67 WW to Messrs Biggs & Cottle, c.2 October 1800; *LWDW*, 1, 303–4

68 STC to Godwin, 8 September 1800; *LSTC*, 1, 620

69 DW to JP, 10 & 12 September 1800; *LWDW*, 1, 296

70 *NBSTC*, 4006

71 Lloyd to Thomas Manning, 26 January 1801; quoted in *WCMY*, 107

72 CL to WW, 30 January 1801; *LCML*, 1, 265–6

73 CL to Thomas Manning, 15 February 1801; *LCML*, 1, 272–3

74 STC to James Webbe Tobin, 17 September 1800; *LSTC*, 1, 623

75 STC to William Godwin, 16 September 1800; *LSTC*, 1, 621–2

76 For an excellent discussion of STC's difficulties with 'Christabel', see Rosemary Ashton: *The Life of Samuel Taylor Coleridge: A Critical Biography* (Oxford, 1996), 181–8

77 *NBSTC*, 848

78 *NBSTC*, 834

79 STC to JW, 1 November 1800; *LSTC*, 1, 643

80 STC to TP, 6 December 1800; *LSTC*, 1, 650

81 STC to Daniel Stuart, c.30 September 1800; *LSTC*, 1, 627

82 In his admirably sceptical book *The Gang*, John Worthen writes 'who did the determining, it is impossible to say' (9). But subsequent letters written by both Wordsworth and Coleridge establish that the decision had been Wordsworth's.

83 STC to Davy, 9 October 1800; *LSTC*, 1, 631

84 WW to Messrs Longman and Rees, 18 December 1799; *LWDW*, 1, 309

85 STC to JW, 1 November 1800; *LSTC*, 1, 643

86 See STC's Preface to the 1816 and subsequent editions

87 STC to TP, c.11 October, & to Stuart, 7 October 1800; *LSTC*, 1, 634 & 629

88 STC to Thomas N. Longman,
15 December 1800; *LSTC*, 1, 654

89 STC to TP, 6 December 1800; *LSTC*,
1, 651

90 STC to JT, 17 December 1800;
LSTC, 1, 656

91 Annotation in Heinrich's
Commentary on the Apocalypse;
quoted in Walter Jackson Bate:
Coleridge (London, 1969), 41

92 STC to FW, 19 December 1800;
LSTC, 1, 658

93 STC to William Godwin, 25 March
1801; *LSTC*, 2, 714

PART III: ACQUAINTANCES

1 *NBSTC*, 1471. The words in
parentheses were added at a later
date to an entry made during the
1803 tour of Scotland.

11 : SUBORDINATION

1 STC to TP, 18 April 1801; *LSTC*, 2,
721

2 DW & WW to MH, 29 April 1801;
LWDW, 1, 330

3 *NBSTC*, 949

4 JW to DW, 28 & 29 March 1801;
Carl H. Ketchman (ed.): *Letters of
John Wordsworth* (Ithaca, 1969), 110

5 *Bondage*, Appendix 1, 493–5

6 STC to TP, 16 & 23 March 1801;
LSTC, 2, 706–7 & 708

7 DW & WW to MH, 29 April 1801;
LWDW, 1, 330

8 STC to RS, 25 July, & to TP, 23 March,
18 April & 5 July 1801; *LSTC*, 2,
747–8, 709–10, 722 & 741–2

9 WW to TP, early July 1801; *LWDW*,
1, 338–40; TP to STC, 14 November
1800, 9 April & 7 May 1801; *Poole*,
175, 186 & 187; STC to TP, 24 March
1801; *LSTC*, 2, 711

10 TP to STC, 7 May & 21 July 1801;
Poole, 187 & 194–5

11 *Opium and the Romantic
Imagination*, op. cit., 26

12 STC to Henry Daniel, 19 May 1814;
LSTC, 3, 496

13 STC to JC, 26 April 1814; *LSTC*, 3, 476

14 STC to TP, 7 September &
21 October 1801; *LSTC*, 2, 756 & 770

15 Sara Hutchinson to Thomas
Monkhouse, 3 May 1819; Kathleen
Coburn (ed.): *Letters of Sara
Hutchinson* (London, 1954), 151

16 DW & WW to Sara Hutchinson,
14 June 1802; *LWDW*, 1, 363

17 DW & WW to MH, 29 April 1801;
LWDW, 1, 330–1

18 *NBSTC*, 979

19 STC to RS, 6 May & 22 July 1801;
LSTC, 2, 728 & 745–6; RS to STC,
11 July 1801; *Life and Correspondence
of Robert Southey*, op. cit., 2, 151

20 STC to RS, 21 October 1801; *LSTC*,
2, 767

21 RS to Charles Danvers, 9 January
1802, quoted in Taussig, op. cit.,
309; RS to John Rickman,
18 October 1802; *NLRS*, 1, 294

22 STC to RS, 21 October 1801; *LSTC*,
2, 767; RS to Charles Danvers,
6 February 1802; *NLRS*, 1, 271–2

23 Geoffrey Yarlott: *Coleridge and the
Abyssinian Maid* (London, 1967),
310–12

24 *NBSTC*, 1065

25 *DWJ*, 9 & 10 November 1801

26 *DWJ*, 29 January 1802

27 STC to William Godwin,
22 January 1802; *LSTC*, 2, 782

28 *NBSTC*, 932

29 STC to Mrs STC, 24 February 1802;
LSTC, 2, 788

30 DW & WW to MH, 29 April 1801;
LWDW, 1, 332

31 John Wordsworth to ?, 24 March
1801; *Letters of John Wordsworth*,
op. cit., 109–10

32 *DWJ*, 2 February 1802

33 *DWJ*, 28 February, 3 & 4 March 1802

34 From the Advertisement to the 1807 edition of WW's poems

35 STC to Mrs STC, [? February], 19 & 24 February 1802; *LSTC*, 2, 785, 786 & 788–9

36 RS to Charles Danvers, 6 February 1802; *NLRS*, 1, 272

37 *NBSTC*, 1151, 1156 & 1157

38 *DWJ*, 24 March 1802

39 *WPW*, 4, 466

40 *NBSTC*, 3304. Worthern (*Gang*, 110 & 317) questions Kathleen Coburn's dating of this note and suggests that the conversation may have taken place in the period missing from DW's journal, 6–9 November 1801.

41 *DWJ*, 15 April 1802

42 *DWJ*, 21 April 1802; Worthern (*Gang*, 1, 48) suggests that the Wordsworths may have already read the poem, in a letter STC sent them before his arrival. Against this must be set DW's reaction on STC's recital.

43 STC to RS, 29 July 1802; *LSTC*, 2, 832

44 *DWJ*, 31 May 1802

45 DW & WW to the Hutchinson sisters, 14 June 1802; *LWDW*, 1, 366–7

46 *NBSTC*, 4006

47 DW & WW to SH, 14 June 1802, & DW to Catherine Clarkson, 21 November 1803, *LWDW*, 1, 362 & 422

48 STC to GB and MB, 13 August 1803; *LSTC*, 2, 966–73

49 STC to RS, 29 July 1802; *LSTC*, 2, 831

50 Letter from John Simpson, Chief Editor of the *Oxford English Dictionary*, *Times Literary Supplement*, 5382 (26 May 2006), 17

51 *NBSTC*, 1250

52 STC to Tom Wedgwood, 20 October 1802; *LSTC*, 2, 875–6

53 STC to Mrs STC, 8, 13, 16, 21 & 22 November, 4 & 5 December 1802; *LSTC*, 2, 879–92

54 Worthern (*Gang*, 314–16) rejects the standard interpretation of the correspondence, ingeniously arguing that Mrs STC could not have been seriously upset by her husband's meeting with Sara Hutchinson who, he believes, was on her way to Keswick to assist Mrs STC in her pregnancy, where she remained throughout the correspondence. The evidence for this is an entry in DW's journal for 8 November: 'Sara is at Keswick, I hope.' But if this had been prearranged, it is difficult to explain why subsequently Coleridge should have pressed his wife more than once to have Sara Hutchinson come to stay; and why Sara Hutchinson should have been at Grasmere the day after the baby was born.

55 STC to Mrs STC, 5 January 1803; *LSTC*, 2, 908

56 STC to Mrs STC, 16 November 1802; *LSTC*, 2, 882–3

57 *Poetry*, 1239–41

58 RS to William Taylor, 14 February & 23 June 1803; J.W. Robberds (ed.): *A Memoir of the Life and Writing of the late William Taylor of Norwich* (London, 1843), 1, 455 & 461–2; RS to STC, quoted in *LSTC*, 2, 829–30n

59 STC to TP, 14 October 1803; *LSTC*, 2, 1012–13

60 STC to William Godwin, 10 June 1803; *LSTC*, 2, 950

61 STC to TP, 20 May 1803; *LSTC*, 2, 945

62 RS to Miss Barker, 3 April 1804; John Wood Worter (ed.): *Selections*

from the Letters of Robert Southey (London, 1856), 1, 271

63 STC to WW, 23 July 1803; *LSTC*, 2, 957–8

64 Tom Mayberry, 'A Newly-discovered letter of Sir George Beaumont, 1803'; *Coleridge Bulletin*, New Series No 1, (Winter 1992/93), 5–7

65 GB to WW, 24 October 1803; *Memoirs*, 1, 259

66 WW to GB, 14 October 1803; *LWDW*, 1, 406–8

67 *NBSTC*, 1451

68 *WPW*, 3, 438–9

69 STC to TP, 3 October 1803; *LSTC*, 2, 1010

70 DW to MB, 27 October 1805; *LWDW*, 1, 632–3; *LSTC*, 2, 1191–2n

71 STC to TP, 3 October 1803; *LSTC*, 2, 1010

72 *NBSTC*, 1670 & 1669

73 STC to TP, 14 October 1803; *LSTC*, 2, 1012–13

74 STC to GB & MB, 1 October 1803; *LSTC*, 2, 999–1004

75 WW to JT, mid-January 1804; *LWDW*, 1, 431–4

76 STC to TP, 14 October 1803; *LSTC*, 2, 1013

77 *Monthly Mirror*, June 1801; Robert Woof (ed.): *Wordsworth: The Critical Heritage*, 1, 1793–1820 (London, 2001), 144

78 STC to GB & MB, 12 August 1803; *LSTC*, 2, 965

79 *NBSTC*, 1606 & 1607

80 *NBSTC*, 1616

81 STC to RS, 12 March 1804; *LSTC*, 2, 1085

82 *NBSTC*, 1577

83 *NBSTC*, 1801

84 STC to Richard Sharp, 15 January 1804; *LSTC*, 2, 1034

85 *WPW*, 4, 418

86 STC to Richard Sharp, 15 January 1804; *LSTC*, 2, 1033

87 DW & WW to STC, 6 March 1804; *LWDW*, 1, 452

88 WW to Thomas De Quincey, 6 March 1804; *LWDW*, 1, 454

89 DW & WW to STC, 29 March 1804; *LWDW*, 1, 462–4

90 STC to RS, 1 August 1803; *LSTC*, 2, 959

91 Humphry Davy to STC, STC to Davy, 25 March 1804; *LSTC*, 2, 1102–3

92 RS to Miss Barker, 3 April 1804 & undated; *Selections from the Letters of Robert Southey*, op. cit., 1, 253 & 270–1

93 *NBSTC*, 1912, 1913. Worthern (*Gang*, 70) assumes that this date records the receipt of SH's letter two years before, i.e. in 1802, but provides no argument to support this. Kathleen Coburn's notes state her belief that the letter was received in 1804.

94 *NBSTC*, 2118, 2036, 2055, 2600, 2638n & 2495

95 *NBSTC*, 3404

96 *NBSTC*, 2998, 2750, 2517, 2549 & 2001

97 *NBSTC*, 2518 & 2861; STC to the Wordsworths, 1 May 1805; *LSTC*, 2, 1168

98 *NBSTC*, 2063, 2703, 2839, & 2712

99 DW & WW to STC, 29 March; & DW to MB, 25 & 30 May 1804; *LWDW*, 1, 463 & 477

100 WW to GB, 25 December 1804, 1 May & 3 June 1805; *LWDW*, 1, 518, 586–7 & 594–5

101 WW to RW, 11 February 1805; *LWDW*, 1, 540

102 WW to GB, c.23 February 1805; *LWDW*, 1, 547

103 WW to GB, 11 February 1805; *LWDW*, 1, 542

104 DW to MB, 4 May 1805; *LWDW*, 1, 591

105 STC to Daniel Stuart, 30 April, &

to the Wordsworths, 1 May 1805;
LSTC, 2, 1164 & 1169

106 DW to MB, 25 & 26 December
1805; *LWDW*, 1, 664

107 *WPW*, 4, 419–20

108 DW to Mrs Thomas Clarkson,
6 January; & to MB, 11 April &
26 August 1805; *LWDW*, 1, 528,
576–7, & 621

109 DW to MB, 20 March 1806;
LWDW, 2, 16

12 : ESTRANGEMENT

1 DW to Catherine Clarkson,
22 December 1805; *LWDW*, 1, 655–6

2 Ernest de Selincourt, editor of
Wordsworth's letters and poetical
works in five volumes, believed that
these were lines from the narrative
poem that would eventually be
published as *The Excursion* (*WPW*,
5, 371). However, more recently
Mark L. Reed (*WCMY* 1806:56) and
Kenneth Johnston (*Wordsworth and
The Recluse*, 218) have argued that it
was more likely to be the
completion of 'Home at Grasmere'.

3 WW to GB, 1 August 1806; *LWDW*,
2, 64

4 Ibid.

5 STC to RS, 19 August 1806; *LSTC*,
2, 1176–7

6 WW to STC, 18 September 1806;
LWDW, 2, 80

7 DW to Catherine Clarkson,
6 November 1806; *LWDW*, 2, 86–7

8 Ibid.

9 STC to the Wordsworths,
c.19 November 1806; *LSTC*, 2, 1200

10 RS to John Rickman, April 1807;
NLRS, 1, 448–9

11 DW to MB, 22 December, & to
Catherine Clarkson, 6 November
1806; *LWDW*, 2, 110 & 88

12 *WPW*, 2, 473–4

13 STC to Mrs STC, 25 December
1806; *LSTC*, 2, 1205

14 DW to MB, 23 December 1806;
LWDW, 2, 121

15 *Poole*, 247–50

16 *NBSTC*, 2938

17 *NBSTC*, 3148; see also 2975, 3328,
3547, 4537

18 *Prelude*, XIII, 411–27, 439–41, 442–8

19 WW to GB, 8 September 1806;
LWDW, 2, 79

20 RS to John Rickman, April 1807;
NLRS, 1, 448–9

21 WW to Walter Scott, end February
1807; *LWDW*, 2, 139

22 STC to Josiah Wade, August 1807;
LSTC, 3, 24–5

23 STC to GC, 2 April 1807; *LSTC*, 3,
6–8

24 WW to MB, 21 May 1807; *LWDW*,
2, 150

25 RS to Mary Barker, 2 February
1808; *WCMY*, 372–3, & Crabb
Robinson's diary for 1808; *HCR*, 1,
10

26 From *The Spirit of the Age, or,
Contemporary Portraits* (1825)

27 *LSTC*, 3, 35n

28 STC to the Morgans, 17 February
1808; *LSTC*, 3, 73–4

29 STC to Mathilda Betham, c.11 May
1808; *LSTC*, 3, 101; *NBSTC*, 3229

30 HCR to Catherine Clarkson, ?3 May
1808; quoted in *NBSTC*, 3291n

31 STC to Mary Evans Todd, 6 April,
& to Daniel Stuart, 18 April 1808;
LSTC, 3, 85–6 & 91

32 DW to MB, 3 January 1808; *LWDW*,
2, 188

33 WW to Walter Scott, 14 May 1808;
LWDW, 2, 238

34 Thomas Frognall Dibdin,
Recollections of a Literary Life
(1836), 1, 253–7; quoted in *S.T.
Coleridge: Interviews and
Recollections*, op. cit., 117–19

35 WW to DW, 25 March 1808;

LWDW, 8, 11; DW to WW, 31 March 1808; *LWDW*, 2, 207

36 STC to Thomas N. Longman, 23 May, & to WW, 21 May 1808; *LSTC*, 3, 115–16 & 107–15

37 *NBSTC*, 3304

38 WW to STC, late May or early June 1809; *LWDW*, 2, 239–45

39 WW to TP, c.30 May 1809; *LWDW*, 2, 352

40 STC to JW, 1 December 1812; *LSTC*, 3, 421

41 STC to Daniel Stuart, 27 February 1809; *LSTC*, 3, 181–2

42 *NBSTC*, 3383, 3386, 3328, 3404, 3547, 3989

43 STC to RS, 20 October 1809; *LSTC*, 3, 253–4 and 254n

44 RS to Charles Danvers, 15 June 1809; *NLRS*, 1, 511

45 *NBSTC*, 3705

46 DW to Catherine Clarkson, 12 April 1810; *LWDW*, 2, 398–400

47 RS to John Rickman, 1 August, & to GCB, 22 December 1810; *NLRS*, 1, 537 & 548

48 Mrs STC to TP, 3 August 1810; *Minnow*, 11

49 *NBSTC*, 3913

50 Ibid., 3995n

51 Ibid., 4005 & 4006; see also 3991, 3993, 3995, 3997, 3999, 4000, & 4001

52 STC to WW, 4 May 1812; *LSTC*, 3, 402

53 DW to Catherine Clarkson, 12 May 1811; *LWDW*, 2, 488–90

54 DW to Catherine Clarkson, 27 December 1811; *LWDW*, 2, 523

55 STC to Daniel Stuart, 28 April 1811; *LSTC*, 3, 319

56 Mrs STC to TP, 30 October 1812; *Minnow*, 16

57 STC to J.J. Morgan, 23 February 1812; *LSTC*, 3, 376.

58 Mrs STC to TP, 30 October 1812; *Minnow*, 16

59 WW to MW, 29 April & 2 May 1812; *LWDW*, 8, 48–52

60 STC to CL, 2 May 1812; *LSTC*, 3, 396

61 STC to WW, 11 May 1812; *LSTC*, 3, 407

62 STC to TP, 13 February 1813; *LSTC*, 3, 437

63 Mrs STC to TP, 30 October 1812; *Minnow*, 16–17

64 STC to WW, 7 December 1812; *LSTC*, 3, 423n

65 STC to MB, 3 April 1815; *LSTC*, 4, 564

66 WW to STC, 22 May, & STC to WW, 30 May 1815; *LSTC*, 4, 570–76

67 *NBSTC*, 5037

68 Referred to in *NBSTC*, 4243n. I have not been able to find the reference itself.

69 RS to Mrs RS, 5 September 1813, & RS to JC, April 1814; *NLRS*, 2, 68 & 97–8

70 Mrs STC to TP, 24 May 1816; *Minnow*, 48

71 *Edinburgh Review* (September 1816); J.R. de J. Jackson (ed.): *Coleridge: The Critical Heritage* (London, 1970), 226–36

72 STC to RS, 29 July 1802; *LSTC*, 2, 830

73 For this point in particular, and for this piece on *Biographia Literaria* in general, I must acknowledge the excellent introduction to the book in the useful Norton anthology of *Coleridge's Poetry and Prose* (New York and London, 2004), selected and edited by Nicholas Halmi, Paul Magnuson and Raimonda Modiano.

74 *NBSTC*, 1515

75 STC to William Sotheby, 28 April 1808, & to HCR, undated; *LSTC*, 3, 95 & 95n

76 Preface to *Sibylline Leaves*; *Poetry*, 1, 1249

77 Paul Cheshire: 'I lay too many Eggs: Coleridge's "Ostrich Carelessness" and the Problem of Publication'; *Coleridge Bulletin*, New Series 23, Spring 2004, 9–10

78 *HCR*, 1, 213

79 *HCR*, 1, 214–16

80 John Keats to George and Thomas Keats, 21 February 1818; Maurice Buxton Forman (ed.): *Letters of John Keats* (London, 3rd edn 1947), 107, 75n

81 Mrs STC to TP, June 1817; *Minnow*, 56

82 Sara Hutchinson to Edward Quillinan, 13 October, & to Thomas Monkhouse, 14 & 18 October 1823; *Letters of Sara Hutchinson*, op. cit., 262–7

83 e.g. in Hazlitt's *Lectures on the English Poets* (1818), in which he described Coleridge as 'the only person I ever knew who answered to the idea of a man of genius'.

84 *NBSTC*, 5904; see also 5892, 5902 & 5909

85 *NBSTC*, 6589

86 Sara Hutchinson to Edward Quillinan, 9 May, & to Mrs Hutchinson, 3–10 August 1834; *Letters of Sara Hutchinson*, op. cit., 414 & 428

87 WW to Henry Nelson Coleridge, 29 July 1834; *LWDW*, 5, 728

88 From a conversation with Robert Perceval Graves, reported in a letter to Felicia Hemans, 12 August 1834; *Memoirs*, 2, 288–90

APPENDIX

1 STC to WW, 30 May 1815; *LSTC*, 4, 573, 574–5

INDEX

(The initials 'STC' refer to Samuel Taylor Coleridge and 'WW' to William Wordsworth; 'Dorothy' signifies WW's sister Dorothy Wordsworth)

STC, 37, 43, 45, 73, 75, 90–1, 95, 404n; marriage, 106n; marriage difficulties, 397; meets STC after Royal Institution lecture, 397
Evans, Tom, 43

Farington, Joseph, 112
Favell, Samuel, 87
Fawcett, Joseph, 9, 98
Fisher, Molly, 286
Flagellant, The (school magazine), 69
Forncett St Peter, Norfolk, 52–3, 55
Fox, Charles James: on French Revolution, xxi, 7, 37; welcomes French victory at Valmy, 22; disbelieves British insurrection, 28–9; on gagging bills, 127; protests against government, 143; and withdrawal of Whigs from Parliament, 278; returns to Commons after three-year absence, 294; STC proposes sending *Lyrical Ballads* second edition to, 324; meets Napoleon in Paris, 353–4
Fox, Dr Edward Long, 147
France: as enemy of Britain, xxiv; power and economic strength, xxiv; WW visits: (1790) 4–5, (1791–2) 10–23; revolutionary governments, 11, 48, 144; war with Austria and Prussia, 12, 22, 27; Republic proclaimed, 13–14, 22, 25; aristocrats in, 15 & n; calendar revised, 15; revolutionary violence and atrocities, 21, 27, 48, 57, 62, 66, 77–80, 158–9; declares war on Britain (1793), 30, 47–8; visitors from England in wartime, 47; WW's supposed 1793 visit, 56–8; proposed peace settlement, 96; annexes Belgium, 127; invasion threat to Britain, 127, 166, 215, 224–5, 365; belligerence, 143–4; attempts invasion of Ireland, 166; STC and WW's differing attitudes to, 178; refuses British peace offer (1797), 214–15; STC and WW's disenchantment

with, 214–15; invades Switzerland, 215, 224; negotiates peace proposals (1801–2), 338, 341; WW and Dorothy visit Annette Vallon in, 348; renewed war with Britain (1803), 357, 365; Trafalgar defeat ends invasion threat, 379
French Revolution: British attitudes to, xxi–xxiv, 7, 27–30, 35–6; Burke on, 7; progress and effects, 11–14, 16–18, 25; WW welcomes, 18; effect abroad, 27; Southey lectures on, 100; and STC's Bristol lectures, 101; dress, 131; STC on failure of, 278; in WW's autobiographical poetry, 377
Frend, William: continental tour, 5; tried and expelled from Cambridge, 38–9, 68, 109; WW visits in London, 97; condemns gagging bills, 128; Mary Hays's attachment to, 274n; *Peace and Union*, 35, 37–8, 128
Frere, John Hookham, 215
Fricker, Mrs (Sara's mother), 208, 226
Fricker, Sara *see* Coleridge, Sara
Friend, The (periodical), 264, 400–4
Frost, John, 30, 34

'gagging bills' (1795), 127–30
Gallow Hill (farm), near Scarborough, 299, 334, 343, 347, 354
Gellet-Duvivier, M. (of Orléans), 15, 48
Gentleman's Magazine, 63n
George III, King of Great Britain, 28, 127–8
George, Prince of Wales (*later* Prince Regent and King George IV), 7
Germany: STC proposes visit to, 223–4, 250; STC and Wordsworths in (1798–9), 252–8; literature in England, 263; STC studies in, 263–9; STC leaves, 269; STC and WW tour (1828), 423
Gerrald, Joseph, 65, 92, 143
Gill, Joseph, 123, 155
Gillman, James, 41–2, 229, 293, 420

reaction against Della Cruscans, 140n; projected, 232–6; publication, 246, 271–2; STC and WW's contributions, 246–7, 324; 'Advertisement', 247; title, 247; Johnson agrees to publish, 251; critical reception, 272–3; second edition displaces STC's 'Ancient Mariner', 276, 310–11; Cottle hopes to sell to Longman, 279n; WW ascribes failure to inclusion of 'Ancient Mariner', 280; WW controls copyright, 306; WW publishes second edition with changes and additions, 306–7, 312–13; sales, 307, 367; WW's preface explaining poetic principles, 308–10, 314, 341, 366, 417–18, 420; STC's 'Christabel' excluded from second edition, 312, 315, 317, 320–4; third edition, 342, 367

Lysons, Dr Daniel, 190–1, 257

Macpherson, James ('Ossian'), 202
Malta: STC departs for, 371–2; STC employed as Governor's Secretary, 374
Malthus, Thomas, 9, 97
Manning, Thomas, 290, 295, 316
Marat, Jean-Paul, 11, 21, 23, 29, 36; assassinated, 48
Margarot, Maurice, 65
Marie Antoinette, Queen of France, 12, 57, 62
Marsh, Peggy, 124
Marshall, Jane (née Pollard): friendship and correspondence with Dorothy, 11, 46, 52–5, 116; and Dorothy's comments on WW's poetry, 64; and Dorothy's move to Racedown Lodge, 111, 125; marriage, 111; and WW's 'Adventures on Salisbury Plain', 145; and Dorothy's financial constraints, 154; Dorothy writes of Dove Cottage to, 288; and Dorothy's misgivings over Lloyd's stay in Lake District, 314

Marshall, John, 111
Mathews, William: and WW's youthful idleness, 9, 63; invites WW to collaborate on periodical, 64–6; WW declines invitation to London, 84; abandons scheme for periodical, 96; and WW's proposed coming to London for newspaper writing, 96–7; visits Godwin with WW, 98; on WW's references to STC, 111n, 112–13; and WW at Racedown, 124–5; and WW's inability to write, 156; and WW's disillusion with Godwin, 161; WW disparages Southey's *Joan of Arc* to, 173
Merry, Robert, 140n
millenarianism, xxi, 137, 220–1
Milton, John, 116n, 141, 166, 170, 174, 200, 253, 298, 306, 354
Monkhouse, Thomas, 334
Monkhouse, William and Ann (née Cooper), 270n
Montagu, Basil: mother murdered, 108–9; WW meets, 108–10, 156; Dorothy cares for at Racedown Lodge, 124; WW lends money to, 154; behaviour, 159; and Godwin, 161; revisits Racedown, 172, 173; moves to Alfoxden, 184, 192; visits Tom Wedgwood, 196–7; and Wordsworths' educational principles, 197; STC discusses tuition scheme with, 208; fails to pay Richard Wordsworth, 271; abandons radicalism, 292; STC dines with in London, 292; marriages, 339n, 405; STC stays with in London, 405–6; visits Grasmere, 405; WW warns about STC's unsociable habits, 405–8; teetotalism, 406; and breach between STC and WW, 410
Monthly Magazine, 5, 200, 203, 209
Monthly Review, 97, 137–8
Moore, Thomas, 417n, 423
Morgan, John, 395, 407, 409, 418
Morgan, Mary (née Brent), 395

Society of Friends of the People, xxiii
Sockburn-on-Tees, 270–1, 279, 284–7
Southey, Edith (*née* Fricker): courtship
with Southey, 88–9; supports Southey
in quarrel with STC, 102; marriage,
103, 107; and STC's first meeting with
WW, 112; invited to Alfoxden, 185,
205; marriage relations, 293; visits
STC at Greta Hall, 336–7
Southey, Margaret (Robert's daughter):
death, 363
Southey, Margaret (Robert's mother),
336–7
Southey, Robert: on reaction to French
Revolution, xxi, 7; reads Godwin's
Enquiry concerning Political Justice,
61; social idealism, 62–3, 69, 71;
background, 68–9; forms friendship
with STC, 68, 70–5, 84, 118; poetry,
69, 76, 82–3; appearance and
character, 70; travels with STC, 76–7;
hears of Robespierre's death, 82–3;
meets opposition to Pantisocracy
scheme, 88–9; relations with and
courtship of Edith Fricker, 88–9;
visits Gerrald in Newgate, 92n; STC
writes sonnet on, 93; letter from STC
on Godwin, 94; STC meets in Bristol,
95–6, 98; modifies Pantisocracy
scheme, 98; supervises STC's Bristol
lectures, 99; lectures in Bristol, 100,
102, 107; Vandyke portrait of, 101;
disagreement with and estrangement
from STC, 102–3, 106–8, 113, 149;
orderly and disciplined ways, 102;
considers Church career, 103–4, 108;
loses enthusiasm for Pantisocracy,
103–4, 107; marriage, 103, 107, 226,
293; offered annuity by friend, 103;
and STC's first meeting with WW,
112–13; WW meets and admires, 113;
letter from STC on writing poetry,
136; reconciliation with STC on
return from Portugal, 149–50; WW
and STC discuss poems by, 173; letter

from STC on WW's move to
Alfoxden, 184; invited to Alfoxden,
185; and Charles Lloyd, 205–6;
sensitivity to STC's criticism, 205–6;
Wordsworths visit in London, 207;
receives annuity from Wynn, 213;
proposes emigrating, 224; and Lloyd's
Edmund Oliver, 238–9; on
autobiography, 260; cares for Sara
Coleridge on son Berkeley's death,
264; criticises *Lyrical Ballads*, 272;
criticises STC's 'Ancient Mariner',
272, 316; renews friendship with STC,
274–5; Sara Coleridge attempts to
reconcile STC with, 274; edits *Annual
Anthology*, 276; and STC's praise of
Napoleon, 278; and STC's
reconciliation with Lamb, 290;
lampooned in 'The New Morality',
293; letters from STC in London,
295–7; ill health, 296; STC considers
living with, 296; leaves for Lisbon,
297, 301; visits STC at Greta Hall, 336;
visit to Ireland, 337; and STC's
proposed trip to south of France, 343;
STC complains to of loss of poetic
genius, 352, 357; STC invites to
accompany abroad, 355; on STC's
poetic genius, 358; and STC's
proposals for new works, 358; on
Hazlitt's portrait of WW, 360; death
of daughter Margaret, 363; poem on
Emmet's death, 366n; and STC's
decision to travel abroad, 368; on
STC's departure for Malta, 372; on
STC's malaise, 372; stays at Greta
Hall, 383, 385, 404; on STC's
separation from wife, 383; blames
Wordsworths for STC's condition,
388; STC blames for cajoling into
marriage, 395; and STC's morbid
pessimism, 397; submits piece to *The
Friend*, 402; and STC's estrangement
from WW, 408; gives up radical
views, 415; as Poet Laureate, 415;

Tribune, The (journal), 139, 143
Tylden, Richard, 5

Ullswater, 348
United States of America: emigration
  to, 63; Coleridge and Southey
  propose utopian settlement in, 71–2,
  87

Vallon, Annette: affair and child with
  WW, 18, 21–2, 26, 31, 46–7, 58, 271;
  writes to WW, 126; and WW's
  marriage to Mary Hutchinson, 340;
  WW visits with Dorothy, 344, 348,
  353
Vallon, Paul (Annette's brother), 48n
Valmy, 22
Vandyke, Peter, 101
Vendée: uprising, 47, 57
Vimiero, battle of (1808), 404n

Wade, Josiah, 132
Wakefield, Gilbert, 35, 214n, 251
Wales: STC and WW's walking tours in,
  9, 49, 51, 73–4, 250, 357
Watchman, The (journal): STC founds
  and promotes, 13, 130–2, 134–6; STC
  poems in, 138; criticises French
  government, 144; ceases publication,
  145; financial losses, 146–7;
  readership, 200; Lamb parodies, 241
Watson, Richard, Bishop of Llandaff, 7,
  32–5, 214n
Watt, Robert, 65
Wedgwood, John, 172, 196, 208
Wedgwood, Josiah, Jr: manages family
  business, 196; introduces STC to
  Stuart, 208; sends money to STC,
  209; annuity to STC, 212–13, 221, 269;
  STC visits in Surrey, 250; and STC's
  separation from WW in Germany,
  254, 256; STC writes to from
  Germany, 269; STC tells of Sara's
  pregnancy, 293; and STC's translation
  of Schiller, 295; and STC's life of

Lessing, 296, 308; and STC's
  adulation of WW, 298; opposes STC's
  move to Keswick, 301; and STC's
  'Christabel', 321; letters from STC,
  330; STC visits at Blandford, 357; STC
  neglects to write to, 385
Wedgwood, Kitty, 213, 333
Wedgwood, Thomas: proposed school
  for genius, 196–7; disparages WW,
  198; introduces STC to Daniel Stuart,
  208; sends money to STC, 209;
  awards annuity to STC, 212–13, 221;
  and STC's adulation of WW, 291, 298;
  and STC's life of Lessing, 296, 308;
  moves to West Indies for health, 301;
  opposes STC's move to Keswick, 301;
  plans trip to Sicily, 331, 333; letter
  from STC on marriage difficulties,
  355; STC accompanies on travels,
  356–7; death, 385
Weekly Entertainer, 165
Weeks, Shadrach, 88
Wellington, Arthur Wellesley, 1st Duke
  of, 404n
Wilberforce, William, 44n, 324; takes
  opium, 332
Wilkinson, Joshua: *The Wanderer*, 5
Windy Brow (farm), near Keswick,
  58–9, 81, 302
Wollstonecraft, Mary, 9, 274n, 290; *A
  Vindication of the Rights of Woman*,
  226; *Wrongs of Women*, 293
Wordsworth, Anne-Caroline (WW's
  daughter by Annette Vallon): birth,
  22, 31; baptised, 46; WW supports,
  340; meets WW, 353
Wordsworth, Catharine (WW and
  Mary's daughter): birth, 400n; death,
  411
Wordsworth, Christopher (WW's
  brother): childhood, 52; criticism of
  WW's poetry, 117; meets STC in
  Cambridge, 117; and Dorothy's stay in
  Germany, 255; engagement to
  Priscilla Lloyd, 314

A Letter to —

April 4, 1802. — Sunday Evening.

Well! if the Bard was weatherwise, who made
The grand old Ballad of Sir Patrick Spence,
This Night, so tranquil now, will not go hence
Unrous'd by winds, that ply a busier trade
Than that, which moulds yon clouds in lazy flakes,
Or the dull sobbing Draft, that drones & rakes
Upon the Strings of this Eolian Lute,
  Which better far were mute.
For, lo! the New Moon, winter-bright!
And overspread with phantom Light,
With swimming phantom Light o'erspread
But rimm'd & circled with a silver Thread)
I see the Old Moon in her Lap, foretelling
The coming-on of Rain & squally Blast —
O! Sara! that the Gust even now were swelling
And the slant Night-shower driving loud &
                                        fast!

A Grief without a pang, void, dark, & drear,
A stifling, drowsy, unimpassion'd Grief
That finds no natural Outlet, no Relief
  In word, or sigh, or tear —
This, Sara! well thou knowst,